TOP TWENTY 1-2-3 COMMANDS

DESCRIPTION	COMMAND
Aligning labels	/Range Label
Attaching an add-in program	/Add-In Attach
Clearing the screen	/Worksheet Erase
Copying a range	/Copy
Deleting rows or columns	/Worksheet Delete
Erasing a range	/Range Erase
Formatting a range of numbers	/Range Format
Formatting all numbers	/Worksheet Global Format
Freezing row or column headings	/Worksheet Titles
Inserting rows or columns	/Worksheet Insert
Moving a range	/Move
Naming a range	/Range Name Create
Printing	/Print Printer
Retrieving a file	/File Retrieve
Saving a file	/File Save
Setting margins	/Print Printer Options Margins
Setting a column width	/Worksheet Column Set-Width
Setting the default column width	/Worksheet Global Column-Width
Sorting a range	/Data Sort
Turning off auto recalculation	/Worksheet Global Recalculation Manual

Computer users are not all alike.
Neither are SYBEX books.

We know our customers have a variety of needs. They've told us so. And because we've listened, we've developed several distinct types of books to meet the needs of each of our customers. What are you looking for in computer help?

If you're looking for the basics, try the **ABC's** series. You'll find short, unintimidating tutorials and helpful illustrations. For a more visual approach, select **Teach Yourself**, featuring screen-by-screen illustrations of how to use your latest software purchase.

Mastering and **Understanding** titles offer you a step-by-step introduction, plus an in-depth examination of intermediate-level features, to use as you progress.

Our **Up & Running** series is designed for computer-literate consumers who want a no-nonsense overview of new programs. Just 20 basic lessons, and you're on your way.

We also publish two types of reference books. Our **Instant References** provide quick access to each of a program's commands and functions. SYBEX **Encyclopedias** provide a *comprehensive reference* and explanation of all of the commands, features and functions of the subject software.

Sometimes a subject requires a special treatment that our standard series doesn't provide. So you'll find we have titles like **Advanced Techniques, Handbooks, Tips & Tricks**, and others that are specifically tailored to satisfy a unique need.

We carefully select our authors for their in-depth understanding of the software they're writing about, as well as their ability to write clearly and communicate effectively. Each manuscript is thoroughly reviewed by our technical staff to ensure its complete accuracy. Our production department makes sure it's easy to use. All of this adds up to the highest quality books available, consistently appearing on best-seller charts worldwide.

You'll find SYBEX publishes a variety of books on every popular software package. Looking for computer help? Help Yourself to SYBEX.

For a complete catalog of our publications:

SYBEX Inc.

2021 Challenger Drive, Alameda, CA 94501

Tel: (415) 523-8233/(800) 227-2346 Telex: 336311

SYBEX   Fax: (415) 523-2373

Understanding 1-2-3 Release 2.3

Understanding 1-2-3® Release 2.3

Rebecca Bridges Altman

SYBEX ®

San Francisco   Paris   Düsseldorf   Soest

Acquisitions Editor: David Clark
Developmental Editor: Christian Crumlish
Editor: David Krassner
Technical Editor: Sheila Dienes
Word Processors: Scott Campbell, Ann Dunn, and Susan Trybull
Book Designer: Eleanor Ramos
Chapter Art: Charlotte Carter
Technical Art: Delia Brown
Screen Graphics: Cuong Le
Desktop Publishing Production: M.D. Barrera
Proofreader: Patsy Owens
Indexer: Anne Leach
Cover Designer: Thomas Ingalls + Associates
Cover Photographer: Michael Lamotte

SYBEX is a registered trademark of SYBEX, Inc.

TRADEMARKS: SYBEX has attempted throughout this book to distinguish proprietary trademarks from descriptive terms by following the capitalization style used by the manufacturer.

SYBEX is not affiliated with any manufacturer.

Every effort has been made to supply complete and accurate information. However, SYBEX assumes no responsibility for its use, nor for any infringement of the intellectual property rights of third parties which would result from such use.

Library of Congress Card Number: 91-65437
ISBN: 0-89588-856-4

Manufactured in the United States of America
10 9 8 7 6 5 4 3 2

To the hundreds of people who have provided me with the experience and groundwork to write this book: the students who have taken 1-2-3 classes from me over the last nine years

Acknowledgments

This book was somewhat of a family affair. First, I'd like to thank my brother, Brian Bridges, who was the "guinea pig" for this book; he tested the exercises in every chapter and let me know when something didn't work just right. My husband Rick was always there to bounce ideas off of, give me suggestions when my creativity lagged, and provide unfailing love, support, and encouragement. And I couldn't have written the section on regression analysis without the help of a rocket scientist—my father-in-law, David Altman.

At Sybex, I'd like to thank my excellent editors, David Krassner and Christian Crumlish; they were a pleasure to work with.

Many thanks to Lotus Development Corporation for providing me with beta software and to Steve Ormsby who patiently researched answers to my many questions.

Contents at a Glance

Table of Contents

PART IV Databases

Chapter 12 **Manipulating a Database** 413

APPENDICES

Introduction

When I first started using Lotus 1-2-3 in 1982 I was intimidated. Although I had mastered dozens of other software programs, 1-2-3 scared me. It seemed so complicated and overwhelming. (Sound familiar?) At the time, there weren't any tutorial books available, so I had to learn the program by reading the 1-2-3 documentation. Not a pleasant experience.

You are more fortunate than I was—*Understanding 1-2-3 Release 2.3* is an easy-to-read book that guides you through the process of learning 1-2-3. Using this book as your teacher, you can become proficient in 1-2-3 without a struggle; it will be a rewarding experience as you achieve things that initially looked incredibly complicated. After teaching 1-2-3 for nine years, I am familiar with the kinds of mistakes beginners make and where novices are likely to trip up. Throughout this book, I warn about common errors you might make and how to correct these mistakes. Keep in mind that making mistakes is part of the learning process.

Understanding 1-2-3 is a tutorial, with step-by-step exercises that you can follow at your computer. This book takes a hands-on approach; you will learn by doing. Pictures of the screen are provided at key points so that you can check to make sure you are on the right track.

You can also use this book as a reference guide when you need to review a topic. Use the Index or the Table of Contents to locate the subject, and then read through the text to refresh your memory.

WHOM THIS BOOK IS FOR

Before you read any further, make sure you have Lotus 1-2-3, *Release 2.3*. There are several different versions of 1-2-3; this book is for those who are using Release 2.3. Some of the exercises will not work properly if you don't have this version of the program.

The first two chapters of this book are for those new to electronic spreadsheets and Lotus 1-2-3. You'll start with the basics and gradually build on the techniques and concepts learned in earlier chapters. Although *Understanding 1-2-3* contains beginning material, if you are an experienced user, there is plenty of advanced information to keep you challenged—data analysis, graphics editing, and macro programming are a few of the more advanced topics covered in this book.

If you have recently upgraded to Release 2.3 from an earlier version of 1-2-3, this book is for you, too. The book explains all new commands and features, and they are marked with 2.3 icons in the margins so that you can easily find them. The chapters devoted entirely to new features contain *Release 2.3* in their titles.

NEW FEATURES IN 1-2-3, RELEASE 2.3

Release 2.3 contains an abundance of new features and commands. Here is a brief list of the most noteworthy ones:

- Mouse support
- Graphical interface and extensive formatting commands, available through an add-in called *Wysiwyg* (this replaces the Allways add-in)
- Ability to erase the current cell with the Del key
- Dialog boxes
- Five add-in programs (Wysiwyg, Macro Library Manager, Viewer File Manager, Auditor, and Tutor)
- New graph types and options
- Background printing
- Ability to specify a range before you give a command

HOW TO USE THIS BOOK

This book is divided into five parts and has four appendices. The first part gives you an overview of 1-2-3 and what it can do for you. The next three parts concentrate on the three primary components of 1-2-3: Spreadsheets, Graphics, and Databases (they make up the *1*, *2*, and *3* of *1-2-3*). The last part discusses how to create macros to automate your commands and tasks.

PART I: INTRODUCTION TO 1-2-3

This part is primarily designed for novices. Chapter 1 explains different ways to use 1-2-3 and discusses the many virtues of electronic spreadsheets. Chapter 2 shows you how to interact with 1-2-3: You will learn how to use the menus, the mouse, the dialog boxes, and the Help feature.

PART II: SPREADSHEETS

Because the spreadsheet is the primary component of 1-2-3, Part II is the heart of the book. In Chapter 3 you will build a spreadsheet from the ground up. You will enter data, make calculations, format the data, and modify the spreadsheet.

Chapter 4 explains how to enhance your spreadsheet with the Wysiwyg commands. By specifying different type styles (bold, italic, and so forth), changing typefaces, creating lines, and adding shades, you can, and will, produce professionally formatted reports.

Chapter 5 covers special topics for working with large spreadsheet projects. This chapter shows you how to protect your spreadsheet from accidental changes, to manage your memory efficiently, and to consolidate data from separate files. You will also learn shortcuts for moving around the spreadsheet.

The discussion of printing is divided into two chapters. Chapter 6 covers all aspects of printing in 1-2-3 while Chapter 7 is devoted to printing in Wysiwyg. You will learn how to set up the page layout, print multiple-page spreadsheets, and print in the background.

In Chapter 8 you will learn all about Release 2.3's text editor. The text editor has all the basic features of a word-processing program—automatic word wrap, editing, centering, and formatting.

PART III: GRAPHICS

Because spreadsheets and graphics are packaged in one program, you can quickly and easily create graphs of your spreadsheet data. Chapter 9 describes the different types of graphs that are available and teaches you how to define a graph. You will also insert a graph into a spreadsheet so you can simultaneously view a spreadsheet and chart.

Graph printing is reserved for Chapter 10. This chapter is arranged into two sections. One section explains how to print graphs in Wysiwyg; the other describes how to use the PrintGraph program.

Chapter 11 explains how to use Release 2.3's graphics editor to spruce up your charts and to design graphics from scratch. In this chapter, you will design a company logo and print it at the top of your spreadsheet reports.

PART IV: DATABASES

With 1-2-3's database features, you can keep track of and analyze information. Chapter 12 shows you how to create, sort, and query a database. Chapter 13 covers advanced database topics such as database functions, data tables, frequency distribution, and regression analysis.

PART V: MACROS

To automate your commands, keystrokes, and tasks you can create *macros*. In Chapter 14 you will create a set of generic macros that automate common spreadsheet tasks such as file-saving, formatting, and column addition.

Chapter 15 describes how to use the Macro Library Manager add-in. With this add-in, you can load your macros into memory and use them in any spreadsheet.

Chapter 16 introduces you to the process of macro programming. To understand this concept, you will write a program that automates database operations.

Chapter 17 is a complete reference guide to all the macro commands in 1-2-3's programming language. Sample programs and explanations are included for each command.

APPENDICES

Appendix A takes you through the steps of copying 1-2-3 to your hard disk. You should turn to this appendix first if you haven't yet installed 1-2-3.

Appendix B is a thorough reference guide to all the spreadsheet functions included in 1-2-3. Each function is illustrated with at least one example.

Appendix C explains different ways of importing and exporting data. You will learn how to get your 1-2-3 files to work with other programs and vice versa.

Appendix D describes how to analyze your spreadsheet with the Auditor add-in program. This add-in helps you locate errors in your formulas.

LIFE IN THE FAST LANE: FAST TRACKS

The beginning page spread of each chapter contains a *Fast Track*—a quick reference to the chapter's main points. In this command summary, you will find the basic steps for doing a task, along with the page number on which the topic is discussed. When you don't have time to complete an entire chapter, you can use the Fast Track to locate the topics you are interested in and go directly to that discussion. It's also a great reference tool when you need to review a command.

PART I
PART II
PART III
PART IV
PART V

Introduction
to 1-2-3

Chapter 1

Chapter 2

Chapter 3

Chapter 4

Chapter 5

Introducing the Electronic Spreadsheet

◄|||| FAST TRACK ||||►

Lotus 1-2-3 is actually three programs in one. First and foremost, 1-2-3 is an electronic *spreadsheet* used for number crunching. Second, Lotus can take your spreadsheet numbers and produce business *graphs* (pies, bars, lines, and so on) for presentations or trend analysis. The third part of 1-2-3, its *database* capabilities, provides tools for you to turn raw data into meaningful information. With the database commands, you can manage and manipulate information such as customer data.

These three components of the program led to the name *1-2-3*. This name is also said to be derived from the well-known expression "It's as easy as 1-2-3." While the program may not be *that* easy, this book will guide you on the quickest path to learning this powerful program.

WAYS TO USE 1-2-3

A spreadsheet is ideal for doing budgets, forecasts, projections, and financial analyses. In my business, I use 1-2-3 to invoice my clients, produce a monthly cash-disbursements journal and an income statement, manage investments, and help me with tax preparation. I also use 1-2-3 for more personal tasks. For example, I created a 1-2-3 database of all the guests I invited to my wedding. Lotus was also a key player when my husband and I were house-hunting. We created a spreadsheet to calculate down payments and mortgage payments according to different home prices and interest rates. I can't tell you how many hours we spent staring at a Lotus spreadsheet, hoping the numbers would magically change to something we could afford!

Though 1-2-3 is primarily designed for numerical work, you can also use it to create columnar tables; the columns are already set up so that you don't have to set tab stops. Furthermore, many people love 1-2-3 so much that they even use it to type letters and memos. My father-in-law is one such person—he never saw any need to learn a word processor because he writes all his letters in 1-2-3. Figure 1.1 shows a memo typed in Release 2.3's text editor.

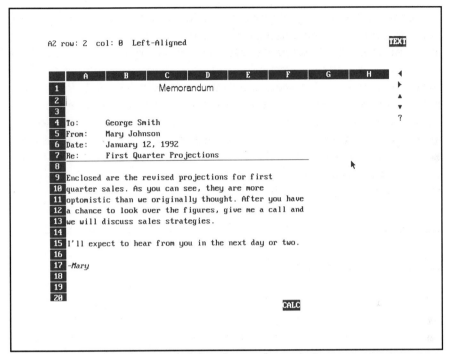

Figure 1.1: You can even use 1-2-3 to do word processing

ADVANTAGES OF AN ELECTRONIC SPREADSHEET

An electronic spreadsheet is a computerized version of ledger paper—you know, the yellow paper with the green and brown lines. Using the old ledger paper has its problems. If you forget a line, you have to redo the spreadsheet, attempt to write in small letters between the lines, or cut-and-paste. In 1-2-3, you simply issue the command to insert a row.

If you enter an incorrect number on ledger paper, you have to white it out or erase it, enter the new number, and then recalculate all the figures that use that number. In 1-2-3, you type the new number (you don't even have to erase the old one), and all the calculations are updated automatically.

One of the biggest advantages of an electronic spreadsheet is its ability to play "what if" games with the assumptions underlying a projection or forecast. I know people who, before electronic spreadsheets, would stay up all night recreating forecasts, a different one for each set of assumptions. For example, they might first develop a spreadsheet projecting a ten-percent increase in the sales of a given product. Then they would get out another piece of paper, rewrite the spreadsheet, and recalculate the results for a fifteen-percent increase. They would repeat this process for each scenario. This doesn't sound like a pleasant way to spend an evening.

With the electronic spreadsheet you can spend your evenings at the movies or at a ballgame instead of recreating spreadsheets. To revise a forecast in 1-2-3, all you have to do is enter the new percentage and you instantly have the revised figures. It takes only seconds to play "what if" games in an electronic spreadsheet—call me a nerd, but I even think it's fun.

WHAT VERSION DO YOU HAVE?

Lotus 1-2-3 comes in so many different varieties and flavors, it's hard to keep up with them all. You may not even know what version you have. To determine your version, read the title screen that appears when you load the program. This book focuses on Release 2.3.

If you are confused about what each version of 1-2-3 offers, read the summary below:

- *Release 1A* was the first version of 1-2-3, released in 1982.

- *Release 2.01* introduced a variety of new menu and macro commands, in addition to new functions that performed calculations on labels.

- *Release 2.2* provided an Undo feature, the Allways spreadsheet formatting program, settings sheets, search-and-replace, macro recording, file-linking, and improved graphics.

- *Release 2.3* offers mouse support, dialog boxes, and the Wysiwyg graphical interface and spreadsheet publisher.

- The key new feature in *Release 3.0* is three-dimensional spreadsheets—multiple spreadsheets in one file. It also allows you to have more than one file open at a time, and offers an Undo feature, search-and-replace, macro recording, file-linking, additional print options, external database manipulation, and improved graphics.

- *Release 3.1* features the Wysiwyg graphical interface, which encompasses advanced spreadsheet formatting and mouse support.

- *1-2-3/G* is a graphical version of 1-2-3 that runs under the OS/2 operating system.

The main advantage to the Release 3.x series is its three-dimensional spreadsheet capability, shown in Figure 1.2. For example, one file can contain data for five different divisions of a company, each division having its own spreadsheet. You can easily consolidate this data by summing the numbers across all five spreadsheets. However, this increased sophistication comes at a high price: the Release 3.x series requires more expensive hardware (it won't work on an IBM PC or XT) and additional memory (at least 1Mb of RAM). Furthermore, the 3.x versions are slower than their 2.x counterparts.

Because the 3.x series is not appropriate for everyone, Lotus Development Corporation is maintaining two separate paths for 1-2-3, and will continue to offer upgrades to both the 2.x and 3.x series in the future.

For the most part, the files created in the various versions of 1-2-3 are compatible. In Release 2.3, you can retrieve 1A, 2.01, and 2.2 files, but you cannot retrieve Release 3.x files that have the extension .WK3. All versions of 1-2-3 can retrieve Release 2.3 files.

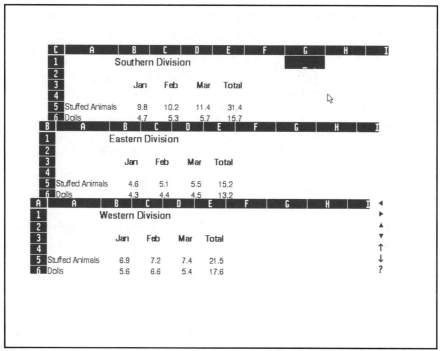

Figure 1.2: The Release 3.x series offers three-dimensional spreadsheets

THE POWER OF 1-2-3

Lotus 1-2-3 is the most popular electronic spreadsheet for good reason: it is extremely fast and powerful. Here are a few staggering specifications:

- The spreadsheet grid contains 256 columns and 8192 rows. While actual spreadsheet size is limited by the amount of memory (RAM) you have available, 2.3 can access up to 640K of conventional and up to 8Mb of expanded memory.

- Over ninety specialized functions are available. These functions do everything from summing a column to calculating a mortgage payment.

- The program offers over 130 menu commands and options.

- You can view your data in seven different types of graphs.

- A database can contain up to 8191 records.

- When you change a number, the spreadsheet instantly and auto-matically recalculates all formulas that refer to that particular value. This feature can be turned off at your discretion.

In addition, Release 2.3 includes several *add-in* programs that make 1-2-3 even more powerful. Probably the most noteworthy of these add-ins is Wysiwyg—which stands for *what you see is what you get*. With this spreadsheet-publishing program, you can create professionally format-ted spreadsheets, as shown in Figure 1.3. In Chapter 4 you will see how to produce enhanced reports such as this one.

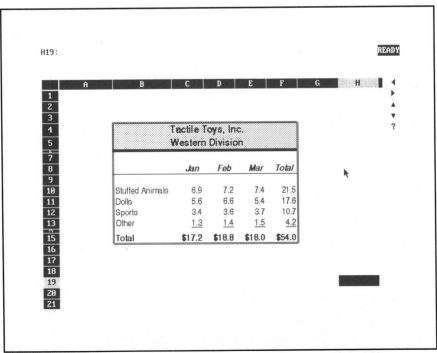

Figure 1.3: Wysiwyg lets you format your spreadsheets with boldface, italics, fonts, shading, and borders.

The other add-ins included with 1-2-3 are:

- *Viewer:* a file manager that lets you look at the contents of files without retrieving them.
- *Macro Library Manager:* stores your macros in memory instead of in each spreadsheet file.
- *Auditor:* analyzes your spreadsheet formulas and flags errors.
- *Tutor:* an on-screen tutorial to help you learn 1-2-3.

These add-ins will be discussed in more detail later in the book.

Chapter 1

Chapter 2

Chapter 3

Chapter 4

Chapter 5

Interacting
with 1-2-3

◄▐▐▐ FAST TRACK ▐▐▐►

To automatically attach Wysiwyg every time you load 1-2-3:   33

Press / to display the 1-2-3 menu and choose Worksheet Global Default Other Add-In Set. (Note: Be sure to choose Update on the Default menu to permanently save this setting.)

To manually attach an add-in (such as Wysiwyg):   34

Press / to display the 1-2-3 menu and choose Add-In Attach.

To detach an add-in: 34

Press / to display the 1-2-3 menu and choose Add-In Detach.

To save a file with a new name: 37

Press / to display the 1-2-3 menu and choose File Save. Then enter the name (up to eight characters).

To resave a file with the same name: 39

Press / to display the 1-2-3 menu and choose File Save. Press Enter to keep the same name and choose Replace.

To retrieve a file: 40

Press / to display the 1-2-3 menu and choose File Retrieve. Then press F3 to see a list and choose the name.

To permanently change the default directory: 42

Press / to display the 1-2-3 menu and choose Worksheet Global Default Directory. Enter the new drive and/or directory and choose Update.

To change the default directory for the current session: 43

Press / to display the 1-2-3 menu and choose File Directory. Enter the new drive and/or directory.

To get help, press F1.   44

Whenever you buy a new electronic toy, whether it be a VCR, a microwave oven, or a PC with 1-2-3, the first thing you have to do after plugging it in is to figure out how it works. You need to know what all the buttons mean, how to give instructions, and how to read or understand the electronic display. This chapter gives you this kind of information for 1-2-3. You will start the program, learn how to use the menus, and learn the significance of what you see on the screen.

STARTING 1-2-3

Complete instructions for setting up 1-2-3 to run on your computer appear in Appendix A. If you haven't yet copied 1-2-3 to your hard disk, you should turn to Appendix A now and return here when you are finished.

Follow these steps to load 1-2-3:

1. At the DOS C:\> prompt, change to the subdirectory where you copied 1-2-3. For example, if you named the subdirectory 123R23, type **CD\123R23** and press Enter.

2. To start the program, type **123** and press Enter.

The *123* command loads the main 1-2-3 spreadsheet program. Another way to load Lotus 1-2-3 is to type **lotus**, instead of **123**. When you start the program this way, you see the Lotus Access Menu, shown in Figure 2.1. This menu gives you access to several programs:

- 1-2-3: the main spreadsheet program

- PrintGraph: prints graphs created in 1-2-3

- Translate: converts files from other software programs so they can be used in 1-2-3, and vice-versa

- Install: lets 1-2-3 know what hardware (monitor, printer, and so on) you have

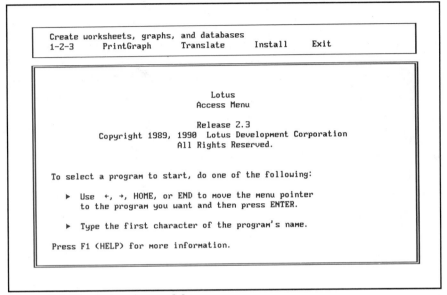

Figure 2.1: The Lotus Access Menu

To load 1-2-3 from the Access Menu, make sure 1-2-3 is highlighted and press Enter.

If you know that you aren't going to be using the other programs, it's faster to simply type **123** to go directly into the spreadsheet.

EXPLORING THE SCREEN

Figure 2.2 points out the various areas of the 1-2-3 screen. The columns are labeled with letters and the rows are numbered. The intersection of a row and a column is called a *cell*. A cell is a box in which you type text or numbers. You refer to a cell by its coordinates, designated by its column letter and row number. Right now the *cell pointer* (the rectangular bar) is in cell A1. Always refer to a cell by its column letter first and then its row number.

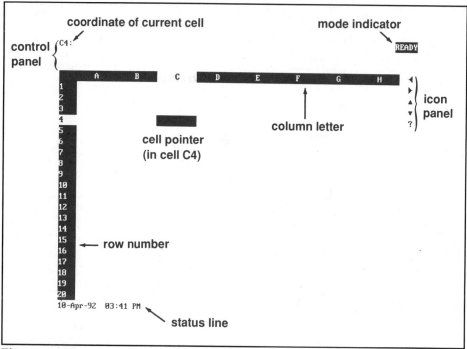

Figure 2.2: The 1-2-3 screen

The *mode indicator* is in the upper-right corner of the screen. Currently, you are in READY mode which means that 1-2-3 is ready for you to move the cell pointer, make an entry into a cell, or give a command. The mode indicator changes according to your current task. If you are in the menu, the indicator reads MENU. If you are typing, it reads either LABEL or VALUE. If you make a mistake, it might read ERROR or EDIT. Keep your eye on the mode indicator because it lets you know what 1-2-3 thinks you are doing, which might be different from what you think you're doing! For example, if 1-2-3 beeps at you when you try to move the cell pointer, check the mode indicator to see what mode you are in.

The *status line* is the last line on the screen. Right now it is displaying the date and time. The status line also lets you know when the Caps Lock, Num Lock, or Scroll Lock keys are turned on: you will see indicators (CAPS, NUM, or SCROLL) in the status line.

The area above the spreadsheet grid, called the *control panel*, is where you enter and edit data, and where menus appear.

MOVING THE CELL POINTER BY USING THE KEYBOARD

For practice, use your arrow keys to move around to different cells in the spreadsheet. When you are in the middle of the screen, it's sometimes difficult to tell what the current cell coordinates are. However, you don't need to guess—just look on the first line of the control panel. The current column letter and row number are also colored or shaded differently.

How large is the spreadsheet grid? To find out, press → to see what happens when you move past the last column on your screen (column H). Is the world flat? Do you fall off the edge? No, you get more columns. Column A scrolls off the screen and you see another column on the right. What happens when you get to column Z? The alphabet starts doubling up (AA, AB, AC,...BA, BB, BC,...CA, CB, CC, etc.) and continues through column IV (the letters *I* and *V*)—making 256 columns.

How many rows are there? Press the Page Down (PgDn) key to see the next twenty rows. If you were to continue pressing PgDn, you would eventually find the bottom of the spreadsheet, but it might take a while: there are 8192 rows.

This spreadsheet grid, containing 2,097,152 cells, should be large enough for most of your computing needs. You would probably run out of computer memory before you ran out of available spreadsheet space.

To bring your cell pointer back to cell A1, the beginning of the spreadsheet, press Home. We'll be learning more ways to move the cell pointer in Chapter 5.

MOVING THE CELL POINTER BY USING THE MOUSE

◀|||| 2.3

If your mouse software is loaded, you see either a small square block or an arrow in the middle of your screen when you start 1-2-3. This symbol is called the *mouse pointer*—it moves as you roll the mouse along your desktop.

To move the cell pointer to another cell on the screen, place the mouse pointer in the cell and click the left mouse button. The cell pointer will then jump to the new cell. To move the cell pointer to a cell off the screen, use the *icon panel* on the right side of the screen. The *icons*, or symbols, in this panel represent the direction the cell pointer will move when you click on the icon. For example, to move to a cell that is to the right of the current screen, follow these steps:

1. Place the mouse pointer on the right-arrow icon.

2. Click the left mouse button. Each time you click, the cell pointer moves one cell to the right.

3. To move continuously to the right, click on the right-arrow icon and hold down the left mouse button.

Another way to scroll through the cells is to drag the cell pointer in the direction you want to go. For example, to move the cell pointer down:

1. Place the mouse pointer on the cell pointer.

2. Click the left mouse button, and hold it down.

3. Move the mouse towards the bottom of the screen.

4. Release the mouse button when you are at the desired cell.

ENTERING DATA

There are two types of data you can enter in a cell: labels (text) and values (numbers or formulas). 1-2-3 determines which type of entry you are making by the first character you enter in the cell. The appropriate mode indicator (LABEL or VALUE) will then display in the control panel.

Entering numbers and text in the spreadsheet is easy. Follow these general steps:

- Place the cell pointer where you want to type the data. You can use the arrow keys or simply click the mouse pointer on the cell.

- Type the data in the cell. As you type, the characters appear in the control panel at the top of your screen—not in the cell.

- If you make a mistake while you are typing, press the Backspace key to back up and correct it. Don't use the left-arrow key because this action moves the cell pointer.

- When you are finished typing the data, you can press Enter to leave the cell pointer on the current cell or press an arrow key to move the cell pointer in the direction of the arrow.

The arrow keys actually perform double-duty. They enter data in a cell *and* move the cell pointer to the location where you want to type next. For example, when entering a column of data, press ↓ instead of pressing Enter and then ↓. This technique saves you one keystroke per cell.

To practice data entry, do the following exercise at your computer:

1. Move the cell pointer to cell A1.

2. Type the word **Sales**. The letters appear on the edit line in the control panel so you can correct any mistakes with the Backspace key. Notice that the mode indicator says LABEL.

3. Press Enter, then look in the control panel. The first line contains the contents of the highlighted cell. Notice that the word is preceded by an apostrophe ('*Sales*). 1-2-3 automatically places an apostrophe in front of labels as a way of distinguishing them from values. This symbol is not inserted in front of numbers.

4. To confirm this rule, put the cell pointer on A2 and type **4000**.

5. Press Enter and study the control panel. As Figure 2.3 shows, the label *Sales* is aligned on the left side of the cell and number *4000* is aligned on the right. These alignments are the defaults

(automatic settings) for labels and values. In Chapter 3 you will learn how to change label alignment.

6. In cell A3, type the date **10-1-91** and press Enter. What happened?! Instead of the date, the cell displays the number –82: the result of 10 minus 1 minus 91. Though you didn't intend to, you just used 1-2-3 as a calculator. Because you began the cell entry with a number, 1-2-3 thought you were typing a value and therefore performed a calculation. In order to see the date, you must make the entry a label by preceding it with an apostrophe—the label symbol.

7. In cell A3, type **'10-1-91** and press Enter. Notice that you didn't have to erase the cell before typing a new entry; the new data automatically replaced the previous contents of the cell.

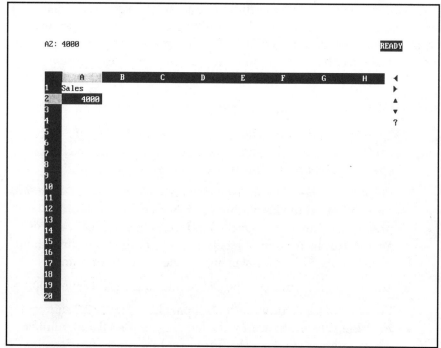

Figure 2.3: Labels are aligned on the left, values on the right.

You should now see the date in the cell. Whenever a label begins with a number or other value character (such as parentheses or a dollar sign), you must type an apostrophe so that 1-2-3 knows that it's a label. Here are a few other examples:

- street addresses
- phone numbers
- social security numbers
- part numbers

Whenever you type a label longer than the current column width, the text automatically runs over into the next cell, assuming the next cell is blank. If the next cell contains an entry, the label is truncated until you widen the column.

If you enter data in the wrong cell, you can use the Delete (Del) key to clear it out.

USING THE MENUS

To display the 1-2-3 menu, as shown in Figure 2.4, press the slash (/) key. This menu has two lines. The top line contains the eleven main menu options (Worksheet, Range, Copy, and so on). The second line is a description of the highlighted option, and will change depending on which option the menu pointer is highlighting. Think of the second line as a help line that gives you additional information about the highlighted option.

Follow these steps to explore the menu:

1. To display the menu, press /. The Worksheet option is high-lighted and the second line displays a description of this option: Global, Insert, Delete, and so forth. These are commands that affect the entire worksheet.

2. Press → to highlight the Range option and you will see that the second line lists a different description: Format, Label, Erase, etc. These commands affect ranges of cells in the spreadsheet.

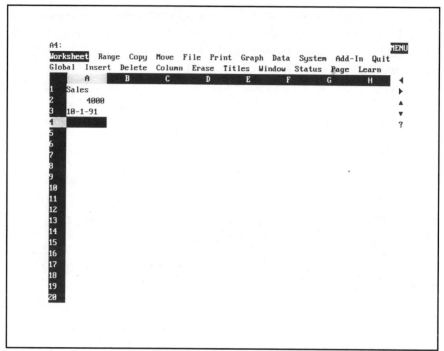

Figure 2.4: The 1-2-3 main menu

3. Continue pressing → and read the second-line descriptions.

The second menu line was designed with the beginning or infrequent 1-2-3 user in mind. Because it's hard to remember which menu option contains a certain command, you can use the help line to refresh your memory.

CHOOSING MENU OPTIONS

1-2-3 offers two ways to select menu options:

- Highlight the option with the arrow keys (or spacebar) and press Enter.
- Type the first letter of the option.

The first method allows you to read the help line, but the second method is faster. As a 1-2-3 novice, you should use the first method. Once you become more experienced with the program, save time by using the second method.

Let's practice selecting menu options:

1. Highlight the Range option, read the description, and press Enter. The Range submenu now appears—the options that were formerly on the description line are now on the top line.

2. Highlight the Name option, read the description, and press Enter.

3. Highlight the Create option, read the description, and press Enter.

You are now several levels deep in 1-2-3 menus. How do you get out of this quagmire? Read on...

ESCAPING FROM THE MENUS

Probably the most often-used key in 1-2-3 is the Escape (Esc) key. Whenever you are either lost or somewhere you don't want to be, press Esc. If you are at the main menu, Esc returns you to READY mode. If you are in a submenu, Esc takes you back to the previous menu. Try it now.

1. Press Esc. The Range Name submenu appears with the options Create, Delete, Labels, etc.

2. Press Esc again. The Range submenu appears.

3. Press Esc a third time. The main menu appears.

4. Press Esc again and you are in READY mode.

Instead of pressing Esc a number of times when you are several layers deep in the menus and want to return to READY mode, you can give the Break command by holding down the Ctrl key and pressing the Break key. If you aren't sure where your Break key is, look at the side of the Scroll Lock or Pause key.

There are a lot of commands in 1-2-3, but don't bother trying to memorize them. Eventually you will remember the commands you use all the time. Until you reach that point, highlight the menu options, and read the descriptions on the second menu line. If you get into the wrong submenu, just press Esc.

2.3 ▐▐▶

OF MICE AND MENUS

The mouse offers another way to activate the menu and select options. Here are a few key points:

- To display the menu, place the mouse pointer in the control panel.

- To select a menu option, place the mouse pointer on the option and click the left mouse button.

- To escape back to the previous menu level, press the right mouse button.

2.3 ▐▐▶

CONVERSING WITH DIALOG BOXES

Several 1-2-3 commands produce *dialog boxes*. A dialog box is a framed set of options. Figure 2.5 shows the Print Settings dialog box. A dialog box offers several nice features. First, you can see all the current settings at once. Second, you can change the settings in the box without having to select menu options.

There are several types of options in a dialog box. These options are pointed out in Figure 2.5 and described in Table 2.1. Some options (*text boxes*) require you to type in numbers or text, and others have you choose from a list (*list boxes*) or turn a setting on or off (*option buttons* and *check boxes*). Sometimes there is a dialog box within a dialog box—called a *popup dialog box*. With few exceptions, each dialog box has two *command buttons*, labeled OK and Cancel. Choose OK when you are finished filling in the box; choose the Cancel button if you decide to cancel the command you issued. It's not important that you memorize the official names of all these types of options—just that you recognize them when you see them.

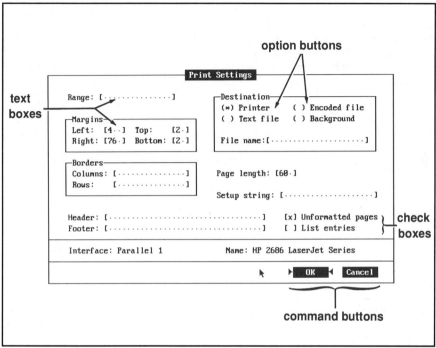

Figure 2.5: The Print Settings dialog box

In the following exercise, you will practice filling in a dialog box. Don't worry about what the particular options mean.

1. Press / to display the 1-2-3 menu.

2. Highlight Print and press Enter.

3. Press Enter to select Printer. The Print Settings dialog box appears.

4. Press F2 to edit the settings. Notice that the first letter of each option is shaded or colored differently. To edit an option in the dialog box, you can either type this highlighted letter or press the Tab key to move from one option to the next. To move to the previous option you can press Shift-Tab.

5. Press **D** to choose Destination.

Table 2.1: Dialog Box Options

OPTION TYPE	DESCRIPTION
Text Boxes	Area into which you type information.
Option Buttons	A set of two or three options that are mutually exclusive (only one option can be selected). An asterisk appears next to the selected option.
Check Boxes	A group of options that are nonexclusive (turn on or off as many as you like). An *X* appears next to the selected option(s).
List Box	A list of choices from which you can select one item.
Command Buttons	Boxed words that carry out a command (OK), cancel the command (Cancel), or display another dialog box.

6. Press **T** to choose Text File. The asterisk option button moves next to Text File.

7. Press **P** (Printer) to change the option back to its original setting.

8. To turn on the Unformatted Pages check box, press **U**.

9. To turn on the List Entries check box, press **L**.

10. To enter text in the Header text box, press **H**.

11. Type **Practice Worksheet** and press Enter.

12. To accept all of the settings in the dialog box, choose the OK command button, or press Shift-Enter.

13. Highlight Quit and press Enter or simply press **Q** to exit the menu.

Filling in a dialog box with the keyboard is a bit cumbersome—the mouse works much better because you can simply click on the options you want to change. Follow these steps if you have a mouse:

1. Place the mouse pointer in the control panel to display the menu.

2. Click on Print.

3. Click on Printer.

4. To edit the settings, click anywhere in the dialog box.

5. Click on Text File to turn on this Destination option. The asterisk option button moves next to Text File.

6. Click on Printer to change the option back to its original setting.

7. Click on Unformatted Pages to turn off this option.

8. Click on Top, a margin setting, and type **6**.

9. Click on OK to accept all the settings in the dialog box.

10. Click on Quit in the menu bar.

The quickest way to cancel a dialog box without saving the changes you made to it is to press Ctrl-Break. You can also press Esc or the right mouse button several times until the dialog box disappears.

Another way to fill in a dialog box is to choose menu options. For example, instead of setting a right margin by editing the Print Settings dialog box, you can choose the following series of commands from the print menu: Options, Margins, Right. Use whichever method you find easier. In most of the exercises in the book, the instructions have you choose menu options, but you can edit the dialog box if you prefer.

WYSIWYG: WHAT YOU SEE IS WHAT YOU GET

◀ ||| 2.3

As mentioned in Chapter 1, Wysiwyg is a graphical interface that offers advanced formatting capabilities. It is a lot like Allways, an add-in that was packaged with Release 2.2. Wysiwyg actually shows bold, fonts, underline, italic, lines, boxes, and shading on the screen to give you a good representation of what your report will look like when printed. Figure 2.6 is a spreadsheet formatted with Wysiwyg. Wysiwyg does a lot more than formatting, however. With Wysiwyg you can do word processing, print a graph without exiting 1-2-3, annotate a graph, adjust column widths and row heights with the mouse, preview a report, and see more columns and rows on the screen.

Wysiwyg is a separate add-in program that you must load or *attach* before you can use it. It does require extra memory—about 108K—so you may not be able to attach it when you are working on large spreadsheets. Because Wysiwyg greatly extends the capabilities of 1-2-3, I recommend that you always attach Wysiwyg. The remainder of this book assumes that Wysiwyg is attached, and many of the exercises use Wysiwyg commands.

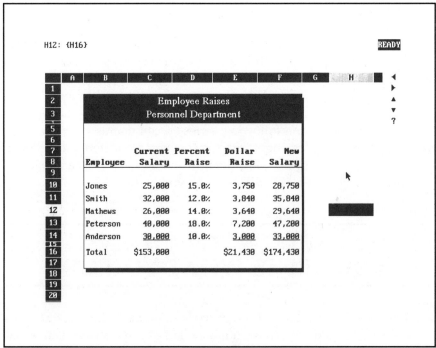

Figure 2.6: A spreadsheet formatted with Wysiwyg

If most of your spreadsheets are large or if you have little interest in advanced formatting capabilities, you can skip over the sections that refer to Wysiwyg.

ATTACHING
WYSIWYG AUTOMATICALLY

To automatically attach Wysiwyg every time you load 1-2-3, follow these steps:

1. Press / to display the 1-2-3 menu and choose:

    Worksheet

    Global

    Default

    Other

    Add-In

    Set

2. The numbers 1 through 8 appear on the menu. You are allowed to automatically attach up to eight add-ins. Choose 1.

3. From the list of add-ins that are displayed, highlight WYSIWYG.ADN and press Enter.

4. Choose No-Key.

5. Choose No because you do not want to automatically invoke the add-in. If you choose Yes, the Wysiwyg menu appears after 1-2-3 is loaded.

6. Choose Quit.

7. Choose Update to save this setting.

8. Choose Quit to return to READY mode.

You can see right away that Wysiwyg is attached because the mouse pointer changes from a square block to an arrow, and the spreadsheet frame (row numbers and column letters) is enhanced. You might also notice that the style of the characters in your cell entries looks a little different when Wysiwyg is attached. The character style depends on your current font, as explained in Chapter 4.

ATTACHING WYSIWYG MANUALLY

If you don't think you'll be using Wysiwyg very often, you can attach it manually whenever you need to. Here's how it's done:

- Press / to display the 1-2-3 menu and choose:

    Add-In

    Attach

- From the list of add-ins that is displayed, highlight WYSIWYG.ADN and press Enter.

- Choose No-Key.

- Choose Quit.

When you are finished using Wysiwyg, detach it with the following procedure:

- Press / to display the 1-2-3 menu and choose:

    Add-In

    Detach

- From the list of add-ins that is displayed, highlight WYSIWYG and press Enter.

- Choose Quit.

By detaching Wysiwyg, you free up 108K of memory, allowing you to work on larger spreadsheets.

THE WYSIWYG MENU

Wysiwyg has its own set of commands, separate from those of the 1-2-3 menu. As you have already seen, the 1-2-3 menu is invoked with the slash (/) key. To display the Wysiwyg menu, press the colon (:) key. The Wysiwyg menu is shown in Figure 2.7. Notice the mode indicator says WYSIWYG. You select options in the Wysiwyg menu the same way you do in the 1-2-3 menu.

To display the Wysiwyg menu with the mouse, place the mouse pointer in the control panel. You will see the menu (1-2-3 or Wysiwyg) you last displayed. If you see the 1-2-3 menu, press the right mouse button. This button switches you back and forth between the two menus. To return to READY mode, press Esc.

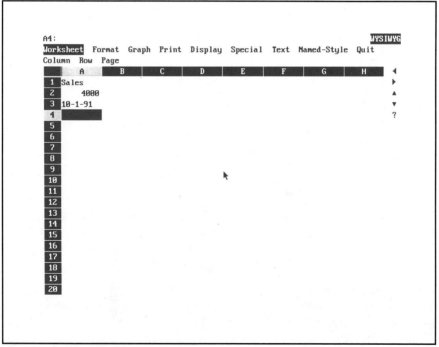

Figure 2.7: The Wysiwyg menu

Most of the Wysiwyg menu options have to do with the formatting of the spreadsheet. You will learn about these options in detail throughout the book.

CHANGING THE SCREEN DISPLAY

When you attach Wysiwyg, the screen colors will be reversed—black characters on a white background. I personally find the white background to be difficult to work with for long periods of time, so I changed Wysiwyg's default colors to white characters on a black background. If you would like to do this, follow these steps:

1. Press **:** to display the Wysiwyg menu and choose:

    Display

    Colors

    Background

    Black

2. To save this setting for future 1-2-3 sessions, choose:

    Quit

    Default

    Update

    Quit

Those with a color monitor might want to change the colors of other parts of the screen, such as the text, cell pointer, and spreadsheet frame. These options are on the :Display Colors menu. If you don't want color, turn on black-and-white mode with the :Display Mode B&W command. (Note: This command may improve legibility on monochrome monitors.) The :Display Options Intensity High command will make your screen brighter. To permanently save the display settings, be sure to use the :Display Default Update command. The settings are saved in a file named WYSIWYG.CNF.

FILE MANAGEMENT

As you make entries into a spreadsheet, your work is stored in the computer's temporary memory (RAM). To keep a permanent copy of a spreadsheet, you need to save it to a disk file. The /File menu, shown in Figure 2.8, is the center for file management in 1-2-3. It is here that you save your work to disk, retrieve existing files, and delete files you no longer need.

SAVING YOUR WORK

Save your work to disk about every fifteen minutes. It doesn't take very long to save, and it could take a long time to recreate something you have typed. Always save before you leave your computer unattended.

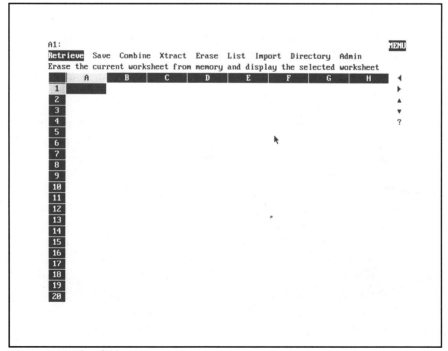

Figure 2.8: The /File menu

All the usual DOS file-naming rules apply to 1-2-3 file names, as follows:

- A file name can be up to eight characters long. Try to make the name descriptive of what is contained in the file.

- A file name can contain letters and numbers.

- Many of the special symbols (such as the * and ?) are not allowed. If you type an invalid character, 1-2-3 displays an error message.

- Do not use spaces or periods.

- Do not type an extension. 1-2-3 automatically assigns the extension .WK1.

Follow these steps to save the spreadsheet you have been working on:

1. Press / to display the 1-2-3 menu. (Remember, you can also display the menu by moving the mouse pointer into the control panel; if necessary, press the right mouse button to display the 1-2-3 menu.) Then choose:

   File

   Save

   At this point, you are asked for a file name. You may find this step to be a little confusing because 1-2-3 displays a list of existing file names. When creating a new file, you should assign a new name—do *not* choose one of the existing names or you will lose the contents of that file. Some people prefer to press Esc to clear the existing file names from the screen before they type the new name. It's not necessary, though.

2. Type **practice** for the file name. As soon as you start typing, the existing names disappear.

3. Press Enter.

After you save a file, the spreadsheet remains on the screen so that you can continue working on it.

RESAVING A FILE

Let's make a change to the spreadsheet and resave the file.

1. Type your name in an empty cell.

2. Press / to display the 1-2-3 menu and choose:

   File

   Save

   The file name, *PRACTICE.WK1*, is automatically filled in for you. If you wanted to save this version of the file under a new name, you would type the new file name (you don't even have to delete the current name). To save the current spreadsheet under the same name, press Enter.

3. Press Enter to save the file with the same name.

4. You are then presented with the following menu:

   Cancel Replace Backup

   Most of the time you will choose the Replace option to update the file. Choosing Cancel does not save the file: it's like pressing Esc several times. The Backup option creates a backup copy of the previous version of the file. For example, the spreadsheet you originally saved (the one without your name typed in it) is saved with the name PRACTICE.BAK. The current spreadsheet is named PRACTICE.WK1. 1-2-3 keeps only one backup copy for each file. While these backup copies do consume extra disk space, the feature can be a life-saver if something happens to your .WK1 file.

5. Choose Replace to update the file.

EXITING TO DOS BY MISTAKE

Here is one of the most common mistakes people make when saving a file:

1. Press / to display the 1-2-3 menu.
2. Highlight the File option.
3. Type **S** to Save.

Oh, no—your spreadsheet has disappeared! The following thoughts are probably whizzing through your head: What happened to my spreadsheet? Did I lose it? Where am I? How did I get here? How can I get back to my spreadsheet? Help!

Don't panic—you haven't lost your spreadsheet. You just temporarily went to the DOS prompt. This happened because you highlighted the File option but you didn't press Enter to choose it. Therefore, when you typed **S** to Save you actually typed **S** for System. The /System command temporarily takes you to DOS so that you can perform DOS operations such as copying files, formatting floppy disks, and checking how much space is available on a drive. To return to your 1-2-3 spreadsheet, type **exit** and press Enter.

I've seen people make this mistake dozens of times. As long as you read the screen (it tells you right at the top to type *exit*), you can safely return to your spreadsheet. But if you panic and try to load 1-2-3 again or you reboot your computer, you will lose your spreadsheet.

RETRIEVING A FILE

To display a spreadsheet you have already saved, use the /File Retrieve command. This command displays the .WK1 files in the current directory path, probably C:\123R23. (The path consists of a drive letter and directory name.) The first five files are listed alphabetically in the control panel. If you have more than five files, you will need to move the pointer over to see them. Actually, there are quite a few shortcuts for moving around the file list. Table 2.2 lists the keyboard shortcuts and Table 2.3 lists the mouse shortcuts. The icons referred to in Table 2.3 are located at the top of the control panel.

Follow these steps to retrieve COLORTST, one of the files that comes with 1-2-3:

1. Press / to display the 1-2-3 menu and choose:

   File

   Retrieve

2. Press F3 or click on the List icon to see a full-screen list of file names.

3. With the arrow keys, highlight the name COLORTST.WK1 (but don't press Enter yet). The control panel displays information about the highlighted file name: date, time, and file size in bytes (characters). The date and time indicate when you last saved the file.

4. Press Enter to retrieve the file.

Table 2.2: Keyboard Shortcuts for File Retrieval

KEY	DESCRIPTION
↓	Lists the next five file names in the control panel
↑	Lists the previous five file names in the control panel
Home	Highlights the first file name
End	Highlights the last file name
F3	Fills the entire screen with file names

Table 2.3: Mouse Shortcuts for File Retrieval

ICON	DESCRIPTION
▼	Lists the next five file names in the control panel
▲	Lists the previous five file names in the control panel
➤	Highlights the next file name
➤	Highlights the previous file name
List	Fills the entire screen with file names

If you have modified the current spreadsheet without saving it, 1-2-3 warns you that your worksheet changes have not been saved. Choose Yes to go ahead and retrieve the file anyway; choose No to cancel the Retrieve command so that you can save the file.

SPECIFYING A DIFFERENT PATH

When you save a file, 1-2-3 automatically saves it in the current path unless you specify otherwise. The default path is your 1-2-3 directory, for example, C:\123R23. You are not forced to save all your files in this directory, however. If you have many spreadsheets, you will want to have several subdirectories for your 1-2-3 files—perhaps one for each project. On occasion you will want to save spreadsheets onto floppy disks for safekeeping or to give a copy to a work associate. 1-2-3 offers three ways to change the path into which your files are saved.

Permanently
Changing the Default Directory

To permanently change the default directory, follow this procedure:

- Press / to display the 1-2-3 menu and choose:

    Worksheet

    Global

    Default

    Directory

- Press Esc to clear the current path.

- Type the new path. For example, **C:\123R23\BUDGET** or **A:\.**

- Press Enter.

- Choose Update to save the setting.

- Choose Quit.

Temporarily
Changing the Default Directory

To change the default directory for your current 1-2-3 session, follow these steps:

- Press / to display the 1-2-3 menu and choose:

    File

    Directory

- Type the new path. For example, **C:\123R23\BUDGET** or **A:**.

- Press Enter.

This directory change applies to each new file you save or retrieve while 1-2-3 is loaded. The next time you load 1-2-3, the directory listed in the Default Settings dialog box is used.

Changing the Directory on the Fly

If you have a single file that needs to be saved to or retrieved from a different path, you can specify the new path on the fly. With the keyboard, press Esc until the current path is cleared and type the new path and file name. For example, to save a file to a floppy disk, type **A:PRACTICE.**

To save to or retrieve from a subdirectory of the current path, you don't need to press Esc or type the path: the subdirectory names are listed at the end of the file list. Just highlight the subdirectory name and press Enter. Let's look at an example. If the current path is C:\123R23 and you want to retrieve a file from C:\123R23\BUDGET, choose /File Retrieve and press F3 so that you can see a full-screen list of names. Highlight \BUDGET, press Enter, and you will see a list of files in the BUDGET directory.

Mouse-users can change the path with the icons at the top of the control panel. To change to a different drive, click on the appropriate drive letter (such as A:). To change to the previous directory level (the parent), click on the double-dot (..) icon.

GETTING HELP

1-2-3 has a comprehensive *online help* facility that is like an onscreen reference manual—complete with an alphabetical index.

1. To display the Main Help Index, press F1 or click on the question mark (?) in the icon panel. The initial help screen is shown in Figure 2.9.

2. Press PgDn to see additional help topics. Mouse-users can click on the down arrow in the lower-right corner of the help box.

3. Press PgUp to display the previous screen, or click on the up arrow.

4. Highlight the topic *Dialog boxes* and press Enter (or click on it).

5. Choose *Dialog Box Definitions.*

6. Read about this help topic. At the end of most help screens is a category called Other Topics. This section lists related topics that you can go to directly. The current topic, *Dialog Boxes*, lists *Using Dialog Boxes*, as an additional topic.

7. Highlight *Using Dialog Boxes* and press Enter.

8. Read about this topic and press F1 to return to the Main Help Index.

Several of the topics on the Main Help Index deserve special discussion, as follows:

- *1-2-3 Command Index* provides an explanation of all of 1-2-3's menu options. The commands are listed in the same hierarchy as the 1-2-3 menus.

- *1-2-3 Commands* explains how to give commands in 1-2-3.

- *1-2-3 Keys* defines the keys used in 1-2-3: the function keys, editing keys, keys for cell pointer movement, and so on.

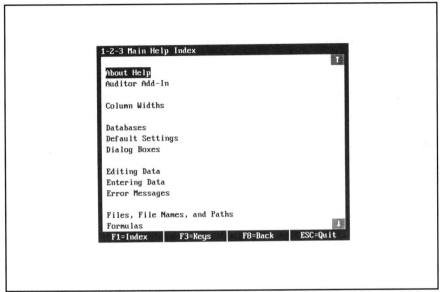

Figure 2.9: The Main Help Index

- *1-2-3 Screen* explains the various parts of the screen. If you don't understand an indicator in the status line or control panel, you can look it up here.

- *Glossary of Terms* is an online dictionary of 1-2-3 jargon.

- *How Do I...?* gives a list of questions of frequently used tasks. Choose a question and the help feature gives you the answer.

The Esc key cancels the Help facility, and returns youto whatever mode you were in before you pressed F1 (for example, READY mode).

Another way to use Help is to press F1 while you are in the middle of a command. 1-2-3 automatically displays the Help screen for the currently highlighted menu option. This feature is called *context-sensitive help*. Thus, if you need help while you are giving a command in the menu, press F1, read the instructions for using that command, then press Esc to continue the command where you left off.

To see how context-sensitive help operates, follow these steps:

1. If necessary, press Esc to exit Help.

2. Press / to display the 1-2-3 menu.

3. Choose Worksheet.

4. Highlight the Erase option (but don't press Enter).

5. Press F1, and read the help screen about erasing a worksheet.

6. Press Esc to clear the help screen.

7. Press Enter to choose Erase.

8. Choose Yes.

PART I

PART II

PART III

PART IV

PART V

Spreadsheets

Chapter 1

Chapter 2

Chapter 3

Chapter 4

Chapter 5

Building a Spreadsheet

◀─┃┃┃ FAST TRACK ┃┃┃─▶

To begin a simple formula: 56

> Type a plus sign (+).

To sum a range of cells: 59

> Type **@SUM(**. Indicate the range to be summed (move the pointer to the first cell in the range, type a period, and move to the last cell in the range). Type **)** and press Enter.

To format the numbers in the entire worksheet: 68

> Press / to display the 1-2-3 menu and choose Worksheet Global Format.

To format a range of numbers: 69

> Press / to display the 1-2-3 menu, and choose Range Format.

To align labels: 71

> Press / to display the 1-2-3 menu and choose Range Label. Then select Left, Right, or Center.

2.3 ┃┃┃▶   **To center a title:**   73

> Press : to display the Wysiwyg menu and choose Text Align Center.

To change the global column width: 77

> Press / to display the 1-2-3 menu and choose Worksheet Global Column-Width.

To change the width of a single column: 78

> Press / to display the 1-2-3 menu and choose Worksheet Column Set-Width.

To erase a range: 80

> Press / to display the 1-2-3 menu and choose Range Erase.

1-2-3's grid of rows and columns is a blank slate onto which you build your spreadsheet. The design of your spreadsheet should begin before you even turn on your computer. To design an effective spreadsheet, you must clearly define the purpose and scope of the project. Think about what you will use the spreadsheet for and what results you would like to get from it. For a complex spreadsheet, you might use paper and pencil to sketch possible layouts. If you have already created the spreadsheet on ledger paper, you can use it as a guide for the layout of your electronic spreadsheet. Always consider how you want the final report to look and design your layout accordingly.

After you have a good idea of your spreadsheet's purpose, you can start entering descriptive labels into spreadsheet cells. Keep the descriptions brief but don't make the labels so cryptic that you won't be able to decipher them a month or a year down the road. Also, keep in mind that someone else may need to read your spreadsheets. In a spreadsheet with many complex calculations, you might want to test them by entering whole round numbers as sample data. If you use simple numbers such as 100 or 1000, you can easily see if your calculations are correct.

Once you have entered the data, the real fun begins: You do your calculations. Initially this may not be your idea of fun, but you might change your mind after you see how 1-2-3 does all the computing for you. All you have to do is specify which cells to add, subtract, multiply, or divide.

CREATING A SPREADSHEET

To create a new spreadsheet, you need to have a blank worksheet on your screen. When you first load 1-2-3, an empty spreadsheet grid appears automatically, but if you are working on another spreadsheet, you must clear the screen with the /Worksheet Erase command.

In this chapter and in Chapter 4 you will work with an employee-raise spreadsheet model. It calculates employee raises and new salaries for a fictitious company's personnel department. The spreadsheet also totals and averages the salaries and raises.

Type the spreadsheet shown in Figure 3.1, keeping the following in mind:

- Type the information in the exact cells shown in Figure 3.1. All examples throughout this and the next chapter refer to these cells. Note that *Employee Raises* is typed in cell A1 and *Personnel Department* is typed in A2.

- If you make a mistake after you press Enter, clear the cell with the Del key and retype the data.

- Do not type commas in the numbers. (Commas are added with a formatting command.)

- Because the alignment settings for text and numbers are automatic, the column headings may not line up with the numbers. You will fix the alignment later.

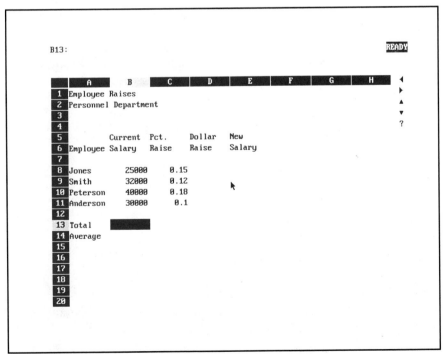

Figure 3.1: The data for the employee-raise spreadsheet

Save the file with the name RAISE, as follows:

1. Press / to display the 1-2-3 menu and choose:

   File

   Save

2. Type **RAISE** and press Enter.

BUILDING FORMULAS

Formulas perform calculations with the numbers in your spreadsheet. In the employee-raise spreadsheet, you will type formulas to calculate the dollar amounts of raises, the new salaries, and the total and average salaries for all employees. You type formulas in the cells where you want the calculations to appear. A formula refers to the cells containing the numbers rather than to the numbers themselves. For example, if you wanted to do a calculation with Jones' salary in Figure 3.1, the formula would refer to cell B4, not the number 25000. That way, no matter what numbers are in the cells, the calculation is accurate.

CREATING SIMPLE FORMULAS

Simple formulas are formulas that refer to individual cells. You can create simple formulas to add, subtract, multiply, or divide the numbers in two or more cells. The Dollar Raise and New Salary columns are simple formulas. The total and average rows use built-in functions and are covered in a later section.

To define simple formulas, use the following mathematical operators:

- \+ Addition
- − Subtraction
- / Division
- * Multiplication

Formulas must begin with a value character. To add cells B14 and C14, you couldn't type *B14+C14* because 1-2-3 would think you were typing a label. The most common way to begin a formula is with the plus sign, for example, *+B14+C14*. The plus sign is a value character and will not affect the result. A minus sign, on the other hand, would make the first cell a negative number. I've seen some people place parentheses around the formula, but this requires extra work.

Typing a Simple Formula

To calculate the dollar amount of the raise, you multiply the salary by the raise percentage. Follow these steps to calculate Jones' raise:

1. Put the cell pointer in cell D8, where you want the answer to appear.

2. Type the formula **+B8*C8**

3. Press Enter.

The answer, *3750*, appears in the cell; the formula appears in the control panel. The formula is permanently recorded in the cell.

To see how 1-2-3 automatically recalculates its formulas when you enter new values, do the following:

1. Put the cell pointer in cell B8.

2. Type **52000**.

3. Press Enter. The new answer, *7800*, is automatically displayed, without your having to do a thing. How's that for powerful!

4. Return B8 to its original value, *25000*.

You are probably wondering how to calculate the raises for the other three employees. You do not need to retype the formula for each row. Because the formula is the same for each employee (the salary multiplied by the raise percentage), you can copy the formula. We will do this a little later in the chapter. For now, let's enter the other formulas.

Entering a Formula by Pointing to Cells

1-2-3 offers another way to enter formulas. The technique you just used to enter the raise formula is called the *typing* method. The alternative technique is called the *pointing* method. With the typing method, you must type everything: the mathematical operators (+, −, *, /) and the cell references. With the pointing method, you still type the operators, but instead of typing the cell references, you can use the cell pointer to specify them.

To try this method, follow these steps to calculate the dollar amount for New Salary (the salary plus the raise amount):

1. Place the cell pointer in cell E8.

2. Begin the formula by typing +.

3. Move the cell pointer to B8 by pressing ←. The control panel displays +*B8*. Do not press Enter yet.

4. Type +. The cell pointer jumps back to where you are building the formula.

5. Move the pointer to D8. The control panel now displays +*B8+D8*.

6. Press Enter to complete the formula. Your spreadsheet should now look similar to Figure 3.2.

The pointing method has several advantages over the typing method. First, you don't have to figure out what cells the numbers are in; you simply put the pointer on the cell and 1-2-3 fills in the cell reference. Second, it is more accurate. It's easy to make a typing mistake when typing a cell reference. For example, you might accidentally type *B88* instead of *B8*. You don't have to worry about this kind of mistake if you select cells with the pointer.

When you create spreadsheets on your own, experiment with the two methods to see which one you prefer. In formulas that refer to cells all over a large spreadsheet, you might find it tedious to point to each cell. In this case, it would be easier to write down the cell coordinates you want to use in the formula and then use the typing method to enter the formula.

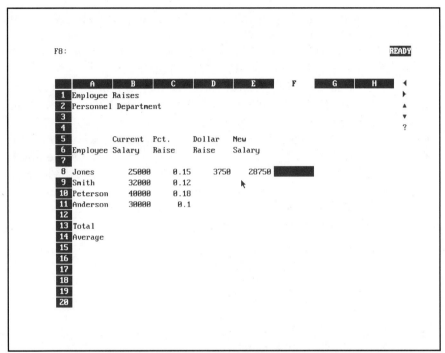

Figure 3.2: The spreadsheet after formulas for Raise and New Salary have been entered

USING BUILT-IN FUNCTIONS

1-2-3 comes with more than ninety built-in functions that you can use in your formulas. These functions are categorized as *mathematical, statistical, engineering, financial, logical, date, string, database,* and *special.* Appendix B contains a list with complete descriptions of each function. All functions begin with the @ sign, which 1-2-3 recognizes as a value symbol. Probably the most commonly used function is @SUM, which totals columns and rows.

Totaling a Column

The @SUM function requires you to indicate the *range* of cells containing the numbers to be totaled. A range is a rectangular group of cells. For example, *@SUM(B8..B11)* totals the range of cells from B8 to B11. One way of indicating a range is to type it; you use one or two periods to separate the beginning cell and the ending cell. The other way to specify a range is to point to it, using either the keyboard or the mouse.

 With the mouse, you can use the *click-and-drag* technique to select the range: Click on the first cell in the range, hold down the left mouse button, move the pointer to the last cell, and release the button.

To select a range with the keyboard, use the arrow keys. Place the pointer on the first cell in the range, press the period to anchor the range, and then move the pointer to the last cell in the range. The range will highlight as you press the arrow key. This is sometimes called *painting* a range.

In the employee-raise spreadsheet, you need to total the Current Salary column. Use the pointing technique to indicate the range.

1. Place the pointer in cell B13.

2. Type **@SUM(** to begin the formula (functions are not case-sensitive, so you can enter them in either upper- or lowercase).

3. Move the pointer up to cell B8.

4. Press the period to anchor.

5. Move the pointer to cell B11. The range B8..B11 is highlighted.

6. Type **)** and press Enter. As shown in Figure 3.3, the answer appears in the cell, and the formula appears in the control panel.

If you are using a mouse, you can use the click-and-drag technique to highlight the range to be summed. Here is the general procedure:

• Click on the cell where you want to enter the formula.

• Type **@SUM(** to begin the formula.

• Click on the top cell to be summed, and hold down the mouse button.

• Drag the mouse down to the last cell.

• Type **)** and press Enter.

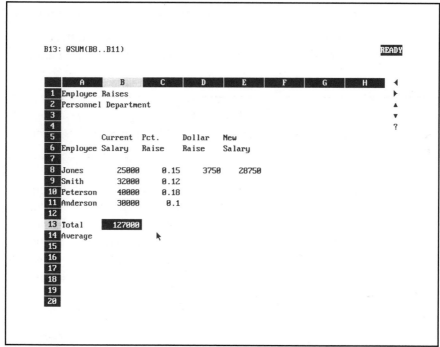

Figure 3.3: Using the @SUM function to add up a column

Finding an Average

Usually, to find an average you have to total the numbers, count how many entries there are, and then divide the total by this number. In 1-2-3, all these steps are built into the @AVG function. All you have to do is indicate the range of numbers to average.

To average the salaries in the employee-raise model, follow these steps:

1. Place the pointer in cell B14.

2. Type **@AVG(** to begin the formula.

3. Move the pointer up to cell B8.

4. Press the period to anchor.

5. Move the pointer to cell B11. The range B8..B11 is highlighted.

6. Type **)** and press Enter. The answer, *31750*, appears in the cell, and the formula, *@AVG(B8..B11)*, appears in the control panel.

COPYING DATA
IN THE SPREADSHEET

You can copy anything in the spreadsheet, including text, numbers, and formulas. 1-2-3 is smart when it comes to copying formulas—it assumes that you want to copy the formula, not the results of the formula. Thus, when a formula is copied, the cell references are changed relative to where you are copying the formula. For example, when you copy the Dollar Raise formula from row 8 to row 9, 1-2-3 adjusts the formula so that the copied formula multiplies the salary and raise percentage in row 9.

The /Copy command asks two questions. First, it asks

Copy what?

This range is the cell or cells you want to copy. Think of it as your *source* range—what you want to copy. Frequently, it is one cell containing a formula. Once you answer this question, you are presented with the second question:

To where?

This range consists of the *blank* cells into which you want to place the copies. Think of this as your *target* range—where you want to copy the cell or cells to. Figure 3.4 indicates the source (Copy what?) and target (To where?) ranges for two different formulas.

Over the years, I have taught 1-2-3 to hundreds of people, and the /Copy command causes more problems than any other command. People tend to forget the command has two steps, and they highlight the source and target ranges at once. The end result is that nothing gets copied. If you can remember that there are two questions, you should have less trouble copying cells.

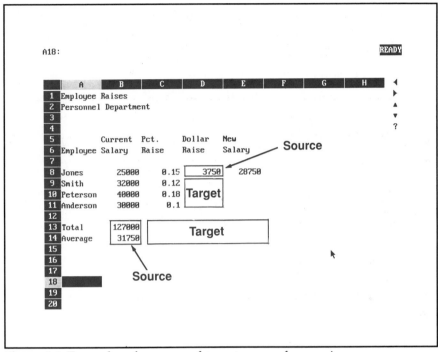

Figure 3.4: Examples of source and target ranges for copying

Follow these steps to copy the raise formula:

1. Place the pointer on cell D8. (You should get in the habit of positioning the pointer on the correct cell before you bring up the menu.)

2. Press / to display the 1-2-3 menu.

3. Choose Copy. For the *Copy what?* range, 1-2-3 suggests the current cell, D8..D8. Because this is the correct source range, you do not need to highlight anything else.

4. Press Enter to accept D8..D8 as the *Copy what?* range. You are then asked "To where?" There are two possible ranges for the second question: D9..D11 (the blank cells you want to copy to) or D8..D11 (the cell containing the formula and the blank cells).

You will get the same results regardless of which range you indicate. You can either type this range or highlight it. Let's try the
highlighting technique:

5. Place the pointer in cell D9 (or leave it on D8).

6. Press the period to anchor the range. This step is very impor-
    tant. If you forget it, you will not be highlighting a range.

7. Move the pointer to cell D11. The range D9..D11 or D8..D11 is
    highlighted.

8. Press Enter.

9. Move the pointer to D9 and look at the control panel. Notice
    that the formula automatically adjusts to the row it is copied
    into.

10. Repeat the steps above to copy the formula for New Salary.

You can copy the Total and Average formulas in a similar fashion. This
time, let's copy both formulas at the same time.

1. Place the pointer on cell B13.

2. Press / to display the 1-2-3 menu.

3. Choose Copy.

4. Move the pointer to B14 to highlight B13..B14 as the *Copy what?*
    range.

5. Press Enter.

6. Place the pointer in cell C13.

7. Press the period to anchor the range.

8. Move the pointer to cell E13. The range C13..E13 is highlighted.
    (It is not necessary to highlight the cells in row 14, though you
    can if you like.)

9. Press Enter.

Your screen should look similar to Figure 3.5. Notice that some of the
numbers have decimal places and some don't, and that the raise percentages

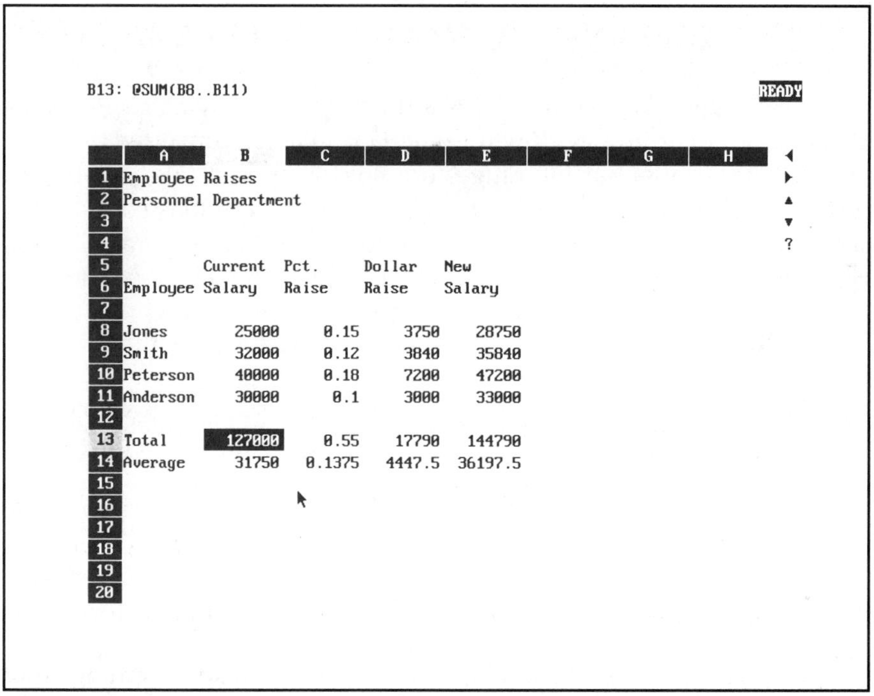

B13: @SUM(B8..B11) READY

	A	B	C	D	E	F	G	H
1	Employee Raises							
2	Personnel Department							
3								
4								
5		Current	Pct.	Dollar	New			
6	Employee	Salary	Raise	Raise	Salary			
7								
8	Jones	25000	0.15	3750	28750			
9	Smith	32000	0.12	3840	35840			
10	Peterson	40000	0.18	7200	47200			
11	Anderson	30000	0.1	3000	33000			
12								
13	Total	127000	0.55	17790	144790			
14	Average	31750	0.1375	4447.5	36197.5			
15								
16								
17								
18								
19								
20								

Figure 3.5: The Total and Average formulas after copying

are displayed without percent signs. These numbers are screaming "Format me!"

TRANSPOSING A RANGE

The /Range Trans command is a copy command with a twist (literally and figuratively). This command copies rows of data into columns and columns of data into rows. You can use this command to reverse the layout of a spreadsheet. Like the /Copy command, you are prompted for source and target ranges. If there are any formulas in the source range, they will be removed and replaced with values.

CONVERTING FORMULAS TO VALUES

The /Range Value command is a third way of copying data—it is a cross between /Copy and /Range Trans. Formulas are converted to values (like /Range Trans) but the ranges are not transposed (like /Copy). In other words, /Range Value freezes the results of formulas so that they remain constant. Why would you want to do this? For several different reasons:

- To conserve memory (values consume less memory than formulas)

- To speed up recalculation (formulas must be recalculated when-ever data changes)

- To delete cells referenced in formulas without complications (if a formula references deleted cells, an error message results; if you convert the formulas to values, you won't have any problem deleting the cells that were originally referenced in the formulas)

You can copy converted values to an empty spreadsheet range, but usually you will be trying to replace formulas with values. Therefore, your source and target ranges should be identical.

BASIC FORMATTING

Although your employee-raise spreadsheet has all the correct results, it doesn't look very pretty. Together, 1-2-3 and Wysiwyg offer numerous formatting options to enhance the spreadsheet. In this chapter, you will learn how to add symbols and punctuation to the numbers (like dollar signs, commas, and decimal places), align the headings with the numbers, and change column widths. Chapter 4 will show you how to use Wysiwyg to further enhance your spreadsheets.

FORMATTING THE NUMBERS

1-2-3 offers a variety of ways to format your numbers; Table 3.1 lists the most common ones. The default format, General, displays numbers with the greatest possible precision. If the number has decimal places, it displays as many decimals as can fit in the column width. If the number is too large, the General format displays exponential notation (for example, the number *1234567890* is displayed as *1.2E+09*).

After you select a numeric format from the Format menu, you are usually asked to enter a number of decimal places. The number you enter controls the digits to the right of the decimal point. For example, the number 1.368 formatted with two decimal places is displayed as *1.37*. Notice that the formatted number is rounded. This rounding applies only to the display of the number; 1-2-3 uses the actual number (*1.368*) in its calculations.

Table 3.1: Number Formats

FORMAT	DESCRIPTION	EXAMPLE
General	No punctuation, variable decimal places	1200.647
Fixed	No punctuation, definable decimal places	1200.65
,	Commas, definable decimal places	1,201
Currency	Dollar sign, comma, definable decimal places	$1,200.65
Percent	Percent sign, definable decimal places	34.25%

This screen rounding can get you into trouble, though. Look at the example below:

Before Formatting	Formatted without Decimals
1.4	1
1.4	1
---	---
2.8 (total)	3 (total)

The apparent mistake in the formatted answer happens because 1-2-3 adds the actual numbers (1.4 and 1.4) in its calculation of the total, not the rounded numbers. Keep your eye out for such rounding problems. You may have to display more decimal places for your results to be precise.

1-2-3 offers two Format commands: one on the /Range menu and one on the /Worksheet Global menu. The /Range Format command lets you indicate which range of cells you want to format. The /Worksheet Global Format command formats all cells, except for those formatted with /Range Format. Decide which format most of the numbers should have and assign this format globally. Then format special ranges individually.

Figure 3.6 displays the formatting for numbers in the employee-raise spreadsheet. The Current Salary, Dollar Raise, and New Salary columns have the comma format, the Pct. Raise column has the Percent format with one decimal place, and the Total and Average rows have the Currency format. Because most of the cells have commas, specify commas as your default format, as follows:

1. Press / to display the 1-2-3 menu and choose:

   Worksheet

   Global

   Format

   , (comma)

2. Type **0** for the number of decimal places.

3. Press Enter.

```
C8: (P1) 0.15                                            READY


        A       B       C       D       E       F       G       H    ◄
  1  Employee Raises                                                 ►
  2  Personnel Department                                            ▲
  3                                                                  ▼
  4                                                                  ?
  5          Current  Pct.    Dollar  New
  6  Employee Salary  Raise   Raise   Salary
  7
  8  Jones      25,000  15.0%   3,750   28,750
  9  Smith      32,000  12.0%   3,840   35,840
 10  Peterson   40,000  18.0%   7,200   47,200
 11  Anderson   30,000  10.0%   3,000   33,000
 12
 13  Total    $127,000  55.0%  $17,790 $144,790
 14  Average   $31,750  13.8%   $4,448  $36,198
 15                        ▸
 16
 17
 18
 19
 20
```

Figure 3.6: The spreadsheet with formatted numbers

All existing numbers, and any new numbers you enter, will be formatted with commas and 0 decimal places. You might be a little concerned about your raise percentages; most of the numbers display zeros right now because the global format does not show decimal places and the numbers are rounded to zero. Don't worry, though, you haven't lost the percentages— you just need to format the range to Percent format. You'll format these numbers after formatting the Total and Average rows to Currency. Follow these steps to format the two rows:

1. Place the pointer in cell B13.

2. Press / to display the 1-2-3 menu and choose:

   Range

   Format

   Currency

3. Type **0** for the number of decimal places.

4. Press Enter.

5. Move the pointer to E14 to highlight the range B13..E14.

6. Press Enter.

Look in the control panel and notice the *(C0)* next to the current cell coordinate. *(C0)* is the code for *Currency format, 0 decimal places*. The control panel indicates the format of any cell formatted with /Range Format. If the control panel doesn't indicate a format, the global format applies to the cell.

1. Place the pointer in cell C8.

2. Press / to display the 1-2-3 menu and choose:

   Range

   Format

   Percent

3. Type **1** for the number of decimal places.

4. Press Enter.

5. Move the pointer down to C14 to highlight the range C8..C14. (All /Range commands are automatically anchored so you don't have to press the period.) Note: mouse users can use the click-and-drag technique to paint the range.

6. Press Enter.

The numbers now display with percent signs and one decimal place. The control panel displays the code *(P1)* for *Percent format, 1 decimal*. Your formatted spreadsheet should now look like Figure 3.6.

If you change your mind about a format, don't erase or delete the cells—just choose a different format. The Reset option on the /Range Format menu removes the format and applies the global format to the specified range.

ALIGNING COLUMN HEADINGS

In their default alignments, labels (text) line up on the left side of the cell and values line up on the right side. However, if you have alphanumeric column headings, they will not line up with the numbers below them. Some of the headings in the employee-raise model are victims of this default situation.

This problem has a simple solution—1-2-3 allows you to align labels on the left, right, or center, as shown in Figure 3.7. You cannot change the alignment of values, however. One way to change label alignment is with a menu option: the /Range Label command. The menu is the way to go if you have already typed in the labels. If you haven't yet typed the label and you know that you want it centered or right-aligned, type an alignment symbol before the text. A quotation mark (") right-aligns and the

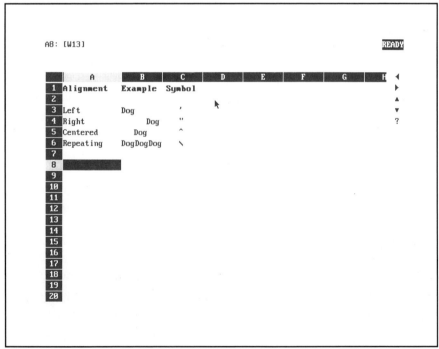

Figure 3.7: Ways to align labels

caret symbol (^) centers the label in the cell. For example, to right-align
the word *Dog*, type **"Dog**.

While you could achieve the same result by pressing the spacebar
several times before the text, the alignment commands and symbols offer
several advantages. First, you don't need to figure out how many spaces
to insert. Second, if you adjust the column width at a later date, you won't
need to realign the text. Right-aligned text remains right-aligned, regardless of the column width.

1-2-3 offers two other alignment symbols or *label prefixes* as they are officially called. The apostrophe is the default label prefix that aligns the
label on the left. You have already seen that 1-2-3 automatically inserts this
symbol in front of your labels. The backslash (\) is the repeating label
prefix; it repeats whatever text comes after the backslash the entire width
of the column. For example, if you type **\Dog**, you see *DogDogDog*. The
repeating label prefix is most commonly used to create lines and borders.
For example, to fill a cell with dashes, type \-. Type \= to create a double-
dashed line. The entire cell will always be filled with dashes, even if you
widen the column. While the repeating label prefix is one way to create
lines, Wysiwyg offers a more professional way. You will learn about this
in Chapter 4.

All the headings over columns of numbers in the employee-raise example need to be right-aligned.

1. Place the pointer on cell B5.

2. Press / to display the 1-2-3 menu and choose:

    Range

    Label

    Right

3. Move the pointer to cell E6 to paint the range B5..E6.

4. Press Enter.

The headings look much better when they are aligned with the numbers, don't they? Notice that the column headings now contain the right-
align symbol, the quotation mark, instead of the apostrophe.

CENTERING A TITLE

Currently the titles at the top of your RAISE spreadsheet are entered into cells A1 and A2, but they would look better if they were centered above the spreadsheet. The /Range Label Center command will not work for this type of centering because it only centers a label within the column width. We want to center them across a range, not just one cell. Wysiwyg to the rescue...

The :Text Align Center command does exactly what we are looking for here: It centers a label across a specified range. Follow these steps to center your titles:

1. Press Home.

2. Press : to display the Wysiwyg menu and choose:

    Text

    Align

    Center

    At this point, you are prompted for the range. You need to high-light the width of the spreadsheet here—all five columns.

3. Move to E2 to paint the range A1..E2.

4. Press Enter.

The titles are now centered, as shown in Figure 3.8.

SETTING COLUMN WIDTHS

The default column width is nine characters, but you can change column widths for a particular column, a range of columns, or all the columns. You will need to widen columns where the number or text doesn't fit in the cell. If a number is too large for the current width, asterisks are displayed instead of the number. Figure 3.9 shows an example of column widths that are too narrow. As you widen the columns, though, the actual numbers reappear. If a text line is longer than the column width, the text automatically displays in the next cell, unless this cell has something in it. If the next

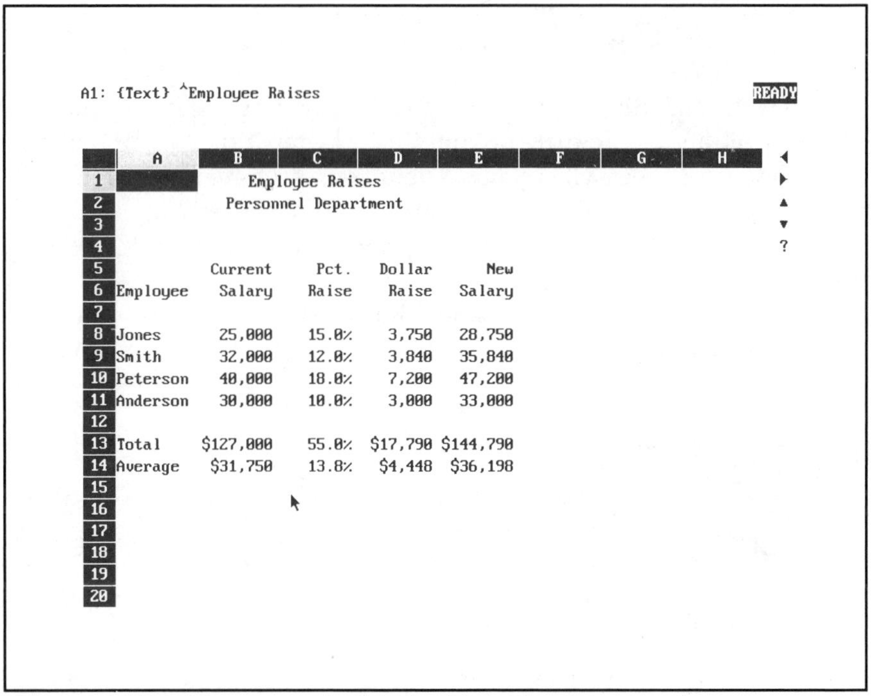

Figure 3.8: The titles centered with the :Text Align command

cell is not blank, the text is truncated (both on the screen and on the print-out). Look at column A in Figure 3.9 for an example of truncated text.

Sometimes you might want to adjust column widths for purely aesthetic reasons. You might think the columns will look better if they have a little more white space between them. Or you might want to narrow a column that contains only a few characters per cell.

There are four commands for setting column widths:

- /Worksheet Global Column-Width sets the width of all columns.

- /Worksheet Column Set-Width sets the width of a single column—the column the cell pointer is in.

- /Worksheet Column Column-Range Set-Width sets the width of a range of consecutive columns.

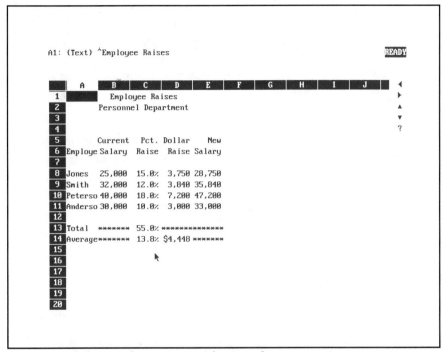

```
A1: {Text} ^Employee Raises                                    READY

         A      B       C       D      E      F    G     H     I     J    ◄
   1            Employee Raises                                           ►
   2            Personnel Department                                      ▲
   3                                                                      ▼
   4                                                                      ?
   5            Current  Pct.  Dollar   New
   6  Employe Salary    Raise  Raise  Salary
   7
   8  Jones    25,000   15.0%  3,750  28,750
   9  Smith    32,000   12.0%  3,840  35,840
  10  Peterso 40,000    18.0%  7,200  47,200
  11  Anderso 30,000    10.0%  3,000  33,000
  12
  13  Total   *******   55.0% ***************
  14  Average*******    13.8%  $4,448 *******
  15
  16                      ▶
  17
  18
  19
  20
```

Figure 3.9: Columns that are not wide enough

- :Worksheet Column Set-Width sets the width of a range of consecutive columns. (It works the same way as /Worksheet
  Column Column-Range Set-Width, but is on the Wysiwyg
  menu.)

Column widths are set in characters; the default global column width
is 9. When you are prompted for a column width, you can either type in
the number or, if you aren't sure what column width you need, press → to
expand or ← to contract the width one character at a time. Your screen
shows you how the column(s) look at each width setting. This technique
allows you to experiment with different column widths without having to
invoke the column-width command several times. Once you are satisfied
with the width, press Enter to accept it.

Changing the Column Width with the Mouse

Wysiwyg offers yet another way to change a column width: with the mouse. Here's how it's done:

- Place the mouse pointer in the spreadsheet frame, on the vertical line to the right of the column letter. For example, to change the width of column B, place the mouse pointer on the line to the right of the *B* in the spreadsheet frame.

- Click and hold the left mouse button. Dotted vertical lines define the current width, as shown in Figure 3.10.

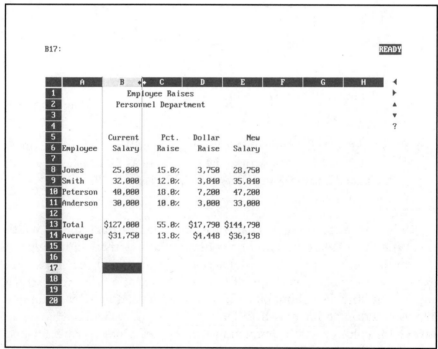

Figure 3.10: Changing the column width with the mouse

- With the mouse button held down, move the pointer to the right to expand the width or to the left to contract.

- When the column is the desired width, release the mouse button.

It takes a lot longer to describe this process in writing than it does to actually change the column width on screen.

Changing the Global Column Width

Now let's change all column widths in the employee-raise spreadsheet. Because you are making a global change, it does not matter where the pointer is.

1. Press / to display the 1-2-3 menu and choose:

    Worksheet

    Global

    Column-Width

2. Type **7** and press Enter.

Because the columns aren't wide enough to display the totals and averages in the currency format, asterisks are displayed in rows 13 and 14. Furthermore, some of the text in column A is truncated. Your spreadsheet is somewhat of a mess, as shown back in Figure 3.9.

To correct these problems, all you need to do is widen the columns. This time, we will enter the column width directly in the Global Settings dialog box.

1. Press / to display the 1-2-3 menu and choose:

    Worksheet

    Global

2. Press F2 to edit the dialog box.

3. Press **C** to choose Column Width.

4. Type **12** and press Enter.

5. Press Enter to choose OK.

6. Press Ctrl-Break to return to READY mode.

Now all the numbers and text are displayed, and you have extra space between columns.

Changing the Width of a Single Column

The Employee and Pct. Raise columns do not really need to be so wide, but because the columns are not adjacent, you must set each one separately.

1. Place the pointer anywhere in column A.

2. Press / to display the 1-2-3 menu.

   Worksheet

   Column

   Set-Width

3. Press ← twice to reduce the width to 10.

4. Press Enter.

5. Following the steps above, set the width of column C to 10.

The [W10] in the control panel indicates that the width of this column has been individually set to 10 characters. When a column is using the global column width, the control panel does not specify the width. The individual column widths override the global setting. To remove an individual column-width setting and reset it back to the global setting, use /Worksheet Column Reset-Width or /Worksheet Column Column-Range Reset-Width.

MODIFYING THE SPREADSHEET

One of the major advantages of an electronic spreadsheet is that you can easily make changes to it. You can edit the contents of cells, insert rows and columns, delete rows and columns, erase cells or ranges, and move cells from one location to another.

EDITING CELLS

You already know one way to change the contents of a cell: If you want something completely different in the cell, you can type over what's already there; when you press Enter, the cell's contents are replaced. However, if you want to make a slight modification to a cell, you can use the Edit function key, F2.

When you press F2, the contents of the cell are displayed in the control panel, with the cursor blinking at the end of the entry. The mode indicator displays EDIT. You can edit with any of the keys described in Table 3.2.

Table 3.2: Cell-Editing Keys

EDITING ACTION	KEYSTROKE
Move left one character	←
Move right one character	→
Move to beginning of entry	Home
Move to end of entry	End
Move left five characters	Ctrl-←
Move right five characters	Ctrl-→
Delete to left	Backspace
Delete	Del (Delete)
Overtype/Insert mode	Ins (Insert)

When you edit, you are automatically in insert mode; to type over text, press the Ins (Insert) key. The status line displays OVR when you are in overtype mode. To return to insert mode, simply press Ins again.

In the employee raise spreadsheet, edit A10 to read *Patterson* instead of *Peterson*.

1. Place the pointer on cell A10.

2. Press F2 to edit the cell.

3. Press Home to move to the beginning of the cell contents.

4. Press → until the cursor is on the first *e*.

5. Type **a**.

6. Press Del to remove the *e*.

7. Type **t**.

8. Press Enter to exit out of Edit mode.

ERASING A RANGE

In Release 2.3, erasing a single cell is easy: place the pointer on the cell and press Del. (The Del key doesn't work in previous versions of 1-2-3.) To erase a range, use the /Range Erase command, which prompts you for a range to erase.

Follow these steps to erase cells in the employee-raise spreadsheet:

1. Place the pointer on cell C13.

2. Press Del.

3. Place the pointer on cell A14.

4. Press / to display the 1-2-3 menu and choose:

   Range

   Erase

5. Move the pointer to E14 to paint the range A14..E14.

6. Press Enter. Your spreadsheet should look similar to Figure 3.11.

Erasing a cell removes the contents but not the formatting. If you move the pointer over to B14, you will still see (C0) in the control panel. Most of the time, this unnecessary formatting doesn't cause any problems. Because cell formatting consumes memory, though, you might want to clear the formatting in blank cells if you are working with a large spreadsheet. The /Range Format Reset command will eliminate the local formatting.

A word of advice: Do not use the spacebar to erase a cell. These extra spaces can cause a number of problems. For example, if you type a long label in A1, it will not display in A2 if this cell contains a space. To locate unwanted spaces, place the pointer on a cell and check the control panel for a lone apostrophe. Remove these spaces with Del or /Range Erase.

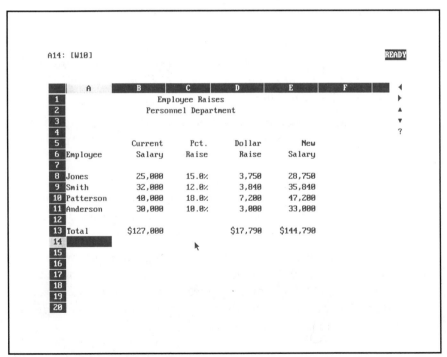

Figure 3.11: After erasing cells

INSERTING ROWS AND COLUMNS

If you discover that you have left out a row or column in your spread-sheet, you can insert one very easily using the /Worksheet Insert command. Rows are inserted above the cell pointer; columns are inserted to the left.

Formulas automatically adjust when you insert rows and columns. If cell locations move after an insertion, 1-2-3 changes the cell references in the formulas. For example, if you insert a row in the middle of a range that is summed, the sum range automatically expands.

To see how this works, insert a row between rows 9 and 10.

1. Place the pointer on any cell in row 10.

2. Press / to display the 1-2-3 menu and choose:

   Worksheet

   Insert

   Row

   To insert more than one row, highlight the number of rows you want to insert (one cell in each row is sufficient). To insert one row, simply press Enter.

3. Press Enter to insert one row. Notice that the inserted row is completely blank. It contains no formulas, nor are any of the cells individually formatted.

4. To make sure your @SUM formulas are still accurate, place the pointer on B14, the Total formula. Before you inserted the row, the formula was *@SUM(B8..B11)*. But after the insertion, 1-2-3 automatically changed the range to *B8..B12*.

5. Type the name, salary and raise percentage for Mathews, as shown in Figure 3.12. Remember, don't type the comma in the number 26,000. (The comma appears automatically because it is the global format.) Also, when you type the raise percentage in cell C10, you must enter *.14*, not *14*.

```
A10: [W10] 'Mathews                                                READY

          A         B          C          D          E          F       ◄
    1                     Employee Raises                                ►
    2                  Personnel Department                              ▲
    3                                                                    ▼
    4                                                                    ?
    5               Current      Pct.     Dollar       New
    6  Employee     Salary      Raise      Raise      Salary
    7
    8  Jones        25,000     15.0%       3,750      28,750
    9  Smith        32,000     12.0%       3,840      35,840
   10  Mathews      26,000     14.0%       3,640      29,640
   11  Patterson    40,000     18.0%       7,200      47,200
   12  Anderson     30,000     10.0%       3,000      33,000
   13
   14  Total       $153,000       ▸      $21,430    $174,430
   15
   16
   17
   18
   19
   20
```

Figure 3.12: The spreadsheet with a row for a new employee, Mathews

6. Format the raise to Percent format with one decimal place (use /Range Format).

7. Copy the formulas in D9..E9 to D10..E10.

More often than not, you will want to insert a new row at the bottom of a range, instead of in the middle. Be careful when doing so—these rows are outside the summed range and therefore are not included in the total. You have to edit the formula to include the new row or rows. If you forget to change the formula, your totals will not be accurate and it will look like you can't add!

1-2-3 does offer a way for you to get around this common problem. In your @SUM range, include the blank cell underneath the last number in the column you want to total, for example, *@SUM(B8..B13)*. Because cell B13 is blank, the total won't be affected. But if you insert rows at the bottom of the range, the formula range expands to include these new rows.

DELETING ROWS AND COLUMNS

Many of the rules you learned for inserting rows and columns apply to deleting them:

- To delete more than one row or column, select a range that includes one cell in each row or column you want to delete.

- Formulas automatically adjust when you delete rows or columns.

- It's OK to delete a row or column in the *middle* of a summed range, but you will run into problems if you delete the beginning or end of a range.

This last rule merits further discussion. If you delete rows 9, 10, or 11 in your current version of the employee-raise spreadsheet, the range in the @SUM formula will contract without a problem. But if you delete row 8 or row 12, you are eliminating the beginning or end of the range. 1-2-3 gets confused when this happens, and you will get ERR (error) messages in the total cells; you then have to reenter your cell references. However, if you include the blank cells at the bottom and top of the column in your @SUM range, you will not be faced with those dreaded ERR messages if you delete the first or last row of data.

Before you delete anything in the spreadsheet, save the file.

1. Press / to display the 1-2-3 menu and choose:

    File
    Save

2. Press Enter to keep the same name.

3. Choose Replace.

4. Place the pointer anywhere in row 10.

5. Press / to display the 1-2-3 menu and choose:

    Worksheet

    Delete

    Row

6. Press Enter to delete the current row (10).

UNDOING MISTAKES

One of the greatest fears new computer users have is making mistakes. To a great extent, this fear can be alleviated in 1-2-3, thanks to its Undo feature. With 1-2-3's Undo command, Alt-F4, you can undo your last action. Undo is a lifesaver if you delete or erase cells accidentally. It is not limited to deleting, however, since you can undo all of the following:

- Commands on the 1-2-3 menu.
- Commands on the Wysiwyg menu.
- Data entry.
- Cell editing.

The Undo command only undoes operations that take you out of READY mode. For example, it will not undo pointer movement commands. One way to use the Undo feature is to temporarily go into another file to look something up:

- While you are in one spreadsheet, retrieve another file.
- Find the information you are looking for—but don't go out of READY mode.
- Press Alt-F4 to undo the file retrieval. Your original spreadsheet will be redisplayed.

Enabling the Undo Feature

Have you ever pressed Alt-F4 only to have nothing happen? Don't worry, your computer is not broken. If Undo is not working, it's because it isn't currently *enabled,* or turned on. By default, Undo is disabled because the feature is such a memory hog. If you are working with a large spreadsheet, you may not have enough memory to enable Undo. Or, if you are using Wysiwyg, you may not be able to turn on the Undo feature even with the smallest of spreadsheets. It all depends on how much and what type of memory your computer has. Before we get into a discussion of memory, try to enable your Undo feature.

Press / to display the 1-2-3 menu and choose:

Worksheet

Global

Default

Other

Undo

Enable

Quit

When Undo is enabled, you will see UNDO in the status line. You may get the following error message when you try to enable Undo:

Cannot enable undo: memory required is already in use

This message means that your data or an add-in (such as Wysiwyg) is using the memory the Undo feature needs. It does not necessarily imply that you don't have enough RAM to enable Undo. The bottom line is that you must enable Undo *before* you attach Wysiwyg (or other add-ins) and *before* you create or retrieve a spreadsheet. To rectify this situation, you must:

- Press Esc and then Ctrl-Break to return to READY mode.
- Save your file, if necessary (/File Save).
- Detach add-ins (/Add-In Detach).
- Clear the screen (/Worksheet Erase).

- Turn on Undo (/Worksheet Global Default Other Undo Enable).
- Attach add-ins (/Add-In Attach).
- Retrieve your file.

Because this requires a lot of steps, Undo should be enabled before you attach any add-ins or begin work on a spreadsheet. To automatically enable Undo, choose the Update option on the /Worksheet Global Default menu.

To see how much memory your computer has, follow these steps:

1. Press / to display the 1-2-3 menu and choose:

    Worksheet

    Status

    Your screen should look something like Figure 3.13, though your numbers will be different. When Undo is enabled, 1-2-3 stores a backup copy of your spreadsheet in memory. This backup copy is stored in expanded memory, if you have enough of it. Otherwise, it is stored in conventional memory, leaving you

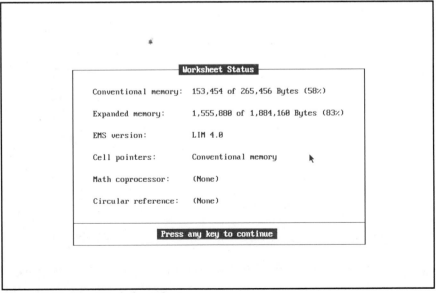

Figure 3.13: The Worksheet Status screen

very little room for your spreadsheets. If you do not have expanded memory, I would advise you *not* to enable the Undo feature, unless your spreadsheets are very small.

2. Press any key.

3. Assuming you have successfully enabled Undo, move the pointer to A1 and press Del.

4. Press Alt-F4 to Undo the deletion.

MOVING CELLS

When you need to reposition cells, rows, or columns, use the /Move command. This command is very similar to /Copy except that the source range is no longer in its original location; it is moved to the target range. The /Move command is potentially dangerous because it overlays cells in the target range. If the "To where?" range is blank, you won't have a problem. But if the target range contains data, you will lose it (unless the Undo feature is enabled). Sometimes you will need to insert blank rows or columns before you invoke the /Move command.

PRINTING IN 1-2-3

There are two ways to print a spreadsheet: with 1-2-3's /Print command or with Wysiwyg's :Print option. Which one should you use? If you haven't used any of Wysiwyg's formatting commands, you can print with either command. Once you start formatting with the :Format commands, though, you will need to print with Wysiwyg's :Print command to see the formatting on the printed page.

CHECKING YOUR PRINTER'S NAME

Before you can print in 1-2-3, you need to specify your printer's name in the Install program. For example, if you have an Epson FX-80, 1-2-3 needs to know that. To see if you have the correct printer installed, follow these steps:

1. Press / to display the 1-2-3 menu and choose

   Worksheet

   Global

   Default

   Printer

   The Default Printer Settings dialog box then appears. Your printer name is displayed near the bottom of this box (it is circled in Figure 3.14). If this is the correct printer, you are ready to print. If no name is listed, you need to run the Install program; refer to Appendix A for details. If the wrong name is listed, 1-2-3 may be installed for more than one printer. To choose a different printer name, follow these steps:

2. Press F2 to edit the dialog box (or click the mouse inside the box).

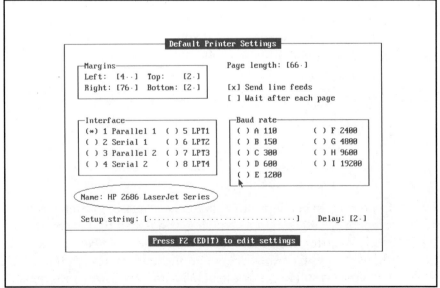

Figure 3.14: The Default Printer Settings dialog box

3. Choose Name.

4. Highlight the correct printer name and press Enter twice.

5. Choose Quit until you are in READY mode.

PRINTING A REPORT

In the employee-raise spreadsheet, you have used only one Wysiwyg formatting command: You centered the titles with :Text Align. When you print this report in 1-2-3, the titles will not be centered. In Chapter 4, you will apply some additional formatting options, and then print the spreadsheet in Wysiwyg. For now, let's print the report in 1-2-3, as follows:

1. Make sure your printer is turned on, has paper, and is online.

2. Press Home.

3. Press / to display the 1-2-3 menu and choose

    Print

    Printer

    While there are a lot of options in the Print Settings sheet, there is only one that you must enter. You must indicate the print range. You might assume that if you don't specify a range, 1-2-3 prints everything. Wrong—nothing prints.

4. Choose Range.

5. Paint the range A1..E14 (don't forget to anchor with the period).

6. Press Enter.

7. Choose Align. (This command lets 1-2-3 know that the printer is at the top of the page. It is a private conversation between 1-2-3 and your printer—nothing happens that you can see.)

8. Choose Go to begin printing. If you have a laser printer, it appears that nothing happened when you issued the Go command. You don't see the report, though the Form Feed button should be lit up on the printer's front panel, indicating that the report is still in the printer. Unlike most software programs,

1-2-3 does not automatically eject the page when a report is finished printing. In order to remove the page from the printer, you have to use either your printer's formfeed button or 1-2-3's Page command on the print menu. The Page command requires less physical labor, so let's do it that way.

9. Choose Page to eject the page. (On some printers that use continuous paper, you may need to choose Page twice to tear off the page.)

10. Choose Quit to exit the print menu.

11. Save the file with the same name (**RAISE**).

Figure 3.15 shows a printed sample of your spreadsheet. The titles are not centered because they were aligned with a Wysiwyg command. In Chapter 4, you will get an opportunity to print the report in Wysiwyg. Chapters 6 and 7 discuss printing in detail.

```
Employee Raises
Personnel Department


                   Current      Pct.     Dollar        New
Employee            Salary      Raise      Raise      Salary

Jones               25,000     15.0%       3,750      28,750
Smith               32,000     12.0%       3,840      35,840
Patterson           40,000     18.0%       7,200      47,200
Anderson            30,000     10.0%       3,000      33,000

Total             $127,000              $17,790    $144,790
```

Figure 3.15: The employee-raise spreadsheet printed with /Print

Chapter 1

Chapter 2

Chapter 3

Chapter 4

Chapter 5

Enhancing a Spreadsheet with Wysiwyg in Release 2.3

FAST TRACK

Once you see some of the formatting options Wysiwyg offers, you will be hooked forever. If done properly, Wysiwyg-formatted reports are more attractive, legible, and professional-looking than bare-bones 1-2-3 reports. Wysiwyg proves that numerical data needn't be boring. Just make sure you don't overdo it. Contrary to popular belief, maximizing the number of different formatting features used on one page is *not* a goal of spreadsheet publishing. Using many fonts, shades, boxes, and lines is not only unattractive, it's distracting and inhibits understanding of the data.

PRESPECIFYING A RANGE

Many 1-2-3 and Wysiwyg commands prompt you for a range. For example, after you issue the /Range Label Right command, 1-2-3 asks you to enter the range of labels. All of the :Format commands outlined in this chapter also require that you specify a range of cells to format. You can either type the range or highlight it with the arrow keys or mouse.

Typically, you invoke a command and then specify a range when prompted. But rather than waiting for 1-2-3 to ask you for a range, you can specify ranges *before* you invoke any commands. To *prespecify* a range, follow this basic procedure:

- Place the cell pointer on the first cell in the range.

- Press F4 to anchor (this works like the period).

- With the arrow keys, move the cell pointer to the last cell in the range. The range will be highlighted.

- Press Enter.

At this point, you can give a 1-2-3 or Wysiwyg command. You will not be prompted for a range; the prespecified range will be used automatically.

The mouse offers another way to prespecify a range, as follows:

- Click on the first cell in the range.

- Drag the mouse to the last cell in the range.

- Release the mouse button.

Prespecifying a range is convenient when you are formatting the same range with several different formatting commands. For instance, suppose you want the column headings formatted in the bold and italic type styles, with a solid line underneath. Because a range will remain highlighted until you move the cell pointer elsewhere, you can invoke one command after another without having to respecify the same range. You will get an opportunity to try this technique later in the chapter.

TYPE STYLES

To emphasize column headings, titles, and totals in your spreadsheets, you can use these *type styles*: bold, italic, and underline. Figure 4.1 illustrates these three styles.

There are three types of underlining styles. Use the single or wide style above column totals, and the double-underline style below bottom-line calculations. Notice that the underlining style underlines only the characters in the cell and does not span the cell width. To get a solid line across the cell, use the Lines formatting option. Or, to produce a line that's even heavier than the wide option, use the Shades command. Both of these options are discussed later in the chapter.

Let's add some style to your employee-raise spreadsheet. If necessary, retrieve RAISE and then follow these steps to bold the titles and column headings:

1. Place the pointer on cell A5.

2. Press : to display the Wysiwyg menu and choose:

    Format

    Bold

    Set

3. Paint the range A5..E6.

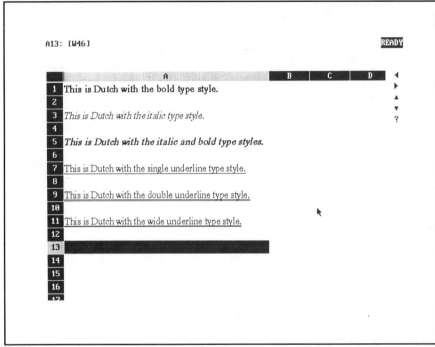

Figure 4.1: The type styles

4. Press Enter. The headings are now in a heavier type. The control panel displays the Wysiwyg format inside braces, in this case *{Bold}*.

5. Follow the steps above to bold the titles in A1..A2. (Remember, the titles are in cells A1 and A2, although it doesn't look like it because they are centered.)

Now, underline the numbers above the totals:

1. Place the pointer on cell B11.

2. Press **:** to display the Wysiwyg menu and choose:

    Format

    Underline

    Single

3. Paint the range B11..E11 and press Enter.

4. To remove the underlining from cell C11, first place the pointer on C11.

5. Then press **:** to display the Wysiwyg menu and choose:

   Format

   Underline

   Clear

6. Press Enter to clear the underlining from cell C11..C11.

Your spreadsheet should look similar to Figure 4.2.

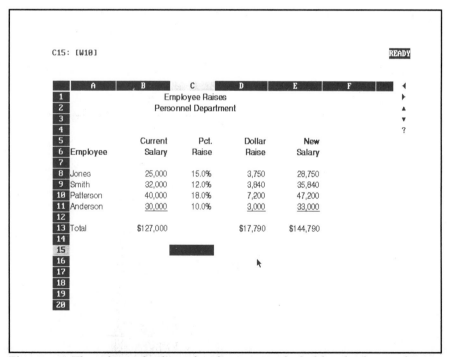

Figure 4.2: The titles and column headings are in the bold style; the numbers above the totals are underlined.

FONTS

Wysiwyg defines the word *font* in a slightly different way from the rest of the world. In Wysiwyg, a font refers to a specific typeface—Helvetica, Times Roman, Courier, Line Printer, etc.—in a specific size. It does *not* refer to a character's type style (light, bold, italic, etc.).

There are two different types of fonts: serif and sans serif. *Serif* fonts have decorative tails at the ends of the strokes of each character. *Sans serif* fonts do not have these decorative touches. Figure 4.3 compares a serif font (Dutch) with a sans serif font (Swiss).

The spacing of a particular font is either proportional or fixed. In a *fixed-space font*, each character is assigned the same amount of space, regardless of how thin or fat the character is. In a *proportional font*, the space each character consumes depends on the size of the character. For example, a lowercase *i* or *t* takes up much less space than an uppercase *M* or *W*. Figure 4.4 compares a fixed-space font (Courier) with a proportional font (Swiss). Proportional fonts are used most often in professional publications.

Dutch is a serif font

Swiss is a sans serif font

Figure 4.3: Comparing two types of fonts (serif and sans serif)

Character sizes are measured in *points*. Points refer to a character's height and width in a given typeface. The larger the point size, the larger the character. There are 72 points to an inch. To give you an idea of what point sizes to use for your text, follow these rough guidelines: most text is usually in 10- or 12-point type, and headings are usually around 14 points. If you want to maximize the amount of text on the page you can choose a smaller size, such as 6 or 8 point.

WHERE DO FONTS COME FROM?

Fonts are generally located in one of three specific areas:

- Inside the printer.
- In cartridges that plug into the printer.
- In files on your hard drive.

This list is ordered by desirability. The most attractive scenario is a printer that already has typefaces built-in, like PostScript printers, and to

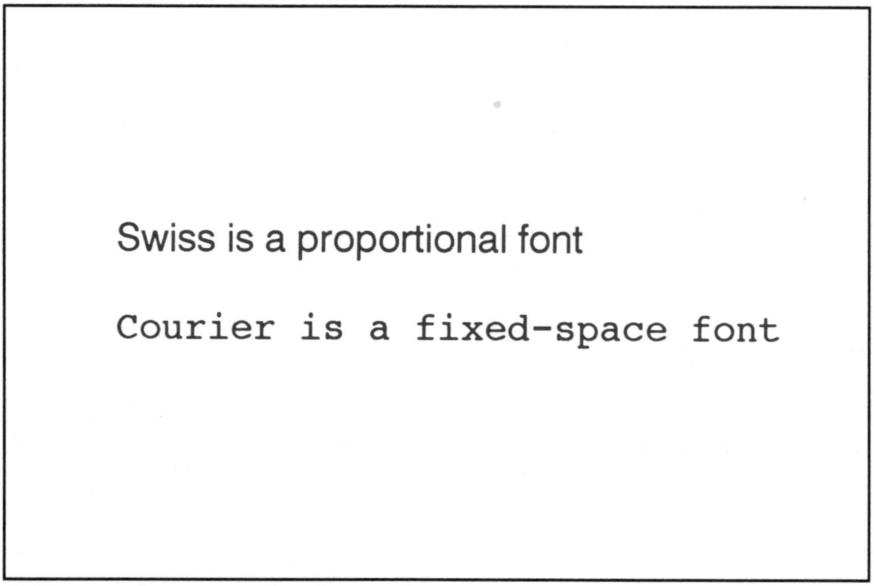

Swiss is a proportional font

```
Courier is a fixed-space font
```

Figure 4.4: Comparing fixed-space and proportional fonts

a lesser degree, HP LaserJet III printers. You can use built-in, or *resident*, typefaces without ever having to worry about such nagging issues as downloading of fonts or font installation. Another advantage to built-in typefaces is that they are *scalable* and can be printed in any size. In 1-2-3, you can produce any point size from 4 to 72.

Cartridges are a close second, although most cartridges designed for the HP LaserJet offer only fixed-size fonts. You enjoy the convenience and speed of resident fonts, but not the versatility of built-in scalable fonts.

Soft fonts are disk files that tell the printer how to produce a font. They must be sent to the printer's memory, or *downloaded*, before the report is printed so that the printer knows how to print the document. Fortunately, Wysiwyg downloads fonts automatically so the process is transparent to you. Soft fonts have three drawbacks: downloading is slow, they take up a lot of space on your hard disk, and they are generally not available in all sizes.

Wysiwyg comes with four soft fonts:

- Swiss, a sans serif, proportional typeface

- Dutch, a serif, proportional typeface

- Courier, a serif, fixed-spaced typeface

- Xsymbol, a set of special effects characters, or *dingbats*

CHANGING FONTS

Each spreadsheet can use up to eight different fonts. Choose :Format Font and you will see the default set of fonts shown in Figure 4.5. Your default font set contains several sizes for two of the soft fonts that are included with Wysiwyg, Swiss and Dutch. (By the way, in case you are wondering what *Bitstream* means, it is the company that makes the fonts.) Font 1, currently 12-point Swiss, is the global font that is assigned to all cells.

One of the most common reasons to change fonts is to enlarge a heading or title. For example, the title in the employee-raise model should be

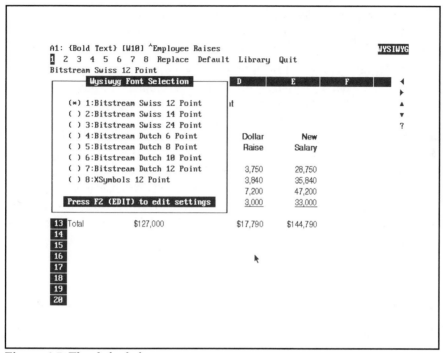

Figure 4.5: The default font set

larger than the rest of the spreadsheet. Follow these steps to assign a different font to the title:

1. Place the pointer in A1.

2. Press : to display the Wysiwyg menu and choose:

   Format

   Font

   The largest sizes on the list are 14-point and 24-point Swiss. Since 24-point would overwhelm your small spreadsheet, choose 14-point. (In the next section you will learn how to add additional sizes to the font set.)

3. Choose 2 to select Bitstream Swiss 14 point.

4. Paint the range A1..A2 and press Enter.

Your titles are now in 14-point Swiss, as shown in Figure 4.6. The control panel displays the typeface, size, and type style: {SWISS14 Bold}. If no font information is displayed for a cell, it is using the global font, font 1.

REPLACING FONTS

You are not limited to the eight fonts on the list. While you can't have more than eight choices on the list, you can substitute different fonts for fonts 1 through 8. Whenever you want to use a typeface or size that's not on the font list, you can replace one of the existing fonts with the one you want. Replace only those fonts you are unlikely to need in the current spreadsheet.

```
A1: {SWISS14 Bold Text} [W10] ^Employee Raises                      READY
```

	A	B	C	D	E	F
1		Employee Raises				
2		Personnel Department				
3						
4						
5		Current	Pct.	Dollar	New	
6	Employee	Salary	Raise	Raise	Salary	
7						
8	Jones	25,000	15.0%	3,750	28,750	
9	Smith	32,000	12.0%	3,840	35,840	
10	Patterson	40,000	18.0%	7,200	47,200	
11	Anderson	30,000	10.0%	3,000	33,000	
12						
13	Total	$127,000		$17,790	$144,790	
14						
15						
16						
17						
18						
19						
20						

Figure 4.6: The titles are formatted to 14-point Swiss bold.

In the previous exercise, you assigned font 2, 14-point Swiss, to cells A1..A2. Let's assume you prefer that the titles be 14-point Dutch, a font not on the list. Which of the eight fonts should you replace? You definitely don't want to replace font 1 because it is the global font. That leaves you with fonts 2 through 8. While you can choose any font you are unlikely to need, font 2 is the best choice because you have already assigned this font to the range. When you format a cell to a specific font number (in this case, font 2), that cell will always be formatted to whatever typeface and size have been assigned to that font number. Follow these steps to replace font 2:

1. Press **:** to display the Wysiwyg menu and choose:

   Format

   Font

   Replace

   2

   The menu lists the four Wysiwyg soft fonts, along with an option for Other. The Other option displays an extended list of fonts that are built into some printers, such as PostScript printers, or available on cartridges for LaserJet printers. Keep in mind that your printer may not have all of the fonts on the extended list. If you choose a font that your printer doesn't have, a similar font that you do have is substituted when you print.

2. Choose Dutch and press Enter.

3. Type **14** for the point size and press Enter. Then choose:

   Quit

   Quit

The titles are now in 14-point Dutch.

CHANGING THE GLOBAL FONT

The most common reason for changing the global font is to reduce the point size so that you can print more on a page. Or perhaps you simply prefer a different typeface. To change the global font, you replace font 1 with a different typeface and/or size. For your employee-raise spreadsheet, change the global font to 12-point Dutch:

1. Press **:** to display the Wysiwyg menu and choose:

   Format

   Font

   Although 12-point Dutch is listed as font 7, you do not want to choose it. To change the global font, you replace font 1 with a new font. To do so, choose:

   Replace

   1

2. Choose Dutch and press Enter.

3. Type **12** for the size and press Enter. Then choose:

   Quit

   Quit

When you change font 1, all cells are automatically assigned this new font, except for cells that have been individually formatted to fonts 2 through 8 (such as your titles in A1 and A2). You do *not* need to highlight any ranges when you change font 1.

Be aware that when you change fonts, you may need to adjust column widths. When you increase the type size, the text may get truncated or asterisks may display in place of numbers—classic symptoms of too-narrow column widths. Conversely, when you decrease the type size, you should reduce the column widths to eliminate unnecessary extra space between them.

CHANGING THE DEFAULT FONT SET

If you find that you are constantly replacing certain fonts, you should change the default font set. When you change the default, any new spreadsheets you create will automatically have these fonts. Use the following general procedure if you ever want to change your default font set:

- Replace fonts as necessary.
- Press : to display the Wysiwyg menu and choose:

    Format

    Font

    Default

    Update

The Restore option replaces the current font set with the default font set.

CREATING FONT LIBRARIES

You may find that there are certain combinations of fonts that you use for different types of spreadsheets. Maybe all your budgets use 10-point Swiss for the global font and 12- and 14-point Swiss for the titles, and all your monthly cash-flow projections use 8-point Line Printer for font 1 and 10-point Swiss for font 2. To save yourself the time and effort of replacing the fonts each time you create a new budget or projection, you can create font libraries. A *library* is a named set of fonts that can be retrieved into any spreadsheet.

To create a font library, follow these general steps:

- Replace fonts as necessary.
- Press : to display the Wysiwyg menu and choose:

    Format

    Font

    Library

    Save

- Type a file name (up to eight characters) and press Enter.

Then, whenever you want to use this font set in a spreadsheet, follow this procedure:

- Press : to display the Wysiwyg menu and choose:

    Format

    Font

    Library

    Retrieve

- Highlight the name and press Enter.
- Choose Quit.

The font list then displays the eight fonts that were stored in the library.

WORKING WITH DINGBATS

One of the soft fonts included with Wysiwyg is called Xsymbol. This typeface is different from the others in that it transforms regular characters into special symbols or *dingbats*. For example, if you type the letter **a** in a cell and format it to Xsymbol, you will see →. Or if you format an asterisk to Xsymbol font, you will see a heart in the cell. Figure 4.7 lists all the symbols in the Xsymbol font. There are six sets of paired columns in the figure. The first column in each pair indicates what character is typed to produce the symbol in the cell to its right. For example, a capital *A* produces a circled number 2 when formatted to Xsymbol.

To format a cell to Xsymbol, choose :Format Font 8 in the default font set. This font is 12-point Xsymbol. To get larger symbols, replace font 8 with a bigger type size. In Figure 4.7, I replaced font 8 with 14-point Xsymbol and assigned this font to the cells in columns B, D, F, H, J, and L.

WORKING WITH FONT CARTRIDGES

If you have font cartridges for your printer, you can access the fonts in Wysiwyg. Let's suppose you have an HP LaserJet II with Hewlett

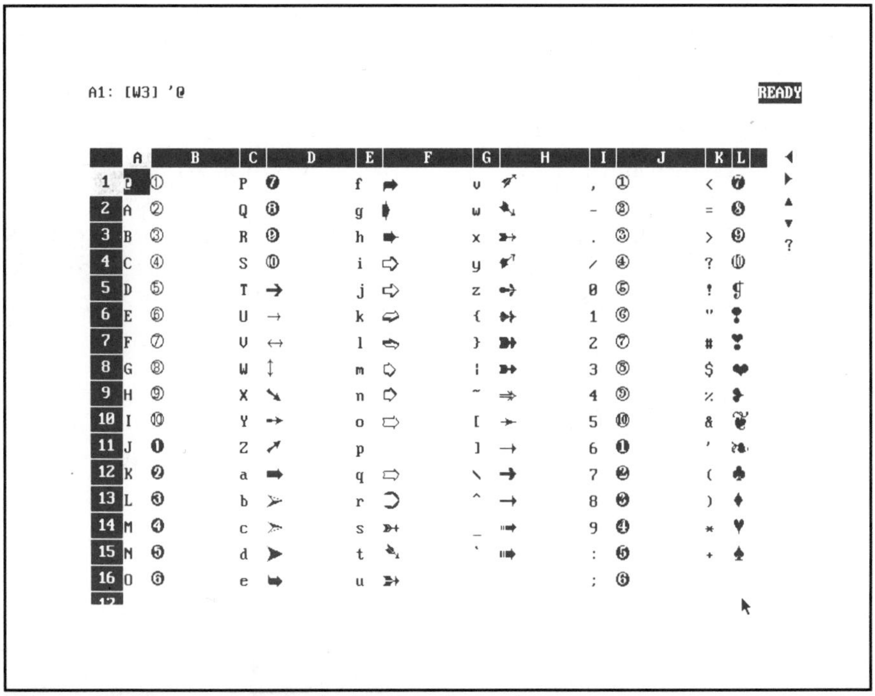

```
A1: [W3] '@                                                    READY
```

Figure 4.7: The symbols in the Xsymbol typeface

Packard's B cartridge inserted into the first (left-hand) slot. This cartridge contains 8- and 10-point Times Roman and 14-point Helvetica.

There are three steps to using font cartridges in Wysiwyg. First, you must select the Extended Capabilities printer driver. This driver allows you to access your printer's internal cartridges. Second, you need to tell Wysiwyg the kind of cartridge you are using and whether it is inserted in the first or second slot. Third, you must include the cartridge fonts in your font set.

Follow this general procedure to configure Wysiwyg for a font cartridge:

- Press : to display the Wysiwyg menu and choose:

    Print

    Config

Printer

- Choose the Extended Capabilities driver.

- Choose 1st-Cart (or 2nd-Cart)

- Select the font cartridge's file name, for example, *HP4-B.CAR*.

To format specific cells with cartridge fonts, you need to replace fonts in the font set. In our B-cartridge example, you might want to replace font 1 with 8-point Times Roman so that this font is the default. You might also want to replace font 2 with 14-point Helvetica. Follow this general procedure to choose a cartridge font as your default (font 1):

- Press : to display the Wysiwyg menu and choose:

  Format

  Font

  Replace

  1

  Other

- In the font list, choose the desired cartridge typeface (for example, *HP Cartridges TmsRmn*).

- Enter the type size.

CHANGING THE ROW HEIGHT

The height of each row is determined by the height of the largest character in the row. When you increase the point size, Wysiwyg automatically increases the row height. But if you want more or less space, you can manually adjust row heights with the :Worksheet Row Set-Height command. There are several occasions when you might want to change the height of a row.

- To get less space between the last number in a column and the totals, or between the column headings and the first row of data, reduce the height of the blank row.

- If two blank rows provide too much space and one row is not enough, increase the height of a single blank row.

- To provide a little extra space between rows of data, increase the row heights of the data range.

Note that you don't normally reduce the height of rows containing characters because you could truncate the top of the characters.

Like fonts, row heights are measured in points. The row height is 120 percent of the font size, rounded to the nearest point. For example, if the font size is 12-points, the row height is 14-points.

Let's adjust some of the row heights in the employee-raise spreadsheet. First, reduce the amount of space above the totals:

1. Place the pointer in row 12.

2. Press : to display the Wysiwyg menu and choose:

   Worksheet

   Row

   Set-Height

3. Press Enter to change the current row. The current row height, 14 points, is displayed. To change the height, you can either type in the value, or press ↑ or ↓ to reduce or expand the height one point size at a time.

4. Type **5**.

5. Press Enter. Because the row is so narrow, the row number (12) in the frame is miniaturized. Now, let's increase the amount of space between the rows of data:

6. Place the pointer in row 8.

7. Press : to display the Wysiwyg menu and choose:

   Worksheet

   Row

   Set-Height

8. Highlight rows 8 through 11 (one cell in each row is sufficient).

9. Press Enter.

10. Press ↓ twice to increase the row height to 16.

11. Press Enter.

Your spreadsheet should look similar to Figure 4.8.

CHANGING THE
ROW HEIGHT WITH THE MOUSE

The mouse offers another way to change a row's height. Figure 4.9 shows a row's height in the process of being changed with the mouse.

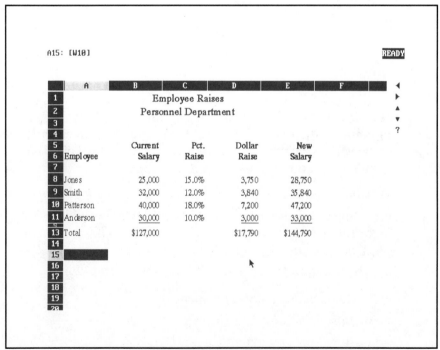

Figure 4.8: The height of row 12 has been decreased while the heights of rows 8–11 have been increased.

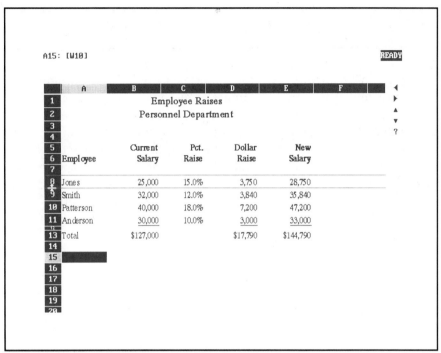

Figure 4.9: Changing a row's height with the mouse

Follow this general procedure:

- Place the mouse pointer in the spreadsheet frame, on the horizontal line below the row number. For example, to change the height of row 8, place the mouse pointer on the line below 8 in the spreadsheet frame.

- Click and hold the left mouse button. Dotted horizontal lines define the current height, as shown in Figure 4.8.

- With the mouse button down, move the pointer down to increase the height or up to reduce it.

- When the row is the desired height, release the mouse button.

CREATING LINES

As you have already seen, the underline format does not underscore the complete width of the cell. To get a solid line, use the :Format Lines command. Unlike with underlining, you are not limited to lines at the bottom of the cell. You can place lines around any part of the cell (left, right, top, bottom, or all sides), or around the periphery of a range (called the *Outline*). Several line styles are available: single, double, wide, and shadow. These styles are pictured in Figure 4.10. Note that the drop shadow is created by using two styles. First, you draw an outline around the range using the default line style. Second, you specify the Shadow style for the same range.

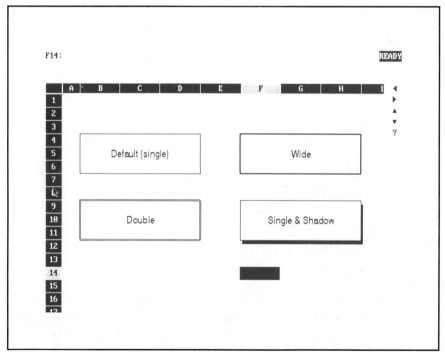

Figure 4.10: Line styles

Add a line underneath the column headings of your RAISE spreadsheet:

1. Place the pointer in cell A6.

2. Press : to display the Wysiwyg menu and choose:

    Format

    Lines

    Bottom

3. Paint the range A6..E6.

4. Press Enter.

Next, create a drop shadow around the entire spreadsheet:

1. Press Home.

2. Press F4 to prespecify the range. Paint the range A1..E14 and
    press Enter. (Since you are going to be assigning two line styles
    to the same range, you can save time by prespecifying the range.)

3. Press : to display the Wysiwyg menu and choose:

    Format

    Lines

    Outline

4. Press : to display the Wysiwyg menu and choose:

    Format

    Lines

    Shadow

    Set

Your spreadsheet should look similar to Figure 4.11. If you were to insert
rows or columns inside the borders, the new cells would be outlined as well.

To remove lines from a range, use the :Format Lines Clear command.
This command applies to the single, double, and wide line styles. To delete
a drop shadow, use :Format Lines Shadow Clear. Because these effects are
overkill for the employee-raise spreadsheet, let's remove the lines.

1. If the range A1..E14 is not still highlighted, prespecify the range (refer to step 2 in the previous task).

2. Press : to display the Wysiwyg menu and choose:

   Format

   Lines

   Clear

   Outline

3. Press : to display the Wysiwyg menu and choose:

   Format

   Lines

   Shadow

   Clear

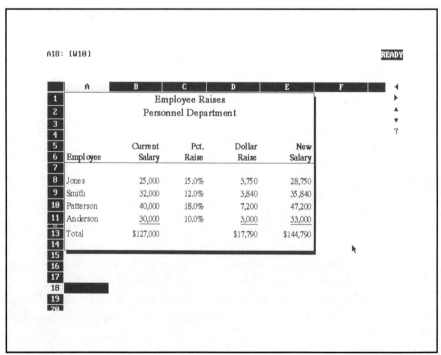

Figure 4.11: A drop shadow around the spreadsheet.

ADDING SHADES

To further emphasize titles, column headings, or important numbers, you can shade them with the :Format Shade command. As shown in Figure 4.12, three levels of shading are available: light grey, dark grey, and solid. The solid shade should be used on blank lines only, because it will block out any text in the shaded range. Solid shading is typically used to create thicker lines than the ones offered in :Format Lines. In the figure, a heavy line was created by using a solid shade on a blank row and then reducing the row height to 3 points. Thus, you control the thickness of the line with the :Worksheet Row Set-Height command.

Here are a few pointers about shades:

- Boldface the characters in a shaded cell to make them easier to read.

- To delineate shaded cells, use :Format Lines Outline to draw a box around the range. This effect was used in Figure 4.11.

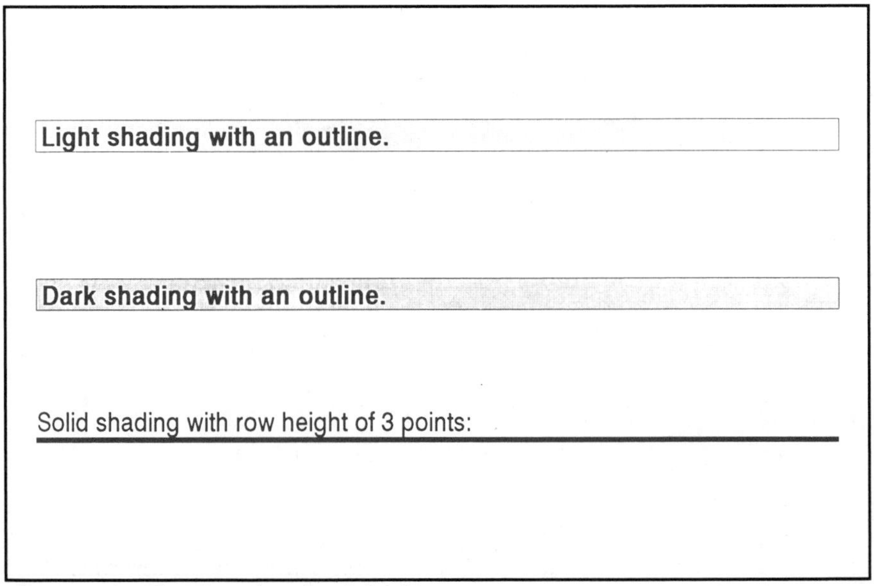

Light shading with an outline.

Dark shading with an outline.

Solid shading with row height of 3 points:

Figure 4.12: The three levels of shading

- On some printers, the light shade may be so faint that it's imperceptible. In this case, you would need to specify dark shading.

- To make a large spreadsheet easier to read, shade every other row.

REVERSING TEXT

An alternative to creating a grey shade is to reverse the text: white text on a black background. This effect is created with the :Format Color Reverse command. In general, large, bold, sans serif fonts are the most legible. Small or serif typefaces tend to be difficult to read when reversed.

In the employee-raise spreadsheet, follow the steps below to reverse the title, as illustrated in Figure 4.13.

1. Press Esc to clear the prespecified range.

2. Press Home.

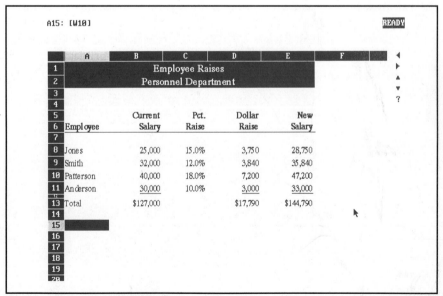

Figure 4.13: Reversed titles

3. Press : to display the Wysiwyg menu and choose:

   Format

   Color

   Reverse

4. Paint the range A1..E2 and press Enter. Your titles should look similar to those in Figure 4.12.

5. Save your file.

PRINTING WYSIWYG-FORMATTED REPORTS

To print a spreadsheet you have formatted with the :Format commands, you must print it with Wysiwyg's :Print command. If you print it with /Print, none of the formatting will appear on the printed report. Printing in Wysiwyg is quite similar to printing in 1-2-3. You specify a print range, and then use the Go option to begin printing. Even though you have already specified a print range in 1-2-3, you must respecify it in Wysiwyg because 1-2-3's print settings are not transferred over into Wysiwyg.

Before you print the report, you need to check to make sure Wysiwyg is configured for the correct printer.

1. Press : to display the Wysiwyg menu and choose:

   Print

   Config

   Printer

   Depending on the type of printer you have, several levels of print qualities are available. The higher the density, the better the quality, but the longer time it will take to print. For a rough draft, choose medium (or low density, depending on your printer) density. For your final printout, choose high density.

2. Highlight your printer's high-density option and press Enter.

3. Choose Quit. The :Print menu should be displayed.

You are now ready to print in Wysiwyg:

1. Choose:

    Range

    Set

2. Paint the range A1..E14 and press Enter.

3. Choose Go. You will obtain a printout similar to Figure 4.14.

Employee Raises Personnel Department				
Employee	Current Salary	Pct. Raise	Dollar Raise	New Salary
Jones	25,000	15.0%	3,750	28,750
Smith	32,000	12.0%	3,840	35,840
Patterson	40,000	18.0%	7,200	47,200
Anderson	30,000	10.0%	3,000	33,000
Total	$127,000		$17,790	$144,790

Figure 4.14: The formatted employee-raise report, printed in Wysiwyg

You will notice right away that printing in Wysiwyg is slower than in 1-2-3. The speed depends on the print density you selected, but even with a low-density choice, printing is slower than in 1-2-3 because of the downloading of the soft fonts. However, the results more than make up for it (compare Figure 4.14 with 3.15). The control panel keeps you posted on the percentage printed. When the report is finished printing, it is automatically ejected from the printer. (In 1-2-3's /Print command, you had to issue the Page command to formfeed the page.)

SAVING WYSIWYG FORMATTING

You should always save your spreadsheets before and after you print. Save before you print just in case something bad happens during the printing process—occasionally, your keyboard will lock up and you will be unable to save the file. Save after you print to store your print settings.

Save your spreadsheet now.

As long as Wysiwyg is attached, your Wysiwyg formatting is saved automatically. The formatting is actually saved in a separate file which has the same first name as your spreadsheet, but has the extension .FMT. For example, your employee-raise spreadsheet is stored in RAISE.WK1 and the formatting is stored in RAISE.FMT. When you retrieve a file when Wysiwyg is attached, the formatting is shown on your screen. If Wysiwyg is not attached when you retrieve the file, it appears as if you have lost all your formatting. But, as soon as you re-attach Wysiwyg, the formatting will reappear.

If you aren't sure whether Wysiwyg is attached, here's a quick test: Press the colon (:). If you see the Wysiwyg menu, the add-in is attached.

Do not modify a Wysiwyg-formatted spreadsheet when Wysiwyg is not attached. If you move cells, insert rows and columns, or delete rows and columns while Wysiwyg is detached, the next time you attach Wysiwyg, you will probably find that the wrong cells are formatted. This mismatching occurs because the .FMT file contains the formatting for the cells in their original locations, and doesn't know that the cells have moved.

CLONING WYSIWYG FORMATS

Once you are satisfied with a particular set of formats for a range of cells, you may want to use the format over and over again. Wysiwyg offers several ways to clone a format. You can:

- copy the format from one range to another

- import the formatting from another file

- assign a code name to a particular style of formatting and then apply this name to other ranges

This section explains each of the above cloning techniques.

COPYING A FORMAT

The /Copy command copies *everything* in the cell: the contents, the numeric formatting, and the Wysiwyg formatting. To copy only the Wysiwyg formatting, use the :Special Copy command. This command is useful when you want to format a cell or a range exactly like a previously formatted range. For example, let's say you formatted a row with bold, light shading, and an outline, and your spreadsheet contains ten rows that should be similarly formatted. Rather than specifying these three attributes for each row, use :Special Copy to copy the formatting.

Like /Copy, :Special Copy prompts you for the source (the formatted range) and the target (the currently unformatted range). If the target range is already Wysiwyg-formatted, the original formatting will be replaced with the copied formatting.

GOING IN STYLE

Named styles allow you to automate the formatting, and the inevitable reformatting, of your spreadsheet. With this feature, you can assign style names to the different elements in the spreadsheet. In your employee-raise spreadsheet, you might want to create names such as Title and ColHed (short for column heading), each of these names having a specific Wysiwyg format associated with it. For instance, all column headings will be 12-point Swiss bold with a line at the bottom, and titles will be 14-point Dutch bold with reversed text. With styles, you need to format only one range. You can then apply this exact formatting to any other range with a few keystrokes or mouse clicks.

Imagine that your spreadsheet contains ten rows of column headings and you have decided that they would look better in italic. Making this formatting change without styles would be a tedious process, requiring you to italicize each range, or to use the :Special Copy command numerous times. But, if all the ranges have been assigned a style name, making this change is easy. Just change one column heading and redefine the style; every range that is assigned the ColHed name changes automatically.

Another benefit to the style feature is the assurance of consistent formatting. When you are formatting ranges one at a time, you risk forgetting to set a particular option. With styles, every range associated with a certain name is formatted identically.

Defining a Style

To create a named style, you first format the range with all the formatting you want associated with the name: the font, type style (bold, italic, underlining), lines, shading, and color. Once you are satisfied with the formatting, you give it a style name with :Named-Style Define.

In the employee-raise spreadsheet, create a style for the column headings, following the steps below:

1. Place the pointer on cell A6—one of the cells that contains the column heading formatting. (You could place the pointer in any of the formatted cells in row 6.)

2. Press **:** to display the Wysiwyg menu and choose:

   Named-Style

   Define

You can define up to eight style names per spreadsheet. Currently, each style is named Normal, and is undefined.

3. Choose 1:Normal.

4. Press Enter to choose A6 as the cell defining the style.

5. Press Esc to clear the current style name, Normal.

6. Type **ColHed** and press Enter. (Six characters is the maximum.)

7. For the description, type **Column Heading** and press Enter.

The control panel displays the name of the style, ColHed. When you define a style, you automatically apply the style name to that highlighted cell.

Applying Styles

The employee-raise spreadsheet doesn't have any other column headings to format with the ColHed style, so to practice assigning styles, let's type a few labels in row 17.

1. Save your file. (Note: you will *not* be saving the following changes you make to your spreadsheet.)

2. Type the following right-aligned labels in the indicated cells:

    A17: **"Jan**
    B17: **"Feb**
    C17: **"Mar**
    D17: **"Total**

3. Place the pointer on cell A17.

4. Press **:** to display the Wysiwyg menu and choose:

    Named-Style
    1:ColHed

5. Paint the range A17..D17 and press Enter. The row is instantly formatted with the ColHed style (12-point Swiss bold, with a bottom line), as shown in Figure 4.15.

6. Follow steps 3 through 5 above to assign the ColHed style to the range B6..E6. This assignment becomes important if you ever change the formatting associated with a style name, as you will see in the next exercise.

Changing a Style

Changing the format associated with a style is a two-step procedure:

- Change the format of one cell.

- Redefine the style, using the same style number.

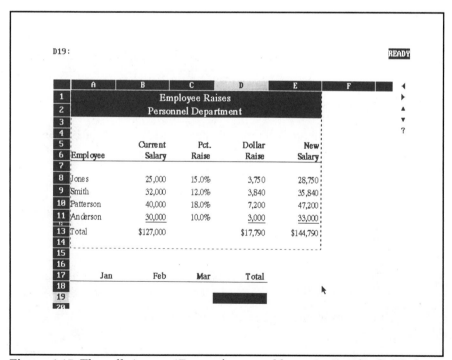

Figure 4.15: The cells in row 17 were formatted by assigning the ColHed style name.

Let's say you want the line under all the column headings to have the wide line style. Follow these steps to change the ColHed style:

1. Place the cell pointer in any cell formatted with the ColHed style.

2. Press : to display the Wysiwyg menu and choose:

   Format

   Lines

   Wide

   Bottom

3. Press Enter to change the current cell only. At this point, only the current cell is changed. You now need to redefine the style.

4. Press : to display the Wysiwyg menu and choose:

   Named-Style

   Define

   1:ColHed

5. Press Enter to associate the style with the format in the current cell.

6. Press Enter to accept the current name, ColHed.

7. Press Enter to accept the current description, Column Heading.

Now, all cells with the ColHed style have wide lines at the bottom. Because this last exercise is not an official part of the RAISE spreadsheet, erase the spreadsheet without saving the changes:

1. Press / to display the 1-2-3 menu and choose:

   Worksheet

   Erase

   Yes

   1-2-3 warns you that your changes have not been saved.

2. Choose Yes to clear the screen without saving.

IMPORTING
FORMATS FROM OTHER FILES

With :Special Import, you can copy all or part of the Wysiwyg formatting in another file. Importing offers the following choices:

- Fonts—the font set in the current spreadsheet will be replaced with the imported font set

- Named-Styles—the current set of styles will be replaced with the imported style set

- Graphs—the imported graphs will be inserted in the same locations as in the source file

- All—each cell will be formatted the same way as in the source file. The font set, named styles, and graphs will be imported as well.

Be very careful with the All option. With this option, all the Wysiwyg formatting in the current spreadsheet is lost and is replaced with the formatting in the source file. If the two spreadsheets are not laid out identically, the wrong cells will be formatted, and you may have a mess on your hands. Figure 4.16 shows a spreadsheet for the Manufacturing Department that is laid out similarly, but not identically, to the employee-raise spreadsheet you have created for the Personnel Department. As you can see, the wrong cells are formatted. *Always save your file* before you import from another spreadsheet. Then, if you get unexpected results, you will be able to retrieve your original file.

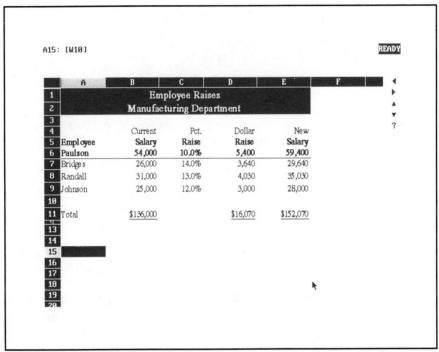

Figure 4.16: If used improperly, the All import option can create a disaster.

Chapter 1
Chapter 2
Chapter 3
Chapter 4
Chapter 5

Working with Large Spreadsheet Projects

◀||||| FAST TRACK |||||▶

To freeze column/row headings on the screen:　　139

Press / to display the 1-2-3 menu and choose Worksheet Titles.

To create windows:　　146

Press / to display the 1-2-3 menu and choose Worksheet Window.

To create a range name:　　153

Press / to display the 1-2-3 menu and choose Range Name Create.

To protect your spreadsheet:　　161

Press / to display the 1-2-3 menu and choose Worksheet Global Protection Enable. Unprotect each data-entry range (see next item).

To unprotect a range:　　161

Press / to display the 1-2-3 menu and choose Range Unprot.

To turn off automatic recalculation:　　167

Press / to display the 1-2-3 menu and choose Worksheet Global Recalculation Manual. Press F9 when you need to recalculate.

**To create a new file out of part
of the current spreadsheet:**　　169

Press / to display the 1-2-3 menu and choose File Xtract Formulas (or Values).

To combine data from separate files:　　172

Press / to display the 1-2-3 menu and choose File Combine Add.

To create a file-linking formula:　　174

Type **+<<*filename*>>cell**, (for example, **+<<JAN.WK1>>C6**).

As your spreadsheets get larger, you are likely to encounter one or all of these problems:

- It takes a long time for you to get to the different parts of your spreadsheet.

- You can't find the section you want to go to.

- Your column and/or row headings scroll off the screen, making it difficult to understand the data.

- Whenever you make a new cell entry, you can't move the cell pointer or give a command until the spreadsheet is finished recalculating.

- You run out of memory (RAM) and can't enter any new data.

Judging from this list, working with large spreadsheets doesn't sound like much fun. However, 1-2-3 provides solutions to each of these problems, as you will see in this chapter.

REVIEW

We will begin this chapter with a review. You will build a spreadsheet to track the sales for a hypothetical company's sales force. Because this exercise is a review, only general steps will be provided, though the basic commands are indicated inside parentheses. If you get stuck, refer to Chapters 3 and 4 for further information.

1. If necessary, clear the screen (/Worksheet Erase).

2. Change the global column width to 12 characters (/Worksheet Global Column-Width).

3. Enter the labels and values shown in Figure 5.1.

4. Right-align the Sales and *% of Total* column headings (/Range Label).

5. Set the width of column D to 9 characters (/Worksheet Column Set-Width).

6. Set the global format to comma with zero decimals (/Worksheet Global Format).

7. Underline C18 (:Format Underline).

8. Boldface the column headings and the title (:Format Bold).

9. Place a line under the column headings (:Format Lines Bottom).

10. Change the font of the title to 14-point Swiss (:Format Font).

11. Center the title (:Text Align).

12. Total the Sales column with the formula @SUM(C6..C18). Your spreadsheet should look similar to Figure 5.2.

13. Save the file with the name **SALES** (/File Save).

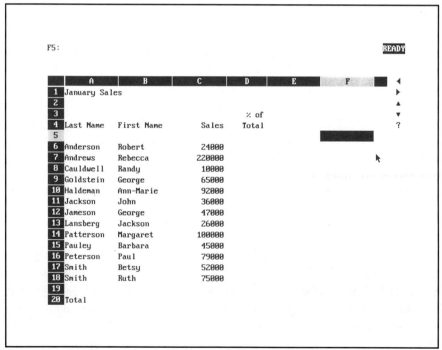

Figure 5.1: The data for the sales spreadsheet

F8:   READY

	A	B	C	D	E	F	
1		January Sales					
2							
3				% of			
4	Last Name	First Name	Sales	Total			
5							
6	Anderson	Robert	24,000				
7	Andrews	Rebecca	220,000				
8	Cauldwell	Randy	10,000				
9	Goldstein	George	65,000				
10	Haldeman	Ann-Marie	92,000				
11	Jackson	John	36,000				
12	Jameson	George	47,000				
13	Lansberg	Jackson	26,000				
14	Patterson	Margaret	100,000				
15	Pauley	Barbara	45,000				
16	Peterson	Paul	79,000				
17	Smith	Betsy	52,000				
18	Smith	Ruth	75,000				
19							
20	Total		871,000				

Figure 5.2: The formatted sales spreadsheet

USING ABSOLUTE REFERENCES IN FORMULAS

As you saw in Chapter 3, when you copy a formula from one cell to another, 1-2-3 automatically adjusts the cell references relative to the new location to which you are copying the formula. For instance, when you copied the formula *@SUM(B8..B11)* to column C, the formula became *@SUM(C8..C11)*. Sometimes, though, you don't want a cell reference to change when you copy; you want it to remain constant. To prevent a cell reference from changing when you copy, you need to turn it into an *absolute reference*.

Figure 5.3 displays an example of a situation where you would want
to use an absolute reference. The *% of Total* formula in column D divides
each person's sales by the total sales. The reference to total sales in cell C20
should be made absolute because you want the formula to always divide
by C20—you do not want C20 to change. Look in the control panel of Figure 5.3. The formula in D6 is +C6/$C$20. The dollar signs do not have
anything to do with currency; they are the symbols that make the cell
absolute. Essentially, the first dollar sign says, "Don't change the column"
and the second dollar sign says, "Don't change the row" when the formula
is copied.

The procedure for making a reference absolute depends on whether
you enter the formula with the typing or pointing method. If you indicate
the cell references by pointing to them as you build the formula, you can
press the Abs key, F4. If you type the formula, you can type in the dollar

```
D6: (P2) [W9] +C6/$C$20                                           READY

           A            B            C        D       E          F
     2              January Sales                                    
     2                                                               
     3                                        % of                   
     4  Last Name    First Name      Sales    Total                  
     5                                                               
     6  Anderson     Robert          24,000   2.76%                  
     7  Andrews      Rebecca        220,000  25.26%                  
     8  Cauldwell    Randy           10,000   1.15%                  
     9  Goldstein    George          65,000   7.46%                  
    10  Haldeman     Ann-Marie       92,000  10.56%                  
    11  Jackson      John            36,000   4.13%                  
    12  Jameson      George          47,000   5.40%                  
    13  Lansberg     Jackson         26,000   2.99%                  
    14  Patterson    Margaret       100,000  11.48%                  
    15  Pauley       Barbara         45,000   5.17%                  
    16  Peterson     Paul            79,000   9.07%                  
    17  Smith        Betsy           52,000   5.97%                  
    18  Smith        Ruth            75,000   8.61%                  
    19                                                               
    20  Total                       871,000                         
```

Figure 5.3: The *% of Total* formula requires an absolute reference.

signs yourself, or press F4 to get 1-2-3 to insert them. Follow these steps to build the *% of Total* formula:

1. Place the cell pointer in D6.

2. Type + to begin the formula.

3. Move the pointer to C6.

4. Type / to divide.

5. Move the pointer to C20 and press F4. The dollar signs are inserted in front of the column letter and the row number.

6. Press Enter to complete the formula. A zero displays because the global format is set to zero decimal places.

7. Format the cell to Percent with two decimal places (/Range Format).

8. Copy the formula in D6 to D7..D18 (/Copy).

Each individual's sales total is now divided by the total sales in cell C20. Creating an absolute reference requires you to think ahead. While you are building the formula, you need to think about whether you need any absolute references when you copy the formula. Frequently, though, you don't think this way. You enter the formula, copy it, and then discover something is awry. If you copy the formula in Figure 5.3 without using an absolute reference, you will get error messages. If you discover that you need an absolute reference *after* you have entered and copied the formula, you must edit the formula, insert the dollar signs in front of the column letter and row number (or press F4), and recopy the formula.

In some cases, you may want *partial absolute references*. For example, you may want the row number to change but the column letter to remain constant when the formula is copied. In this case, you only need one dollar sign: in front of the column letter (such as $B2). To keep only the row constant, the dollar sign should be in front of the row number (such as B$2). The first time you press F4 the reference changes from relative to absolute. The second time you press F4 the reference changes to row-only absolute, the third time to column-only absolute, and finally it begins the cycle again with relative.

FREEZING THE TITLES

Your sales spreadsheet currently fits perfectly on the screen—you can see every cell clearly. In the real world, however, your spreadsheets will likely be longer and/or wider than the screen. It's time for us to move into the real world...

Let's increase the height of the rows of data to add some breathing room between them:

1. Place the pointer in cell A6.

2. Press **:** to display the Wysiwyg menu and choose:

    Worksheet

    Row

    Set-Height

3. Paint the range A6..A18 and press Enter.

4. Type **20** for the height and press Enter.

Reality hits—some of your spreadsheet doesn't fit on the screen. Move the cell pointer down to the totals, row 20, and notice that the column headings scroll off the screen. Without the headings it's difficult to understand the data. In a wide spreadsheet, you'd have a similar problem because the row headings in column A would scroll off the screen.

The /Worksheet Titles command is a quick fix to this problem: It freezes the column and/or row headings on the screen so that they won't scroll off. You can choose to freeze horizontally (in other words, the column headings), vertically (the row headings), or both. The position of your cell pointer is especially important with the Titles command because

1-2-3 doesn't prompt you for a range. When freezing horizontally, all rows above the cell pointer are frozen on the screen. When freezing vertically, all columns to the left are frozen. Therefore, the cell pointer should be positioned below and to the right of your headings.

In the SALES spreadsheet, freeze the titles horizontally, as follows:

1. Press Home.

2. Move the pointer to row 6.

3. Press / to display the 1-2-3 menu and choose:

    Worksheet

    Titles

    Horizontal

4. Move the pointer to the totals in row 20, and you will see that the column headings do not scroll off the screen, as shown in Figure 5.4.

5. Press Home.

When titles are frozen, you cannot use your keyboard controls (such as the arrow keys or Home) or the mouse to move the cell pointer into the frozen area. If you need to edit in this area, you have two alternatives:

- Unfreeze the titles with /Worksheet Titles Clear
- Use the Goto key, F5, to move to the cell

This last method is a bit confusing because it temporarily makes a duplicate copy of the frozen rows or columns. Make your desired change, and then move the pointer off the screen and back again to remove the duplicate rows or columns.

Before continuing, unfreeze the titles by pressing / to display the 1-2-3 menu and choosing:

Worksheet

Titles

Clear

```
F21:                                                     READY

         A            B            C         D       E         F
  1                January Sales
  2
  3                                        % of
  4  Last Name   First Name     Sales     Total
  5
 11  Jackson      John           36,000    4.13%
 12  Jameson      George         47,000    5.40%
 13  Lansberg     Jackson        26,000    2.99%
 14  Patterson    Margaret      100,000   11.48%
 15  Pauley       Barbara        45,000    5.17%
 16  Peterson     Paul           79,000    9.07%
 17  Smith        Betsy          52,000    5.97%
 18  Smith        Ruth           75,000    8.61%
 19
 20  Total                      871,000
 21
 22
```

Figure 5.4: The spreadsheet with frozen horizontal titles

EXPANDING THE SPREADSHEET

Let's assume the February sales figures have just arrived, and you want to create a spreadsheet for this data. Because February's spreadsheet format is identical to January's, let's just copy the spreadsheet to another location in the same file, and then change the numbers.

1. Press Home.

2. Press / to display the 1-2-3 menu.

3. Choose Copy.

4. For the *Copy what?* range, paint the range A1..D20 and press Enter.

5. For the *To where?* range, move the pointer to A30 and press Enter.

Now enter the February data. Position the copied spreadsheet in the upper-left corner of the screen. One way to do this is with the Goto key, F5.

1. Press F5.

2. Type **A30** for the cell to go to and press Enter.

3. Use the F2 key to edit cell A30 so that it reads *February Sales*.

4. Edit the *% of Total* formula in D35 so that it divides by $C$49. (Because $C$20 is an absolute reference, it didn't change when you copied the range.)

5. Copy the formula to D36..D47.

6. With the /Range Erase command, erase the range C35..C47. ERR messages display in the *% of Total* column because the formulas are dividing by zero. As soon as you enter numbers in column C, the ERR messages will disappear.

7. Enter the data shown in column C of Figure 5.5.

8. Use the :Worksheet Row Set-Height command to increase the height of rows 35 through 47 to 20 points. (The /Copy command does not copy the row heights.)

Later in the chapter, you will learn a way to avoid the extra formatting and editing that you had to do for the February sales data.

GETTING AROUND THE SPREADSHEET

A large spreadsheet can be cumbersome to work with unless you know a few tricks. Now that the SALES file has grown, it's time to learn some faster ways of getting to a specific cell or range.

```
F35:                                                              READY

            A          B          C        D         E          F
    30                February Sales
    31
    32                                    % of
    33 Last Name   First Name      Sales  Total
    34
    35 Anderson    Robert         31,000   3.24%
    36 Andrews     Rebecca       250,000  26.12%
    37 Cauldwell   Randy          21,000   2.19%
    38 Goldstein   George         70,000   7.31%
    39 Haldeman    Ann-Marie      93,000   9.72%
    40 Jackson     John           39,000   4.08%
    41 Jameson     George         52,000   5.43%
    42 Lansberg    Jackson        38,000   3.97%
    43 Patterson   Margaret       86,000   8.99%
    44 Pauley      Barbara        39,000   4.08%
    45 Peterson    Paul           90,000   9.40%
    46 Smith       Betsy          63,000   6.58%
    47 Smith       Ruth           85,000   8.88%
    48
    49 Total                     957,000
```

Figure 5.5: February sales data

KEYS FOR MOVING THE CELL POINTER

Up to this point, you haven't used many shortcuts for moving the cell pointer because you haven't needed to. You've used the arrow keys to move the pointer a cell at a time, Home to go to the beginning of the file, and you just learned how to use the F5 key to go to a specific cell. Table 5.1 summarizes the keyboard shortcuts for moving the cell pointer.

The End key deserves special discussion. When you press End, the status line displays END, indicating that 1-2-3 is waiting for you to specify which direction you want to move. If you then press an arrow key, the cell pointer is moved to the next block in that direction. A *block* is a range of cells that is bordered by blank cells. The block commands jump the cell pointer from one block to another, in the direction of the arrow you press. For example, if the pointer is on cell A33 and you press End and ↓, the

Table 5.1: Moving the Cell Pointer

DESTINATION	KEYSTROKE
Beginning of file	Home
End of file	End Home
Next screen	PgDn
Previous screen	PgUp
Screen right	Ctrl-→ or Tab
Screen left	Ctrl-← or Shift-Tab
Next block down	End ↓
Previous block up	End ↑
Block to the right	End →
Block to the left	End ←
Specific cell	F5

pointer moves to the beginning of the next block, A35. Press End ↓ again and the pointer moves to the end of the block, cell A47. The third time you press End ↓ the pointer moves to the next block, cell A49. The block commands use blank cells as their "stop signs."

You can also use these shortcuts when painting a range to sum, format, erase, print, and so on. Suppose you have just issued the /Range Erase command, and the pointer is on cell C35. The fastest way to paint the range C35..C47 is to place the pointer on C35 and press End and ↓. You'll find that these keyboard shortcuts are big time-savers.

One special note about the Goto key, F5: Don't overuse it! If you are in cell B5 and want to go to B7, just use your arrow keys. Typically, you will use Goto to move the pointer to a cell off the screen.

1-2-3 DOES WINDOWS

1-2-3 can't wash your windows for you, nor is it a Microsoft Windows application that can simultaneously show you multiple spreadsheets in their own windows, but it can create two windows on the screen. The windowing feature allows you to view two widely separated parts of your spreadsheet at the same time. In Figure 5.6, the SALES spreadsheet has been divided into horizontal windows. The January total in row 20 appears in the top window and the February total in row 49 appears in the bottom half of the screen. With windows, you can easily compare these totals.

The /Worksheet Window command lets you create horizontal or vertical windows. As with frozen titles, the position of your cell pointer is crucial. For horizontal windows, the rows above the cell pointer are placed in the top window. For vertical windows, the columns to the left of the cell pointer are placed in the left window. Most of the time, you will want to create windows of approximately the same size. To create two equal-sized windows, just place the cell pointer in the middle of the screen.

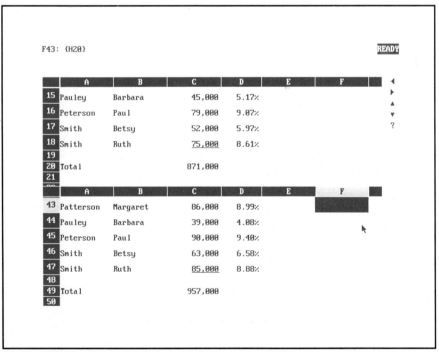

Figure 5.6: Horizontal windows

Creating a Window

Follow these steps to create a horizontal window in the SALES spreadsheet:

1. Press Home, and then place the pointer in row 8. (Row 8 is approximately the center row on the screen.)

2. Press / to display the 1-2-3 menu and choose:

   Worksheet

   Window

   Horizontal

   A second set of column letters appears for the bottom window, and the cell pointer is in the top window. First, position the January total in the top window, and then position the February total in the bottom window.

3. Move to row 20.

4. Press F6 to move the cell pointer to the other window.

5. Move to row 49.

You have now reached your objective: You can simultaneously see and compare the January and the February totals.

The F6 function key jumps you back and forth between the windows. You can move the cell pointer to display whatever range you want in each window. Windows are stored with the file, and will remain until you remove them with the /Worksheet Window Clear command. Each window can have its own global column width, individual column widths, and global format. When you print, the settings in the current window are used. The windows themselves do not print.

Getting Out of Sync

The window feature has two settings: Sync and Unsync. The default setting is synchronized (Sync), which means that the two windows scroll together. To see how this works, press → several times until you see additional columns. Both windows display the same columns (for example, C through H). With unsynchronized windows, you are able to see different columns in the top and bottom windows. The top window might display columns A through F and the bottom window might show columns P through V. When you need to view two ranges that are not only widely separated but also in completely different rows and columns, create the window and then use /Worksheet Window Unsync to unsynchronize the scrolling.

Before you continue, clear the windows:

1. Press / to display the 1-2-3 menu and choose:

   Worksheet

   Window

   Clear

2. Press Home.

VIEWING MORE OF THE SPREADSHEET ◀ⅢⅡ 2.3

Wysiwyg offers several ways to maximize the number of rows and columns you can see on your screen at one time. These options are located on the :Display menu and have no impact on the appearance of your printed reports.

Displaying More Rows

With :Display Rows you can specify the number of rows (between sixteen and sixty) displayed on the screen. Figure 5.7 shows a spreadsheet with 29 rows displayed. Depending on how many rows you display, the tops of the characters may be truncated to provide space for the additional rows. However, this truncation will have no effect on the printed report.

The number of rows displayed on the screen may not exactly correspond to the number you specify with :Display Rows. You may get fewer or more rows depending on the following factors: the type of graphics card you have, the typeface and size of the default font, and

A4: [W5]   READY

	A	B	C	D	E	F	G	H	I
1			Employee Database						
2									
3									
4									
5									
6	ID	Last	First	Dept	Exempt	Hire Date	Salary	Raise %	New Sal.
7	1000	Anderson	Jane	MIS	Yes	08/02/85	34,000	13.0%	38,420
8	1001	Andrews	Andy	MIS	Yes	08/27/89	61,000	14.0%	69,540
9	1002	Bradford	William	Sales	Yes	09/10/86	60,000	10.0%	66,000
10	1003	Bradley	Brad	Sales	No	02/26/85	54,000	8.0%	58,320
11	1004	Gibson	Pamela	Eng.	No	11/26/89	45,000	12.0%	50,400
12	1005	Ingram	Greg	Mfg.	No	09/30/90	21,000	6.5%	22,365
13	1006	Jones	Carolyn	MIS	Yes	10/17/84	62,000	11.0%	68,820
14	1007	Jones	Mary	Sales	No	10/15/88	29,500	11.0%	32,745
15	1008	Kline	Harry	Sales	No	03/25/88	26,000	7.0%	27,820
16	1009	Manley	Martin	Mfg.	No	03/09/91	26,000	7.0%	27,820
17	1010	Meyers	Andrew	MIS	Yes	12/01/88	41,000	9.0%	44,690
18	1011	Peterson	Pete	MIS	Yes	07/21/82	21,000	12.0%	23,520
19	1012	Slater	Peter	Mfg.	No	01/05/82	20,000	8.0%	21,600
20	1013	Smith	Charles	Mfg.	Yes	06/29/84	25,000	7.0%	26,750
21	1014	Smith	Paul	Mfg.	No	06/10/87	27,000	10.0%	29,700
22	1015	Smothers	Stacey	Mfg.	No	05/01/87	24,000	7.5%	25,800
23	1016	Smythe	Jennifer	Eng.	Yes	11/13/90	34,000	6.0%	36,040
24	1017	Tucker	Brian	Eng.	Yes	04/22/88	39,000	9.0%	42,510
25	1018	Wilson	Robert	Eng.	Yes	10/14/83	36,000	15.0%	41,400
26	1019	Anderson	Jane	MIS	Yes	08/02/85	34,000	13.0%	38,420
27	1020	Andrews	Andy	MIS	Yes	08/27/89	61,000	14.0%	69,540
28	1021	Bradford	William	Sales	Yes	09/10/86	60,000	10.0%	66,000
29	1022	Bradley	Brad	Sales	No	02/26/85	54,000	8.0%	58,320

Figure 5.7: You can show more rows on the screen with the :Display Rows command.

whether you are zoomed in or out (discussed in the next section).

To return the screen to its default number of rows, choose :Display Default Restore. Most monitors display twenty rows in the default font (12-point Swiss). However, when you install 1-2-3, you can choose a text-display driver that displays more rows. For example, VGA monitors can display 25, 43, or 50 lines. Note that these numbers include the control panel and the status line, not just the spreadsheet rows. (See Appendix A for details on using the INSTALL program.)

Zooming In and Out

The :Display Zoom command reduces or enlarges cells on the screen. By reducing cells (zooming out), you can see more rows and columns. By

enlarging cells (zooming in), you can see small type sizes more clearly.
Five levels of magnification are available:

Size	Description
Tiny	Reduces cells to 63 percent
Small	Reduces cells to 87 percent
Normal	The default
Large	Enlarges cells to 125 percent
Huge	Enlarges cells to 150 percent

If none of these sizes is appropriate, you can set your own magnification level with the Manual option. The minimum reduction is 25 percent; the maximum enlargement is 400. Figure 5.8 shows a spreadsheet in Tiny magnification while Figure 5.9 is enlarged with the Large zoom option.

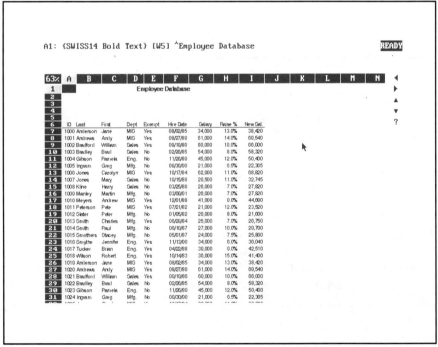

Figure 5.8: The Tiny zoom option

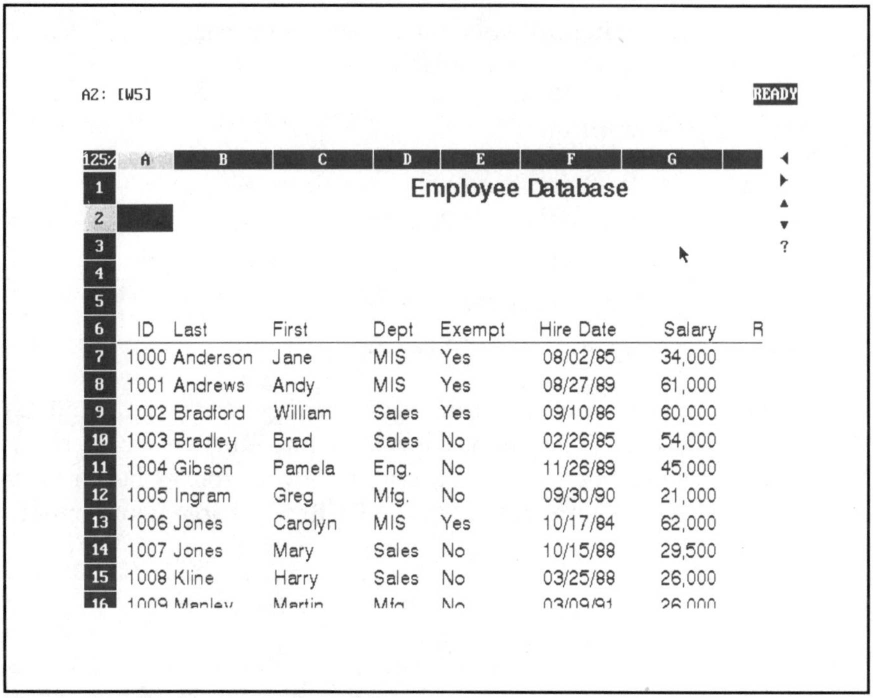

Figure 5.9: The Large zoom option

The zoom percentage appears in the upper-left corner of the spreadsheet frame (see Figures 5.8 and 5.9).

Displaying the Grid

When you display more of the spreadsheet with the :Display Rows or :Display Zoom commands, you may find it helpful to display the spreadsheet grid lines—dotted lines that outline each cell (see Figure 5.10). To display grid lines, use the :Display Options Grid Yes command. If you have a color monitor, you may want to change the color of the grid lines with :Display Colors Grid.

SEARCHING THE SPREADSHEET

Locating a particular area or cell in a large spreadsheet can be tedious and frustrating. When you need to look up a number, correct a mistake, or update data, you have to scroll screen by screen, scanning for the item you want. An easier method is to use the search feature and have 1-2-3 do the scanning for you.

In the SALES spreadsheet, correct the February sales for Paul Peterson. Use the /Range Search command to take you there directly:

1. Press / to display the 1-2-3 menu and choose:

   Range

   Search

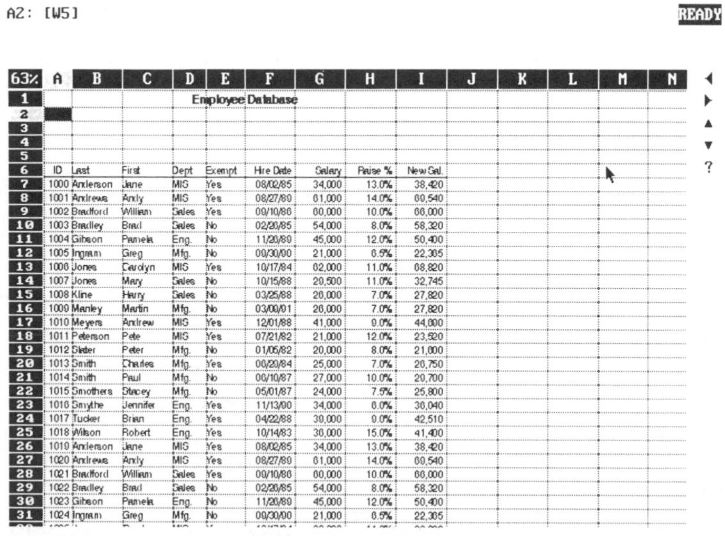

Figure 5.10: Non-printing grid lines outline each cell

You are prompted for a search range. The quickest way to paint the entire spreadsheet is to press Home, type a period to anchor, press End and then Home. *End Home* moves the cell pointer to the lower-right corner of the spreadsheet.

2. Paint the range A1..D49 and press Enter.

3. Type **Peterson** for the search string and press Enter. (A *string* is a series of characters.) Then choose:

    Labels

    Find

    The cell pointer moves to the first occurrence of *Peterson*, and the control panel displays two choices, Next and Quit. If this were the *Peterson* you were searching for, you would choose Quit to stop the search. Because you are looking for Peterson's February data, you need to continue the search with the Next option.

4. Choose Next, and the cell pointer moves to Peterson in the February spreadsheet. This is the one you want.

5. Choose Quit.

6. Change Peterson's sales in C45 from *90000* to *92000*.

2.3 ▐▐▐▶   If you aren't sure of the exact spelling of a word you want to search for, you can use wildcards. In poker, a wildcard can be any card you choose it to be; frequently, the joker is declared as a wildcard. In 1-2-3's /Range Search command, the asterisk and question mark are your *wildcards*—symbols that take the place of one or more characters in a search string. Use these wildcards when you don't know the exact contents of a search string. The asterisk matches any group of characters in the position where you type it; the question mark is a placeholder for a single character. Here are a few examples:

* *J*son* matches all strings that have one or more letters between *J* and *son* (like Jackson and Jameson).

* *Thomps?n* finds all strings that have a single character in the position of the question mark (like Thompsen and Thompson).

- *5?0* finds all strings in labels or formulas that have a single character between *5* and *0* (like 500, 510, and 540).

Follow these steps to search for someone whose name starts with *P* and ends in *son*:

1. Press / to display the 1-2-3 menu and choose:

   Range

   Search

2. Press Enter to accept the previously defined search range (A1..D49).

3. Press Esc to clear out the previous search string.

4. Type **P*son** for the search string and press Enter.

5. Choose:

   Labels

   Find

The cell pointer moves to the first string that starts with *P* and ends in *son*—*Patterson*. Choose Next to find the next string—*Peterson*. Continue choosing Next until no more matching strings are located. Press Esc or Enter when you see the message

   No more matching strings

The /Range Search command has two options: Find and Replace. As you just saw, the Find option is a quick way of moving the cell pointer to a particular cell. The Replace option, which makes global editing changes to a spreadsheet, is explained in Chapter 8.

ASSIGNING RANGE NAMES

Another way to get around a large spreadsheet is to assign names to its different sections, and then use the F5 key to go to them. Besides letting you quickly move to any section of your spreadsheet, range names can be used in formulas and to specify ranges to print, erase, format, etc. The

/Range Name Create command lets you assign a meaningful name to a cell or a range of cells.

Going to a Range Name

The F5 key moves the pointer to a specific cell, assuming you know the exact cell coordinates of where you want to go. But how often does that happen? Because it's difficult to remember cell coordinates, 1-2-3 offers a way to assign names to your ranges. And you don't even have to remember the exact name—you can choose it from a list.

In the SALES spreadsheet, assign the name *January* to the range of January sales data and the name *February* to the February data.

1. Press Home.

2. Press / to display the 1-2-3 menu and choose:

   Range

   Name

   Create

3. Type **JANUARY** for the name and press Enter.

4. Paint the range A1..D20 and press Enter.

5. Repeat the above steps to assign the name **FEBRUARY** to the range A30..D49.

When you create range names, you do not see anything different in the spreadsheet. But rest assured that the names are now part of the spreadsheet and can be referred to. Let's go to the January data.

1. Press F5, the Goto key.

2. Press F3, the Name key. This function key displays the range names in the current spreadsheet.

3. Highlight JANUARY and press Enter.

4. Follow the above steps to go to FEBRUARY.

Here are a few more notes about range names:

- Range names can be up to fifteen characters long, and may consist of numbers, letters, spaces, or symbols.

- Be sure not to assign a cell coordinate as a range name. For instance, don't create the name *Q1* for first quarter sales because Q1 is a cell. You will get unexpected results if you make this mistake.

- If you insert additional rows and columns *inside* the named range, the range associated with the name automatically expands.

- If you add rows or columns *outside* the named range, you will need to adjust the range associated with the name (using the /Range Name Create command again).

- Deleting the first or last row or column in a named range will destroy the range associated with the name. In such cases, you will need to redefine the range.

Using Range Names in Commands

Any time a 1-2-3 or Wysiwyg command prompts you for a range, you can press the F3 key and choose a range name from a list. Don't do this now, but if you wanted to eliminate the February data from the spreadsheet, you could give the /Range Erase command, press F3, and choose FEBRUARY. The range name saves you from having to manually paint the range. Remember when you copied the January data to A30? Instead of painting the range A1..D19, you could have chosen JANUARY as your *Copy what?* range.

Probably the most frequently used command in which range names are used is printing (/Print Printer Range or :Print Range Set). In a large spreadsheet with several different ranges to print, you can assign a name to each range and then select the appropriate name when specifying the print range.

Follow these steps to print the January data:

1. Press **:** to display the Wysiwyg menu and choose:

    Print

    Range

    Set

2. Press F3 to see a list of names.

3. Highlight JANUARY and press Enter. The name *JANUARY* fills in next to Print Range in the Wysiwyg Print Settings dialog box.

4. Make sure your printer is turned on, is online, and has paper.

5. Choose Go.

After a few minutes, the January sales data prints.

Note that the F3 key also works if you are editing the Print Settings dialog box directly. After choosing the Print Range option in the dialog box, press F3 to see the Range Names dialog box, such as the one shown in Figure 5.11. The range associated with the highlighted range appears in the bottom of the dialog box.

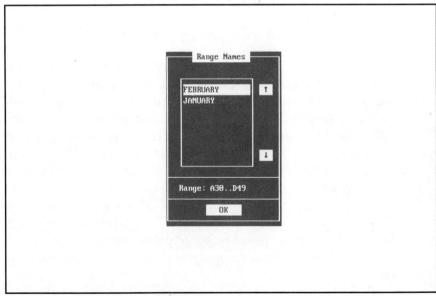

Figure 5.11: Range Names dialog box

Using Range Names in Formulas

Another place to use range names is in formulas. Formulas are much easier to understand when they refer to names instead of cell coordinates. Here are a few examples of ways to use range names in the SALES spreadsheet's formulas:

- If you name C20 *JAN TOTAL*, all the *% of Total* formulas would be easier to understand. For example, the formula in D6 would read *+C6/$JAN TOTAL* and the formula in D7 would read *+C7/$JAN TOTAL*.

- If you name C6..C18 *JAN SALES*, the total formula in C20 would then read *@SUM(JAN SALES)*.

Let's create the aforementioned names in addition to names for the February data.

1. Place the cell pointer in C20.

2. Press / to display the 1-2-3 menu and choose:

    Range
    Name
    Create

3. Type **JAN TOTAL** for the name.

4. Press Enter to accept C20..C20 as the range.

5. Follow the steps above to create the following range names:

    JAN SALES   C6..C18
    FEB TOTAL   C49
    FEB SALES   C35..C47

6. Place the pointer on one of the formulas, such as C49, and look at the control panel. The range name (for example, *FEB SALES*) appears in the formula, as shown in Figure 5.12.

C49: @SUM(FEB SALES)   `READY`

	A	B	C	D	E	F
36	Andrews	Rebecca	250,000	26.07%		
37	Cauldwell	Randy	21,000	2.19%		
38	Goldstein	George	70,000	7.30%		
39	Haldeman	Ann-Marie	93,000	9.70%		
40	Jackson	John	39,000	4.07%		
41	Jameson	George	52,000	5.42%		
42	Lansberg	Jackson	38,000	3.96%		
43	Patterson	Margaret	86,000	8.97%		
44	Pauley	Barbara	39,000	4.07%		
45	Peterson	Paul	92,000	9.59%		
46	Smith	Betsy	63,000	6.57%		
47	Smith	Ruth	85,000	8.86%		
48						
49	Total		959,000			
50						

Figure 5.12: The range name appears in the formula

If you name a range *after* you have built a formula, the name is automatically substituted in the formula. If you name a range *before* you build the formula, you can either type the name yourself, or press F3 to choose the name from a list. You cannot refer to a range name in a formula before you have created that name.

Creating a Range-Name Table

The /Range Name Table command helps you to keep track of all your range names. This command creates an alphabetical list of the names and their associated ranges. Figure 5.13 shows a range-name table for the SALES spreadsheet. You can create this table in any unused area of the

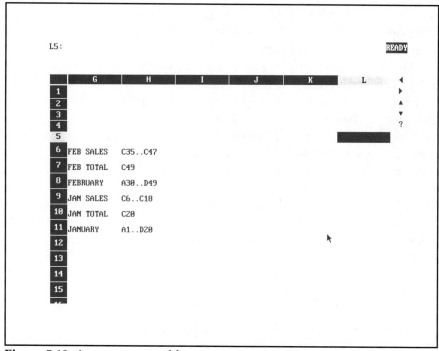

Figure 5.13: A range-name table

spreadsheet grid, for example, to the right of your active spreadsheet area. Make sure the target location for the range-name table is empty because it will overwrite data.

Create a range-name table in your SALES spreadsheet:

1. Move the cell pointer to a blank area of the spreadsheet, such as G6.

2. Press / to display the 1-2-3 menu and choose:

   Range
   Name
   Table

3. Press Enter.

Check your names and ranges against the ones shown in Figure 5.9. The exercises in the remainder of the chapter won't work properly unless your range names are accurate.

The range-name table is not dynamic, meaning that when you add, delete, or change a range name, the table does not automatically update. You need to reissue the /Range Name Table command whenever you change range names.

One reason to build a table of range names is to verify the accuracy of the ranges associated with the names. First, check for ERR messages that indicate you have deleted the first or last row or column of a named range. Also, keep your eye out for nonsensical ranges such as K5..IV8192. (These bizarre ranges sometimes occur when you move part of the range.) To redefine the range of an existing name, reissue the /Range Name Create command. When you are finished checking a range name table, you can either leave it in the spreadsheet, print it, or erase it.

Deleting Range Names

When you no longer need a particular range name, delete it with the /Range Name Delete command. Any formula that contained a reference to this name would then refer to the cell coordinates. For example, if you deleted the name JAN SALES, the total formula would read @SUM(C6..C18). The Reset option on the /Range Name submenu deletes all names in the current spreadsheet.

PROTECTING YOUR SPREADSHEET

1-2-3 offers two ways to safeguard your spreadsheet. The protection feature protects against accidental errors such as inadvertently typing over or erasing a formula. But if someone is out to sabotage your spreadsheet, the protection feature is not much of a deterrent. To safeguard against snoopers and saboteurs, you need to password-protect your spreadsheet. This section discusses both of these topics.

AVOIDING ACCIDENTAL CHANGES

When entering data into the spreadsheet, it's all too easy to type the data in the wrong cell, perhaps overwriting an important formula. This is especially true in some spreadsheets where formulas appear in the middle of data-entry ranges. To prevent changing the wrong cells, you can use the protection feature.

This feature is commonly used when someone builds a spreadsheet into which another person will be entering data. Frequently, the person doing the data entry doesn't have much experience with 1-2-3, and is more likely to make mistakes. The protection feature prevents a novice user from inadvertently entering data in the wrong cells and erasing formulas.

This feature works differently from how you might expect it to. Rather than protecting the cells you don't want changed (for example, your formulas), you start out by protecting everything and you unprotect the cells you do want to change. Thus, protection is a two-part process. First, you enable the protection feature with /Worksheet Global Protection Enable. This command protects every cell in the spreadsheet. At this point, you can't enter new labels or values, nor can you change existing data. You then unprotect the data-entry cells with /Range Unprot.

When a cell is protected, you *cannot*

- Change its contents with F2 or by typing over the current cell contents.

- Erase the cell with Del or /Range Erase.

- Delete the row or column it's in.

- Move or copy another cell to a range that contains a protected cell.

Even though you can't change the contents of a protected cell, you can format them. For example, you can add punctuation to numbers with /Range Format, align labels with /Range Label, and add underlining with :Format Underline.

Protecting the Sales Spreadsheet

In the SALES spreadsheet, there are only two ranges into which data is entered: JAN SALES (C6..C18) and FEB SALES (C35..C47). All other cells are either labels, formulas, or blank. Follow the steps below to protect the SALES spreadsheet. First, turn on the protection feature:

1. Press / to display the 1-2-3 menu and choose:

    Worksheet

    Global

    Protection

    Enable

    Look in the control panel and you will see PR (for protected) indicated for each cell. You cannot change any cells in the spreadsheet until you unprotect ranges.

2. Press / to display the 1-2-3 menu and choose:

    Range

    Unprot

3. Press F3 to display a list of range names.

4. Highlight JAN SALES and press Enter. On most monitors, the unprotected cells are very easy to spot because they appear brighter or in a different color. The control panel indicates an unprotected cell with the letter U.

5. Follow steps 2 through 4 above to unprotect the FEB SALES range.

Try typing something in a protected cell. When you press Enter, you will see the Protected Cell error box. Press Esc to clear this message (Enter also works), or press F1 to see a help screen that describes the problem. This help screen is shown in Figure 5.14. After reading this screen, press Esc twice to return to READY mode.

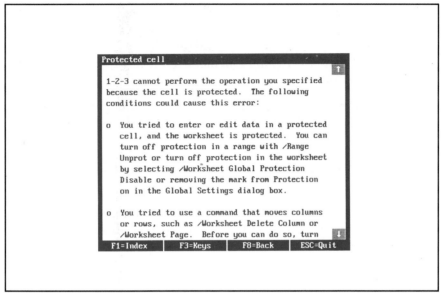

Figure 5.14: The help screen for the Protected Cell error message

Entering Data into an Unprotected Range

Since you can't edit protected cells, you will not need to move the cell pointer to them during data entry. Therefore, when you are entering data, you can use the /Range Input command to limit cell pointer movement to unprotected cells. Follow this basic procedure:

- Press / to display the 1-2-3 menu and choose:

    Range

    Input

- When prompted for the data input range, highlight your column and row headings as well as the unprotected cells. The first cell in the range will be placed at the upper-left corner of the screen.

- Enter your data into unprotected cells. When you press ↓ at the bottom of a column in the input range, the pointer will move to the top of the next column. Likewise, when you press → at the end of a row, the pointer will move to the beginning of the next line.

- To cancel the /Range Input command, press Esc or Enter when you are in READY mode.

Modifying a Protected Spreadsheet

You shouldn't enable protection until you are finished building a spreadsheet, because once protection is enabled, your command and data-entry options are severely restricted. You can't insert and delete rows and columns, and you can only type in the ranges you have specifically unprotected.

Inevitably, after protection is enabled, you will want to change the spreadsheet in some way. You might discover an error in one of the formulas or you might want to insert a new row. To make these modifications, you need to temporarily turn off the protection feature with the /Worksheet Global Protection Disable command. After you have made your changes, enable protection again.

Because we are not finished with the SALES spreadsheet, you should disable the protection. Press / to display the 1-2-3 menu and choose:

Worksheet

Global

Protection

Disable

Even though you have disabled protection, the ranges that you unprotected still retain their unprotected status. If you were to later enable protection again, you wouldn't need to unprotect the data entry ranges.

PASSWORD-PROTECTING YOUR SPREADSHEET

For confidential data, consider password-protecting the spreadsheet. When a file is password-protected, you cannot retrieve it unless you know the password. Your spreadsheet will be safe from prying eyes.

It will also be off-limits from *you* if you forget your password. Use the same password for all your spreadsheets so that you only have one to memorize.

Follow this procedure to password-protect a file:

- Issue the /File Save command.

- Type the filename, press the spacebar, and type **p**—for example, *sales p*. Press Enter.

- When prompted, enter your password. It can be up to fifteen characters long, and can contain any combination of letters, numbers, spaces, and symbols. As you type, you will not see the characters on the screen. Instead, you will see boxes in place of each character. (This way, if someone is looking over your shoulder at the screen, he or she won't be able to read your password.) Press Enter.

- You are then asked to verify the password by typing it again. If you make a typing mistake, you are told that the two passwords don't match and you must start over with the first step.

Once a file is password-protected, you must know the password to retrieve the file. If 1-2-3 refuses to accept your password, it's possible that you entered the capitalization differently from how it was originally created. Passwords are case-sensitive, so pay attention to distinctions in upper- or lowercase.

When you resave a password-protected file, you will see *[PASSWORD PROTECTED]* after the file name. To continue protecting the file with a password, simply press Enter here. If you no longer want to protect the file, press Backspace to remove this message and press Enter.

MANAGING YOUR MEMORY

A spreadsheet's size is limited by the amount of temporary memory (RAM) in your computer. As you learned in Chapter 3, the /Worksheet Status command shows how much memory is currently available. It's a fact of life that the larger the spreadsheet, the more memory it consumes. When you have less than 4096 bytes of memory available, the status line flashes a MEM indicator. If you ignore this indicator and continue to increase your spreadsheet size, you will eventually run out of memory. 1-2-3 then displays a Memory Full error message, and you may lose your work.

Memory management is a complicated issue and the specific details of how 1-2-3 uses memory are beyond the scope of this book. In this section, I limit my discussion to practical ways of maximizing the amount of memory available for your spreadsheets. Here are a few tips for memory conservation:

- Don't format blank cells unnecessarily. The control panel displays the current cell's format (for example, (C2) or {Bold}). If you discover a range of blank formatted cells, remove the formatting with /Range Format Reset and/or :Format Reset.

- Erase data ranges you no longer need. (And not with the spacebar because spaces consume memory!)

- Delete unused range names with the /Range Name Delete command.

- Eliminate blank cells in the middle of a column by deleting rows or moving ranges. For example, if you enter data in cells A1 and A8192, 1-2-3 consumes memory for all 8192 cells, even though 8190 of them are blank. This memory gluttony is not true for blank cells in the middle of *rows*, however. In general, arrange your spreadsheets as compactly as possible.

- Disable the Undo feature—it's a big memory hog.

- Detach add-in programs, such as Wysiwyg.

- Divide large spreadsheets into several smaller files, and then use file linking or combining to consolidate the data. (These topics are discussed later in the chapter.)

After you use the above methods to conserve memory, you may need to save the file and retrieve it again before the additional memory is available.

TURNING OFF
AUTOMATIC RECALCULATION

As a spreadsheet gets larger, you may begin to notice a delay when you enter new data, format and copy ranges, and so on. It's almost as if 1-2-3 needs a moment to think before it continues. This delay occurs because 1-2-3 checks all cells to see if the change you made requires a recalculation of the formulas. The recalculation process takes longer in large spreadsheets simply because there are more cells to check. One solution is to divide the large file into several smaller files; this technique is discussed in the next section. Another solution is to turn off the automatic recalculation feature. When it's turned off, you don't experience any delays when you change the spreadsheet, because 1-2-3 doesn't recalculate your formulas until you explicitly give a command to do so.

Although the SALES spreadsheet isn't large enough to justify turning off automatic recalculation, we'll go through the motions so that you can see how it's done:

1. Press / to display the 1-2-3 menu and choose:

   Worksheet

   Global

   Recalculation

   Manual

2. Change Betsy Smith's January sales to **58000**. Notice that the total did not update to reflect the new value you entered. The CALC message in the status line indicates that you need to manually recalculate the spreadsheet.

3. Press F9, the Calc key.

The total now includes the revised sales figure for Betsy Smith, and the CALC indicator disappears. When automatic recalculation is turned off, it's important to remember to recalculate the spreadsheet before you attempt to analyze the data or to print a report. Otherwise, you will be looking at inaccurate results.

To see whether a spreadsheet is set for automatic or manual recalculation, display the Global Settings dialog box (/Worksheet Global). An X by Automatic indicates automatic recalculation is turned on.

Before continuing, turn automatic recalculation back on. Press / to display the 1-2-3 menu and choose:

Worksheet

Global

Recalculation

Automatic

The F9 key can also be used to do quick calculations in the control panel. Try this:

1. In cell C17, type **4500*12**—but don't press Enter.

2. Press F9. 1-2-3 calculates the answer (54000) and displays it where the calculation was. To place the result in the current cell, press Enter. To clear the computation, press Esc.

3. Press Enter.

You can do these on-the-fly calculations regardless of whether you are using automatic or manual recalculation.

CREATING SMALLER FILES OUT OF A LARGE SPREADSHEET

There are a number of good reasons for creating several smaller files instead of one large spreadsheet. First, you may not have enough memory to store all the data in one file. Second, calculations are slower with a large spreadsheet. Third, it takes longer to retrieve and save the file. And fourth, it's generally more cumbersome to work with a huge file.

Despite all these good reasons for creating smaller files, you may still be thinking that you need to store everything in one file because you have to create a single report of this data. This is not a major concern, though, because 1-2-3 offers several techniques for consolidating data from separate files, as you will soon see.

Now that you are (I hope) convinced that good things come in small packages, let's analyze the SALES spreadsheet you have been working with in this chapter. It currently contains the data for two months of sales. If you were to continue adding each subsequent month's data to this file, you might eventually run out of memory. It therefore makes sense to place each month's data in its own file.

The /File Xtract command copies a range from the current spreadsheet into a separate file; although the command's name implies otherwise, the data is not removed from the current spreadsheet. It copies values, labels, formulas, column widths, numeric formatting, and range names. It does not copy Wysiwyg formatting. In the SALES spreadsheet, copy the JANUARY and FEBRUARY ranges into their own spreadsheets, as follows:

1. Press / to display the 1-2-3 menu and choose:

   File

   Xtract

   Formulas

2. Type **JAN** for the file name and press Enter.

3. When prompted for the range to extract, press F3 twice to see a complete list of range names.

4.   Choose JANUARY and press Enter.

5.   Press / to display the 1-2-3 menu and choose:

File

Xtract

Formulas

6.   Type **FEB** for the file name and press Enter.

7.   Press F3 to see a list of range names.

8.   Choose FEBRUARY and press Enter.

Now, let's take a look at the JAN file, illustrated in Figure 5.15.

1.   Save the SALES spreadsheet.

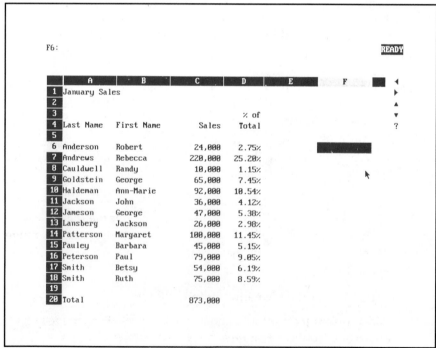

Figure 5.15: The JAN file

2. Retrieve the JAN file. As shown in Figure 5.15, the file contains the January data, but none of the Wysiwyg formatting. To format this file like the SALES spreadsheet, you can import the format.

3. Press : to display the Wysiwyg menu and choose:

    Special

    Import

    All

4. When asked for the format file name to import, choose *SALES.FMT*. This file contains the Wysiwyg formatting for the SALES spreadsheet.

5. Save the JAN file and repeat the above steps to import the SALES format into the FEB file.

6. Save the FEB file.

CREATING A TEMPLATE

Another reason to create separate files for each month's data is to avoid having to go through the copy-edit-erase-and-format routine you went through earlier. An easier way is to create a reusable *template* that you retrieve each month. A template is a formatted spreadsheet that contains labels and formulas but no values. You retrieve the blank template, enter data into it, then save the file with a new name so that the template always remains blank.

It wouldn't take much effort to make a template for the monthly sales data. Just erase the values in column C, delete the unnecessary range names, and save the file with a new name. The FEB file should still be on your screen.

1. Use the /Range Erase command to clear the range FEB SALES (C6..C18). Don't worry about the ERR messages—they will disappear as soon as you enter values in column C.

2. Press / to display the 1-2-3 menu and choose:

    Range

    Name

    Reset

3. Press / to display the 1-2-3 menu and choose:

    File

    Save

    The current file name, FEB.WK1, is suggested. You want to assign a new name here, so don't press Enter. You do not need to erase the current name before typing a new one.

4. Type **TEMPLATE** and press Enter.

CONSOLIDATING DATA FROM SEPARATE FILES

1-2-3 offers several ways to transfer data between files. First, you can use /File Combine to copy all or part of another file into the current spreadsheet. This command even has calculating capabilities—as you copy numbers, you can add them to or subtract them from the existing values.

Another way to exchange data between spreadsheets is to create formulas that refer to cells in other spreadsheets. This technique is called *file linking*.

We'll use both methods to consolidate the sales data.

COMBINING DATA

In the following exercise, you will copy the monthly sales data into the template you just created. When you are finished with the exercise, the Sales column will contain the total sales for the two months.

1. Edit cell A1 with the F2 key so that it reads *Year-to-Date Sales*.

2. Place the cell pointer in C6. Cell pointer location is very important because you will not be asked for a target range: the data is copied to the current cell.

3. Press / to display the 1-2-3 menu and choose:

    File

    Combine

    Add

    Named/Specified-Range

4. Type **JAN SALES** for the range name and press Enter.

5. Choose JAN.WK1 for the file name. The January data is copied into the spreadsheet.

6. Press / to display the 1-2-3 menu and choose:

    File

    Combine

    Add

    Named/Specified-Range

7. Type **FEB SALES** for the range name and press Enter.

8. Choose FEB.WK1 for the file name. The February data is added to the current values. The Sales column now displays a consolidation of January and February data, as shown in Figure 5.16.

9. Save the file with the name **YTDSALES**.

While the /File Combine command is quite powerful, it has one serious limitation. If any of the sales figures in JAN or FEB were to change, the values in YTDSALES would not update. To display the correct year-to-date figures, you would have to erase the existing data in YTDSALES and reissue the /File Combine command. When you suspect the values in the source files might change, a better route is to use the file linking technique.

```
C6: {H20} 55000                                              READY
```

	A	B	C	D	E	F	
1		Year–to–Date Sales					◄
2							►
3				% of			▲
4	Last Name	First Name	Sales	Total			▼
5							?
6	Anderson	Robert	55,000	3.00%			
7	Andrews	Rebecca	470,000	25.66%			
8	Cauldwell	Randy	31,000	1.69%			
9	Goldstein	George	135,000	7.37%			
10	Haldeman	Ann-Marie	185,000	10.10%			
11	Jackson	John	75,000	4.09%			
12	Jameson	George	99,000	5.40%			
13	Lansberg	Jackson	64,000	3.49%			
14	Patterson	Margaret	186,000	10.15%			
15	Pauley	Barbara	84,000	4.59%			

Figure 5.16: The Sales column is a consolidation of January and February data.

FILE LINKING

With the /File Combine command, no relationship exists between the source (JAN and FEB) and the target (YTDSALES) files. But with file-linking formulas, you can create a dynamic interaction between spreadsheet files. When you change a value in a source file, the target file (the one containing the linking formula) automatically reflects the change when you retrieve it. Figure 5.17 illustrates file linking.

A file-linking formula refers to a single cell in another file. For example, the formula +<<JAN>>C6 brings in the value of cell C6 from the file named JAN. Notice that the file name is enclosed in double angle brackets. As always, there are two ways to enter formulas: by typing or by pointing. Because the cell is in a separate file, you need the help of an add-in if you want to use the pointing method. The *Viewer* add-in that comes

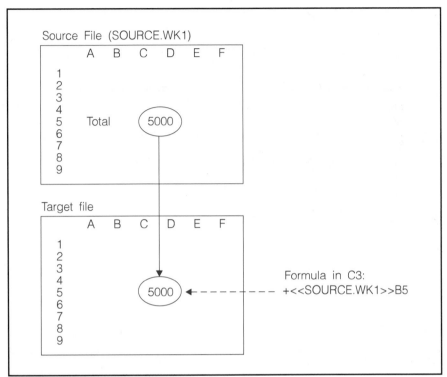

Source File (SOURCE.WK1)

Target file

Formula in C3:
+<<SOURCE.WK1>>B5

Figure 5.17: File-linking formulas

with Release 2.3 lets you point to a cell in another file, and it actually builds the entire file-linking formula for you.

Creating a Quarterly Sales Report

The goal in this exercise is to create the quarterly sales report shown in Figure 5.18. This report brings in the sales data from the JAN and FEB files, using file-linking formulas. The March column is currently empty, but is ready for the data when it's available.

Before you enter the formulas, you need to do a bit of prep work, as follows:

1. Retrieve TEMPLATE.

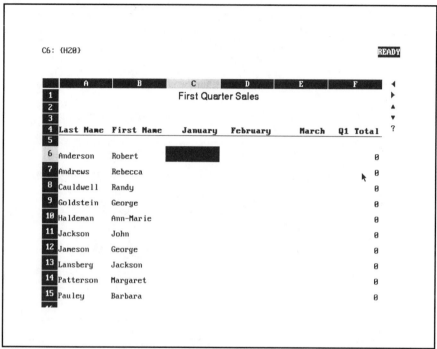

C6: {H20}   READY

	A	B	C	D	E	F	
1			First Quarter Sales				
2							
3							
4	Last Name	First Name	January	February	March	Q1 Total	?
5							
6	Anderson	Robert				0	
7	Andrews	Rebecca				0	
8	Cauldwell	Randy				0	
9	Goldstein	George				0	
10	Haldeman	Ann-Marie				0	
11	Jackson	John				0	
12	Jameson	George				0	
13	Lansberg	Jackson				0	
14	Patterson	Margaret				0	
15	Pauley	Barbara				0	

Figure 5.18: First Quarter Sales report, created with file-linking formulas

2. Delete the *% of Total* column (D) with /Worksheet Delete Column.

3. Enter the title and column headings as shown in Figure 5.14.

4. Use the :Text Align command to recenter the title.

5. Use the :Special Copy command to format the new column headings the same way as the existing headings.

6. Use the /Copy command to copy the total formula in C20 to D20..F20.

7. In the *Q1 Total* column, create a formula to total the January, February, and March data. (Hint: The formula in cell F6 should be @SUM(C6..E6). Use the /Copy command to copy the formula down the column.)

Now that the report is formatted and laid out properly, you are ready to enter the file-linking formulas. To enter the first formula, you'll use the typing method.

1. Place the pointer in cell C6.

2. Type **+<<JAN>>C6** and press Enter. The number 24,000 is brought into the spreadsheet. You can now copy this formula down the column. Copying a file-linking formula is no different from copying a regular formula. The file reference in the formula will remain constant, but the cell reference will adjust relative to where you are copying the formula.

3. Use the /Copy command to copy C6 to C7..C18. Your spreadsheet should look similar to Figure 5.19.

4. Save the file with the name **1STQTR**.

```
C6: {H20} +<<JAN.WK1>>C6                                          READY

         A         B          C        D        E        F      ◄
   1                      First Quarter Sales                    ►
   2                                                             ▲
   3                                                             ▼
   4  Last Name  First Name   January  February   March  Q1 Total  ?
   5
   6  Anderson   Robert        24,000                      24,000
   7  Andrews    Rebecca      220,000                     220,000
   8  Cauldwell  Randy         10,000                      10,000
   9  Goldstein  George        65,000                      65,000
  10  Haldeman   Ann-Marie     92,000                      92,000
  11  Jackson    John          36,000                      36,000
  12  Jameson    George        47,000                      47,000
  13  Lansberg   Jackson       26,000                      26,000
  14  Patterson  Margaret     100,000                     100,000
  15  Pauley     Barbara       45,000                      45,000
```

Figure 5.19: The Jan Sales column contains file-linking formulas.

Attaching the Viewer Add-In

The purpose of the Viewer add-in is to help you find, view, and link files on your hard disk. First, we'll take a look at how to use the Viewer to enter a file-linking formula. Later, we'll retrieve a file with the Viewer.

The Viewer must be attached before you can use it. It uses about 35K of conventional memory. Follow these steps to attach the Viewer:

1. Press / to display the 1-2-3 menu and choose:

   Add-In

   Attach

2. Choose VIEWER.ADN. A menu displays so that you can choose how you will invoke the Viewer—with No-Key or with the function keys 7, 8, 9, or 10. Alternatively, you can invoke the Viewer with the /File View command. For example, if you choose 7, you will bring up the Viewer menu with Alt-F7. Unlike Wysiwyg, which is invoked with the colon, the Viewer doesn't have a single keystroke to invoke the menu. Choose:

   7

   Quit

The Viewer is now attached and available for use.

Entering a File-Linking
Formula with the Viewer

The Viewer makes it easy to enter a file-linking formula because you don't have to memorize the source file name or the cell coordinate. Furthermore, you don't even need to copy the formula. Follow these steps to build the file-linking formula for the February data:

1. Place the pointer in D6, the target cell.

2. Press Alt-F7 to display the Viewer menu.

3. Choose Link.

4. Press ↓ and highlight FEB.WK1. Your screen should look similar to Figure 5.20. The Viewer screen contains two windows. The left window lists your worksheet files alphabetically, and the right window shows you the contents of the files. As you highlight different file names with ↓, the Viewer shows you the contents of the file in the right window. In Figure 5.20, the file name *FEB.WK1* is highlighted and the contents of the file are shown in the right window.

5. Press → to move into the right window. You now have a cell pointer in A1 and can move to the cells you want to link to. The top line of the screen lets you know what to do next:

    Select cell or range and press [Enter] to link

6. Paint the range C6..C18 and press Enter.

7. Save the file.

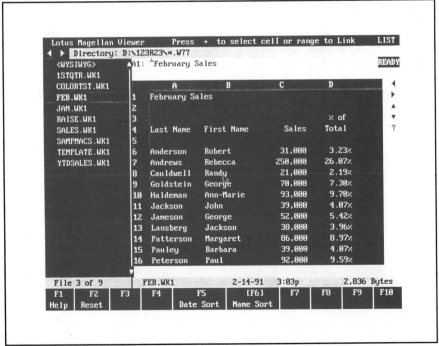

Figure 5.20: The Viewer screen

The data from FEB.WK1 is imported into the current spreadsheet at the cell pointer location, as shown in Figure 5.21. In the control panel, look at the formula that the Viewer built for you. The only difference between the formula you typed and the Viewer formula is that the Viewer specified the complete path of the file name (for example, D:\123R23\FEB.WK1). This extra information is actually good to include so that 1-2-3 knows exactly where the source file is located. If you later were to change the default drive or directory (with /File Directory or /Worksheet Global Default Directory), 1-2-3 would not be able to locate the JAN.WK1 file because the complete path was not specified in the formula.

Retrieving Files with the Viewer

To see how the 1STQTR file is dynamically linked to its source files, let's change a number in the JAN file. This exercise will show you how to

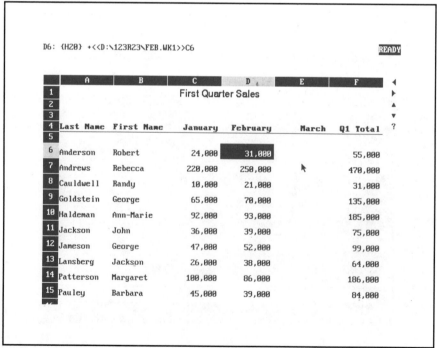

Figure 5.21: The January and February sales data are linked to their source files.

use the Viewer to retrieve the file. The advantage to retrieving a file this way, as opposed to with /File Retrieve, is that the Viewer lets you peek at the contents of the file before you retrieve it. This could save you time if you aren't sure which file you want. Without the Viewer, you have to retrieve files one at a time, until you find the one you are looking for.

Follow these steps to retrieve the JAN file and change a sales figure:

1. If necessary, save the 1STQTR file. Make a note of John Jackson's January sales amount (36,000).

2. Press / to display the 1-2-3 menu and choose:

   File

   View

   Retrieve

3. Press ↓. The right window displays the contents of the high-lighted file name.

4. Highlight JAN.WK1 and press Enter. The JAN file is retrieved.

5. Move to C11 and enter **26000**.

6. Save the file.

7. Follow steps 2 through 5 to retrieve the 1STQTR file.

Because of file-linking formulas, John Jackson's sales figure is automatically entered in this spreadsheet.

Chapter 5

Chapter 6

Chapter 7

Chapter 8

Chapter 9

Printing
Spreadsheet Reports
in 1-2-3

◄IIII FAST TRACK IIII►

As you saw in chapters 3 and 4, you can print a spreadsheet with two different commands: /Print in 1-2-3 and :Print in Wysiwyg. In general, you will use :Print when you have enhanced the spreadsheet with Wysiwyg formatting and alignment commands. If you haven't formatted the spreadsheet with Wysiwyg commands, it doesn't matter which print command you choose. Of course, if Wysiwyg is not attached, you must print the report with /Print.

This chapter covers all aspects of printing with 1-2-3's /Print command, while Chapter 7 describes the Wysiwyg :Print options. If you don't plan on ever printing with the /Print command, you can skip this chapter and turn directly to Chapter 7.

In this chapter, you will learn how to specify print ranges, determine appropriate page-layout settings, print multipage spreadsheets, change the default print settings, print in the background while you continue to work, and print to a file.

PRINTING BASICS

In Chapter 3 you learned the basic procedure for printing a report. To refresh your memory, the steps are repeated here:

- Turn on the printer and make sure it is online. Also, on some printers, you may need to manually align the top of the page with the print head.

- Retrieve the file to print.

- Press / to display the 1-2-3 menu and choose:

  Print

  Printer

  Range

- Indicate the range to be printed. (The next section explains the different ways to specify a print range.)

- Choose:

  Align

  Go

  Page

  Quit

The Align command lets 1-2-3 know that the printer is at the top of the page—make sure the printer is indeed at the top of the page before you issue this command. The Page command ejects the last page of the report from the printer. While you can eject the page with your printer's formfeed button, there are three good reasons why you should use the Page command instead.

First, choosing Page is easier than taking your printer offline, pressing formfeed, and placing the printer back online. Second, the Page command will print the footer on the last page of your report; the formfeed button will not. (Footers are discussed later in the chapter.) Third, 1-2-3 does not know you are at the top of the page when you use your printer's controls to feed the paper; it still thinks you are in the middle of the page where the report finished printing. This last reason creates a problem only if you don't use the Align command before your print the next report. In other words, if you use the printer controls to feed out the page *and* you don't choose Align before your next printing job, your future reports may contain a set of blank lines somewhere in the middle. These blank lines occur where 1-2-3 thinks it should issue a formfeed.

STOP THE PRESSES!

If you need to stop printing for one reason or another (for example, if you have the wrong paper in the printer, or if you discover a mistake in the printout), press Ctrl-Break. Printing may not stop immediately, however, if your printer has a large *buffer*. A buffer is an area of memory storage inside the printer, where the document is placed temporarily until the printer is ready to print it out. A buffer is necessary because the computer can send information much faster than the printer can print it. If your printer has a one-line buffer, printing stops almost immediately when you press Ctrl-Break. But if your printer has a four-page buffer, four pages will print after you cancel printing.

SPECIFYING PRINT RANGES

There is only one setting you absolutely must specify before you can print a spreadsheet in 1-2-3: the range to print. Either use the /Print Printer Range command or fill in the Printer Settings dialog box directly. There are a variety of ways to specify the print range:

- Type the range name.
- Press F3 to choose a range name from a list.
- Type the cell coordinates (for example, A1..G40).
- Paint the range. The quickest way to paint the entire spread-sheet is to press Home, period, and then End Home.

2.3 |||▶   You can also specify the print range before you bring up the Print Settings dialog box, as follows:

- Place the cell pointer in the upper-left corner of the print range.
- Press F4 to anchor.
- Move the pointer to the lower-right corner of the range and press Enter.
- Press / to display the 1-2-3 menu and choose:

   Print
   Printer
   Range

The print range will then be entered into the Print Settings dialog box.

CHANGING A PRINT RANGE

1-2-3 remembers the last range you specified in the Print Settings dialog box, and the next time you choose the /Print Printer Range command, 1-2-3 will suggest the previously entered range. To specify a range that has the same beginning cell coordinate, use the arrow keys to expand or contract the current range. To specify a completely different range, press Esc or Backspace to clear the range and unanchor the cell pointer. The difference between the two keys lies in where the cell pointer ends up. The Esc key places the cell pointer in the upper-left corner of the previously defined print range. The Backspace key, on the other hand, places the cell pointer where it was positioned before you brought up the menu.

For example, suppose the original print range was A1..G40 and you now want to print A50..G100. Place the pointer in the upper-left corner of the new range (cell A50) and choose /Print Printer Range. If you press Esc, the cell pointer is in A1; but if you press Backspace, the pointer is where you prepositioned it: cell A50. Thus, when you preposition the pointer in the new range, press Backspace to clear the old range. Pressing Esc just creates extra work.

Another way to cancel a range is to use the /Print Printer Clear Range command. The print range is then eliminated from the Print Settings dialog box.

EXCLUDING DATA
FROM A PRINT RANGE

1-2-3 offers several commands for excluding data in the middle of a print range. If you don't want to print a column or a range of columns, you can hide them. If you don't want to print certain rows, you can make them non-printing lines. And, if you have a range you don't want printed, you can specify a hidden format. These techniques are discussed below.

Hiding Columns

When you have columns of data in the middle of a print range that you don't want to print out, you can hide them with the /Worksheet Column Hide command. For example, suppose you have a spreadsheet that has quarterly totals interspersed between monthly data. To print only the quarterly totals, you can hide the columns containing the monthly data.

In the 1STQTR spreadsheet you created in Chapter 5, hide the columns of monthly data:

1. Retrieve 1STQTR.

2. Place the cell pointer in column C.

3. Press / to display the 1-2-3 menu and choose:

   Worksheet

   Column

   Hide

4. Highlight one cell each in columns C, D, and E (for example, C1..E1).

5. Press Enter.

The three columns disappear, and your spreadsheet should now look like Figure 6.1. You know that this spreadsheet has hidden columns because the column letters in the spreadsheet frame do not list C, D, and E. If you were to specify A1..F20 as the print range, 1-2-3 would print only the displayed columns.

Although the columns are hidden, 1-2-3 always displays them whenever you are prompted for a range. For example, if you were to give the /Range Erase command, columns C through E would temporarily display so that you can paint a range in the hidden area. During this temporary display of hidden columns, an asterisk appears in the spreadsheet frame next to the column letter of the hidden columns. Once you finish the range command, the hidden columns go back into hibernation.

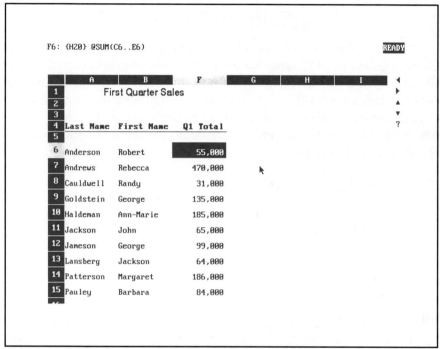

Figure 6.1: Columns C through E are temporarily hidden.

Redisplaying Hidden Columns

To unhide a column, use the /Worksheet Column Display command. Follow these steps to unhide columns C through E:

1. Press / to display the 1-2-3 menu and choose:

   Worksheet

   Column

   Display

2. Paint one cell each in columns C, D, and E (for example, C1..E1).

3. Press Enter.

Hiding Rows

While 1-2-3 does not offer a command for hiding rows, you can exclude rows from a print range by inserting a vertical bar (|) in the first cell of the row. You still see the row on your screen but it will not print. One way to create a non-printing line is to edit the first cell in the row and insert the vertical bar at the beginning of the cell contents. Let's practice this in the 1STQTR spreadsheet. Follow the steps below to exclude row 11 (Jackson's data) from the report:

1. Place the cell pointer on A11.

2. Press F2 to edit.

3. Press Home to move the cursor to the beginning of the cell contents.

4. Type | and press Enter. (The vertical bar is located on the same key as the backslash.)

As Figure 6.2 displays, you don't see the vertical bar in the cell itself (only in the control panel). This symbol creates a non-printing line, and the entire row will be eliminated when you print. It must appear in the first column of the print range, in the row you want to exclude. Now, print the spreadsheet:

1. Press / to display the 1-2-3 menu and choose:

   Print

   Printer

   Range

2. Paint the range A1..D18 and press Enter. (You don't want to include the totals or *% of Totals* because the values would be incorrect without Jackson's data.)

3. Choose:

   Align

   Go

```
A11: (H20) :'Jackson                                          READY

        A         B          C          D        E        F       ◄
 1                         First Quarter Sales                     ►
 2                                                                 ▲
 3                                                                 ▼
 4  Last Name  First Name    January   February    March  Q1 Total  ?
 5
 6  Anderson   Robert          24,000    31,000             55,000
 7  Andrews    Rebecca        220,000   250,000            470,000
 8  Cauldwell  Randy           10,000    21,000             31,000
 9  Goldstein  George          65,000    70,000            135,000
10  Haldeman   Ann-Marie       92,000    93,000            185,000
11 'Jackson    John            26,000    39,000             65,000
12  Jameson    George          47,000    52,000             99,000
13  Lansberg   Jackson         26,000    38,000             64,000
14  Patterson  Margaret       100,000    86,000            186,000
15  Pauley     Barbara         45,000    39,000             84,000
```

Figure 6.2: Row 11 is a non-printing line.

Page

Quit

Row 11, Jackson's data, is excluded from this report. To re-include this row in the report, just edit A11 and delete the vertical bar. (Note: The Wysiwyg formatting doesn't print when you use /Print.)

If you have many rows you don't want to print, it would be tedious to insert the vertical bar in each cell. An easier way is to enter the vertical bars in a newly inserted blank column. Here is the basic procedure:

- Insert a column to the left of the print range.

- Narrow the column width to 1 character.

- Enter the vertical bar in this column at the beginning of each row you don't want to print. If you have several consecutive non-printing rows, use the /Copy command. The cells will appear to be empty because the vertical bar does not display in the cell (only in the control panel).

- Be sure to include the new column in the print range.

To include these rows in the report at a later date, you can either delete the entire column or selectively erase the cells containing the vertical bars.

Hiding Ranges

To hide the contents of a range of cells, both on the screen and on the printed report, use the /Range Format Hidden command. The cells' contents are actually there—you just can't see them unless you place the pointer on the cell and look in the control panel. (Note: If global protection is enabled, the control panel does *not* display the contents of hidden cells.) A2 in Figure 6.3 is a hidden cell, and you can see the cell contents in the control panel. When you print the report, the hidden cells will appear blank.

To unhide the cells, use the /Range Format Reset command.

PRINTING MULTIPLE RANGES ON A SINGLE PAGE

You may have been wondering why the /Print command doesn't automatically formfeed the page after you print a range. There is a good reason: so that you can print more than one range on a page. If you have two short reports that are related in some way, you may want to print them both on the same page. Here's the general procedure:

- Specify the first print range.

- Choose:

  Align

  Go

```
A2: (H) 'Note: When March data comes in, enter a file-linking formula.    READY
```

	A	B	C	D	E	F
1			First Quarter Sales			
2						
3						
4	Last Name	First Name	January	February	March	Q1 Total
5						
6	Anderson	Robert	24,000	31,000		55,000
7	Andrews	Rebecca	220,000	250,000		470,000
8	Cauldwell	Randy	10,000	21,000		31,000
9	Goldstein	George	65,000	70,000		135,000
10	Haldeman	Ann-Marie	92,000	93,000		185,000
11	Jackson	John	26,000	39,000		65,000
12	Jameson	George	47,000	52,000		99,000
13	Lansberg	Jackson	26,000	38,000		64,000
14	Patterson	Margaret	100,000	86,000		186,000
15	Pauley	Barbara	45,000	39,000		84,000

Figure 6.3: A2 is a hidden cell.

- To get blank lines between each report, choose the Line command a few times.

- Specify the second print range.

- Choose:

    Go

    Page

    Quit

Notice that you do not choose Align before you print the second range. Remember, the Align command tells 1-2-3 that the printer is at the top of the page. Since you are in the middle of a page, you don't want to align.

SETTING UP THE PAGE LAYOUT

By default, 1-2-3 prints on an 8½-by-11" letter-size page in *portrait* (vertical) orientation using the printer's default font. This section will show you how to change the margins, page length, font, and orientation in 1-2-3. Refer to Figure 6.4 throughout this section.

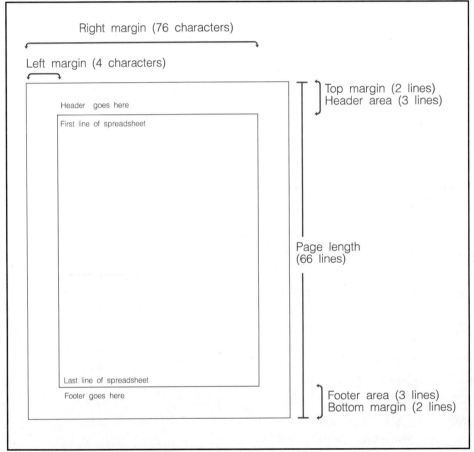

Figure 6.4: Page layout in 1-2-3

CHANGING THE MARGINS

When printing a spreadsheet in 1-2-3, you change margins with the /Print Printer Options Margins command. You can also choose /Print Printer, and then edit the margins in the Print Settings dialog box. Left and right margins are measured in characters while top and bottom margins are measured in lines. Table 6.1 indicates the default and maximum margin settings.

The best way to explain the layout of a 1-2-3 page is with a picture. As indicated in Figure 6.4, both the left and right margins are measured from the left edge of the page. To calculate how many characters will fit on a printed line, subtract the left from the right margin. With the default margins, up to 72 characters will print per line. This page width will print eight spreadsheet columns, assuming you haven't changed the default column width of 9 characters. After adjusting column widths and left and right margins, you may be able to fit more or fewer columns across.

You can increase the number of characters that print on a line by taking advantage of some of the unique capabilities your printer offers:

- Some printers have wide carriages that allow you to use 14"-wide paper.

- Laser printers can print the spreadsheet sideways on the page; this is called *landscape orientation.*

- Almost all printers can print in smaller, or compressed, type.

Read the upcoming section on Setup Strings to find out how to use the last two printer features.

Table 6.1: 1-2-3's Margin Settings

MARGIN	DEFAULT SETTING	MAXIMUM SETTING
Left	4 characters	240 characters
Right	76 characters	240 characters
Top	2 lines	32 lines
Bottom	2 lines	32 lines

Now, let's look at the vertical page measurements. A letter-size piece of paper contains 66 lines (11 inches multiplied by 6 lines per inch), and 66 is the default Page-Length setting. Notice that three lines are reserved for a header—regardless of whether you have one. (A *header* is a standard line of text, such as a title or date, that automatically prints at the top of every page.) Therefore, even if you specify a top margin of zero and don't have a header, you will get three blank lines at the top of each page when you print. The same rules apply for the bottom margin.

The None margin option (/Print Printer Options Margins None) sets the top, bottom, and left margins to zero and the right margin to the maximum (240 characters). However, this command still reserves three lines each for the header and footer. This option is typically used to create ASCII files, as discussed later in the chapter.

PAGE LAYOUT ON A LASER PRINTER

If you have a laser printer, you must adjust your margins and page-length settings because this type of printer cannot print all the way to the edges of the page. At the top and bottom of the page, there is a half-inch (three lines) you can't print on, and on the left and right, there is an unusable quarter-inch (2 characters). For all intents and purposes, the laser page is 8" by 10". Figure 6.5 shows the layout of a page printed on a laser printer. The shaded area represents the part of the page on which the laser can't print.

The margins you enter in the Print Settings dialog box are added to the built-in margins on the laser printer. Therefore, when you set your margins, you should subtract the built-in margins from the desired margin. For example, to get three blank lines above the header, set a top margin of 0. Or, to get five spaces at the left of the page, set a left margin of 3.

Because of the three built-in lines at the top and bottom of the page, you must also change the page length to 60 lines instead of 66. The page length is changed in the Print Settings dialog box or with /Print Printer Options Pg-Length. See *Changing Printer Defaults* later in this chapter for information on permanently changing page-length settings.

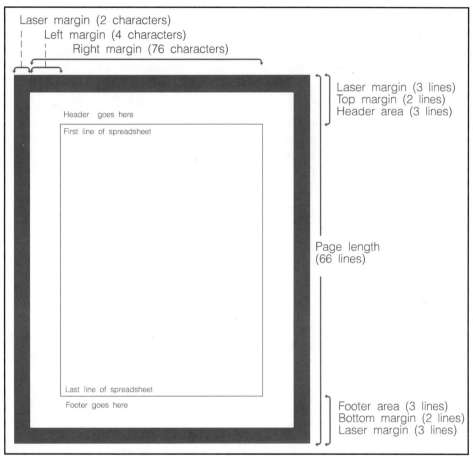

Figure 6.5: Layout of page printed on a laser printer

SETUP STRINGS

While 1-2-3 does not have the extensive formatting options that Wysiwyg offers, you can change fonts, type style, and page orientation using *setup strings*. Setup strings are codes that give special instructions to your printer. For example, the code \015 tells an Epson printer to print in condensed mode, and \027(s16.66H tells an HP LaserJet to use the 8.5-point Line Printer font. As you can see, these codes are quite cryptic and not nearly as easy to use as Wysiwyg's menu options. But if you want to print the spreadsheet with a different font or type style using 1-2-3's /Print command, you need to use setup strings. (Note: Some printers have buttons to change to different fonts or modes; you can press these buttons instead of specifying setup strings.)

You can enter the setup string directly in the Print Settings dialog box or with the /Print Printer Options Setup command.

Each printer has different capabilities and unique codes for producing these effects. How do you know what your printer's setup strings are? Tables 6.2 and 6.3 list some of the codes for two popular printers—the Epson RX-80 and the HP LaserJet II. If you have a different printer, it may be compatible with the Epson or LaserJet and use the same codes. If not, you will need to look up the codes in your printer manual and translate them into the proper format for 1-2-3 setup strings. For example, the documentation may say that the code for emphasized print is *Esc E*. This code translates into the setup string \027E. All setup strings must begin with a backslash. Note that 027 is the string for Esc (Escape). In fact, most codes begin with Esc, so the printer codes are sometimes referred to as *escape codes* or *escape sequences*. The codes are case-sensitive, so make sure you enter them with the exact upper- and lowercase indicated in the tables or in your printer manual.

Table 6.2: Setup Strings and Settings for the Epson RX-80

FUNCTION	STRING	RIGHT MARGIN	PAGE LENGTH
Reset to defaults	\027@	80	66
Emphasized	\027E		
Italics	\0274		
17 cpi	\015	136	
12 cpi	\027M	96	
8 lines per inch	\0270		88

Table 6.3: Setup Strings and Settings for the HP LaserJet II

FUNCTION	STRING	RIGHT MARGIN	PAGE LENGTH
Reset to defaults	\027E	80	60
Bold	\027(s3B		
Portrait, 16.66 cpi	\027(s16.66H	133	
Portrait, 8 lpi	\027&l8D		80
Landscape, 10 cpi	\027&l1O	106	45
Landscape, 16.66 cpi	\027&l1O\027 (s16.66H	175	45

A MATH LESSON: CALCULATING YOUR LAYOUT SETTINGS

When you specify a setup string that changes the number of characters that can fit on each line, you must adjust the right margin. Two types of strings affect the right margin—namely, type size and page orientation. With smaller type sizes (12 or 17 characters per inch) and in landscape (sideways) orientation, you can fit more characters on a line, and you will therefore need to increase the right margin. If you don't change the margin, the data will not print all the way across the page. Similarly, when you change the number of lines that can fit on each page, you must change the page length setting. Strings that control lines-per-inch settings and orientation affect the page length. Tables 6.2 and 6.3 indicate the margin and page length for the strings that affect these settings. If no value is listed, the string has no effect on the setting.

Use the following formula to calculate the value for the right margin:

- Multiply the page width in inches by the number of characters per inch (cpi). This product is the total number of characters that can fit across the page.

- Subtract the left margin from the total page width. (Tables 6.2 and 6.3 assume a left margin of 0.)

To calculate the value for the page length, use this formula:

- If you are printing on a laser printer, subtract one inch from the page length. The difference is the usable page length.

- Multiply the usable page length by the lines per inch (lpi).

Setup strings are a complicated issue and definitely not for the casual 1-2-3 user. Some of the codes are quite long and it's all too easy to make a typing mistake. Because Wysiwyg offers a much easier way to give the same printing instructions, stick with the :Format and :Print Layout commands until you feel more confident.

PRINTING MULTIPAGE SPREADSHEETS

Even after compressing the print horizontally and vertically, the spreadsheet may still print onto several pages. 1-2-3 automatically divides your print range into multiple pages when all the columns or rows can't fit on a single page. Unfortunately, in 1-2-3, there is no easy way to predetermine whether the report will fit on one page or where the page breaks will occur, without actually printing the report. (Wysiwyg, however, provides this option, as you will see in Chapter 7.)

When a report runs over one page, you have several special requirements that you don't have with single-page reports. You might want to number the pages, print a title on each page, repeat the column or row headings on every page, and insert page breaks. These topics are covered here.

CREATING HEADERS AND FOOTERS

A *header* is a single line of text that automatically prints at the top of each page while a *footer* is text that prints at the bottom. Figures 6.4 and 6.5 illustrate exactly where headers and footers appear on the page. There are always two blank lines that separate the header and footer from the body of the spreadsheet report.

Headers and footers are ideal places for documenting your spreadsheet. By including the date, the title, the name of the file, and your name in the header and footer, you eliminate guesswork if you (or someone else) find a printed report lying around. Other types of information you can include in a header or footer are page numbers, titles, revision numbers, warning messages about confidentiality, and so on.

You can enter the header or footer text in the Print Settings dialog box or use the /Print Printer Options Header (Footer) commands. You do not actually see the headers and footers in your spreadsheet—they appear only when you print.

Special Codes for Headers and Footers

In addition to text, there are several special codes you can use in your headers and footers:

#	Inserts the page number
@	Inserts the current date
\	Inserts the contents of the specified cell
|	Aligns the text in the center
| |	Aligns the text on the right

When you print, the number sign (#) will be replaced with the page number, and the at sign (@) will be replaced with the date you print the report. It's a good idea to include the date in a header or footer so that you can readily identify whether you are looking at the most current printout of the spreadsheet. To specify the contents of a cell as your header or footer, type a backslash (\) followed by a cell coordinate or range name. For example, if A1 contains the label *January Sales*, type **\A1** as the header text.

The vertical bar (|) is an alignment command. By default, your headers and footers print at the left margin. To center a header or footer, place one vertical bar before the text. To align a header or footer at the right margin, use a second vertical bar.

Let's look at some examples. The footer, | #, centers the page number at the bottom of each page. The header, @ | *1992 Budget* | *BUDGET92.WK1*, places the date at the left margin, centers the title *1992 Budget* and aligns the file name at the right margin. The footer, @ | | *Page* #, places the date at the left margin and the word *Page* followed by the page number at the right margin.

Troubleshooting

Here are a few common problems you may experience with headers and footers.

Problem: A header or footer doesn't look properly aligned.

Solution: It's possible that your margins aren't quite right. Perhaps your right margin is set to 132 but your spreadsheet is only 70 characters wide. Check your right margin and reduce it if necessary.

Problem: The footer does not print on the last page of the report.

Solution: Footers do not automatically print on the final page unless you formfeed the paper with the /Print Printer Page command. If you use your printer's formfeed button or manually roll the paper out of the printer, you will not get the footer on the last page.

Problem: Your pages aren't numbered correctly (for example, the first page is numbered 5).

Solution: You didn't choose the Align option before you printed. One of the functions of the Align command is to set the starting page number to 1. To begin numbering the report with 1, be sure to choose Align before you print the report with the Go option.

REPEATING A RANGE ON EACH PAGE

Figure 6.6 shows what happens when you print a spreadsheet that doesn't fit on a single page. The first seven columns print on page one and the remaining columns print on page two. Here's the problem: When you look at page two, you have no idea what the data means unless you somehow cut and paste it to page one.

A cleaner solution is to use the Borders option to print the column A headings on every page. This option is similar to the /Worksheet Titles command discussed in Chapter 5. Instead of freezing the titles on the screen, though, the Borders command freezes the titles on the printed report. When you use borders, all pages can be read independently, as shown in Figure 6.7.

The /Print Printer Options Borders command offers two options: Columns and Rows. The columns you specify are repeated on the left side of each page while rows are repeated at the top of each page. Border

	Jan	Feb	Mar	Apr	May	Jun
Mid Atlantic	100,000	101,000	102,000	103,000	104,000	105,000
South	100,500	101,500	102,500	103,500	104,500	105,500
Mid West	200,000	202,000	204,000	206,000	208,000	210,000
Pacific	201,000	203,000	205,000	207,000	209,000	211,000
Total	601,500	607,500	613,500	619,500	625,500	631,500

Jul	Aug	Sep	Oct	Nov	Dec	Total
106,000	107,000	108,000	109,000	110,000	111,000	1,266,000
106,500	107,500	108,500	109,500	110,500	111,500	1,272,000
212,000	214,000	216,000	218,000	220,000	222,000	2,532,000
213,000	215,000	217,000	219,000	221,000	223,000	2,544,000
637,500	643,500	649,500	655,500	661,500	667,500	7,614,000

Figure 6.6: The second page of this report can't be understood without the first page.

columns are ideal for wide spreadsheets while border rows are typically used for long reports. Use both column and row borders if your spreadsheet is long and wide.

Rows and columns you specify as borders should *not* be part of your print range. In the example shown in Figure 6.6, column A would be the border column, and the print range would be B1..N8. A common mistake is to include the border in the print range. When you do this, the border range prints twice on the first page.

Follow this general procedure to specify print borders:

- Press / to display the 1-2-3 menu and choose:

  Print

  Printer

  Options

  Borders

  Columns (or Rows)

- Highlight the columns or rows to be repeated on each page. (One cell in each row or column is sufficient—you don't have to highlight the entire range.)

- Press Enter.

- Choose:

  Quit

  Range

```
                Jul        Aug        Sep        Oct        Nov        Dec

Mid Atlantic   106,000    107,000    108,000    109,000    110,000    111,000
South          106,500    107,500    108,500    109,500    110,500    111,500
Mid West       212,000    214,000    216,000    218,000    220,000    222,000
Pacific        213,000    215,000    217,000    219,000    221,000    223,000
               -------------------------------------------------------------
Total          637,500    643,500    649,500    655,500    661,500    667,500
```

Figure 6.7: The row headings in column A are repeated on page two so that each page stands by itself.

- Specify the range to be printed. Be sure you do not include the border rows or columns.
- Press Enter.

INSERTING PAGE BREAKS

When 1-2-3 prints a long spreadsheet, it automatically divides the report into multiple pages. The layout settings determine exactly how many rows can fit on the page. To compute the number of spreadsheet rows that will print on each page:

- Add together the top and bottom margins and the header and footer areas.
- Subtract this total from the page length.

With the default margins, 56 spreadsheet rows fit on a page (50 rows on a laser printer).

After you print a report, you may discover that the pages break in inappropriate places, such as in the middle of a section that begins at the bottom of one page and continues onto another. To manually force a page break, follow this general procedure:

- Place the cell pointer where you want to insert the page break. The pointer should be in the first column of the print range.
- Press / to display the 1-2-3 menu and choose:

  Worksheet

  Page

The /Worksheet Page command inserts a row above the cell pointer and enters the page-break symbol into the cell above, as shown in Figure 6.8. When you print, 1-2-3 will place the data below this symbol on the next page.

If 1-2-3 ignores your page break when you print, the page-break symbol is in the wrong place. It may be outside of the print range, or not on the left edge of the range. For example, the page will not break properly if the symbol is in B45 and the print range is A1..G90. In this case, the symbol needs to be in column A, the first column in the print range.

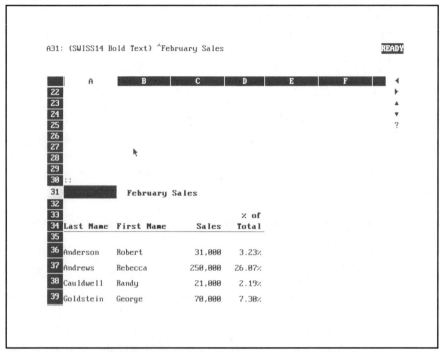

Figure 6.8: A page break inserted above row 30

To remove a page break, either erase the cell that contains the page-break symbol or delete the entire row. Before you delete the row, make sure there isn't any data on it.

HANDS-ON PRACTICE: PRINTING A MULTIPAGE REPORT

To practice some of the printing options discussed in this chapter, you will print out both ranges (the January and February data) in the SALES file.

1. Retrieve SALES. To place the February data on its own page, you will insert a page break.

2. Place the pointer in A30.

3. Press / to display the 1-2-3 menu and choose:

   Worksheet

   Page

4. The page break symbol is inserted above the current row. Now, specify the entire spreadsheet as the print range. Press / to display the 1-2-3 menu and choose:

   Print

   Printer

   Range

5. To highlight the entire spreadsheet, press Home, period, End, and Home.

6. Press Enter.

Change the left and right margins so that the spreadsheet is centered on the page:

1. Choose:

   Options

   Margins

   Left

2. Type **15** and press Enter.

3. Choose:

   Margins

   Right

4. Type **65** and press Enter.

5. Now, create a footer that prints the file name at the left margin, centers the page number, and inserts the current date at the right margin. Choose Footer.

6. Type **SALES.WK1 | Page # | @** and press Enter.

7. If you are printing on a laser printer, change the page length to 60 lines.

Your Print Settings dialog box should look similar to Figure 6.9. You are now ready to print the report. When you complete the following steps, the second page of the report should look similar to Figure 6.10.

```
                         ┌─Print Settings─┐

    Range: [A1..D50········]      ┌─Destination──────────────┐
                                  │ (*) Printer     ( ) Encoded file │
    ┌─Margins─────────────┐       │ ( ) Text file   ( ) Background   │
    │ Left:  [15·] Top:   [2·]│   │                                  │
    │ Right: [65·] Bottom: [2·]│  │ File name:[···················]  │
                              └──────────────────────────────┘

    ┌─Borders─────────────┐
    │ Columns: [··············]     Page length: [60·]
    │ Rows:    [··············]
                                    Setup string: [···················]

    Header: [·······························]    [ ] Unformatted pages
    Footer: [SALES.WK1¦Page #¦@···········]      [ ] List entries

    Interface: Parallel 1          Name: HP 2686 LaserJet Series

                 ┌─Press F2 (EDIT) to edit settings─┐
```

Figure 6.9: The Print Settings dialog box for the SALES report

```
        February Sales

                                             % of
        Last Name   First Name      Sales    Total

        Anderson    Robert          31,000   3.23%
        Andrews     Rebecca        250,000  26.07%
        Cauldwell   Randy           21,000   2.19%
        Goldstein   George          70,000   7.30%
        Haldeman    Ann-Marie       93,000   9.70%
        Jackson     John            39,000   4.07%
        Jameson     George          52,000   5.42%
        Lansberg    Jackson         38,000   3.96%
        Patterson   Margaret        86,000   8.97%
        Pauley      Barbara         39,000   4.07%
        Peterson    Paul            92,000   9.59%
        Smith       Betsy           63,000   6.57%
        Smith       Ruth            85,000   8.86%

        Total                      959,000
```

Figure 6.10: Page 2 of the sales report

1. Choose:

   Quit

   Align

   Go

   Page

   Quit

2. Save the file with the name **123SALES**.

Because you printed with 1-2-3's /Print command, none of the Wysiwyg formatting appears in the printout.

CHANGING PRINTER DEFAULTS

If you find that you are constantly changing certain page layout settings when you print reports, consider modifying the printer defaults. Change these defaults in the Default Printer Settings dialog box, shown in Figure 6.11. You can display this dialog box with the /Worksheet Global Default Printer command.

Some of the settings pertain to printer configuration (interface, baud rate, automatic line feed, and printer name); these options are discussed in Appendix A. Other settings affect the page layout (margins, page length, and setup string).

If there is a certain setup string you want to use more often than not, then specify it here. That way, you won't have to enter the string for each report. Or, you may want to specify your printer's reset code (\027E on an HP LaserJet, \027@ on an Epson RX-80) to cancel any codes that may already be in the printer's memory.

Laser printer owners should change the default page length to 60 lines. You may also want to reduce the default margins since the laser has its own built-in margins.

Very important: To permanently change the printer defaults, you must choose the Update option on the /Worksheet Global Default menu. If you skip this step, your changes will not be saved.

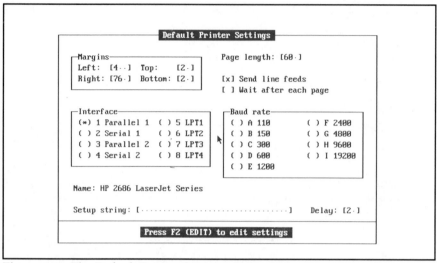

Figure 6.11: The Default Printer Settings dialog box

2.3 ⏭ BACKGROUND PRINTING

While a report is printing, 1-2-3 displays a WAIT indicator in the control panel. You cannot work on the current spreadsheet, print another range, or retrieve a different file until this message disappears. If you have a slow printer or long reports, this waiting period can seem endless. Release 2.3 has an alternative for those who hate waiting: background printing. When you tell 1-2-3 to print a spreadsheet in the background, you can be productive while a report is printing.

LOADING BPRINT

Before you can use the /Print Background command, you must first load a small 6K program called BPRINT. The BPRINT program is stored in your 1-2-3 directory, and must be loaded before you load 1-2-3. To load

BPRINT, follow these steps:

1. Quit 1-2-3.

2. If necessary, change to the subdirectory where 1-2-3 is located. For example, if the subdirectory is named 123R23, type **CD\123R23** and press Enter.

3. Type **BPRINT** and press Enter. (Note: If your printer is not connected to the first parallel port, refer to the next section.)

4. Type **123** and press Enter.

If you plan to do a lot of background printing, you should include BPRINT in your batch file for loading 1-2-3. (See Appendix A.)

Now, print the SALES spreadsheet in the background:

1. Retrieve 123SALES.

2. Press / to display the 1-2-3 menu and choose:

    Print

    Background

3. You are asked to enter a name for the background file. When printing a file in the background, 1-2-3 creates a temporary file with an .ENC (for encoded) extension. This file is erased after the file is printed. Type **123SALES** and press Enter.

4. Choose:

    Align

    Go

    Quit

While the report is printing, you can continue working on the current spreadsheet or even retrieve another file. One of the features of BPRINT is that you can print one range after another, without having to wait for the previous ranges to finish printing. Each print range is stored in its own .ENC file and placed in a *print queue* (a line-up) in the order you gave the print request. 1-2-3 automatically issues a formfeed after each report—you do not need to give the Page command to eject the page.

BPRINT COMMANDS

When you simply type BPRINT, the program will send your reports through the first parallel port (LPT1) during background printing. Most printers are connected to LPT1, but if your printer is attached to a different port, you must specify a parameter when you load BPRINT, as follows:

Port	Description	Command
LPT2	(second parallel port)	BPRINT -P=2
COM1	(first serial port)	BPRINT -S=1
COM2	(second serial port)	BPRINT -S=2

To cancel or temporarily pause the printing of a file, you can use the following commands:

Command	Description
BPRINT -PA	Temporarily pauses printing
BPRINT -R	Resumes printing after a pause
BPRINT -C *filename*	Cancels a specified file from the queue (you must include the complete path)
BPRINT -T	Cancels (terminates) all files in the queue

The above commands must be typed at the DOS prompt. Instead of quitting 1-2-3, a faster way is to use the /System command. This option takes you to DOS temporarily so that you can give DOS commands and then returns you to 1-2-3 when you type **EXIT**.

CREATING PRINT FILES

The /Print menu contains two options that create disk files instead of directly printing the report: File and Encoded. The File option creates a text file, otherwise known as an ASCII file. (ASCII is an acronym that stands for *American Standard Code for Information Interchange*.) This file contains only text—no formulas, fonts, type styles, or other formatting. You will create ASCII files when you want to transfer a 1-2-3 spreadsheet into another program. Since each program (1-2-3, WordPerfect, Microsoft Word, dBASE, Excel, etc.) has its own unique way of storing its files and usually cannot understand other program's file formats, a standard format, ASCII, was developed so that data could be transferred easily between programs.

CREATING AN ASCII FILE

Suppose you typed a report in your word processor and you want to include a 1-2-3 spreadsheet in the middle of it. While a few word-processing programs allow you to retrieve .WK1 files, most do not. You will therefore need to convert the spreadsheet into a format that your word-processing program can understand, ASCII. To create an ASCII file out of a 1-2-3 spreadsheet, you print it to a file, as follows:

- Retrieve the spreadsheet file.

- Press / to display the 1-2-3 menu and choose:

  Print

  File

- Enter a file name. If you don't type an extension, 1-2-3 assigns .PRN to the name.

- Specify the range.

- To eliminate margins, page breaks, headers, and footers from the file, choose:

  Options

  Margins

  None

  Other

  Unformatted

  Quit

- To create the ASCII file, choose:

    Align

    Go

    Quit

This file can then be brought into any program that accepts ASCII files. Refer to the documentation on the destination software for details on importing or retrieving ASCII files. For information on importing ASCII files into 1-2-3, see Appendix C.

CREATING AN ENCODED FILE

You may not personally own a laser printer, but that doesn't mean you can't print your spreadsheet reports on one of these fast, high quality printers. Check around your office—maybe someone else has one who won't mind if you print an occasional document. Or call your friendly neighborhood copyshop; many of these shops rent time on PCs connected to laser printers. Some shops charge by the page, others by the hour. *The computer hooked up to the remote printer does not even need to have 1-2-3.*

To use a remote printer, though, you must first use the INSTALL program to install 1-2-3 for the printer. Refer to Appendix A for details on installing printer drivers. You will also need to designate this printer as your default with the /Worksheet Global Default Printer Name command; you can then devise setup strings specific to it.

To create the encoded file, follow this general procedure:

- Retrieve the spreadsheet file.

- Press / to display the 1-2-3 menu and choose:

    Print

    Encoded

- Enter a file name. 1-2-3 automatically assigns .ENC to the name.

- Specify the range.

- Set the margins, page-length, and setup strings appropriate for the remote printer.

- Choose:

    Align

    Go

    Quit

You will then need to copy the .ENC file to a floppy disk and take it to the remote printer. To print the encoded file, use the following command at the DOS prompt:

COPY A:*filename*.enc/B LPT1

Substitute the actual name of the encoded file in place of *filename*. The above command assumes the file is on a floppy disk in drive A, and that the printer is connected to the first parallel port (LPT1). You may need to change these parameters.

Chapter 5

Chapter 6

Chapter 7

Chapter 8

Chapter 9

Printing Spreadsheet Reports in Wysiwyg with Release 2.3

◀|||| FAST TRACK ||||▶

To stop printing: 223

> Press Ctrl-Break.

To change to landscape (sideways) orientation: 233

> Press : to display the Wysiwyg menu and choose Print Config Orientation Landscape Printer.

To fit a print range on a single page: 233

> Press : to display the Wysiwyg menu and choose Print Layout Compression Automatic.

To number pages of a multipage report: 238

> Press : to display the Wysiwyg menu and choose Print Layout Titles Footer. To create a centered page number, type | # and press Enter.

To repeat a range (border) on each page: 240

> Press : to display the Wysiwyg menu and choose Print Layout Borders Top (or Left).

To insert a page break: 241

> Place the cell pointer where you want to insert the page break. Horizontal page breaks are inserted above the pointer and vertical breaks are inserted to the left of the pointer. Press : to display the Wysiwyg menu and choose Worksheet Page Row (or Column).

To change the page layout defaults: 244

> Make desired changes (margins, page size, etc.). Press : to display the Wysiwyg menu and choose Print Layout Default Update.

To load the background print utility (BPRINT):   246

> Quit 1-2-3. If necessary, change to the subdirectory where 1-2-3 is located. For example, if the subdirectory is named 123R23, type **CD\123R23** and press Enter. Type **BPRINT** and press Enter. Type **123** and press Enter.

Load the BPRINT utility (see previous step). Press : to display the Wysiwyg menu and choose Print Range Set. Paint the print range and press Enter. Choose Background and enter a name for the temporary encoded file. Choose Go.

CHAPTER SEVEN

If you have used any of Wysiwyg's formatting or alignment options, you must use the :Print command in order for these effects to print, because the /Print command ignores Wysiwyg formatting. You may even want to use :Print for spreadsheets with no Wysiwyg formatting, because of its enhanced printer controls. Besides being able to print fonts, lines, and shading, Wysiwyg's :Print command offers several features unavailable in 1-2-3:

- a print preview command that allows you to see how your spreadsheet looks on the page before you actually print

- a menu option to change the page orientation from portrait (vertical) to landscape (sideways)

- a command that automatically changes the type size so that a large spreadsheet range can fit on a single page

- options to print grid lines and the worksheet frame

These special printing options, in addition to the standard settings, are discussed in this chapter. You will learn how to specify print ranges, determine appropriate page layout settings, print multipage spreadsheets, change the default printing settings, print in the background while you continue working, and print on a remote printer.

PRINTING BASICS

In Chapter 4 you learned the basic procedure for printing a report. To refresh your memory, the steps are repeated here:

- Turn on the printer and make sure it is online. Also, on some printers you may need to manually align the top of the page with the print head.

- Retrieve the file to print.

- Press **:** to display the Wysiwyg menu and choose:

    Print

> Range
>
> Set

- Indicate the range to be printed.
- Choose Go.

STOP THE PRESSES!

If you need to stop printing for one reason or another (for example, if you have the wrong paper in the printer, or if you discover a mistake in the printout), press Ctrl-Break or Esc. Printing may not stop immediately, however, if your printer has a large *buffer*. A buffer is an area of memory storage inside the printer where a document is placed temporarily until the printer is ready to print it out. A buffer is necessary because the computer can send information much faster than the printer can print it. If your printer has a one-line buffer, printing stops almost immediately when you press Ctrl-Break. But if your printer has a four-page buffer, four pages will print after you cancel printing.

CHANGING PRINT DENSITY

When you selected a printer name in Chapter 4, you also chose a print density. The print density controls the quality of your printed output. Figure 7.1 compares LaserJet output of two different print densities. The higher the density, the better the output quality, but the longer the print time. You may want to print your first drafts in medium density, and then select high density for your final report. For high-density printing, consider background printing, as discussed later in the chapter.

If you have an HP LaserJet printer, you will have a choice for *Extended Capability* on your printer list. This driver allows you to access internal font cartridges. See Working with Font Cartridges in Chapter 4 for more details.

When you choose a different print density with the :Print Config Printer command, that density becomes the default for any new files you create in the current 1-2-3 session. The print density is also stored with the file when you save.

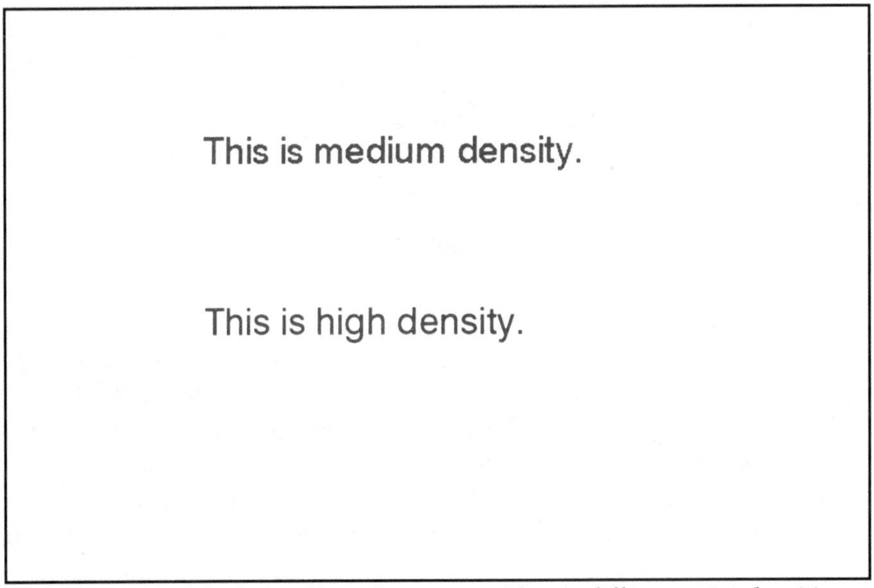

This is medium density.

This is high density.

Figure 7.1: A comparison of LaserJet ouput with two different print densities

However, the next time you load 1-2-3, no printer driver will be selected; fortunately there is a way to specify a default printer. Follow these steps:

1. Press **:** to display the Wysiwyg menu and choose:

    Print

    Config

    Printer

2. Highlight the printer driver you want to be the default and press Enter.

3. Quit to READY mode.

4. To save the configuration defaults, press **:** to display the Wysiwyg menu and choose:

    Display

Default

Update

It may seem odd that you save your printing defaults on the Display menu. While this procedure is in no way intuitive, it does work.

SPECIFYING PRINT RANGES

There is only one setting you absolutely must specify before you can print a spreadsheet in Wysiwyg: the range to print. Either use the :Print Range Set command or fill in the Wysiwyg Printer Settings dialog box directly. There are a variety of ways to specify the print range:

- Type the range name.

- Press F3 to choose a range name from a list.

- Type the cell coordinates (for example, A1..G40).

- Paint the range. The quickest way to paint the entire spreadsheet is to press Home, period, and then End Home.

You can also specify the print range before you bring up the Print Settings dialog box, as follows:

- Place the cell pointer in the upper-left corner of the print range.

- Press F4 to anchor.

- Move the pointer to the lower-right corner of the range and press Enter.

- Press **:** to display the Wysiwyg menu and choose:

    Print

    Range

    Set

The print range will then be entered into the Wysiwyg Print Settings dialog box.

CHANGING A PRINT RANGE

Wysiwyg remembers the range most recently specified in the Wysiwyg Print Settings dialog box, and the next time you choose :Print Range Set, Wysiwyg will suggest the previously entered range. To specify a range that has the same beginning cell coordinate, use the arrow keys to expand or contract the current range. To specify a completely different range, press Esc or Backspace to clear the range and unanchor the cell pointer. The difference between the two keys lies in where the cell pointer ends up. The Esc key places the cell pointer in the upper-left corner of the previously defined print range. The Backspace key, on the other hand, places the cell pointer where it was positioned before you brought up the menu.

For example, suppose the original print range is A1..G40 and you now want to print A50..G100. Place the pointer in the upper-left corner of the new range (cell A50) and choose :Print Range Set. If you press Esc, the cell pointer is in A1; but if you press Backspace, the pointer is where you prepositioned it: cell A50. Thus, when you have prepositioned the pointer in the new range, press Backspace to clear the old range. Pressing Esc just creates extra work.

Another way to cancel a range is to use the :Print Range Clear command. The print range is then eliminated from the Wysiwyg Print Settings dialog box.

DETERMINING HOW MUCH WILL FIT ON A PAGE

Several factors determine how much of your spreadsheet can fit on a page. The page size, left and right margins, column widths, page orientation, and font determine the number of spreadsheet columns that print on each page. With the default settings, eight spreadsheet columns can fit across the page (seven columns with a laser printer). After adjusting any of the aforementioned settings, you may be able to fit more or fewer columns across.

The number of rows that can print on each page is determined by the page size, the top and bottom margins, the font, row heights, page orientation, and the use of headers and footers. With the default settings, fifty-one spreadsheet rows can fit on the page (forty-six rows with a laser printer). You may be able to fit more or fewer lines after adjusting any of the previously mentioned settings.

So how do you determine whether your spreadsheet will fit on a single page? In 1-2-3 you need to do a bit of math to calculate how many columns and rows will fit on the page; Wysiwyg offers an easier way. After you define a print range, Wysiwyg draws dashed lines around each page. Before you print, you can see exactly how much will print on each page, and where the page breaks are. If you don't like where the page breaks occur, you can change them. If you want to try to fit the entire range on a single page, you can take action before you waste paper.

Let's see how this works in the SALES spreadsheet you created in Chapter 5. Follow these steps to specify the entire sales spreadsheet as the print range:

1. Retrieve the SALES file. Because you defined the January data as the print range, dotted lines appear around the range A1..D20.

2. Press : to display the Wysiwyg menu and choose:

    Print

    Range

    Set

3. The current print range, A1..D20, is highlighted. You need to expand this range to include the February data. Press End and Home to paint the entire spreadsheet (A1..D49), and press Enter.

4. Choose Quit so that you can look at the print-range definition lines.

5. Press PgDn until you see the dotted line across the middle of the February data, as shown in Figure 7.2. This line represents a page break.

Because you wouldn't want the February sales data to be split onto two pages, you should adjust the page break. You will learn how to do this later in the chapter.

F41: {H20}   READY

	A	B	C	D	E	F
35	Anderson	Robert	31,000	3.23%		
36	Andrews	Rebecca	250,000	26.07%		
37	Cauldwell	Randy	21,000	2.19%		
38	Goldstein	George	70,000	7.30%		
39	Haldeman	Ann-Marie	93,000	9.70%		
40	Jackson	John	39,000	4.07%		
41	Jameson	George	52,000	5.42%		
42	Lansberg	Jackson	38,000	3.96%		
43	Patterson	Margaret	86,000	8.97%		
44	Pauley	Barbara	39,000	4.07%		
45	Peterson	Paul	92,000	9.59%		
46	Smith	Betsy	63,000	6.57%		
47	Smith	Ruth	85,000	8.86%		
48						
49	Total		950,000			

Figure 7.2: The dotted horizontal line represents a page break.

INCLUDING GRID LINES
AND THE SPREADSHEET FRAME

Two printing options that 1-2-3 doesn't offer in its Print Settings dialog box are Grid and Frame. The :Print Settings Grid option prints narrow lines between rows and columns, as shown in Figure 7.3. This option is equivalent to using the :Format Lines All command on the entire spreadsheet range. The only difference between the two commands is that with the Print setting you don't see the grid lines on the screen. (The :Display Options Grid command displays dotted lines on the screen.) Grid lines can make a large spreadsheet easier to read.

The :Print Settings Frame option places column letters across the top and row numbers down the left of the printed spreadsheet. The report in Figure 7.3 was printed with the Frame option.

	A	B	C	D
1		January Sales		
2				
3				% of
4	Last Name	First Name	Sales	Total
5				
6	Anderson	Robert	24,000	2.75%
7	Andrews	Rebecca	220,000	25.20%
8	Cauldwell	Randy	10,000	1.15%
9	Goldstein	George	65,000	7.45%
10	Haldeman	Ann–Marie	92,000	10.54%
11	Jackson	John	36,000	4.12%
12	Jameson	George	47,000	5.38%
13	Lansberg	Jackson	26,000	2.98%
14	Patterson	Margaret	100,000	11.45%
15	Pauley	Barbara	45,000	5.15%
16	Peterson	Paul	79,000	9.05%
17	Smith	Betsy	54,000	6.19%
18	Smith	Ruth	75,000	8.59%
19				
20	Total		873,000	

Figure 7.3: The Grid option prints lines on the worksheet grid; the Frame option prints the column letters and row numbers.

EXCLUDING DATA FROM A PRINT RANGE

1-2-3 offers several commands for excluding data in the middle of a print range. If you don't want to print a column or a range of columns, you can hide them. If you don't want to print certain rows, you can make them non-printing lines. And, if you have a range you don't want printed, you can specify a hidden format. Chapter 6 discusses these commands in detail; refer to the section *Excluding Data from a Print Range.*

Sometimes you may want to print only certain pages of a long report. By default, Wysiwyg prints the entire print range, but you can print a range of pages with the :Print Settings Begin and End commands. For example, to print only page 2 of a four-page report, enter 2 for the beginning and ending page numbers.

SETTING UP THE PAGE LAYOUT

By default, Wysiwyg prints on an 8½-by-11" letter-size page in *portrait* (vertical) orientation. This section will show you how to change the margins, page size, and orientation in Wysiwyg.

PREVIEWING ON THE SCREEN

One way to see your current page layout is to preview the report on the screen. The :Print Preview command gives you an idea of what your printed page will look like without wasting time and paper. Though the preview does not show you the data in detail, you can see what the whole page looks like with the current margins, page size, and orientation.

Follow these steps to preview the SALES report:

1. Press **:** to display the Wysiwyg menu and choose:

   Print

   Preview

2. Your screen should look similar to Figure 7.4. The black area outside the dotted lines represents the margins. The current screen shows the first page of the report. To see the next page, press PgDn.

3. Press any key to return to the :Print menu.

4. Because you don't want to print the report yet, choose Quit to return to READY mode.

CHANGING THE MARGINS

When printing a spreadsheet in Wysiwyg, you change margins with the :Print Layout Margins command. You can also choose :Print and then edit the margins in the Wysiwyg Print Settings dialog box. The default

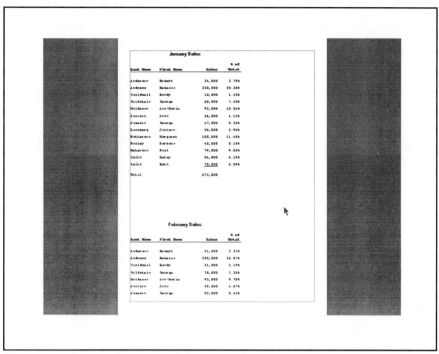

Figure 7.4: A screen preview of the printed page

margins are:

Margin	Default Setting
Left	0.5"
Right	0.5"
Top	0.5"
Bottom	0.55"

Margins are calculated quite differently in Wysiwyg than in 1-2-3. First of all, margins are measured in inches, not in characters or lines. Second, the right margin is measured from the right edge of the page, not the left. Third, no lines are reserved for the header or footer if they aren't used.

PAGE SIZE

The default page size is letter—8½" by 11". With the :Print Layout Page-Size command, you can specify a variety of page sizes. Table 7.1 describes these options.

For printers that use continuous, fanfold paper, specify option 3, 4, or 5, depending on the exact size of the paper. If you are using a non-standard paper size, choose the Custom option and enter the paper width and length in inches.

PAGE LAYOUT ON A LASER PRINTER

If you have a laser printer, you must adjust your margins and page size, because laser printers cannot print all the way to the edges of the page. At the top and bottom of the page, there is a half-inch that you cannot print on, and on the left and right, there is an unusable quarter-inch. For all intents and purposes, the laser page is 8" by 10".

The margins you enter in the Wysiwyg Print Settings dialog box are added to these built-in margins on the laser printer. Therefore, when you set your margins, you should subtract the built-in margins from the desired margin. For example, to obtain a half-inch margin above the header, set the top margin to 0. To get a half-inch margin at the left edge of the page, set the left margin to 0.25.

Table 7.1: Page Sizes

OPTION	DESCRIPTION
1:Letter	8½" by 11" (the default)
2:A4	210mm by 297mm (an international paper size)
3:80 × 66	8" by 11" fanfold paper (80 columns by 66 lines)
4:132 × 66	13.2" by 11" fanfold paper (132 columns by 66 lines)
5:80 × 72	8" by 12" fanfold paper (80 columns by 72 lines)
6:Legal	8½" by 14"
7:B5	176mm by 250mm (an international paper size)

Because of these built-in margins, you must choose a custom page size of 8" by 10". The page size is changed in the Wysiwyg Print Settings dialog box or with :Print Layout Page-Size Custom.

If you print primarily on a laser printer, you should change the default settings so you don't have to change the layout for each new spreadsheet you create. See the section *Changing Printer Defaults* later in this chapter.

CHANGING THE ORIENTATION

Laser printers can print reports either vertically (portrait orientation) or horizontally (landscape orientation). Because landscape mode prints more spreadsheet columns across the page, it is commonly used for wide spreadsheets. Figure 7.5 compares a portrait page with a landscape page.

To print in landscape mode in 1-2-3, you have to enter a complex printer-control code. In Wysiwyg, it's simply a matter of choosing landscape orientation. You can turn on this option in the Wysiwyg Print Settings dialog box, or use the :Print Config Orientation command.

The orientation you specify here is saved with the file and does not affect the orientation of any other spreadsheets.

COMPRESSING
A REPORT ONTO A SINGLE PAGE

A typical goal when printing a report is to get the entire range to print on a single page. So far, you have learned the following techniques to maximize the amount of data that prints on a page:

- Specify a smaller font size (in other words, replace font 1).
- Reduce column widths and row heights.
- Specify smaller margins.
- Use landscape orientation.
- If your printer can accept it, use a larger paper size.

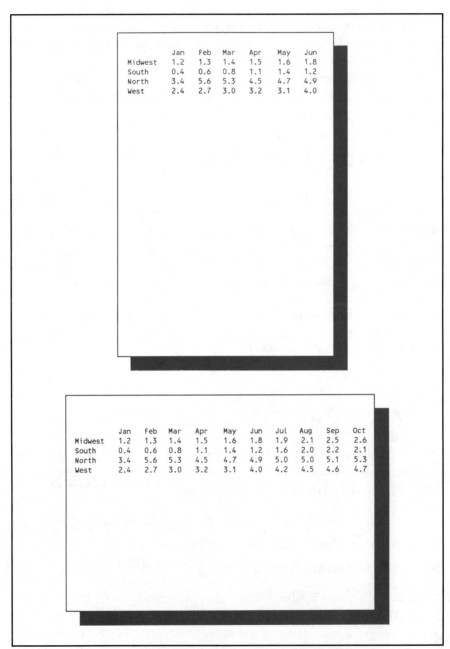

Figure 7.5: The page on the top is in portrait orientation; the page on the
bottom is in landscape.

As an alternative to (or perhaps in addition to) making the above changes, you can tell Wysiwyg to reduce the entire spreadsheet so that it fits on a single page. The command is :Print Layout Compression Automatic. It is usually quicker to turn on automatic compression than to play around with font sizes until you hit upon the largest size that will keep the spreadsheet on one printed page.

Even with automatic compression, very large spreadsheets still may not be able to fit on a single printed page. Wysiwyg will do its best, but it may have to divide the report onto multiple pages.

This feature automatically calculates how much the range needs to be reduced to fit it on a single page. With the :Print Layout Compression Manual option you can enter the reduction percentage yourself. In fact, you can even enlarge the page if you want to. This command is similar to the reduction and enlargement settings on a photocopy machine. As on a copy machine, you specify a percentage of the current page size. Enter a number less than 100 to reduce the print range. For example, to reduce the print range to seventy percent of its current size, enter 70. Enter a number greater than 100 to enlarge the data. A range cannot be reduced to less than fifteen percent of its current size, nor can it be expanded by more than 1000 percent.

Bear in mind that the more a spreadsheet is reduced, the harder it is to read. Reducing the page doesn't do you much good if no one can read it.

PRINTING
MULTIPAGE SPREADSHEETS

Even after compressing the print horizontally and vertically, the spreadsheet may still print on several pages. Wysiwyg automatically divides your print range into multiple pages when all the columns or rows can't fit on a single page. You can see where the page breaks will occur by looking at the page definition lines after you specify your print range or by using :Print Preview.

When a report is several pages long, you have several special requirements that you don't have with single-page reports. You might want to number the pages, print a title on each page, repeat the column or row headings on every page, and insert page breaks. These topics are covered here.

CREATING HEADERS AND FOOTERS

A *header* is a single line of text that automatically prints at the top of each page while a *footer* is text that prints at the bottom. Figure 7.6 illustrates exactly where the header and footer appear on the page. There are always two blank lines that separate the header and footer from the

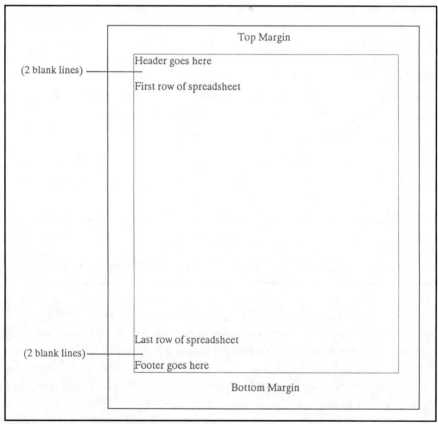

Figure 7.6: Header and footer placement

body of the spreadsheet report. When you have headers and footers, you cannot print as many rows on the page.

Headers and footers are ideal places for documenting your spreadsheet. By including the date, the title, the name of the file, and your name in the header and footer, you eliminate guesswork if you (or someone else) find a printed report lying around. Other types of information you can include in a header or footer are page numbers, titles, revision numbers, warning messages about confidentiality, and so on.

Enter the header or footer text in the Wysiwyg Print Settings dialog box, or use the :Print Layout Titles command. You do not actually see the headers and footers in your spreadsheet—they appear only when you print or preview.

Special Codes for Headers and Footers

In addition to text, there are several special codes you can use in your headers and footers:

#	Inserts the page number
@	Inserts the current date
\	Inserts the contents of the specified cell
|	Aligns the text in the center
||	Aligns the text on the right

When you print, the number sign (#) will be replaced with the page number and the at sign (@) will be replaced with the current date. It's a good idea to include the date in a header or footer so that you can readily identify whether you are looking at the most current printout of a spreadsheet. To specify the contents of a cell as your header or footer, type a backslash (\) followed by the cell coordinate or range name. For example, if A1 contains the label *January Sales*, type **\A1** as the header text.

The vertical bar (|) is an alignment command. By default, your headers and footers print at the left margin. To center a header or footer, place one vertical bar before the text. To align a header or footer at the right margin, use a second vertical bar. (The vertical bar is located on the same key as the backslash.)

Let's look at some examples. The footer, | #, centers the page number at the bottom of each page. The header, @ | *1992 Budget* | *BUDGET92.WK1*, places the date at the left margin, centers the title *1992 Budget* and aligns the file name at the right margin. The footer, @ | | *Page* #, places the date at the left margin and the word *Page* followed by the page number at the right margin.

Page Numbering

When you include the number sign (#) in a header or footer, Wysiwyg inserts the appropriate page number at the top or bottom of each page: number 1 on the first page of the print range, 2 on the second page, 3 on the third, and so on. To begin page numbering with a number other than 1, change the starting number in the Wysiwyg Print Settings dialog box. The :Print Settings Start-Number command lets you begin with any number. You might want to change the starting page number if the current print range is a continuation of another report.

PAPER FEEDING

If you have to (or choose to) manually feed single sheets of paper into your printer, you will need to tell Wysiwyg to pause between pages of a multipage report. To turn on the pause feature, choose the :Print Settings Wait Yes command. Then, when you print, Wysiwyg will display the following message in the control panel:

Press a key when ready to print (ESC to cancel)

Insert a sheet of paper, and press any key to print the page. You will see the same message for each page in the report.

Some printers, such as certain models of the HP LaserJet, have two paper trays so that you can print on two different types of paper. For instance, you can put plain paper in the top tray and letterhead in the bottom. To tell Wysiwyg which paper tray to access, use the :Print Config Bin

Upper-Tray or Lower-Tray command. This setting will be stored with the file when you save.

REPEATING A RANGE ON EACH PAGE

Figure 7.7 shows what happens when you print a spreadsheet that doesn't fit on a single page. The first seven columns print on page one and the remaining columns print on page two. Here's the problem: When you look at page two, you have no idea what the data means unless you tape it to page one.

A cleaner solution is to use the Borders option to print the column A headings on every page. This option is similar to the /Worksheet Titles

	Jan	Feb	Mar	Apr	May	Jun	Jul
Mid Atlantic	100,000	101,000	102,000	103,000	104,000	105,000	106,000
South	100,500	101,500	102,500	103,500	104,500	105,500	106,500
Mid West	200,000	202,000	204,000	206,000	208,000	210,000	212,000
Pacific	201,000	203,000	205,000	207,000	209,000	211,000	213,000
Total	601,500	607,500	613,500	619,500	625,500	631,500	637,500

Aug	Sep	Oct	Nov	Dec	Total
107,000	108,000	109,000	110,000	111,000	1,266,000
107,500	108,500	109,500	110,500	111,500	1,272,000
214,000	216,000	218,000	220,000	222,000	2,532,000
215,000	217,000	219,000	221,000	223,000	2,544,000
643,500	649,500	655,500	661,500	667,500	7,614,000

Figure 7.7: The second page of this report can't be understood without the first page.

command discussed in Chapter 5. Instead of freezing the titles on the screen, though, the Borders command freezes the titles on the printed report. When you use borders, all pages can be read independently, as shown in Figure 7.8.

The :Print Layout Borders command offers two options: Top and Left. The columns you specify are repeated on the left side of each page while rows are repeated at the top of each page. Left borders are ideal for wide spreadsheets while top borders are typically used for long reports. Use both top and left borders if your spreadsheet is long and wide.

Rows and columns that you specify as borders should *not* be part of your print range. In the example shown in Figure 7.7, column A would be the border column, and the print range would be B1..N8. A common mistake is to include the border in the print range. When you do this, the border range prints twice on the first page.

Follow this general procedure to specify print borders:

- Press : to display the Wysiwyg menu and choose:

  Print

  Layout

  Borders

  Top (or Left)

- Highlight the columns or rows to be repeated on each page. (One cell in each row or column is sufficient—you don't have to highlight the entire range.)

- Press Enter.

	Aug	Sep	Oct	Nov	Dec	Total
Mid Atlantic	107,000	108,000	109,000	110,000	111,000	1,266,000
South	107,500	108,500	109,500	110,500	111,500	1,272,000
Mid West	214,000	216,000	218,000	220,000	222,000	2,532,000
Pacific	215,000	217,000	219,000	221,000	223,000	2,544,000
Total	643,500	649,500	655,500	661,500	667,500	7,614,000

Figure 7.8: The row headings in column A are repeated on page two so that each page stands by itself.

- Choose:

    Quit

    Range

    Set

- Specify the range to be printed. Be sure you do not include the top or left borders.

- Press Enter.

INSERTING PAGE BREAKS

When Wysiwyg prints a long spreadsheet, it automatically divides the report onto multiple pages. As mentioned previously, the margins, page size, font, row heights, column widths, orientation, and existence of headers and footers determine exactly how many rows and columns can fit on the page. With the default settings, 51 spreadsheet rows fit on a page. If you use a header or a footer, 48 spreadsheet rows will print (45 if you use both a header and a footer). If you are printing a report on a laser printer, three fewer rows will print on each page.

After you print a report, you may discover that the pages break in inappropriate places. For example, a section might begin at the bottom of one page and continue onto another. Wysiwyg lets you control exactly where the pages break, both horizontally and vertically. To insert a page break, follow this general procedure:

- Place the cell pointer where you want to insert the page break. Horizontal page breaks are inserted above the pointer and vertical breaks are inserted to the left of the pointer.

- Press : to display the Wysiwyg menu and choose:

    Worksheet

    Page

- Choose Row to insert a horizontal page break or Column to insert a vertical break.

- Choose Quit.

Manual page breaks look a little different from automatic breaks (the dashes are longer). Figure 7.9 shows a horizontal page break that was inserted above row 30. When you print, Wysiwyg will place the data below this dashed line on the next page.

1-2-3 offers another way to insert horizontal page breaks: the /Worksheet Page command. The 1-2-3 page breaks are honored when you print in Wysiwyg, but Wysiwyg page breaks are ignored when you print with 1-2-3's /Print command. For further information on /Worksheet Page, see Chapter 6.

To remove a row page break, place the cell pointer underneath the dashed line and choose :Worksheet Page Delete. To remove a column page break, place the pointer to the right of the dashed line and choose the same command.

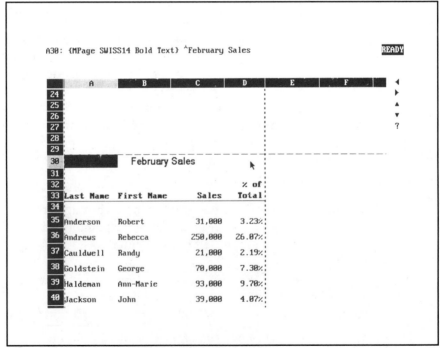

Figure 7.9: A page break inserted above row 30

HANDS-ON PRACTICE: PRINTING A MULTIPAGE REPORT

To practice some of the printing options discussed in this chapter, you will print out the entire SALES file. SALES should still be on your screen, and A1..D49 should be set as the print range.

To place the February data on its own page, insert a page break:

1. Place the pointer in row 30.

2. Press : to display the Wysiwyg menu and choose:

    Worksheet

    Page

    Row

    Quit

The page break is inserted above the current row. Change the left and right margins so that the spreadsheet is centered on the page:

1. Press : to display the Wysiwyg menu and choose:

    Print

    Layout

    Margins

    Left

2. Type **1.5** and press Enter.

3. Choose Right.

4. Type **1.5** and press Enter.

Create a footer that prints the file name at the left margin, centers the page number, and inserts the current date at the right margin:

1. Choose:

    Quit

    Titles

Footer

2. Type **SALES.WK1 | Page # | @** and press Enter.

3. If you are printing on a laser printer, choose a custom page size of 8" by 10".

Your Wysiwyg Print Settings dialog box should look similar to Figure 7.10. You are now ready to print the report:

1. Quit to the main :Print menu and choose Go.

2. Save the file with the name **WWSALES**.

Figure 7.11 shows page 2 of the sales report.

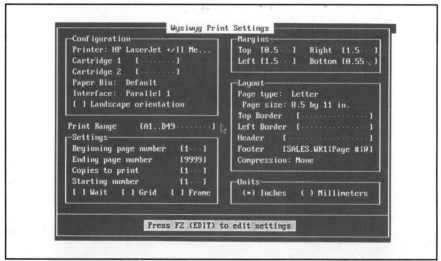

Figure 7.10: The Wysiwyg Print Settings dialog box for the SALES report

CHANGING PRINTER DEFAULTS

If you find that you are constantly changing certain page-layout settings when you print reports, consider modifying the printer defaults. Set

February Sales

Last Name	First Name	Sales	% of Total
Anderson	Robert	31,000	3.23%
Andrews	Rebecca	250,000	26.07%
Cauldwell	Randy	21,000	2.19%
Goldstein	George	70,000	7.30%
Haldeman	Ann–Marie	93,000	9.70%
Jackson	John	39,000	4.07%
Jameson	George	52,000	5.42%
Lansberg	Jackson	38,000	3.96%
Patterson	Margaret	86,000	8.97%
Pauley	Barbara	39,000	4.07%
Peterson	Paul	92,000	9.59%
Smith	Betsy	63,000	6.57%
Smith	Ruth	85,000	8.86%
Total		959,000	

Figure 7.11: Page 2 of the sales report

the page size, margins, borders, header, and footer to your desired default settings, then choose :Print Layout Default Update. From this point forward, any new spreadsheets you create will automatically have this page layout. For example, if you commonly print on 8½"-by-14" fanfold paper, this page size should be your default.

The section *Changing Print Density* earlier in the chapter describes how to change your default printer. This same procedure applies to all configuration (:Print Config) settings.

For the most part, print settings are saved with the current file. The exceptions are:

- Beginning page number

- Ending page number
- Starting number
- Copies to print
- Wait

CREATING PAGE LAYOUT LIBRARIES

If there is a special page layout for a particular type of report that you frequently produce, you can save the settings in a layout library. The :Print Layout Library Save command saves the current layout settings in a library file with the name you specify. Wysiwyg adds the extension .ALS to library files. When you wish to use these settings in another file, use the :Page Layout Library Retrieve command.

BACKGROUND PRINTING

While a report is printing, the control panel displays a status report of the percentage printed. You cannot work on the current spreadsheet, print another range, or retrieve a different file until this message disappears. If you have a slow printer, long reports, or are printing with a high-density printer driver, this waiting period can seem endless. Release 2.3 has an alternative for those who hate waiting: background printing. When you tell Wysiwyg to print a spreadsheet in the background, you can be productive while a report is printing.

Before you can use the :Print Background command, you must first load a small 6K program called BPRINT. Chapter 6 includes a complete discussion on how to load and use the BPRINT program. The instructions in the *Background Printing* section of Chapter 6 apply to printing both in 1-2-3 and Wysiwyg. The only difference is that in Wysiwyg you use :Print Background instead of /Print Background.

PRINTING
ON A REMOTE PRINTER

You may not personally own a laser printer, but that doesn't mean you can't print your spreadsheet reports on one of these fast, high-quality printers. Check around your office—maybe someone else has one and won't mind if you print an occasional document. Or call your friendly, neighborhood copyshop; many of these shops rent time on PCs connected to laser printers. Some shops charge by the page, others by the hour. *The computer hooked up to the remote printer does not even need to have 1-2-3.*

To print a spreadsheet on a remote printer, you create an *encoded* file. This file contains text along with printer formatting codes. You can take the encoded file to another computer that's connected to a high quality printer (such as a laser) and print the report from the DOS prompt.

Before you create the encoded file, you must use the INSTALL program to install 1-2-3 for this printer. Refer to Appendix A for details on installing printer drivers. You will also need to designate this printer as your default with the :Print Config Printer command. You can then format the spreadsheet with fonts that work with this remote printer.

To create the encoded file, follow this general procedure:

- Press : to display the Wysiwyg menu and choose:

  Print

  File

- Enter a file name. Wysiwyg automatically assigns .ENC to the name.

- Specify the range.

- Set the margins and page size appropriate for the remote printer.

- Choose Go.

You will then need to copy the .ENC file to a floppy disk and take it to the remote printer. To print the encoded file, use the following command at the DOS prompt:

COPY A:*filename.enc*/B LPT1

Substitute the actual name of the encoded file in place of *filename*. The above command assumes the file is on a floppy disk in drive A, and that the printer is connected to the first parallel port (LPT1). You may need to change these parameters.

CREATING ASCII FILES

An ASCII file contains only text—no formulas, fonts, type styles, or other formatting. You will create ASCII files when you you want to transfer a 1-2-3 spreadsheet into another program. Since each program (1-2-3, WordPerfect, Microsoft Word, dBASE, Excel, etc.) has its own unique way of storing files and usually cannot understand other program's file formats, a standard format, ASCII, was developed so that data could easily be transferred between programs. ASCII is an acronym that stands for *American Standard Code for Information Interchange*.

To create an ASCII file out of a 1-2-3 spreadsheet, you print it to a file, using 1-2-3's /Print File command. The *Creating an ASCII File* section in Chapter 6 contains explicit steps on how to produce an ASCII file.

Chapter 5

Chapter 6

Chapter 7

Chapter 8

Chapter 9

Using 1-2-3 as a Word Processor in Release 2.3

◀▌▌▌▌ FAST TRACK ▌▌▌▌▶

You may want to use Wysiwyg's text editor to type short letters and memos instead of exiting 1-2-3 and loading your word-processing program. The text editor has all the basic features of a word-processing program. While it cannot check spelling, indent paragraphs, set tabs, or look up words in a thesaurus, it does let you perform the following tasks:

- type paragraphs with the automatic word-wrap feature
- correct mistakes (insert, delete, overtype)
- change attributes (font, bold, underline, and so on)
- center titles
- justify a paragraph so that the right margin is aligned
- change the line length

You will find that the text editor comes in handy whenever you need to type an explanatory paragraph about your spreadsheet data.

TYPING A MEMO

Figure 8.1 is the final printout of the memo you will create in this chapter. This memo contains three distinct areas. The top of the memo was typed into spreadsheet cells—just the way you normally enter data. The paragraphs in the middle of the memo were typed in Wysiwyg's text editor. The spreadsheet at the bottom was copied from the JAN.WK1 file.

TYPING THE MEMO HEADINGS

Because you can't set tabs in the text editor, you are better off typing the memo headings (*To:*, *From:*, and so on) in separate cells. Follow the steps below to create the memo headings:

1. If necessary, clear the screen (/Worksheet Erase).

2. Type the labels shown in columns A and B of Figure 8.2.

3. Format the Memorandum title to 14-point Swiss (:Format Font 2).

4. Create the line in A7..G7 (:Format Lines Bottom).

Memorandum

To: Richard Bell
From: Paula Montgomery
Date: February 25, 1992
Subject: January Sales

Below are the January sales figures for the people in your district. As you can see, *Becky Andrews* had an <u>outstanding</u> month. She sold 25% of the district total. Becky deserves special recognition, don't you think? Have any ideas of what we can do to reward her for these amazing sales efforts?

Randy Cauldwell, on the other hand, is not pulling his weight. Perhaps you should talk to him to see what the problem is.

Please give me a call if you have any questions.

Last Name	First Name	Sales	% of Total
Anderson	Robert	24,000	2.78%
Andrews	Rebecca	220,000	25.49%
Cauldwell	Randy	10,000	1.16%
Goldstein	George	65,000	7.53%
Haldeman	Ann–Marie	92,000	10.66%
Jackson	John	26,000	3.01%
Jameson	George	47,000	5.45%
Lansberg	Jackson	26,000	3.01%
Patterson	Margaret	100,000	11.59%
Pauley	Barbara	45,000	5.21%
Peterson	Paul	79,000	9.15%
Smith	Betsy	54,000	6.26%
Smith	Ruth	75,000	8.69%
Total		863,000	

Figure 8.1: The memo you will create in this chapter

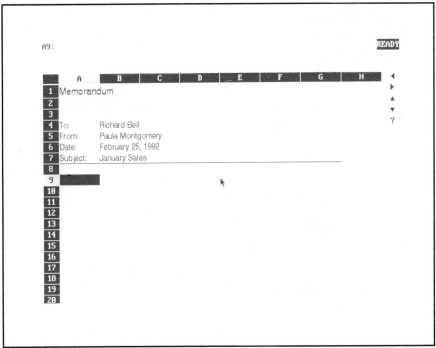

Figure 8.2: The memo heading

TYPING IN THE TEXT EDITOR

To load Wysiwyg's text editor, use the :Text Edit command and indicate the range into which you want to type the text. The width of the range controls how many words will fit on each line. The length of the range controls how many lines of text you can type. In the memo, the text range will be A9..G20.

Figure 8.3 shows the memo paragraphs after they have been typed into the text editor. The screen is a little different when you are actually in the text editor. You will notice the following changes:

- The mode indicator displays TEXT.

- You have a vertical-line cursor instead of a cell pointer, and cursor movement is restricted to the defined text range.

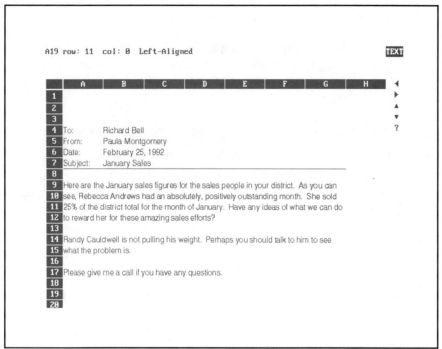

Figure 8.3: Wysiwyg's text editor

- The first line of the control panel displays the cursor's location, for example, *row: 3 col: 10*. The row number refers to the number of the line within the text range, not the actual row number in the spreadsheet grid. The column number is the number of characters from the left edge of the text range.

- The control panel indicates the current text alignment (for example, *Left-Aligned*).

- The status line sometimes says CALC. This indicator is insignificant and can be ignored.

Follow these steps to load the text editor now:

1. Press : to display the Wysiwyg menu and choose:

   Text

   Edit

2. Paint the range A9..G20 and press Enter.

When you type in the text editor, the words automatically wrap to the next line. This feature is called *automatic word wrap*. To start a new paragraph, take one of the following actions, depending on how you want the text to look:

- Press Enter twice to leave a blank line between paragraphs.

- Press Enter once and press the spacebar one or more times at the beginning of the paragraph to create an indent.

- Press Ctrl-Enter. A non-printing paragraph symbol (¶) appears.

As you type the paragraphs in Figure 8.3, let the text automatically wrap to the next line. Press Enter *only* to end paragraphs and to create blank lines. Also, don't worry about mistakes. As you will soon see, correcting your typing errors is quick and easy. To correct a mistake as you are typing, use the Backspace key.

EXITING TEXT MODE

When you are in the text editor, you cannot give commands from the 1-2-3 or Wysiwyg menu. If you press the slash or colon, these characters will appear in the document. To give commands, you must exit TEXT mode by pressing Esc or the right mouse button.

Follow these steps to save your file:

1. Press Esc or the right mouse button to exit the text editor. The mode indicator now displays READY and the cell pointer has returned.

2. Save the file with the name **JANMEMO**.

When you exit TEXT mode, you will see that each line of text is entered as a long label in the first column of the text range. For example, the control panel in Figure 8.4 shows the contents of the current cell, A9. Each cell in the text range also displays {Text} in the control panel. This indicator signifies that the cell has been assigned the {Text} attribute.

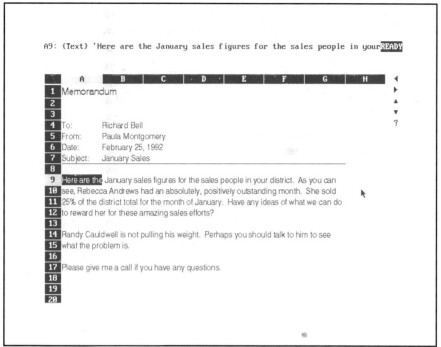

A9: {Text} 'Here are the January sales figures for the sales people in your`READY`

	A	B	C	D	E	F	G	H
1	Memorandum							
2								
3								
4	To:	Richard Bell						
5	From:	Paula Montgomery						
6	Date:	February 25, 1992						
7	Subject:	January Sales						
8								
9	Here are the January sales figures for the sales people in your district. As you can							
10	see, Rebecca Andrews had an absolutely, positively outstanding month. She sold							
11	25% of the district total for the month of January. Have any ideas of what we can do							
12	to reward her for these amazing sales efforts?							
13								
14	Randy Cauldwell is not pulling his weight. Perhaps you should talk to him to see							
15	what the problem is.							
16								
17	Please give me a call if you have any questions.							
18								
19								
20								

Figure 8.4: The control panel in READY mode indicates that the text is actually entered into a spreadsheet cell as a long label.

RETURNING TO TEXT MODE

You can use the F2 key to correct typing mistakes in your text range, but it's much easier to use the text editor. There are two ways to edit an existing text range. The mouse offers the easiest way: double-click on any cell in the range you want to edit. The other way is to use the same command you used to initially type the text—the :Text Edit command. Let's try this second method:

1. Place the cell pointer anywhere in the text range.

2. Press : to display the Wysiwyg menu and choose:

    Text

    Edit

3. Wysiwyg suggests the same range you indicated initially, A9..G20. Press Enter to accept the text range.

CORRECTING MISTAKES

The three most common typing mistakes are to leave out characters, to type the wrong characters, or to type extra characters. If you discover that you have left out text, you need to insert new text; if you have typed wrong or extra characters, you need to delete or overtype them.

Before you edit the memo, you need to learn a few shortcuts for moving the cursor around. Table 8.1 lists the cursor movement keys available in the text editor. Practice these commands before continuing to the next section.

Note that you cannot move the cursor outside of the text range. If you try, your computer will beep at you. Furthermore, you cannot move the cursor with the mouse.

Table 8.1: The Text Editor's Cursor Movement Keys

KEY	DESCRIPTION
→	Character to the right
←	Character to the left
↑	Up one line
↓	Down one line
Ctrl-→	Next word
Ctrl-←	Previous word
Home	Beginning of line
End	End of line
PgDn	Next screen
PgUp	Previous screen

DELETING TEXT

To delete unwanted text, place the cursor to the left of the first character you want to delete, and press Del (or Delete). The character will be removed and characters to the right shift over to take the deleted character's place. Alternatively, you can delete with the Backspace key. While Del removes the character to the *right* of the cursor, Backspace deletes the character to the *left* of the cursor. The Del and Backspace keys delete only one character at a time. Unlike most word-processing programs, the text editor does not offer any shortcuts for deleting larger chunks of text.

The underlined text in Figure 8.5 indicates which words need to be deleted from your memo. Follow these steps to delete the indicated text:

1. Place the cursor in the first row of the text range—look at the control panel for the row number.

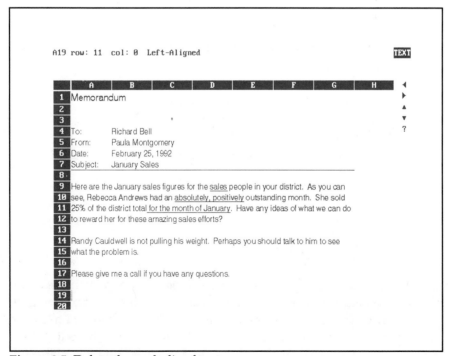

Figure 8.5: Delete the underlined text

2. Press Ctrl-→ to move to the second *sales* in this row.

3. Press Del until this word is deleted. After deleting *sales*, the text in this row will be shorter than the other lines. You will need to reformat this paragraph after you have finished all the editing.

4. Delete the other text indicated in Figure 8.5.

INSERTING TEXT

The text editor is automatically in insert mode—whatever you type, wherever you type it, the text is added to whatever is already there. Text is inserted to the left of the cursor, and text to the right of the cursor is pushed forward as you type.

If you insert more text than can fit in your specified text range, you will see the message

Text input range full

You will then need to press Esc and expand the text range with :Text Edit.

In your memo, follow these steps to insert the underlined text in Figure 8.6. (Note: Your text will not be underlined.)

1. Move the cursor to the word *Have* in row 3.

2. Type **Rebecca deserves special recognition, don't you think?**

3. Press the spacebar after the question mark.

4. Insert **on the other hand** in row 7. (Don't forget the commas.)

OVERTYPING TEXT

The Ins (or Insert) key toggles you between insert and overtype mode. In overtype mode, the existing text is replaced with the new text you type. You may want to use overtype mode when you have transposed two characters or to convert a lowercase letter to uppercase. Sometimes it is faster to use overtype mode than to insert new text and delete old. The status line

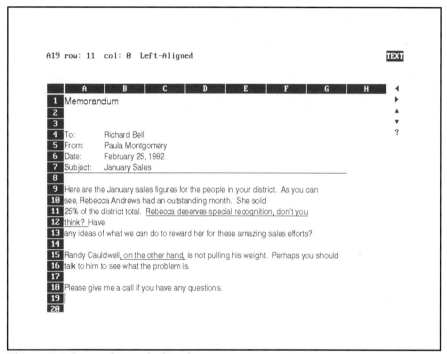

Figure 8.6: Insert the underlined text

at the bottom of the screen displays OVR when you are in overtype mode.

In the memo, use overtype mode to replace the word *Here* with *Below*, as follows:

1. Place the cursor on the word *Here* in the first row.

2. Press Ins to go into overtype mode. The status line should display OVR. If it doesn't, you may have accidentally pressed Ins twice and turned off overtype mode.

3. Type **Below**.

4. Press Ins to return to insert mode.

5. Press the spacebar to insert a space between the words.

REFORMATTING PARAGRAPHS

After you insert and delete text, some lines may end up shorter than the width you originally specified for your text range. For instance, in your memo, the second and fourth rows are quite short. To reformat the paragraphs so that each line extends to the end of the text range, you need to use the :Text Reformat command.

Reformat the paragraphs in your memo:

1. Press Esc to exit TEXT mode. (Remember, you cannot give menu commands from the text editor.)

2. Make sure the cell pointer is within the text range.

3. Press : to display the Wysiwyg menu and choose:

   Text

   Reformat

4. Press Enter to accept the text range, A9..G20.

This command rearranges the text so that the paragraphs are properly aligned, as shown in Figure 8.7.

Reformatting into a Different Range

Another function of the :Text Reformat command is to arrange the paragraphs into a wider or narrower range. After typing the text, you might decide that the paragraphs should flow into nine columns instead of seven, or into five columns instead of eight. Reformatting into a wider range is not a problem—you just give the :Text Reformat command and highlight the additional column(s) into which you want the text to flow. Specifying a narrower range is not as straightforward, however.

To experience why this is a problem, let's arrange the memo paragraphs into six columns instead of seven:

1. Place the cell pointer in the text range.

2. Press : to display the Wysiwyg menu and choose:

   Text

Reformat

3. Press ← to highlight the range A9..F20.

4. Press Enter.

Nothing happens. The reason Wysiwyg ignored your request is that the cells in column G have the {Text} attribute assigned to them. Wysiwyg gives this attribute greater significance than it gives to your specified reformat range. The solution is to clear the {Text} attribute from the cells in column G before you reformat the paragraphs. It's an extra step, but a necessary one to work around this problem.

Follow these steps to *successfully* reformat the paragraphs:

1. Place the pointer in cell G9. Notice the {Text} indicator in the control panel.

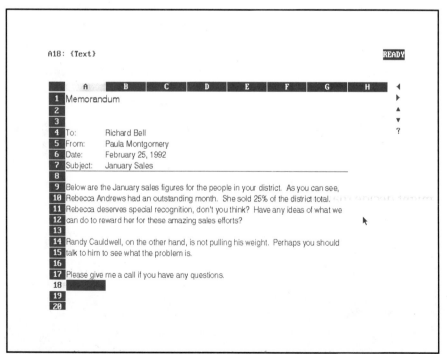

Figure 8.7: After reformatting, the paragraphs are properly aligned.

2. Press : to display the Wysiwyg menu and choose:

   Text

   Clear

3. Paint the range G9..G20 and press Enter. The control panel no longer displays {Text} for these cells.

4. Press : to display the Wysiwyg menu and choose:

   Text

   Reformat

5. Press ← to highlight the range A9..F20.

6. Press Enter. Your paragraphs now reformat into columns A through F, as shown in Figure 8.8.

7. Remove the line from cell G7 (:Format Lines Clear Bottom).

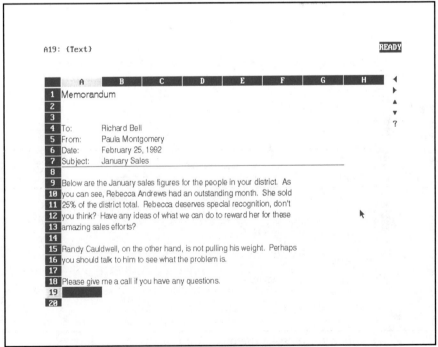

Figure 8.8: The paragraphs have been reformatted into fewer columns.

When you reformat paragraphs into fewer columns, the text will consume extra space vertically. Therefore, make sure the range you specify is long enough to accommodate these extra lines. If the range is too short, you will get the *Text input range full* message. If you have data directly below the text range, you will need to insert space with the /Worksheet Insert Row command. Then reissue the :Text Reformat command, and specify additional rows.

What's a Paragraph?

As you have seen, the :Text Reformat command fills each line with text, pulling text from subsequent lines when necessary. It will not pull text from the next paragraph, however. How does Wysiwyg know what a paragraph is? Wysiwyg considers the following to be paragraphs:

- text that ends with two carriage returns
- text that begins with one or more spaces and ends with a carriage return
- text that ends with a paragraph symbol (Ctrl-Enter)

When :Text Reformat encounters any of the above situations, it will not pull text from the subsequent line.

ALIGNING TEXT

In Chapter 3, you learned several ways to align text. The /Range Label command aligns a label within the column width—on the left, right, or center. The :Text Align command, on the other hand, aligns the text across a range of cells. You used :Text Align Center to center a title over a spreadsheet. The :Text Align command has several other alignment options as well. Figure 8.9 illustrates each of these alignments.

Specify even alignment for the body of the memo:

1. Place the cell pointer in the text range.

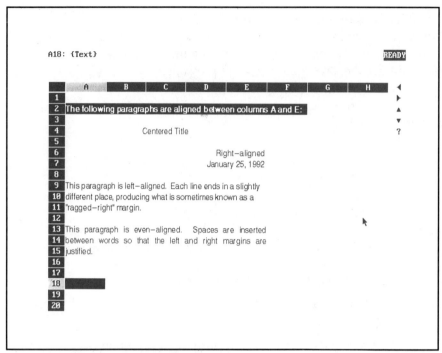

Figure 8.9: Text alignment options

2. Press **:** to display the Wysiwyg menu and choose:

   Text

   Align

   Even

3. Press Enter to accept the range A9..F20.

Spaces are inserted between words so that each line is perfectly aligned with the left and right edge of the text range (except for the last line of each paragraph). Your screen should look similar to Figure 8.10.

Now, center the word *Memorandum* over the memo:

1. Place the pointer on cell A1.

2. Press **:** to display the Wysiwyg menu and choose:

   Text

Align

Center

3. Paint the range A1..F1 and press Enter. The title is now centered.

Each alignment option has its own special symbol that is inserted at the beginning of each text line:

Symbol	Alignment
'	Left
"	Right
^	Center
'|	Even (Justified)

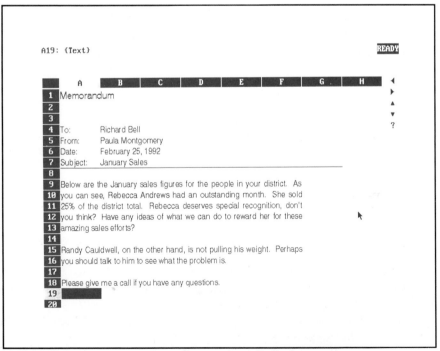

Figure 8.10: The paragraphs with even (justified) alignment

You see these symbols only when you place the pointer on a cell and look at the cell's contents in the control panel. These symbols are similar to the ones inserted with the /Range Label command. However, 1-2-3 interprets the symbols differently when the cell has the {Text} attribute.

When you are in TEXT mode, you do not see these symbols. Instead, the control panel displays the current alignment (Left-Aligned, Right-Aligned, Centered, or Justified).

FORMATTING CHARACTERS

The :Format commands you learned in Chapter 4 apply to a cell or a range of cells. In the text editor, you have the ability to format individual characters within a cell. For example, you can specify bold, italics, or underline for a single word or letter. You can even change the font for part of a line. This capability is not limited to the text editor, however. By inserting special codes, you can format specific characters in a cell or a header or footer.

FORMATTING IN THE TEXT EDITOR

To format in the text editor, press F3 and an attribute menu displays in the control panel, as shown in Figure 8.11. Table 8.2 describes these attributes.

The general procedure for formatting characters in TEXT mode is:

- Load the text editor.
- Place the cursor to the left of the first character to be formatted.
- Press F3.
- Select the formatting attribute from the menu.

At this point, the attribute is applied from the cursor to the end of the line. To end the attribute before the end of the line:

- Place the cursor to the right of the last character to be formatted.

- Press F3.
- Choose Normal.

In the memo, let's format the text so that it looks similar to Figure 8.12.

1. Place the cell pointer in A1.

2. Load the text editor. (If you have a mouse, double-click on cell A1. Otherwise, use :Text Edit.)

3. Place the cursor to the left of *Memorandum*.

4. Press F3 to display the attributes menu.

5. Choose Outline.

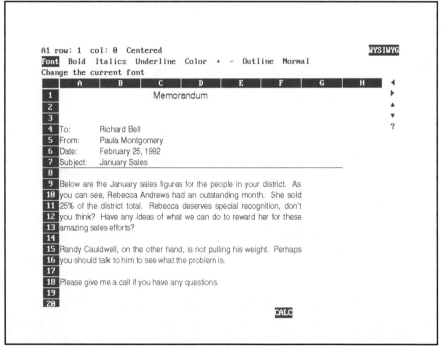

Figure 8.11: The attributes menu

Table 8.2: Formatting Attributes in the Text Editor

MENU OPTION	DESCRIPTION
Font	Displays a menu of the eight fonts in the current font set
Bold	Boldfaces specified text
Italics	Italicizes specified text
Underline	Single-underlines specified text
Color	Displays a menu of color choices
+	Raises (superscripts) the specified characters above the current line (e.g., [1] *Assumes 5 percent yearly increase*)
–	Lowers (subscripts) the specified characters below the current line (e.g., H_20).
Outline	Traces the outline of each character—the inside of the character is hollow
Normal	Removes all attributes

The entire line is displayed with the outline attribute, as shown in Figure 8.12.

Italicize *Rebecca Andrews* and *Randy Cauldwell*:

1. Press Esc to exit TEXT mode.

2. Move the pointer to the other text range (A9..F20) and load the text editor.

3. Place the cursor to the left of *Rebecca*.

4. Press F3 to display the attributes menu.

5. Choose Italics. The remainder of the line is italicized. Because you want only two words in italics, you need to turn off the attribute.

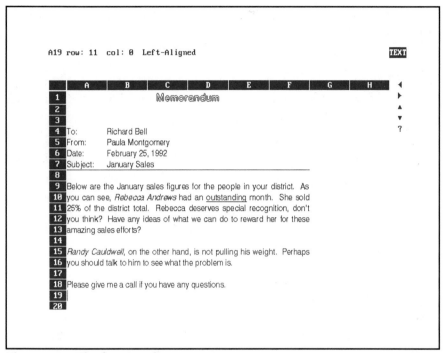

A19 row: 11 col: 0 Left-Aligned   TEXT

	A	B	C	D	E	F	G	H
1				Memorandum				
2								
3								
4	To:	Richard Bell						
5	From:	Paula Montgomery						
6	Date:	February 25, 1992						
7	Subject:	January Sales						
8								
9	Below are the January sales figures for the people in your district. As							
10	you can see, *Rebecca Andrews* had an <u>outstanding</u> month. She sold							
11	25% of the district total. Rebecca deserves special recognition, don't							
12	you think? Have any ideas of what we can do to reward her for these							
13	amazing sales efforts?							
14								
15	*Randy Cauldwell*, on the other hand, is not pulling his weight. Perhaps							
16	you should talk to him to see what the problem is.							
17								
18	Please give me a call if you have any questions.							
19								
20								

Figure 8.12: The formatted text

6. Move the cursor to the right of *Andrews*.

7. Press F3.

8. Choose Normal.

9. Repeat the above steps to italicize *Randy Cauldwell*.

Now underline *outstanding*:

1. Place the cursor to the left of *outstanding* in row 2.

2. Press F3 to display the attributes menu.

3. Choose Underline.

4. Move the cursor to the right of *outstanding*.

5. Press F3.

6. Choose Normal. Your memo should look similar to Figure 8.12.

Here are a few pointers about character formatting in the text editor:

- To remove an attribute, specify the Normal format at the beginning of the formatted text. (The next section shows another way.)

- You may want to increase the height of rows containing super- or subscripted characters.

- Most formatting attributes change the size of the characters so you may need to reformat the paragraphs (:Text Reformat) after choosing an attribute. For example, bold and outlined characters are larger than normal, and super- and subscript characters are smaller.

FORMATTING CHARACTERS WITHIN A CELL

You needn't go into the text editor to format characters within a cell. While you are initially typing the cell's contents, or when you go back to edit a cell, you can insert special codes that tell 1-2-3 where to begin and end a specific attribute. These codes are called *formatting sequences*.

To understand how this works, it's helpful to look at the codes that the text editor inserts when you specify an attribute. You don't see these codes in TEXT mode—only in READY or EDIT mode. The control panel in Figure 8.13 shows the codes in cell A10. The ▲ indicates the beginning of an attribute change. The character(s) immediately after this symbol indicates which attribute to use (for example, *i* for italic or _ for underlining). The ▼ indicates the end of the attribute change.

Now that you see what's going on behind the scenes, here's how you specify attributes when you are not in the text editor:

- If the text has already been entered, press F2 to edit the cell.

- Place the cursor on the first character to be formatted.

- Press Ctrl-A to insert the begin-attribute code (▲).

- Type one of the codes in Table 8.3.

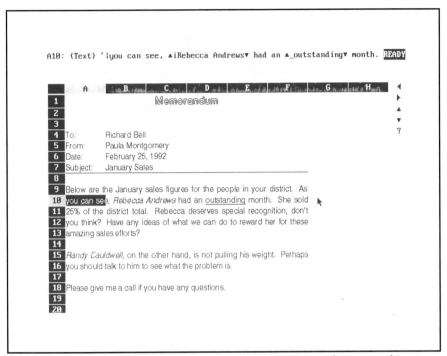

A10: {Text} 'you can see, ▲iRebecca Andrews▼ had an ▲_outstanding▼ month. READY

Memorandum

To: Richard Bell
From: Paula Montgomery
Date: February 25, 1992
Subject: January Sales

Below are the January sales figures for the people in your district. As you can see, *Rebecca Andrews* had an outstanding month. She sold 25% of the district total. Rebecca deserves special recognition, don't you think? Have any ideas of what we can do to reward her for these amazing sales efforts?

Randy Cauldwell, on the other hand, is not pulling his weight. Perhaps you should talk to him to see what the problem is.

Please give me a call if you have any questions.

Figure 8.13: The control panel displays the formatting codes entered in cell A10.

Table 8.3: Formatting Codes

CODE[†]	DESCRIPTION
b	Bold
i	Italics
1_	Single underlining
2_	Double underlining
3_	Wide underlining
4_	Outline box around characters
5_	Strike-through characters
d	Subscript
u	Superscript

Table 8.3: Formatting Codes (continued)

CODE[†]	DESCRIPTION
x	Makes characters backward
y	Places characters upside down
1c	Default color
2c	Red
3c	Green
4c	Dark blue
5c	Cyan
6c	Yellow
7c	Magenta
8c	Reversed text
1F	Font 1 from the current font set
2F	Font 2 from the current font set
3F	Font 3 from the current font set
4F	Font 4 from the current font set
5F	Font 5 from the current font set
6F	Font 6 from the current font set
7F	Font 7 from the current font set
8F	Font 8 from the current font set
1o to 255o	Character outline (hollow inside)

[†] *To begin an attribute, press Ctrl-A followed by one of the codes above. To end all attributes, press Ctrl-N. To end one attribute, press Ctrl-E followed by one of the codes above.*

- Place the cursor to the right of the last character to be formatted.
- Press Ctrl-N to insert the end-attribute code (▼).

Note that the Ctrl-N command removes all formatting attributes. If you have more than one attribute in effect, and you want to turn off only one of them, don't press Ctrl-N. Instead, press Ctrl-E and enter the code to discontinue. For example, if bold and italic are in effect, press Ctrl-E and type *i* to remove the italic formatting. The Ctrl-E command produces the following codes: ▲0.

Here are a few tips about formatting sequences:

- The codes are case-sensitive so be sure to use the exact upper- and lowercase letters shown in Table 8.3.

- To specify multiple format attributes, press Ctrl-A before each code. For example, to specify bold and italic, press Ctrl-A and type *b*, then press Ctrl-A and type **i**.

- To remove all formatting sequences, edit the cell and delete all of the codes. This also applies to formatting attributes that were added in the text editor.

- You can include formatting sequences in your header and footer text.

REPLACING DATA

In Chapter 5 you learned how to use the /Range Search command to move the cell pointer directly to a specified text string in the spreadsheet. This command offers an option that takes the searching capability one step further: You can search for a string (text, a cell coordinate, a range name, or a number within a formula) and replace it with something else. There are many applications for this feature:

- If you find that you have consistently misspelled a word throughout a spreadsheet, you can search for the incorrectly spelled word and replace it with the correct one.

- To take an existing spreadsheet and customize it for a similar project, you can replace the data that is unique to each spread-sheet. For example, if one spreadsheet contains references to

1991 data, and you want to customize it for 1992 data, you can search for the string *1991* and replace it with *1992*.

- My favorite way to use the replace feature is to have it replace shorthand codes I've typed throughout the spreadsheet. If there is a long word or phrase that appears frequently in a spreadsheet, I type an abbreviation in its place. Then, I use the replace command to replace all the shorthand codes with the long phrase.

- To change a cell reference or range name in a series of formulas, the replace command can go through and quickly make all these replacements.

Unfortunately, the replace feature does not have a dialog box. Instead, you are prompted with a series of questions and submenus. Here is the general procedure for using the replace feature:

- Press / to display the 1-2-3 menu and choose:

  Range
  Search

- Indicate the search range. To search the entire spreadsheet, press Home, period, and End Home.

- Enter the search string. The string can be up 240 characters long, and it doesn't matter whether you type the text in upper- or lowercase. You can search for numbers only if they are part of a label or a formula.

- Choose Formulas, Labels, or Both, depending on what type of cell contents you want to search.

- Choose Replace.

- Enter the replacement string, up to 240 characters. Be sure to type the text exactly the way you want it to appear, including proper capitalization.

- When 1-2-3 finds the search string, you are presented with the following menu options:

  Replace All Next Quit

Choose Replace to replace the currently highlighted string and find the next one. Choose All to replace all remaining search strings with the replacement string. Choose Next to skip over the current string and proceed to the next one. Choose Quit to cancel the command.

Be very careful when you use the All option. If you are not 100-percent certain that you want every occurrence automatically replaced, choose Replace, not All. Let's say you want to replace all occurrences of *her* with *him* in a text range, and you choose the All option. 1-2-3 will replace the letters *h-e-r* with *h-i-m*—even if they are part of a word. For example, the word *other* becomes *othim*. You can end up with some pretty funny-looking words. If you have the Undo feature enabled, you can press Alt-F4 to reverse the replacements. (Otherwise, you must use the /Range Search command again and search for *him* and replace it with *her*—but this time choose Replace, not All.)

In the memo document, use the /Range Search command to replace the name *Rebecca* with *Becky*:

1. Press / to display the 1-2-3 menu and choose:

   Range

   Search

2. Paint the entire memo (A1..F20) and press Enter.

3. For the search string, type **Rebecca** and press Enter.

4. Choose:

   Labels

   Replace

5. For the replacement string, type **Becky** and press Enter.

6. In the control panel, 1-2-3 highlights the first search string that it finds. To replace all occurrences, choose All.

After making replacements in a text range, you may need to reformat the text if the search and replacement strings are different lengths. Because *Becky* is several characters shorter than *Rebecca*, there is extra space in these lines. Follow these steps to reformat the text range so that it looks like Figure 8.14:

1. Place the cell pointer anywhere within the paragraphs of the memo.

2. Press **:** to display the Wysiwyg menu and choose:

   Text

   Reformat

3. Press Enter.

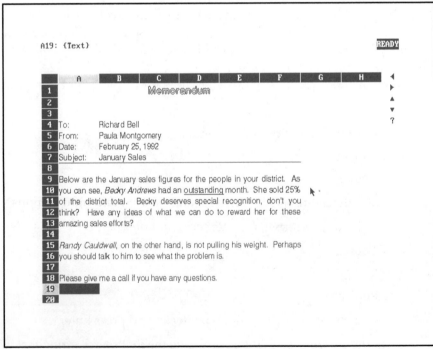

Figure 8.14: The name *Rebecca* was replaced with *Becky*.

SHIPPING IN
THE SPREADSHEET DATA

The final step to completing the memo is to copy in the spreadsheet data from the JAN file. You learned how to combine data from separate files in Chapter 5, so the following steps should be review for you:

1. Place the pointer in cell B21.

2. Press / to display the 1-2-3 menu and choose:

   File

   Combine

   Copy

   Entire-File

3. Choose JAN.WK1 for the file name. The January data is copied into the spreadsheet.

This spreadsheet still needs a bit of formatting before it's finished:

1. Delete rows 21 and 22 (/Worksheet Delete Row).

2. Add commas to the sales figures (/Worksheet Global Format).

3. Save the file as **JANMEMO**.

4. Specify A1..F38 as the print range, set the left and right margins to 1.25", and print memo.

Your printed memo should now resemble Figure 8.1.

PART I
PART II
PART III
PART IV
PART V

Graphics

Chapter 5

Chapter 6

Chapter 7

Chapter 8

Chapter 9

Creating Graphs

FAST TRACK

The old adage "a picture is worth a thousand words" might have been coined with business graphs in mind. You can get dizzy trying to interpret a spreadsheet that has column after column of numbers. But if you create a graph of that data, you may instantly notice a trend that was not readily apparent in the spreadsheet. Even if you don't plan to print any graphs for presentations or reports, you still can use the graphing feature to perform quick, on-screen analyses of your data. How quick is quick? Is ten seconds fast enough for you?

If you have ever created a graph by hand, you know that it's time-consuming, and if incorrect data is used, the graph must be redrawn. However, 1-2-3's graphing feature makes creating graphs fast, easy, and even fun. You do not need to be a graphic artist to create a beautiful chart in 1-2-3. All you have to do is tell the /Graph command what spreadsheet ranges you want to graph and 1-2-3 takes care of the rest. Throw out your ruler, compass, and colored pens. Needless to say, the graphs you can print in 1-2-3 look much more professional than anything the average person could draw. And you can be assured that all the data points are accurate.

One of the advantages of 1-2-3's integrated spreadsheet and graphing capabilities is that you can change any of the numbers in the spreadsheet and the graph will automatically reflect the revised data. If you create a graph by hand and someone revises a number, you have to redraw the entire chart.

This chapter covers all aspects of chart creation; to print your graphs, refer to Chapter 10.

THE FIRST STEP: ENTER THE DATA

The first step to creating a graph does not even involve the /Graph command. Before you can create a graph, you need spreadsheet data. For the exercises in this chapter, you will create various graphs of the data in Figure 9.1. This spreadsheet compares Tactile Toys' (a fictional toy manufacturing company) domestic and international sales for the period 1984 through 1991.

G17:   READY

	A	B	C	D	E	F	G	H
1	U.S. and International Sales							
2	Tactile Toys, Inc.							
3	(In Millions)							
4								
5		U.S.	Intnl.	Total	Avg			
6								
7	1984	0.5	0.1	0.6	0.30			
8	1985	0.9	0.2	1.1	0.55			
9	1986	1.7	0.7	2.4	1.20			
10	1987	1.1	0.5	1.6	0.80			
11	1988	3.2	1.1	4.3	2.15			
12	1989	5.6	1.9	7.5	3.75			
13	1990	8.1	2.3	10.4	5.20			
14	1991	10.4	4.5	14.9	7.45			
15								
16								
17								
18								
19								
20								

Figure 9.1: The data for the graphs you will be creating

Follow these steps to create the spreadsheet:

1. If necessary, clear the screen (/Worksheet Erase).

2. Type the data shown in Figure 9.1. Be sure to enter the data in the exact cells indicated in the figure. (Columns D and E are formulas.)

3. If you like, use Wysiwyg to format the text.

4. Save the file with the name **SALESHIS**.

Figure 9.2 shows the first graph you will create—a line graph. This figure defines the different components of a graph. The horizontal axis is called the *x-axis*. In most graphs, labels appear on this axis, and usually these labels are units of time: years, months, quarters, etc. In this example, the years in the range A7..A14 are the x-axis labels. The vertical axis is the *y-axis* and displays numbers on the *y-scale*. 1-2-3 automatically determines an appropriate y-scale based on the numbers in your spreadsheet. In the SALESHIS spreadsheet, you are graphing two ranges of data: the U.S. data in B7..B14 and the international data in C7..C14. 1-2-3 allows up to six data ranges, and each range can have an infinite number of values.

When you have more than one data range, it's important to have *legends* that describe the data. Without the legends in Figure 9.2, you wouldn't know which line represents U.S. data and which represents international sales. *Titles* are also vital for interpreting the data. The *grid lines* extend from each tick mark on the y-axis and help you read the specific data points on the graph.

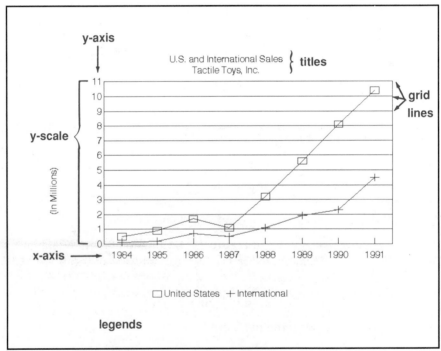

Figure 9.2: A line graph

DEFINING THE RANGES

1-2-3 does not automatically know what data you want to graph, so you must define these ranges with the /Graph command. There are actually two ways to specify graph ranges: individually or as a group (all ranges indicated at once). We'll look at both ways in this section.

Refer to the Graph Settings dialog box shown in Figure 9.3, and locate the Ranges area of the dialog box. Each range is designated by a code letter. X signifies the x-axis range, and A through F refer to the six data ranges.

DEFINING RANGES INDIVIDUALLY

You can specify ranges in the /Graph menu or directly in the Graph Settings dialog box (see Figure 9.3). However, because you can't see your spreadsheet when the dialog box is displayed and you can't paint ranges when you fill in a dialog box, it's easier to define the ranges with the menu options. If you prefer editing the dialog box but you can't remember the ranges, press the F6 key to temporarily remove the dialog box so that you

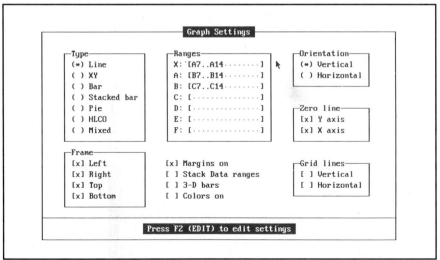

Figure 9.3: The Graph Settings dialog box

can see the spreadsheet; to return to the dialog box, press F6 again.
Follow these steps to define the graph ranges:

1. Press / to display the 1-2-3 menu and choose:

   Graph

   X

2. Paint the range A7..A14 and press Enter.

3. Choose A to specify the first data range.

4. Paint the range B7..B14 and press Enter.

5. Choose B to specify the second data range.

6. Paint the range C7..C14 and press Enter.

7. Choose View to display the graph.

8. Press any key to return to the /Graph menu.

DEFINING A GROUP RANGE

With the /Graph Group command, you can specify the X and A–F
ranges all at once. In order for this to work properly, the data ranges must
be in consecutive rows or columns. Make sure there are no blank rows or
columns in the group range. Follow this general procedure to define a
group range:

- Press / to display the 1-2-3 menu and choose:

  Graph

  Group

- Paint the x-axis range and all the y-axis ranges (A7..C14 in the
  current example)

- Press Enter.

- Choose Columnwise or Rowwise, depending on how the data is
  organized. In the SALESHIS spreadsheet, each individual data
  range is in a column, so Columnwise would be the correct
  choice.

When you select Columnwise, the first column in the range becomes the x-axis range, the second column is the A data range, the third column is the B range, and so on. When you select Rowwise, the first row becomes the x-range, the second row is the A range, the third row is the B range, etc. Because of the way ranges are automatically assigned, it's important that there are no blank rows or columns in the group range.

The Columnwise/Rowwise choice is confusing for some people (like me). So I ask myself the following question when I'm trying to decide which choice is appropriate: Are the x-axis labels in a row or a column? If they are in a row, choose Rowwise; otherwise, choose Columnwise.

CHOOSING A GRAPH TYPE 2.3

As you just saw, the default graph type is line. 1-2-3 offers six other types of graphs: line, XY, bar, stacked-bar, pie, high-low-close-open (otherwise known as *HLCO*), and a combination line and bar (known as *mixed*). The HLCO and Mixed types are new to Release 2.3. Examples of each of these graph types are given throughout this chapter. Here is a brief explanation of the graphs:

- In a *line* graph, data points are connected with lines to show a trend. Line graphs can consist of one to six ranges of data.

- An *XY* graph has numbers on both the x- and y-axis, and illustrates whether a correlation exists between the x and y values. XY graphs can consist of one to six ranges of data.

- In a *bar* graph, bars are placed side by side to compare the values in one to six data ranges.

- In a *stacked bar*, the bars are placed on top of one another to show the total of the data ranges. A stacked bar can consist of two to six data ranges.

- Each slice in a *pie* graph represents a percentage of the total. Only one range of values can be graphed in a pie.

- An *HLCO* (high-low-close-open) graph is used primarily for graphing stock-market data. Each increment on the x-axis has a mark representing a high, a low, an opening, and a closing value. HLCO graphs can consist of one to four data ranges.

- A *mixed* graph displays both lines and bars. It can contain two to six ranges of data.

Variations of the above graph types are available by specifying options. For example, you can transform a normal line graph into an area chart by turning on an option.

Follow these steps to experiment with several of the other graph types (you should still be in the /Graph menu):

1. To display the data in a bar graph, choose:

   Type
   Bar
   View

2. Press any key to return to the menu.

3. To display the data in a stacked bar graph, choose:

   Type
   Stack-Bar
   View

4. Switch back to your original graph type, Line.

AUTOMATIC GRAPH RECALCULATION

Remember back in Chapter 3 when you changed a value and the formulas automatically reflected this change? You can do the same type of thing with your graphs—change a value, and the graph changes the data points and scale accordingly. Let's try it:

1. Choose Quit to return to READY mode.

2. To see the current graph, press F10.

3. Note the 1984 U.S. sales on the graph.

4. Press any key to return to READY mode.

5. Move to cell B7 and enter **13.5**.

6. Press the Graph key, F10, to display the new graph. The first data point on the graph instantly reflects the revised value.

7. Return B7 to its original value (0.5).

8. View the graph.

At the end of this chapter you will see how to simultaneously display a graph and spreadsheet so you don't have to use the F10 key.

ADDING LEGENDS, TITLES, AND DATA LABELS

A good graph should not require a human interpreter. As your graph now stands, it's not apparent what data you are graphing—it desperately needs legends and titles. You specify these labels in the Graph Legends & Titles dialog box. This box is displayed when you choose /Graph Options Legend or /Graph Options Titles. Or, if you have a mouse, you can edit the Graph Settings dialog box and click on the Legends & Titles command button.

When you specify your legends and titles, you can either enter the label yourself, or if the label appears in a spreadsheet cell, you can type a backslash followed by the cell reference (for example, \A1).

CREATING LEGENDS

Legends are imperative when you have more than one data range. The current graph needs legends to explain that the line with the square symbols refers to United States data, while the line with the plus symbols indicates international data.

Enter the legends for your SALESHIS graph:

1. To specify the legend for the first data range, press / to display the 1-2-3 menu and choose:

    Graph

    Options

    Legend

    A

2. Type **United States** and press Enter.

3. To enter the legend for the second data range, choose:

    Legend

    B

4. Type **International** and press Enter.

After specifying your legends, you remain in the /Graph Options menu. To view your graph, you don't need to quit the Options menu and choose View—there's a shortcut. Any time you want to see the current graph—whether you are in the 1-2-3 or Wysiwyg menu, editing a dialog box, or in READY mode—press F10. Press the F10 key now to see your legends.

If a range of spreadsheet cells contains text you would like to use as your legends, you can paint this range with the /Graph Options Legend Range command. In the current example, you could indicate B5..C5 as the legend range, and *U.S.* and *Intnl.* would appear as the legends.

ENTERING TITLES

Each graph can have two titles at the top, a title on the x-axis, and a title on the y-axis. Because the titles entered in the current spreadsheet will work as graph titles, you can reference the appropriate cells instead of typing each title. Follow these steps to add titles to your graph (the /Graph Options menu should still be displayed):

1. To specify the cell containing the first top title, choose:

    Titles

    First

2. Type **\A1** and press Enter.

3. To specify the second top title, choose:

    Titles

    Second

4. Type **\A2** and press Enter.

5. To specify the y-axis title, choose:

    Titles

    Y-Axis

6. Type **\A3** and press Enter.

7. Press F10 to view the graph. It should look similar to Figure 9.4.

ADDING DATA LABELS

The purpose of a spreadsheet is to give you precise numbers with accurate calculations. The purpose of a graph, on the other hand, is to give you an overall picture of the relationship between different series of data or to illustrate trends and correlations. But a graph can give you precise data, too, if you use *data labels*. Data labels are cell contents (usually your graph data ranges) that can be placed right next to the data points on a graph. Although they are called data labels, they can be either labels or values; in fact, data labels are most often values.

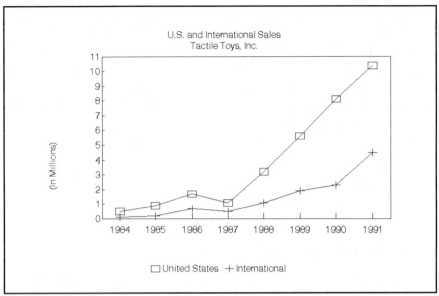

Figure 9.4: A graph with titles and legends

Figure 9.5 shows data labels that have been added to a line graph. Follow this general procedure to add data labels:

- Press / to display the 1-2-3 menu and choose:

    Graph

    Options

    Data-Labels

- Choose the letter of the data range (A–F) to which you want to add data labels, or choose Group to specify all ranges at once.

- Paint the range containing the labels or values you want placed next to the data points; press Enter.

- Choose where you want the labels placed with respect to the data points (Center, Left, Above, Right, or Below).

- If necessary, repeat for other data labels.

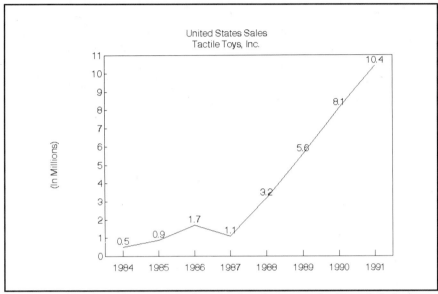

Figure 9.5: To place the numeric data on the chart, use the Data-Labels option.

In Figure 9.5, the data-label range is B7..B14 and the labels are placed above the data points.

MODIFYING THE SCALES

Although 1-2-3 automatically calculates the y-axis scale for you, the scale can be modified. You can change the upper and lower limits, format the numbers, add grid lines that extend from each tick mark, and display a duplicate scale on the right side of the graph. Most of these options also apply to x-axis scales in XY graphs.

ADDING GRID LINES

Grid lines can help you figure out which data point corresponds to which axis label. Horizontal grid lines are placed from each y-axis tick mark, across the width of the graph. Vertical grid lines extend upwards from each x-axis increment. It is rare to have vertical grid lines only; more commonly, they are used in combination with horizontal grid lines, or horizontal grid lines are used alone.

Follow these steps to place horizontal grid lines on your practice graph (you should still be in the /Graph Options menu):

1. Choose:

    Grid

    Horizontal

2. Press F10 to view the graph. Your graph should look similar to Figure 9.2.

Another way to turn on grid lines is by editing the Graph Settings dialog box. It's especially easy with a mouse: click inside the box and then click on the horizontal grid lines option.

SPECIFYING YOUR OWN SCALE

1-2-3 determines the lower and upper limits of the y-scale by looking at the numbers in your graph ranges. In the current example, the values range from 0.1 to 10.4. Consequently, the y-scale ranges from 0 to 11, with increments of 1. There is no way to change the increments, but you can change the upper and lower limits. Sometimes you may want a little extra space at the top of the graph—you can get this extra space by increasing the upper limit. Here's the general procedure for changing the y-scale:

• Press / to display the 1-2-3 menu and choose:

    Graph

    Options

    Scale

    Y-Scale

    Manual

- Choose Lower and specify the value for the bottom of the y-scale.

- Choose Upper and specify the value for the top of the y-scale.

To return to 1-2-3's default upper- and lower-limit settings, use the /Graph Options Scale Y-Scale Automatic command; you do not need to clear the limits you set manually.

DISPLAYING TWO Y-SCALES

The Display option allows you to place the y-scale on the left, right, neither, or both sides of the graph. By default, the y-scale appears only on the left side of the graph, but it's easier to interpret the data points on the right side of the graph if they have their own scale.

Follow these steps to display the y-scale on the left and right (the /Graph Options menu should be displayed):

1. Choose:

    Scale

    Y-Scale

    Display

    Both

    Quit

2. Press F10 to view the graph.

Notice that the y-axis title is repeated on both y-scales.

FORMATTING THE Y-SCALE

Regardless of your worksheet's global format or the specific format of the graph range, the y-scale is in General format. The Format option lets you add punctuation to the y-scale. Follow these steps to add dollar signs to the y-scales (the /Graph Options menu should be displayed).

1. Choose:

   Scale

   Y-Scale

   Format

   Currency

2. Type **0** for the number of decimal places and press Enter.

3. Choose Quit and view the graph.

Both y-scales now have dollar signs, as shown in Figure 9.6.

TURNING OFF THE SCALE INDICATOR

The Indicator option controls whether the (*Thousands*) or (*Millions*) indicator is displayed when the values in the graph range exceed 1000. There

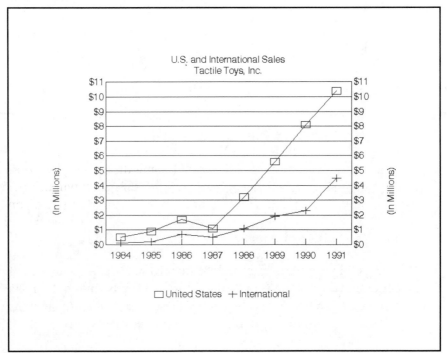

Figure 9.6: The graph with two y-scales formatted to Currency

is no indicator in the SALESHIS spreadsheet because you abbreviated the numbers (for example, 5.1 instead of 5,100,000) and entered a y-axis title that indicates the numbers are in millions. But, if you had entered the full numbers, a *(Millions)* indicator would appear along the y-axis. You would therefore not need the *(In Millions)* y-axis title, because the indicator already specifies that the scale is millions. If you prefer your *(In Millions)* title to the automatic *(Millions)* indicator, turn off the indicator instead of eliminating the y-axis title. All the Indicator option does is turn the indicator on or off.

CREATING MULTIPLE GRAPHS

Your SALESHIS spreadsheet currently has only one graph—a line graph comparing domestic and international data—but 1-2-3 has the ability to manage an infinite number of graphs in each file, memory permitting (each graph consumes about 700K). To create multiple graphs in a spreadsheet, you need a system for storing and retrieving them. Without such a system, you would need to recreate each graph every time you wanted to look at it or print it.

NAMING A GRAPH

Let's say you want to create a new graph to plot total yearly sales. Before you create the new graph, you must name the current one with /Graph Name Create. If you forget this important step, you will need to redefine all the graph settings if you want to work with the comparison chart again.

Follow these steps to name the current graph:

1. Quit to the main /Graph menu and choose:

   Name

   Create

2. Type **COMPARISON** and press Enter. (The name can be up to fifteen characters long, and can contain letters, numbers, special characters, and spaces.)

CLEARING EXISTING SETTINGS

If your new graph will use different data ranges and options than the current graph, you should clear the existing settings with the /Graph Reset command. This command lets you cancel all ranges and options (the Graph option), individual ranges (X, A–F), all data ranges (the Group option), or all options (legends, titles, grid, etc.).

The graph you will be creating here has the same x-axis range and uses most of the same options. Therefore, the fastest way to create the graph is to clear the A and B ranges, as follows (you should be at the /Graph menu).

Watch the Graph Settings dialog box as you choose:

Reset

A

B

Quit

When you choose A and B on the /Graph Reset menu, the ranges are cleared from the dialog box. Notice that the X range and all the option settings remain.

The new graph has only one data range (D7..D14), and should not have horizontal grid lines or a right y-scale. Follow these steps to create the graph (you should be at the /Graph menu):

1. Choose A and define the range D7..D14.

2. To turn off the grid lines, choose:

Options

Grid

Clear

3. To display only a left y-scale, choose:

Scale

Y-Scale

Display

Left

Quit

4. When you have only one data range, you don't need a legend. To clear the A range legend, choose:

Legend

A

5. Press Esc to clear the original graph's legend and press Enter.

6. Press F10 to view the graph. It should look similar to the one in Figure 9.7.

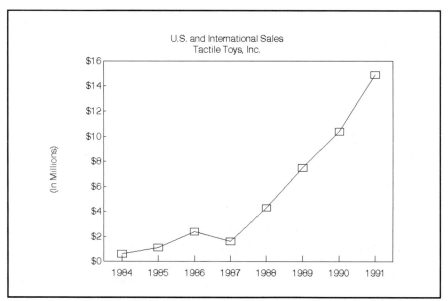

Figure 9.7: A line graph that plots total sales

Now assign a name to your new graph:

1. Quit to the main /Graph menu, and choose:

   Name

   Create

2. Type **TOTAL** and press Enter.

RETRIEVING A NAMED GRAPH

When you press F10 or choose /Graph View, 1-2-3 shows you the current graph. To make a different named graph current, so you can view or modify it, use the /Graph Name Use command.

Follow these steps to practice retrieving graphs:

1. To retrieve the COMPARISON graph, choose:

   Name

   Use

2. Select COMPARISON and press Enter. The line graph with two data ranges is displayed. COMPARISON is now the current graph.

3. To retrieve the TOTAL graph, choose:

   Name

   Use

4. Select TOTAL and press Enter. The line graph with the single data range is now displayed.

MANAGING NAMED GRAPHS

Here are several tips for managing your named graphs:

• Be sure to name the current graph before clearing the settings with /Graph Reset.

- To save all your graphs you must save the spreadsheet file (/File Save).

- After modifying a named graph, you need to resave it with /Graph Name Create.

- There is no way to rename a graph. To change a name, assign a new name to the graph (/Graph Name Create) and then delete the old (/Graph Name Delete).

- Be careful with the /Graph Name Reset option—it deletes all named graphs in the current spreadsheet.

- To see a list of graphs in the current spreadsheet, use the /Graph Name Table command. This command inserts a three-column table into the spreadsheet. It lists the graph names, types, and titles (see Figure 9.8).

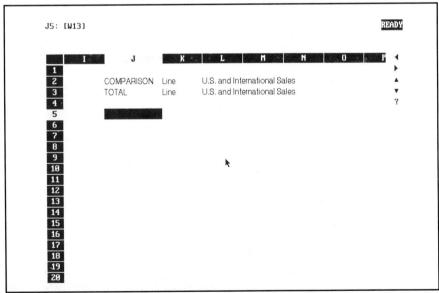

Figure 9.8: A graph name table

EXPLORING GRAPH TYPES

1-2-3 offers special options and features to enhance each particular type of graph. For example, you can create area charts out of line graphs, define the patterns in a pie chart, and use three-dimensional effects with bar graphs. This section explores the enhancements available for each type of graph.

LINE GRAPHS

The default line graph has a symbol at each data point and lines connecting each symbol. If you are working in color (/Graph Options Color), each line is assigned a unique color. For example, in your COMPARISON chart, the U.S. data is represented with square symbols and the international data has plus signs. Each data range (A–F) has its own symbol associated with it:

Data Range	Symbol	Color
A	□	Blue
B	+	Green
C	◇	Cyan
D	Δ	Red
E	×	Magenta
F	∇	Yellow

While you can't assign a different color or symbol to a particular data range, you can assign the data to a different range letter (A–F). For example, if you prefer diamonds instead of squares, assign the data to range C instead of A. (You would also need to assign the legend to C.)

The /Graph Options Format command lets you display or remove the lines and symbols in any graph type that has lines (Line, XY, and Mixed). You can choose Lines, Symbols, Both, or Neither for each individual data range or all ranges. Here are several examples of when you might want to change the combination of lines and symbols:

- If you have only one data series, you don't really need the symbols.

- If you have two data ranges, only one of the series needs to have symbols.

- If you are printing the graphs in color, each line is a different color, so you don't really need the symbols to differentiate the data ranges.

- When you use data labels, you may want to remove the lines and symbols (see Figure 9.9).

Area Graphs

An *area graph* is a cross between a line and a bar chart. Like a line chart, lines connect each data point. Like a bar chart, patterns or colors are used

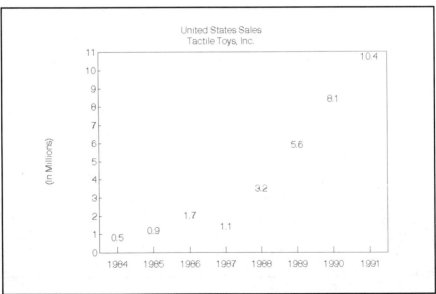

Figure 9.9: A line graph with data labels and no lines or symbols

to represent each data range. Figure 9.10 shows an example of an area graph.

I always have a hard time remembering where the Area option is located because it's not where I think it should be (on the /Graph Type menu). The Area option is tucked away in the /Graph Options Format menu.

Follow these steps to create an area graph out of the COMPARISON chart (the /Graph menu should be displayed):

1. To retrieve the COMPARISON chart, choose:

    Name

    Use

    COMPARISON

2. To create an area chart, choose:

    Options

    Format

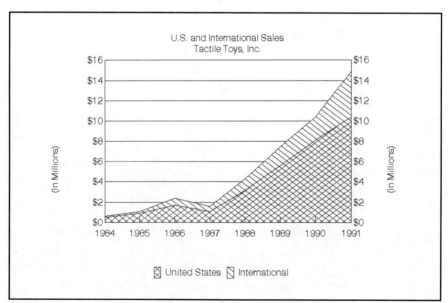

Figure 9.10: An area graph

Graph

Area

Quit

Quit

3. View the chart. It should look similar to Figure 9.10.

There is one difference between your graph and the one shown in Figure 9.10. On your graph, there is a margin on the left and right; in the figure, the first and last data points are plotted right on the frame around the graph. Because area graphs look a little strange with this margin, you should turn it off with the following command:

1. From the main /Graph menu, choose:

Type

Features

Frame

Margins

No

Quit

Quit

2. Assign the name **AREA** to this graph.

Cumulative Line Graphs

Compare the graph in Figure 9.11 with Figure 9.6, and see if you can figure what is unique to Figure 9.11. First, the y-scale's upper limit is 16 instead of 11. Second, it appears as if the international sales are higher than the U.S. sales. What's going on here? As the title indicates, this is a cumulative graph—each data range is added to the previous data range. Thus, the data points on the international line represent the accumulation of U.S. and international sales. This effect is similar to the one achieved with a stacked bar; consequently the option is called Stacked.

The option appears in the Graph Settings dialog box as *Stack data ranges*. To turn on the stacked option in the menu, use the /Graph Type Features Stacked Yes command. This feature stacks ranges in the following graph types: Line, XY, Mixed, and Bar (same as Stack-Bar).

BAR GRAPHS

Bar graphs come in two basic varieties: standard and stacked. A standard bar graph places the bars side by side so that you can compare the data ranges. A stacked bar graph places the bars on top of each other giving you an additional piece of information: the total of the ranges.

1-2-3 assigns each data-range bar a unique hatching pattern if you are working in black-and-white (/Graph Options B&W) or a different color if you are working in color (/Graph Options Color). Figure 9.12 indicates the colors and hatching patterns for each data range (A–F).

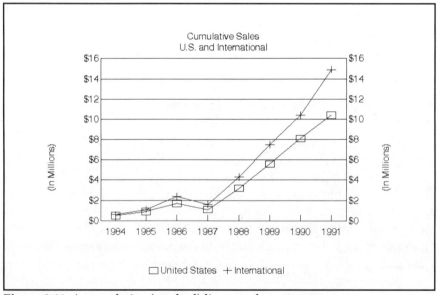

Figure 9.11: A cumulative (stacked) line graph

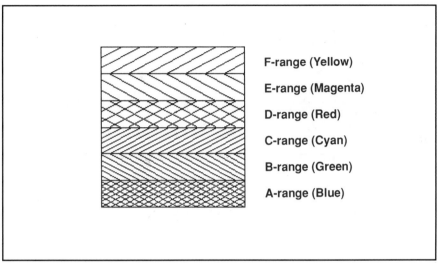

F-range (Yellow)

E-range (Magenta)

D-range (Red)

C-range (Cyan)

B-range (Green)

A-range (Blue)

Figure 9.12: Hatching patterns and colors for bar graphs

Three-Dimensional Bar Graphs

With the 3D-Effect feature you can create three-dimensional bars, as shown in Figure 9.13. This feature works with any graph type that contains bars (Bar, Stack-Bar, and Mixed).

Let's create a three-dimensional stacked bar. This graph will have all the settings of the COMPARISON graph, so you should begin by retrieving this named graph:

1. Retrieve the COMPARISON graph (/Graph Name Use).

2. Change the type to Stack-Bar.

3. To create the 3-D effect, choose:

   Type
   Features
   3D-Effect
   Yes
   Quit

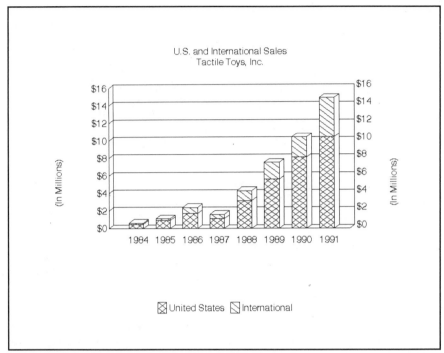

Figure 9.13: A three-dimensional stacked-bar graph

4. View the graph. It should look similar to Figure 9.13.

5. Assign the name **3D BAR** to this graph.

2.3 ▶

Horizontal Charts

Another way to view a bar graph is horizontally, as shown in Figure 9.14. In a horizontal chart, the x- and y-axes are reversed. The x-axis labels appear on the left side of the graph and the y-axis labels display along the top. If you want the labels to appear at the bottom instead of the top, change the display of the y-scale (use the /Graph Options Scale Y-Scale Display Right command).

This feature applies to all graph types, but is most commonly used with bars and stacked-bars. To turn on this feature, use the /Graph Type Features Horizontal command. To return to the standard arrangement, choose /Graph Type Features Vertical.

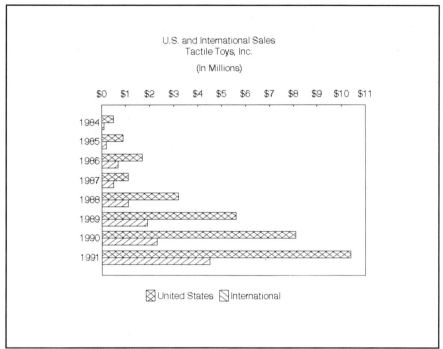

Figure 9.14: A horizontal bar chart

MIXED CHARTS

◀▐▐▐ 2.3

The Mixed graph type displays a combination of lines and bars. One way to use this type of graph is to show an average of the other data ranges: the specific data ranges are displayed as bars and the averages are displayed in a line. Figure 9.15 shows a mixed graph of your SALESHIS spreadsheet.

How do you indicate which ranges are bars and which are lines? The A, B, and C ranges will be bars and the D, E, and F ranges will be lines. Now that you know the "trick" for creating mixed graphs, let's create the graph shown in Figure 9.15:

1. Retrieve the COMPARISON graph (/Graph Name Use).

2. Specify E7..E14 as the D data range.

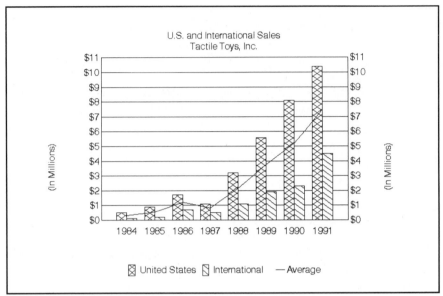

Figure 9.15: A mixed graph

3. Assign the legend **Average** to the D range (/Graph Options Legend D).

4. Choose the Mixed type and view the graph.

5. There is no need for symbols in the line—let's remove them (/Graph Options Format D Lines).

6. View the graph.

7. Assign the name **MIXED** to this graph (/Graph Name Create).

8. Save the spreadsheet file (/File Save).

PIE CHARTS

A pie chart is one of the most commonly used business charts. By looking at the relative size of the pie slices and their accompanying percentage figures, you can clearly see the relationships between the items.

The basic pie graph has only two ranges. The X range contains the labels for each slice, and the A range contains the values you are graphing.

1-2-3 then calculates and displays percentages for each slice.

The SALESHIS spreadsheet doesn't have any data appropriate for a pie graph, so let's create a new one. This spreadsheet, shown in Figure 9.16, contains Tactile Toys' 1991 sales by product line. Only the four major product lines are included (Stuffed Animals, Action Figures, Dolls, and Sports); the other products are lumped into a category called Other. (Although a pie can have an unlimited number of slices, a chart with many small slices is difficult to read. For a more attractive chart, consider combining some of the slices into a single slice labeled "Other," as we did here.)

To create this spreadsheet, follow these steps:

1. Clear the screen (/Worksheet Erase).

2. Create the spreadsheet shown in Figure 9.16.

3. Save the file with the name **PRODUCTS**.

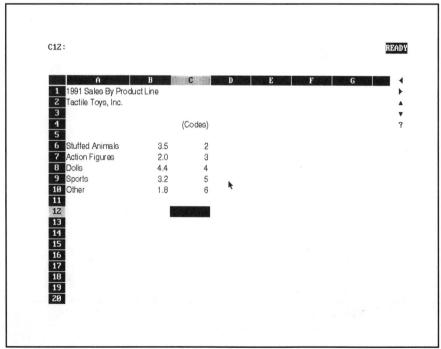

Figure 9.16: The data for the pie graph

Note that the codes in column C indicate color and hatching pat-terns—you'll be using them in the next section. Now, follow the steps below to create a pie chart of this data:

1. To specify the graph ranges, press / to display the 1-2-3 menu and choose:

   Graph

   Group

2. Paint the range A6..B10 and press Enter.

3. Choose Columnwise.

4. Select the Pie graph type.

5. View the graph. Your pie should look similar to the one shown in Figure 9.17.

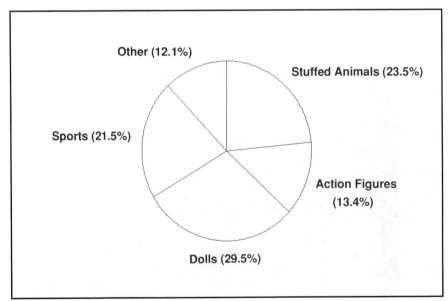

Figure 9.17: A pie graph

Adding Patterns to a Pie Graph

A pie graph is pretty boring without colors or patterns. By specifying a B range of pattern codes, each slice will be a different hatching pattern. If you are working in color (/Graph Options Color), each slice will be patterned in a different color. Eight different patterns and colors are available, as indicated in Figure 9.18. To choose patterns, enter the appropriate code (0 though 7) in the B range. Now you know why you entered the codes in column C of your spreadsheet—all that's left to do is specify this column as the B range, as follows:

1. Choose B, paint the range C6..C10, and press Enter.
2. View the graph.

A patterned pie graph is much more interesting, don't you think?

If your pie has more than eight slices, you will need to use codes more than once. You can enter codes greater than 7, but they will be duplicates of the patterns and colors associated with the eight standard codes (0 through 7).

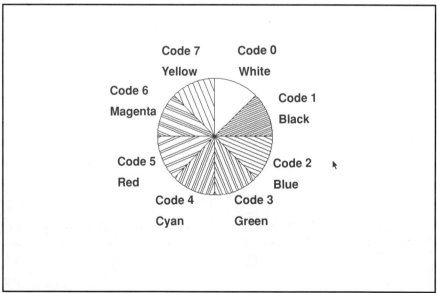

Figure 9.18: Pie graph patterns and colors

Exploding a Pie Slice

You can call attention to a particular slice by separating it from the rest of the pie; this is referred to as *exploding* the slice. To explode a slice of the pie, enter a value over 100 in the B range. For example, to explode the Sports slice, enter 105 in cell C9. Your pie graph would then look similar to Figure 9.19.

You can explode as many slices as you like, but this effect loses its impact if you cut out more than one or two segments.

If you forget to clear an old B range before you create a pie graph and this B range contains values greater than 100, every single slice of the pie will be exploded (see Figure 9.20). To fix this mistake, clear the B range (/Graph Reset B) or enter a new B range with pattern codes less than 100.

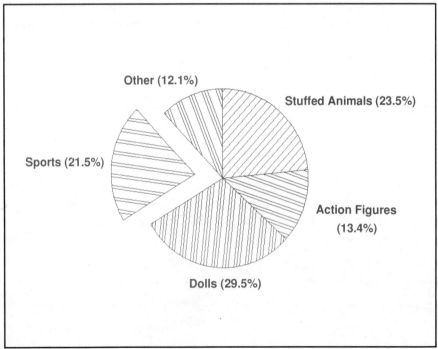

Figure 9.19: An exploded pie slice

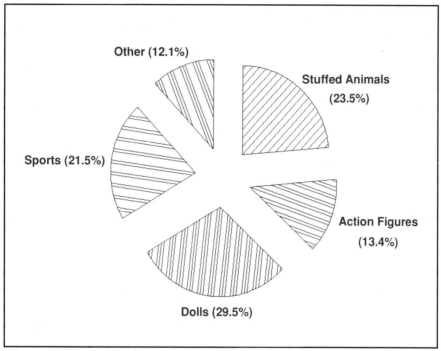

Figure 9.20: A pie graph in which all slices are exploded

HLCO GRAPHS

The primary use for the high-low-close-open (HLCO) chart is to graph fluctuations in stock prices. This chart type usually tracks four data ranges over a specific period: High, Low, Close, and Open. The A range contains the stock's highest price, the B range contains the stock's lowest price, the C range is the closing price, and the D range is the initial price. The time period can be a day, month, quarter, or year.

Figure 9.21 is an example of this graph type. The high and low data points are connected to form a vertical line. The opening price is a horizontal line that extends to the left of the vertical line, and the closing price is the horizontal line to the right of the vertical line.

This chart type is not restricted to stock data. You can also graph other types of high/low data such as temperatures, test scores, sales, and project bids.

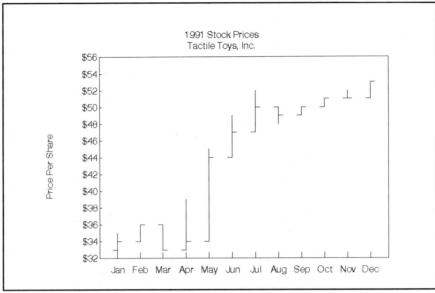

Figure 9.21: An HLCO graph

Although the HLCO graph can plot up to four data ranges, you do not need to use all four; just specify the data ranges you have. Pay attention, though, to how 1-2-3 represents the different data ranges in the HLCO graph. For example, the high and low values should be specified as the A and B ranges.

INSERTING A GRAPH
INTO THE SPREADSHEET

Earlier in the chapter, you entered different values in the spreadsheet and then pressed F10 to view the revised graph. Another way to play "what-if" games is to insert the graph directly into the spreadsheet. When you do this, each time you make a spreadsheet change, the graph is instantly redrawn with the new data. This technique offers several advantages. First, you don't need to press F10. Second, you can see both the spreadsheet and the graph at the same time (see Figure 9.22). Third, you can print the graph without having to exit 1-2-3. Fourth, you can print the graph and the spreadsheet together on one page. (Chapter 10 discusses these last two items in detail.) Finally, you can enhance the graph with Wysiwyg's graphics editor, as explained in Chapter 11.

To insert a graph into a spreadsheet, you must have Wysiwyg attached.

ADDING A GRAPH

The :Graph Add command inserts the current or a named graph into the specified spreadsheet range. Follow these steps to insert the COM-PARISON graph into the SALESHIS spreadsheet:

1. If you haven't done so already, save the PRODUCTS file.

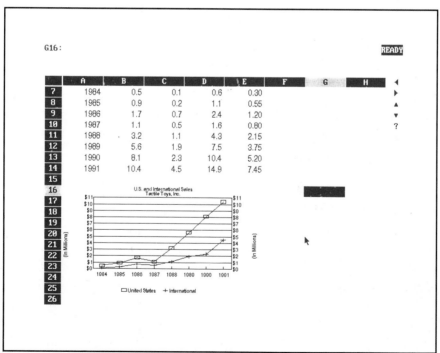

Figure 9.22: A graph inserted into a spreadsheet range

2. Retrieve SALESHIS.

3. Press **:** to display the Wysiwyg menu and choose:

    Graph

    Add

    Named

    COMPARISON

4. Paint the range A16..E26 to insert the graph below the spread-sheet; press Enter. Your screen should look similar to Figure 9.22.

5. Now, change a spreadsheet value. Move to cell B7 and enter **13.5**. The first data point on the graph instantly reflects the revised value.

6. Return B7 to its original value (0.5).

On some computers, you may find this automatic redrawing to be slow. If so, you can turn it off with the :Graph Settings Sync No command. (This graph command is the equivalent of the spreadsheet's manual recal-culation option.) Then, when you want to see your graph with the new data, choose the :Graph Compute command.

Note that inserting a graph does *not* make it current. If you press F10 now you will see the last graph you worked on, not the COMPARISON graph. If you decide to change the COMPARISON graph after it's been added to the spreadsheet, you will need to follow these basic steps:

• Use /Graph Name Use to make COMPARISON the current graph.

• Make your desired changes to the graph.

• Use /Graph Name Create to save the changes.

• Use :Graph Compute to redraw the graph with the revised settings.

REPOSITIONING A GRAPH

After you insert a graph with :Graph Add, you may discover that the graph has inappropriate dimensions, is located in the wrong place, or you may even find that you inserted the wrong graph. Wysiwyg offers commands to remedy each of these situations.

Resizing a Graph

The range you specify when you add the graph determines the chart's size on the screen and on a printed report. As a general rule, the width-to-length ratio of a graph should be approximately three-to-two. If you deviate too much from this ratio, your graph will be distorted, as shown in Figure 9.23. To resize a placed graph, use :Graph Settings Range. With this command, you can expand or contract the current size, or select a completely different range in another part of the spreadsheet. Make sure the range you specify conforms to the 3:2 ratio.

Moving a Graph

If you are pleased with the graph's size, but the chart is in the wrong part of the spreadsheet, use :Graph Move. This command prompts you for the graph to move (indicate one cell anywhere in the graph range) and then asks you to enter the upper-left corner of the new position (one cell is sufficient).

The :Graph Settings Range command is another way to move a graph. However, you must respecify the size of the graph in addition to the new location. Therefore, use :Graph Move to keep the size constant; use :Graph Settings Range to define both a different size and a different location.

Removing a Graph

Wysiwyg offers two ways to remove a graph from a spreadsheet range. If you don't want any graph at the current graph location, use :Graph Remove. If you want a different graph at the same location and with the same dimensions as the current graph, you can replace the graph

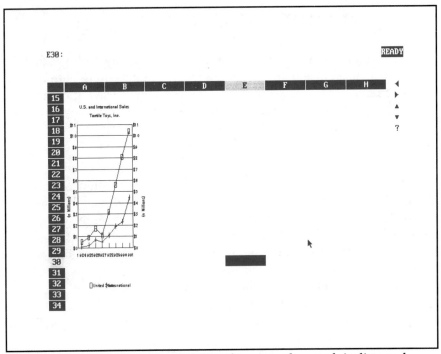

Figure 9.23: Because the range is tall and narrow, the graph is distorted.

with :Graph Settings Graph. Neither of these commands deletes the graph name or settings—they simply remove the graph from the spreadsheet range.

Follow these steps to replace the COMPARISON chart with the 3D BAR graph:

1. Press **:** to display the Wysiwyg menu and choose:

   Graph

   Settings

   Graph

2. Move the pointer to a cell within the graph range and press Enter.

3. To select the new graph, choose:

   Named

   3D BAR

   Quit

The three-dimensional bar graph now displays in place of the line graph. Save the file.

Chapter 10

Chapter 11
Chapter 12
Chapter 13
Chapter 14

Printing Graphs

◀▐▌▌▌ FAST TRACK ▌▌▌▐▶

To print a graph in Wysiwyg: 332

Insert the graph into a spreadsheet range with the :Graph Add command. Specify the graph range as the print range, and print the graph with :Print Go.

To change the size of a graph to be printed in Wysiwyg: 333

Press : to display the Wysiwyg menu and choose Graph Settings Range.

To reduce or enlarge graph text in a graph to be printed in Wysiwyg: 339

Press : to display the Wysiwyg menu and choose Graph Edit. Move the pointer inside the graph range and press Enter. Choose Options Font-Magnification. Enter a percentage to enlarge (over 100) or reduce (under 100).

To create a graph file for printing in PrintGraph: 345

Press / to display the 1-2-3 menu and choose Graph Save. Enter a filename.

To load PrintGraph: 346

Exit 1-2-3. If necessary, change to your 1-2-3 directory. For example, type **CD\123R23** if your directory is called *123R23*. Type **PGRAPH** and press Enter.

To change the print density in PrintGraph: 347

From the main PrintGraph menu, choose Settings Hardware Printer. Highlight the printer with the desired print density and press the spacebar; press Enter.

To print a graph in PrintGraph: 349

Create graph files in 1-2-3 (/Graph Save). Exit 1-2-3 and load PrintGraph. Choose Image-Select. Highlight the graph to print and press the spacebar; press Enter. If necessary, change the Hardware settings (Printer, Interface, and so on). If desired, change any of the Image settings (Size, Font, or Range-Colors). To print the graph, choose Align Go.

To print several graphs at once in PrintGraph: 351

From the main PrintGraph menu, choose Image-Select. Highlight each graph name to print and press the spacebar; press Enter when finished. To turn on the Eject option, choose Settings Action Eject Yes. Quit to the main PrintGraph menu and choose Align Go. Go out to lunch or take a break while the graphs are printing.

You can print your graphs in Wysiwyg or with 1-2-3's PrintGraph program. To print from Wysiwyg, you must insert your graph into a spreadsheet range with the :Graph Add command and specify this range as the print range. To print from PrintGraph, save the graph in a separate graph file, quit 1-2-3, and load the PrintGraph program. Each method has its own advantages and drawbacks.

Graph printing in Wysiwyg has two main advantages. First, you can print a graph without exiting 1-2-3. Second, you can easily print a spreadsheet and a graph on the same page. But don't completely disregard PrintGraph—it has its share of assets. You don't have to attach Wysiwyg (in large spreadsheets, this could be a major consideration) and it's easier to specify the graph size.

2.3 ▶ PRINTING GRAPHS IN WYSIWYG

There is nothing tricky about printing a graph in Wysiwyg. In fact, you already know how to do it, because you learned how to print in Wysiwyg in Chapter 7 and you learned how to insert a graph into a spreadsheet range in Chapter 9. Let's add the pie graph to the PRODUCTS spreadsheet and then print the graph. Follow these steps:

1. Retrieve PRODUCTS.

2. Press **:** to display the Wysiwyg menu and choose:

   Graph

   Add

   Current

3. Indicate the range A16..D26, and then choose Quit. (This graph lacks titles—we'll add them later.)

4. To specify the print range, press **:** to display the Wysiwyg menu and choose:

   Print

   Range

Set

5. Paint the entire graph range (A16..D26) and press Enter.

6. Choose Go. Your printed graph should look similar to Figure 10.1.

Just as with any Wysiwyg report, use the :Print Config command to specify the orientation (landscape vs. portrait) and density. For the most attractive printed graphs, choose your printer's highest print density.

SPECIFYING A GRAPH SIZE

While PrintGraph allows you the option of printing the graph half- or full-page size, Wysiwyg doesn't. Your graph's size is determined by the range you indicate when you place the graph. Wysiwyg's method is a bit cumbersome and imprecise because you have to figure out how many rows and columns will give you the desired size. Wouldn't it be nice if you could enter the size in inches instead of rows and columns?

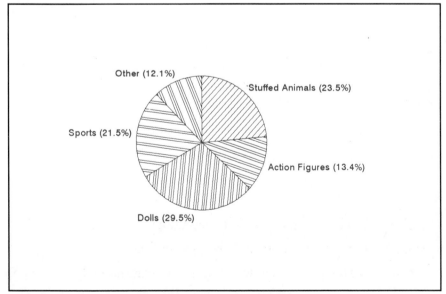

Figure 10.1: A pie graph printed on an HP LaserJet II

You can—sort of. Wysiwyg has an option to display inch marks instead of column letters and row numbers in the spreadsheet frame. With this type of frame, you can measure the width and length of the graph as you are defining its range. Consider this frame type to be a temporary setting, though; for most of your work, you will need the column letters and row numbers.

Follow these steps to display the inch rulers:

1. Press : to display the Wysiwyg menu and choose:

   Display

   Options

   Frame

   Special

   Inches

2. To zoom in so you can see more on your screen, choose:

   Quit

   Zoom

   Tiny

   Quit

As shown in Figure 10.2, your screen now shows more of the spreadsheet (eleven inches across and six inches down). Change the size of your pie graph as follows:

1. Press : to display the Wysiwyg menu and choose:

   Graph

   Settings

   Range

2. Move the cell pointer into the graph range and press Enter.

3. Paint a range that is about 7" by 3¼" and press Enter.

4. Change the print range so that it includes the larger graph range.

5. Use the :Print Preview command to view the graph on the screen.

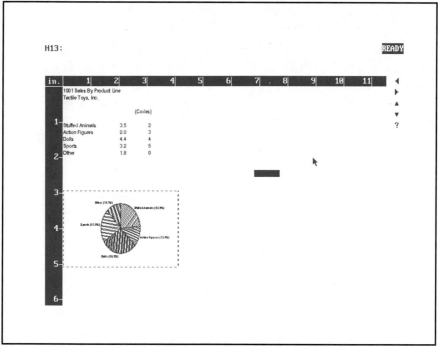

Figure 10.2: A spreadsheet frame with inch markings

Now return the frame to its normal display of rows and columns:

1. Press : to display the Wysiwyg menu and choose:

   Display
   Options
   Frame
   Enhanced

2. To zoom out to your normal screen, choose:

   Quit
   Zoom
   Normal
   Quit

FORMATTING THE GRAPH TEXT

All labels, titles, and numbers in the graph are the same typeface as the spreadsheet's default (font 1). The point size of the text depends on the size of the graph range; a large range will naturally have larger text. In the following exercises, you will learn how to change the typeface, size, and type style of the text in your charts.

Changing the Typeface

To change the typeface of the text in the chart, replace font 1 with a different typeface. Follow these steps to change the font to 12-point Dutch:

1. Press : to display the Wysiwyg menu and choose:

   Format

   Font

   Replace

   1

   Dutch

2. Press Enter to accept the size (12).

3. Quit to READY mode. The pie slice labels are now in Dutch.

Of course, when you replace font 1, you are not just changing the text in the graph—you are also changing the spreadsheet's default font. While Wysiwyg offers no other way to change the typeface of the graph labels and values, you can choose a different typeface (and style) for the titles and legends.

Formatting the Titles and Legends

In Chapter 8 you learned how to format characters within a cell by embedding formatting codes; you can use these same codes (reprinted in Table 10.1 for your convenience) in your graph titles and legends. To refresh your memory, here are the basic steps for embedding formatting codes:

- Place the cursor on the first character to be formatted.
- Press Ctrl-A to insert the begin-attribute code (▲).
- Type one of the codes in Table 10.1.

Table 10.1: Formatting Codes

CODE	DESCRIPTION
b	Bold
i	Italics
1_	Single underlining
2_	Double underlining
3_	Wide underlining
4_	Outline box around characters
5_	Strike-through characters
d	Subscript
u	Superscript
x	Makes characters backward
y	Places characters upside-down
1c	Default color
2c	Red
3c	Green
4c	Dark blue
5c	Cyan
6c	Yellow
7c	Magenta
8c	Reversed text
1F	Font 1 from the current font set
2F	Font 2 from the current font set

Table 10.1: Formatting Codes (continued)

CODE	DESCRIPTION
3F	Font 3 from the current font set
4F	Font 4 from the current font set
5F	Font 5 from the current font set
6F	Font 6 from the current font set
7F	Font 7 from the current font set
8F	Font 8 from the current font set
1o to 255o	Character outline (hollow inside)

- Place the cursor to the right of the last character to be formatted.
- Press Ctrl-N to insert the end-attribute code (▼).

Note that formatting codes do *not* work with titles and legends that are cell references (for example, \A1)—the codes must surround actual text. In your pie chart, enter and format a title, as follows:

1. Press / to display the 1-2-3 menu and choose:

   Graph

   Options

   Titles

   First

2. Press Ctrl-A to insert the begin-attribute code.

3. To insert the italics code, type **i** (make sure you type a lower-case i).

4. Press Ctrl-A to insert another begin-attribute code.

5. To format the text with the second font, type **2F** (make sure you type a capital *F*).

6. Type **1991 Sales by Product Line** (don't press Enter yet).

7. Press Ctrl-N to insert the end-attributes code, and press Enter.

8. Quit to READY mode.

9. To see the revised graph in the spreadsheet range, press : to display the Wysiwyg menu and choose:

   Graph

   Compute

10. Print the graph again. It should look similar to Figure 10.3.

Changing the Text Size

Wysiwyg offers several ways to change the size of text in a graph:

- Use formatting codes in titles and legends to switch to another font size.

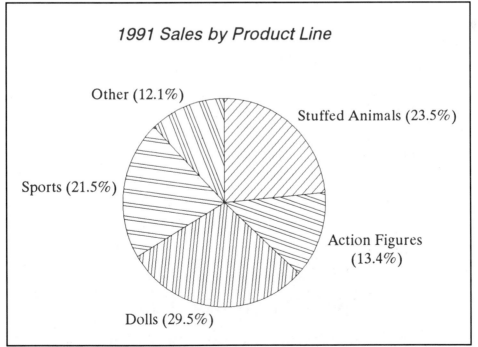

Figure 10.3: The printed pie graph with a formatted title

- Replace font 1 with a smaller or larger font size.

- Use the *font-magnification* feature to enlarge or reduce all graph text by a certain percentage.

Font-magnification overcomes some of the limitations that the other two options have. First, it adjusts the size of *all* text in the chart—formatting codes are limited to legends and titles. Second, it does not affect the spreadsheet's default font—replacing font 1 formats the spreadsheet as well as the graph.

By default, font-magnification is set to 100 percent. To enlarge the text, enter a value over 100. To reduce, enter a value less than 100. This option is available in Wysiwyg's graphics editor—a special area where you can enhance your charts. Chapter 11 discusses the graphics editor in detail.

Follow the steps below to enlarge all the text in your pie graph:

1. To load the graphics editor, press : to display the Wysiwyg menu and choose:

   Graph

   Edit

2. Place the cell pointer anywhere in the graph range and press Enter. The pie graph is loaded into the graphics editor, and a menu automatically displays.

3. To specify the font magnification, choose:

   Options

   Font-Magnification

4. Type **125** and press Enter. This number enlarges the text by 25 percent of its default size. Your pie should look similar to Figure 10.4.

5. Save the file.

TURNING OFF GRAPH DISPLAY

You may notice a delay each time a graph is redrawn on the screen, for example, when you move the pointer to a cell off of the screen. (Try it now.)

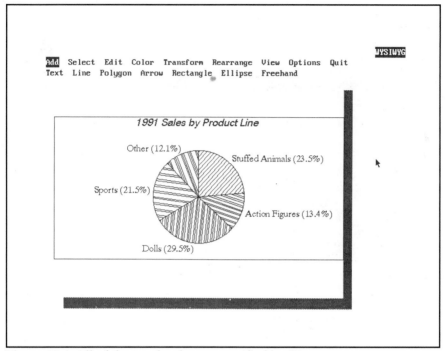

Figure 10.4: All of the text has been magnified by 25 percent.

This delay can be annoying, so once you have perfected your graph, you may want to hide the graph with the :Graph Settings Display No command. You will then see a shaded box that represents the graph (see Figure 10.5). When the graph is hidden, you won't experience a screen redrawing delay. Even though you cannot see the graph on your screen, when you print or preview, you will see the actual graph. To temporarily look at the hidden graph, use :Graph Zoom. To redisplay the graph, use :Graph Settings Display Yes.

PRINTING
A SPREADSHEET WITH A GRAPH

Printing a spreadsheet range on the same page as a graph is easy—just include both areas in the print range. Figure 10.6 shows a printout of the

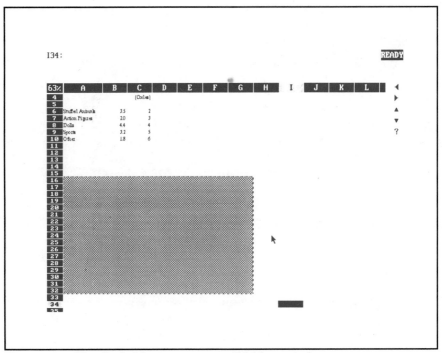

Figure 10.5: The shaded box represents a hidden graph.

SALESHIS spreadsheet and the three-dimensional bar graph. The print range is A1..E25.

PRINTING IN COLOR OR GRAY SHADES

If you have turned on the color option (/Graph Options Color) and have a color monitor, each data range displays in a different color. On a color printer or plotter, Wysiwyg prints the chart with the colors shown on the screen.

If the color option is turned on and you print the graph on a black-and-white printer, Wysiwyg prints each data range in a different shade of gray

Figure 10.6: A spreadsheet and graph printed on a single page

instead of with a hatching pattern. The results are much more attractive. Compare the two bar graphs in Figure 10.7. The graph on the top, which has hatching patterns, was created with the black-and-white option turned on (/Graph Options B&W), while the graph on the bottom, which has gray shades, was created with the color option turned on (/Graph Options Color).

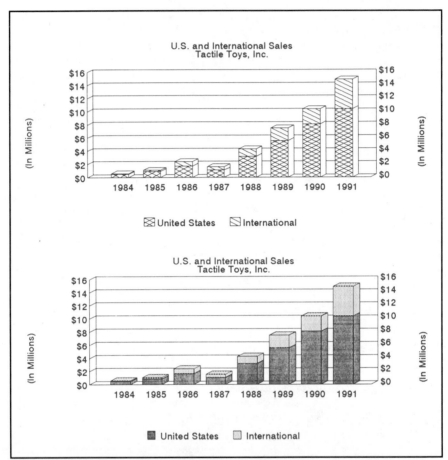

Figure 10.7: The top graph uses hatching patterns while the bottom graph displays gray shades.

PRINTING
GRAPHS WITH PRINTGRAPH

If you aren't using Wysiwyg, the only way to print your 1-2-3 graphs is with a separate software program. The one included in your 1-2-3 package is PrintGraph, though other programs, such as Harvard Graphics and PageMaker 4.0, can import and print graphs created in 1-2-3. Regardless of which program you are using to print the graphs, you need to create a special graph file as described in the next section. The rest of this chapter describes how to print your 1-2-3 graphs with PrintGraph.

CREATING GRAPH FILES

You cannot load the PrintGraph program and tell it to print named graphs from a spreadsheet file; you need to save each graph in its own special picture file. You create these graphs with the /Graph Save command; 1-2-3 automatically assigns the file extension .PIC (*PIC* stands for *picture*).

Unless you have a color printer or plotter, you should turn on the black-and-white graph option (/Graph Options B&W) before you create the picture files. If you save the graph in color, the colors print in solid black.

In the SALESHIS spreadsheet, let's create picture files for the COMPARISON and the 3D BAR graphs. You need to retrieve the appropriate graph before creating the picture file. Follow these steps:

1. Save PRODUCTS.

2. Retrieve SALESHIS.

3. To retrieve the COMPARISON graph, press / to display the 1-2-3 menu and choose:

   Graph

   Name

   Use

   COMPARISON

4. To create the picture file, choose Save.

5. Type **COMPARE** and press Enter. (As with all file names, picture files can contain a maximum of eight characters.)

6. Retrieve the 3D BAR graph.

7. Create a picture file with the name **3DBAR**. (Note: While spaces are acceptable in graph names, they are not allowed in file names.)

8. Save the SALESHIS spreadsheet file.

LOADING PRINTGRAPH

There are two ways to load PrintGraph, and the method you choose depends on how you initially loaded 1-2-3. If you typed **123** to start the program, you type **PGRAPH** from the DOS prompt. If you typed **LOTUS**, you can select PrintGraph from the Lotus Access System menu.

Follow these steps to load PrintGraph:

1. To quit 1-2-3, press / to display the 1-2-3 menu and choose:

   Quit

   Yes

2. If you see the Lotus Access System menu (see Figure 2.1), choose PrintGraph. After a moment, you will see the screen shown in Figure 10.8. If you aren't in the Lotus Access System, complete the following steps.

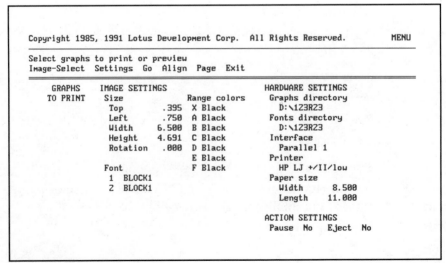

Figure 10.8: The PrintGraph screen

3. If necessary, change into your 1-2-3 directory. For example, type **CD\123R23** if your directory is called *123R23*.

4. Type **PGRAPH** and press Enter. After a moment, you will see the screen shown in Figure 10.8.

Notice that there is already a menu at the top of the screen—you do not need to press / to display the menu.

CHANGING
THE DEFAULT HARDWARE SETTINGS

The right-hand column of your PrintGraph screen indicates all your hardware settings. Before you can print, these settings must be accurate. First of all, you need to choose a graphics printer and density. The first time you use PrintGraph, no printer is selected. To choose a printer, follow these steps:

1. From the main PrintGraph menu, choose:

   Settings

   Hardware

   Printer

2. With the arrow keys (the mouse doesn't work in PrintGraph), highlight the graphic printer you want to use. When you select a printer name, you also choose a print density. The print density controls the quality of your printed output. The higher the density, the better the output quality, but the longer the print time. You may want to print first drafts at low density, and then select a higher density for your final graphs.

3. To select the printer, press the spacebar. A number sign (#) appears next to the name.

4. Press Enter to return to the hardware settings menu.

Study the other hardware settings on the PrintGraph screen: Graphs directory, Fonts directory, Interface, and Paper size. The *Graphs directory* is where your .PIC files are stored. Unless you created an additional subdirectory and are storing your files there, the default path should be accurate. The *Fonts directory* is where the PrintGraph font files are stored. When you install 1-2-3, they are copied into your 1-2-3 directory, so you shouldn't need to change this path unless you moved the .FNT files. The *Interface* is where your printer is connected to the computer. The default setting of *Parallel 1* works for most printers. The *Paper size* refers to the dimensions of the paper on which you are printing. Unlike in 1-2-3, when you print on a laser printer, you do not need to adjust the page length and width; the default size of 8½ by 11" works fine.

1. If necessary, change any of the other hardware settings.

2. To permanently save these settings, choose:

   Quit

   Save

The two Action settings are hardware-related. If you need to manually insert sheets of paper into your printer or plotter, and you are printing more than one graph, you should set the Pause option to Yes. If you want to print more than one graph on a page, leave the Eject option at its default setting (No). The graphs you will be printing in this chapter will be on separate pages, so let's turn on this option, as follows:

1. Choose:

   Settings

   Action

   Eject

   Yes

2. Quit to the main PrintGraph menu.

When you set the Eject option to Yes, you do not need to issue the Page command when the graph is finished printing. (Don't you wish 1-2-3's /Print command had an option like this?)

SELECTING THE GRAPH TO PRINT

When you print a report in 1-2-3, you indicate what you want to print by selecting a print range. To tell PrintGraph which graph to print, you select one or more .PIC files with the Image-Select command. Figure 10.9 shows the list of picture files that appears when you choose Image-Select. The right half of this screen gives you instructions on how to choose graphs to print. Use the arrow keys to highlight each graph you want to print and press the spacebar; a number sign (#) appears next to selected graph names. To unselect a graph, press the spacebar again; the number sign disappears. If your graph names are somewhat vague and you forget which graph is in a particular file, you can press F10 to view the graph.

Follow these steps to select and print the COMPARE graph:

1. From the main PrintGraph menu, choose Image-Select. Your screen should look similar to Figure 10.9. If you get a message that no graph files were found, either you did not save your graphs with /Graph Save or your graph directory is incorrect.

```
Copyright 1985, 1991 Lotus Development Corp.  All Rights Reserved.       POINT

Select graphs to print


  GRAPH FILE  DATE     TIME    SIZE
  ------------------------------------    Space bar marks or unmarks selection
  3DBAR       03-05-91 14:48   6727       ENTER selects marked graphs
  COMPARE     03-05-91 14:47   1510       ESC exits, ignoring changes
                                          HOME moves to beginning of list
                                          END moves to end of list
                                          ↑ and ↓ move highlight
                                            List will scroll if highlight
                                            moved beyond top or bottom
                                          GRAPH (F10) previews marked graph
```

Figure 10.9: The Image-Select screen

To change to a different graph directory, use the Settings Hardware Graph-Directory command.

2. Highlight the name COMPARE and press F10 to see which graph this is; then press any key.

3. Press the spacebar to select COMPARE.

4. Press Enter to return to the main PrintGraph menu. The screen now lists the graph name under the heading *Graphs to Print*.

5. To print the graph, choose:

   Align

   Go

If you selected a high-density printer, or if you have a slow printer, you will need to be very patient while the graph is printing. You may even want to take a coffee break. A high-density graph on an HP LaserJet II takes about a minute and on an Epson RX-80 about eight minutes. Your graph should look similar to the one in Figure 10.10.

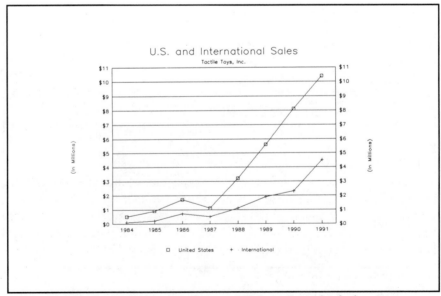

Figure 10.10: A line graph printed on an HP LaserJet at high density

Batch Printing

Because graph printing is a slow process and there is no way to print graphs in the background, you might want to print all your graphs at once—and then have lunch or go home for the day. Printing a group of graphs with a single print command is called *batch printing*.

Follow these steps to select and print a batch of graphs:

1. From the main PrintGraph menu, choose Image-Select.

2. Highlight each graph name you want to print and press the spacebar; press Enter when finished.

3. To print the selected graphs, choose:

   Align

   Go

The Eject option is important for batch printing because it places each graph on its own page. Also, when you batch print, each graph has the same format (size, fonts, and colors). These formatting options are described in the next section.

FORMATTING THE GRAPH

The Image Settings section of the PrintGraph screen displays the three ways you can format your graphs: Size, Font, and Range Colors.

Changing the Graph's Size

As you can see, the default graph size prints on half the page. Print-Graph also offers a full-page option that prints the graph sideways (even if you don't have a laser printer), and a manual option where you can specify the exact size and position of the graph on the page. The Half option creates a graph that is about $6\frac{1}{2}$ inches wide by $4\frac{1}{2}$ inches long. The

Full option creates a graph that is about 9½ by 7 inches, rotated 90 degrees (sideways). The Manual option presents you with the following menu choices:

Top Left Width Height Rotation

Use the Top and Left margin choices to position the graph on the page, and the Width and Height to specify the graph size. The Rotation option lets you print the graph sideways (a setting of 90 or 270 degrees), upside-down (180 degrees), or right-side up (0 degrees).

Follow these steps to change the graph size:

1. To specify a full-page graph, choose:

   Settings

   Image

   Size

   Full

2. Quit to the main PrintGraph menu.

Notice that when you choose the Full option, the size settings in the PrintGraph screen change. Because the graph prints sideways, the Rotation is set to 90 degrees. The other settings also reflect the full-page size, but the margins and size are defined according to a *vertical* page layout. Regardless of the graph's rotation, the dimensions are measured as if the graph were not rotated. Therefore, when you rotate the graph, none of the settings are what you might think they should be. The height setting is actually the width on a rotated graph and vice versa. On a 90-degree rotated graph, the top margin is actually the right margin, and the left margin is the top margin. If you find this to be terribly confusing, join the club. Fortunately, the Full option makes the appropriate settings for you. You need to interpret the settings only when you must change them manually.

To further complicate this issue, the margin settings are inaccurate for laser printers. As when you print reports with 1-2-3's /Print command, the laser's built-in margins are added to the specified margin settings. Thus, a $\frac{1}{2}$-inch top margin setting actually gives you a 1-inch margin.

Changing Fonts

Figure 10.11 lists the fonts that are available in PrintGraph. Many of the typefaces come in two different weights. For example, Block2 is the same typeface as Block1, but it is bolder. The "2" fonts are always heavier than the "1" fonts.

You can have two different fonts on your graph. *Font 1* controls the typeface of the first title on the graph. *Font 2* formats all other text on

This is an example of Block1

This is an example of Block2

This is an example of Bold

This is an example of Forum

This is an example of Italic1

This is an example of Italic2

This is an example of Lotus

This is an example of Roman1

This is an example of Roman2

This is an example of Script1

This is an example of Script2

Figure 10.11: PrintGraph fonts

the page. Usually you will want to use the heavier fonts for the main title (the fonts with *2* in their names or *Bold*) and the lighter fonts for the remaining text (the fonts with *1* in their names or *Lotus* or *Forum*).

Follow these steps to select new fonts for the graph:

1. To change Font 1, choose:

    Settings

    Image

    Font

    1

2. Highlight ROMAN2 and press the spacebar. A number sign appears next to the font name.

3. Press Enter.

4. To change Font 2, choose:

    Font

    2

5. Highlight ROMAN1 and press the spacebar.

6. Press Enter.

7. Quit to the main PrintGraph menu.

Now, let's print the 3DBAR graph with the revised settings you have made in the last several sections:

1. To make graph selections, choose Image-Select. Currently, both graphs are selected.

2. To unselect COMPARE, highlight it and press the spacebar. The number sign disappears from this name.

3. Press Enter.

4. To print the graph, choose:

    Align

    Go

Your printed graph should look similar to Figure 10.12. Notice that it was printed full-page size and rotated 90 degrees. The first title is in the ROMAN2 font and the other text is in ROMAN1.

Choosing Colors

PrintGraph prints your graphs in black and white—unless you assign colors with the Settings Image Range-Colors command. (Of course, you can print in color only if you have a color printer or plotter.) Each data

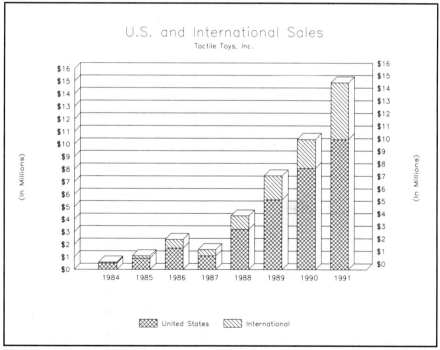

Figure 10.12: The 3DBAR graph, printed full-page size on an HP LaserJet II

range (X, A–F) can print in a different color: black, red, green, cyan, blue, magenta, and yellow.

RETURNING TO 1-2-3

When you are finished printing graphs and want to return to 1-2-3, follow these steps:

1. From the main PrintGraph menu, choose:

   Exit

   Yes

2. If you see the Lotus Access System menu, choose 1-2-3. Otherwise, at the DOS prompt, type **123** and press Enter.

MODIFYING A GRAPH

After you look at your printed graphs, you may discover a mistake or an ommission. To modify and reprint the graph, follow these general steps:

- In 1-2-3, retrieve the file.
- Retrieve the graph you wish to change (/Graph Name Use).
- Make the desired change.
- Save the revised settings under the same name (/Graph Name Create).
- Create a graph file with the same name as your previous .PIC file (/Graph Save).
- Save the spreadsheet file (/File Save).
- Quit 1-2-3, load PrintGraph, and print the revised graph file.

Chapter 10

Chapter 11

Chapter 12

Chapter 13

Chapter 14

Enhancing Graphs with the Graphics Editor in Release 2.3

◀▌▌▌ FAST TRACK ▌▌▌▶

To load the graphics editor: 363

Press : to display the Wysiwyg menu and choose Graph Edit. Move the cell pointer to any cell in the graph range and press Enter.

To load the graphics editor with the mouse: 363

Double-click on the graphic.

To preselect an object with the mouse: 377

Click on the object.

To preselect an object in the graphics editor: 378

From the main graphics editing menu, choose Select One. Place the cursor on the object to select and press Enter.

To magnify a portion of the graphic: 387

From the main graphics editing menu, choose View In. With the mouse, use the click-and-drag technique to draw a box around the area to be zoomed. If you don't have a mouse, place the cursor above and to the left of the area to be zoomed, and press the spacebar. Move the cursor below and to the right of the area, and press Enter.

To create an original graphic: 393

Press : to display the Wysiwyg menu and choose Graph Add Blank. Indicate a range the approximate size of the graphic you will be creating. Load the graphics editor and add text and shapes to create your design.

To import a graphic from another file: 401

Press : to display the Wysiwyg menu and choose Special Import Graphics. Select the name of the format file.

To import a graphics metafile: 404

Press : to display the Wysiwyg menu and choose Graph Add Metafile. If necessary, specify the path that contains the .CGM file, and press

Enter. Choose the .CGM file. Indicate a range that corresponds to the desired size of the graphic. If necessary, load the graphics editor and modify the graphic.

The graphics editor is a free-form drawing program that is part of Wysiwyg. With the editor, you can enhance your graphs with additional text, lines, shapes, and clip art. For example, you may want to explain an unusually high or low data point on a bar graph. Or perhaps you want to draw a box around your legends. You have the freedom of placing the supplemental text and graphics *anywhere* on the chart. This feature gives you the opportunity to be creative. You can even use the graphics editor to create your own graphic designs or to import external graphic images.

Be aware, though, that the graphics editor lets you add only *new* elements to your 1-2-3 graphs. Except for the colors of the data ranges, you cannot modify any part of the underlying graph.

Although you can use the mouse or the keyboard in the graphics editor, the mouse is infinitely faster and more convenient. Mouse users can simply point and click. Keyboard users must tap the arrow keys repeatedly and press Enter—it's awkward and cumbersome, to say the least. I highly recommend you use a mouse in the graphics editor.

LOADING THE GRAPHICS EDITOR

Before you can go into the graphics editor, you need a graph range in the spreadsheet. To edit an existing 1-2-3 graph, you insert it into a spreadsheet range with :Graph Add Named (or Current), as explained in Chapter 9. Later in the chapter you will learn how to use the graphics editor to draw graphics from scratch and to work with external graphic images.

There are two ways to load a graph into the graphics editor. The easiest way is with the mouse: place the mouse pointer on the graph and double-click. The alternative is to choose :Graph Edit and indicate which graph you want to edit.

In this part of the chapter, you will use the graphics editor to annotate a data point on the three-dimensional bar graph you created in Chapter 9. The annotated chart is shown in Figure 11.1. In this simple example you will learn how to add text, ellipses, and arrows.

Let's retrieve the SALESHIS file and annotate the 3D BAR graph in the graphics editor.

1. Retrieve SALESHIS. The 3D BAR graph has already been inserted into a spreadsheet range (A16..E26).

2. If you have a mouse, double-click on the graph to load the graphics editor. Otherwise, press **:** to display the Wysiwyg menu and choose:

   Graph

   Edit

3. Place the pointer anywhere in the graph range and press Enter.

Figure 11.2 shows the 3D BAR graph in the graphics editing window. When you are in the graphics editor, it's almost as if you were in a different program—a drawing program. First of all, your spreadsheet grid is not visible. The window restricts your view to the graph so you can concentrate on the task at hand. Second, the editing menu automatically displays at the top of the screen and is available at all times; you don't have

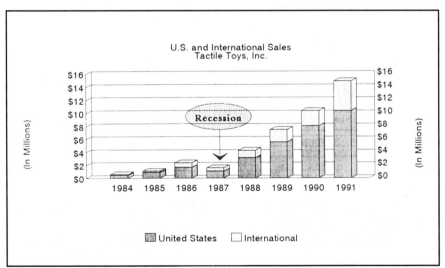

Figure 11.1: A chart annotated with the graphics editor

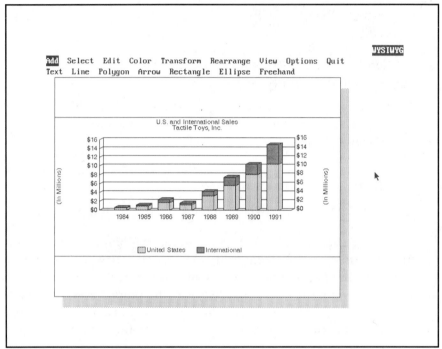

Figure 11.2: The 3D BAR graph in the graphics editing window

to press slash or colon to access it. To exit the graphics editor, you must choose Quit or press Ctrl-Break. (Pressing Esc or the right mouse button does not clear the menu.)

ADDING GRAPHIC ELEMENTS

Use the Add menu option to supplement your charts with graphic elements: text, lines, arrows, polygons, rectangles, and ellipses. You can even draw freehand if you have an artistic bent. Let's look at each of these elements in detail.

ADDING TEXT

With 1-2-3's /Graph commands, there are limitations to where you can place text. You can have titles and legends, but what if you want your chart to display additional comments or descriptions? That's where the graphics editor comes in handy—you can add text anywhere you find room for it.

Here are the basic steps for adding text to a chart:

- Choose:

    Add

    Text

- Type a single line of text (up to 240 characters). Alternatively, you can reference a cell that contains the text you want to add (for example, \A5). To format the text with special attributes (such as bold, italics, and outline), insert formatting codes as explained in Chapter 8. Refer to Table 8.3 for a list of formatting codes.

- Press Enter.

- Use the mouse or arrow keys to position the text on the graph.

- To confirm the final destination of the text, click the left mouse button or press Enter. Small boxes, called *selection indicators*, then surround the text. These boxes indicate that the object is selected and that you can perform another operation on it (delete, move, edit, and so on).

Let's add some text to the current graph:

1. Choose:

    Add

    Text

2. Next to *Text* at the top of the screen, type **Recession** and press Enter. The text is placed somewhere on the chart. If you don't spot it right away, move the mouse or press the arrow keys until you can see it.

3. With the mouse or arrow keys, move the text to the position shown in Figure 11.3. The X and Y coordinates at the top of the screen help you to position the object precisely. The X-value measures the number of units from the left edge of the window while the Y-value measures the units from the top. The text in Figure 11.3 was placed at X=1924 and Y=1502. (There are 4095 units both across and down in the graphics editing window.)

4. Click the left mouse button or press Enter to confirm this position.

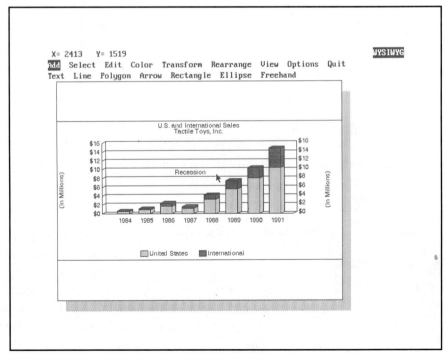

Figure 11.3: Text added to the 3D BAR graph

Editing Text

After you add text to a graph, you may discover that you have made a typing mistake or have forgotten to add formatting codes. The Text command on the Edit menu lets you modify the contents of text added with the graphics editor. To edit the text, you can use all the editing keys available in 1-2-3's EDIT mode. (For a list of cell-editing keys, refer to Table 3.2 in Chapter 3.) Note that you *cannot* edit text that you added with /Graph.

If the text is already selected (as *Recession* is now), you will not be asked to select the text to edit. Otherwise, you will need to move the cursor (shaped like a small cross) to the text and press Enter or click the mouse.

Follow these steps to insert formatting codes in the text you just added:

1. Choose:

    Edit

    Text

2. Press Home to move the cursor to the beginning of the text.

3. Press Ctrl-A to insert a begin-attribute code (▲) and type **b** for bold.

4. Press End to move the cursor to the end of the text.

5. Press Ctrl-N to insert an end-attribute code (▼).

6. Press Enter. The word *Recession* is now bolded.

Changing the Font

The text you insert in the graphics editor uses the default spreadsheet typeface and size (font 1). To use a different font, you can either insert formatting codes in the text or use the Font command on the Edit menu. The fonts available in the graphics editor are the eight fonts in the spreadsheet's font set. If you want to use a typeface or size that's not in the current font set, you must quit the graphics editor and replace one of the existing fonts (:Format Font Replace).

In Chapter 10, you learned another way to change the size of text in a graph: with the Font-Magnification command on the Options menu. To enlarge the text, enter a value over 100 (1000 is the maximum). To reduce, enter a value less than 100. Remember, this command changes the size of *all* the text in the chart, text added in the graphics editor as well as text in the underlying graph.

Let's change the font to 12-point Dutch (font 7). Choose:

> Edit
>
> Font
>
> 7

Note that this command does *not* allow you to change the font of text you have added with /Graph.

Changing the Color of Text

By default, the text you add in the graphics editor will print in black. (Note: If the background color of your screen is black, text appears white on the screen but prints in black.) If you have a color output device, you may want to print the text in a different color. To change colors, choose the Text option on the Color menu, and select one of the following colors: Black, White, Red, Green, Dark-Blue, Cyan, Yellow, or Magenta. You can only select text that you have created with the Add Text command. To change the color of your titles and legends, you must insert formatting codes (see Chapter 10). To change the color of the other text on the graph (the y-scale, x-axis labels, etc.), see the section *Specifying Colors and Gray Shading* later in this chapter.

DRAWING RECTANGLES AND ELLIPSES

You can use rectangles or ellipses to enclose text and other objects. In the current chart, you will enclose the word *Recession* in an ellipse. When you draw rectangles or ellipses, you need to indicate the upper-left and lower-right corners of the object.

To create a perfect circle or square, hold down the Shift key as you are drawing the shape.

Creating Shapes with the Mouse

If you have a mouse, follow these steps to draw an ellipse around the word *Recession*:

1. From the main graphics editing menu, choose:

   Add

   Ellipse

2. Place the cursor slightly above and to the left of the word *Recession*. Refer to Figure 11.4 for exact placement.

3. Click and hold the left mouse button as you drag the mouse slightly below and to the right of the word (see Figure 11.4). As you drag the mouse, a rectangle appears around the text. This rectangle, called a *bounding box*, will be replaced by an ellipse as soon as you finish drawing.

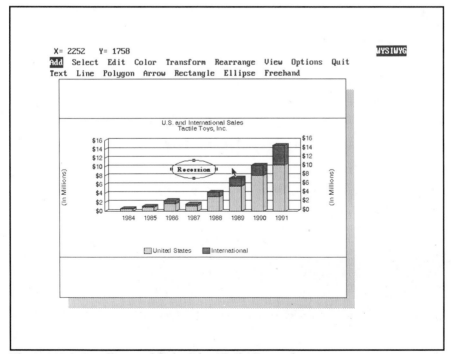

Figure 11.4: An ellipse added to the 3D BAR graph

4. Release the mouse button. The word is now enclosed in an ellipse.

Creating Shapes with the Keyboard

If you don't have a mouse, follow these steps to draw an ellipse around the word *Recession* with the keyboard:

1. From the main graphics editing menu, choose:

   Add

   Ellipse

2. With the arrow keys, place the cursor slightly above and to the left of the word *Recession*. Refer to Figure 11.4 for exact placement.

3. Press the spacebar.

4. Use → and ↓ to draw a box around the word. (This box, called a *bounding box*, will be replaced with an ellipse as soon as you finish drawing.)

5. When the lower-right corner is slightly below and to the right of the word (see Figure 11.4), press Enter. The word is now enclosed in an ellipse.

Changing the Line Style

The Line-Style option on the Edit menu controls the appearance of the outline around the object. The default style is solid. Figure 11.5 shows examples of the six line styles that are available. These line styles apply to any object that contains lines, not just rectangles and ellipses.

Changing Line Widths

The Width option on the Edit menu changes the line width of selected object(s) from very narrow (the default) to very wide. Figure 11.6 shows

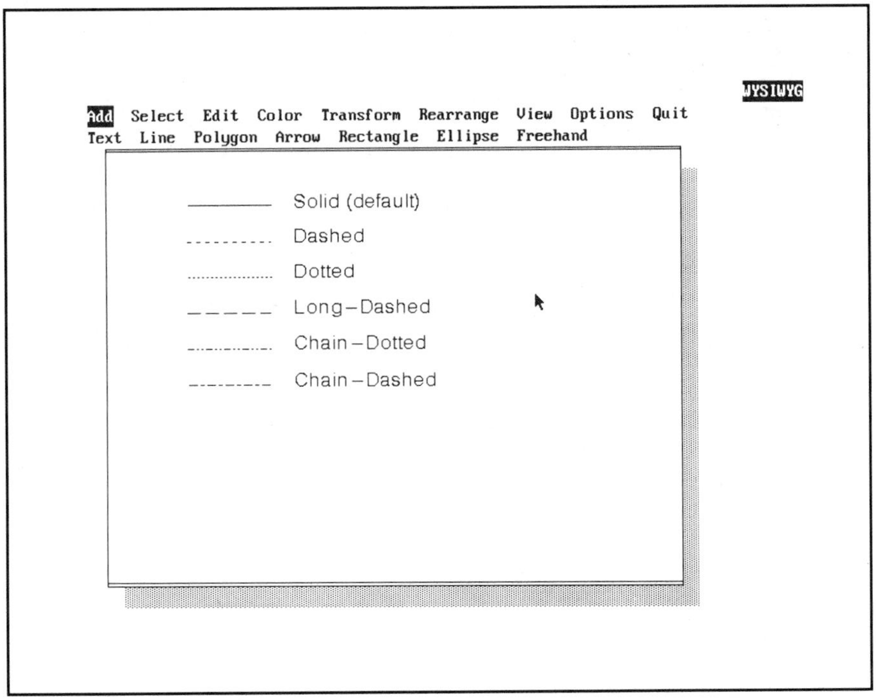

Figure 11.5: Line styles

examples of these line widths. Again, this option applies to any object created in the graphics editor that contains lines (lines, arrows, polygons, etc.).

Changing Line Colors

By default, the shapes you add in the graphics editor will print in black. (Note: If the background color of your screen is black, the shapes appear white on the screen but print in black.) If you have a color output device, you may want to print the lines in a different color. To change colors, choose the Lines option on the Color menu, and select one of the following colors: Black, White, Red, Green, Dark-Blue, Cyan, Yellow, or

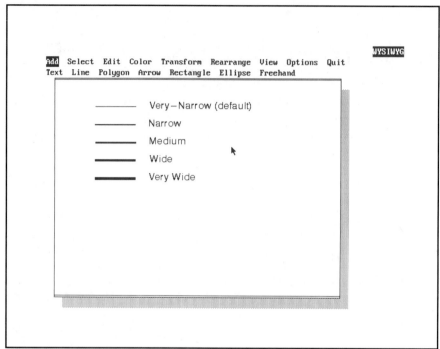

Figure 11.6: Line widths

Magenta. You can select any object that was created in the graphics editor—lines, arrows, ellipses, and so forth. To change the color of the other lines on the graph (the axes, frame, and grid lines), see the section *Specifying Color and Gray Shading* later in this chapter.

Smoothing the Angles

The Smoothing option on the Edit menu changes the angles of an object. With this option, you can create smooth curves out of sharp angles, or sharp angles out of smooth curves. The most common use for this option is to create a rectangle with rounded corners. Three different levels of smoothing are available. *Tight* smoothing slightly rounds the object's angles. *Medium* smoothing rounds the angles to an even greater degree. *None* replaces curves with 90-degree angles. Figure 11.7 compares a rectangle with different levels of smoothing.

Notice that Medium smoothing turns a rectangle into an ellipse. To turn an ellipse into a rectangle, use the None option.

In addition to rectangles and ellipses, smoothing applies to polygons, freehand drawings, and line segments that are connected.

ADDING LINES AND ARROWS

Whether you are creating a straight line or an arrow, the procedure is the same: You indicate where you want the line to begin and where you

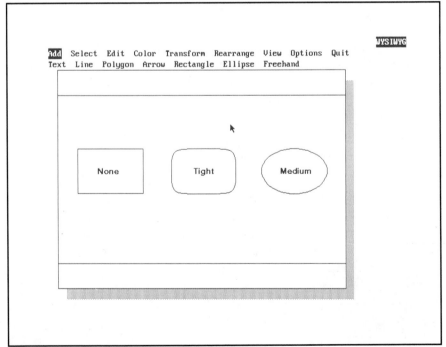

Figure 11.7: The three levels of smoothing

want it to end. In the case of an arrow, the beginning of the line is the tail and the end of the line is the arrowhead. As you are drawing a line, you may notice that it looks a little jagged. To straighten the line, hold down Shift. The Shift key rotates the line to the closest 45 degree angle. For example, to draw a vertical line, hold down Shift before you specify the end of the line.

After you create lines and arrows, you can change the line style and width with the appropriate options on the Edit menu.

Creating an Arrow with the Mouse

If you have a mouse, follow these steps to draw an arrow from the ellipse to the 1987 bar:

1. To create an arrow, choose:

    Add

    Arrow

2. The top of the screen displays the prompt, *First point*. The arrow should begin at the edge of the ellipse, as shown in Figure 11.8. Place the center of the cursor at the edge of the ellipse and click the left mouse button.

3. The top of the screen displays the prompt *Next point*. Hold down the Shift key to keep the line straight, and place the center of the cursor slightly above the 1987 bar. A line draws as you move the mouse.

4. Double-click the left mouse button to complete the arrow. If you single-click instead of double-click, 1-2-3 thinks you want to keep drawing lines, and you will be asked for the *Next point* again; if this happens, press the right mouse button to cancel and try again. Your graph should look similar to Figure 11.8.

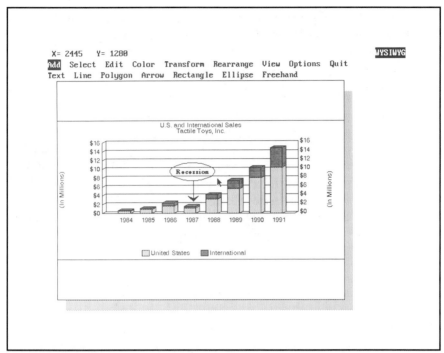

Figure 11.8: An arrow was drawn from the ellipse to the 1987 data point.

Creating an Arrow with the Keyboard

If you don't have a mouse, follow these steps to draw an arrow from the ellipse to the 1987 bar:

1. To create an arrow, choose:

    Add

    Arrow

2. The top of the screen is prompting you for the *First point*. The arrow should begin at the edge of the ellipse, as shown in Figure 11.8. With the arrow keys, place the center of the cursor at the edge of the ellipse and press the spacebar.

3. The top of the screen prompts you for the *Next point*. Hold down the Shift key and place the center of the cursor slightly above the 1987 bar.

4. Press Enter to complete the arrow. Your graph should look similar to Figure 11.8.

Modifying the Arrowhead

The arrowhead automatically points from the second point you indicate. If you want to point the arrow in the opposite direction, or in both directions, you can use the Arrowhead option on the Edit menu. Four options are available. *Switch* moves the arrowhead to the opposite end of the line, *One* turns a line into an arrow, *Two* adds arrowheads to both ends of the line, and *None* turns an arrow into a line.

CREATING POLYGONS

A *polygon* is a shape bounded by three or more line segments. Triangles, rectangles, and octagons are examples of polygons. Note that it's not necessary to connect the last side of the polygon—Wysiwyg automatically connects the first and last points so that the shape is completely enclosed. Here is the basic procedure for creating a polygon:

- Choose:

    Add

    Polygon

- Move the cursor to the first point of the polygon.

- Press the spacebar or left mouse button to add this point.

- Move the cursor to the next point and press the spacebar or left mouse button to add the point. A line connects these two points. Repeat this step for each point.

- When you are finished, double-click the left mouse button or press Enter. (Remember, you don't have to connect the first and last points.)

SELECTING OBJECTS

Once you add objects to a graph, you can edit or modify them in different ways. With text, you can change the font or color. With shapes and lines, you can change the line style, width, or color. Any of the objects can be moved, sized, copied, or deleted. Regardless of what command you issue, you must select the object you want to modify. If you just added the item, it is already selected. When an object is selected, it has small selection indicators on or around it.

When you issue commands that change an existing object, the graphics editor will change the object that is currently selected—the one that has the selection indicators around it. If no object is selected, the graphics editor will ask you to select an object. Let's look at an example. Let's say you want to change the width of the lines in the ellipse. If the ellipse is selected when you give the Edit Width command, the ellipse's line widths will be changed—just what you wanted. However, if the arrow is selected, the arrow's line width will be changed because you aren't given an opportunity to select a different object.

Therefore, you should keep a sharp eye on which item is selected before you issue a command, or you might end up modifying the wrong object. One solution to this problem is to select the appropriate object *before* you issue a command. An alternate solution is to select no objects so that the graphics editor will prompt you to select an object.

PRESELECTING WITH THE MOUSE

Preselecting with the mouse couldn't be easier: just click on the object. You must be at the graphics editing main menu to preselect objects; if you are in a submenu, you will get beeped at. To unselect all objects, click anywhere in the graphics editing window except on an object.

Follow these steps to select and modify the ellipse with the mouse:

1. If necessary, press Esc until the main graphics editing menu displays.

2. To preselect the object, click on the outline of the ellipse. (Because the text is so close to the ellipse, you may accidentally select the wrong object. Keep trying until the outline of the ellipse displays selection indicators.)

3. To modify the selected object, choose:

   Edit

   Width

   5:Very-Wide

4. Because this line width is inappropriate, return the width to Very-Narrow.

PRESELECTING WITH THE KEYBOARD

Preselecting with the keyboard is not nearly as simple as with the mouse. You have to choose the One option on the Select menu, then use the arrow keys to move the cursor to the object you want to select, and press Enter. To unselect all objects, choose the None option on the Select menu. You can see why I recommend a mouse for the graphics editor!

Follow these steps to select and modify the ellipse:

1. To preselect the object, choose:

   Select

   One

2. Move the cursor to the outline of the ellipse and press Enter.

3. To modify the selected object, choose:

   Edit

   Width

   5:Very-Wide

4. Because this line width is inappropriate, return the width to Very-Narrow.

PRESELECTING MULTIPLE OBJECTS

If you want to make the same modifications to several objects, you can preselect all of them before you issue the command. For example, suppose you have added three lines of text to a graph and you want to change the font of all three lines. Instead of selecting and issuing the Edit Font command for each one, you can preselect the three objects and issue the Edit Font command once. Another instance where you might want to preselect multiple objects is when you need to move related items to another location. For example, suppose you want to move the ellipse, the text, and the arrow. If you select all three items, you can move them as a single unit.

To select multiple objects with the mouse, hold down the Shift key as you click on each object. If you want to select all the objects in a certain area (for example, the ellipse, text, and arrow), you can use the click-and-drag technique to draw a box around the objects. As soon as you release the mouse button, the box will disappear, but each of the objects inside the box will be selected.

The Select menu offers several options for preselecting multiple objects:

- *All*—selects all items added with the graphics editor
- *More/Less*—lets you point to the objects you want to select
- *Cycle*—one at a time, it goes around to each object, and gives you the opportunity to select it
- *Graph*—selects the underlying graph

With the More/Less option, you point to each object you want to select or unselect and press the spacebar. When you are finished, press Enter. The Cycle option cycles through all the objects, one at a time, letting you select as many objects as you like. Each time you press an arrow key (any arrow), a different object is surrounded with small hollow boxes. When this occurs you can select the object by pressing the spacebar. If the object is already selected, pressing the spacebar unselects it. Continue pressing the arrow key and the spacebar until you have selected all desired objects. Press Enter when you are finished.

SPECIFYING
COLORS AND GRAY SHADING

Even if you do not have a color monitor or a color output device, don't skip over this section! The graphics editor's Color option also lets you fill in your shapes with gray shades. For example, the ellipse in Figure 11.9 is filled in with a light shade of gray.

You can change the color or shade of the following items:

- *Lines* (includes lines, arrows, and the outlines of ellipses, rectangles, polygons, and freehand drawings)

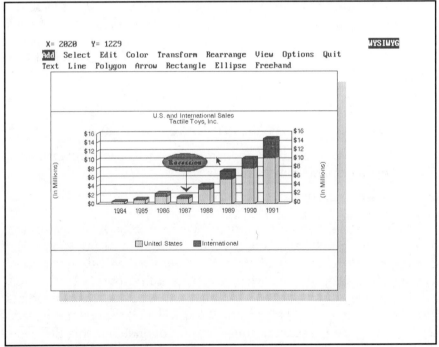

Figure 11.9: The ellipse is filled with a light shade of gray.

- *Inside* (the area inside ellipses, rectangles, polygons, and freehand drawings)

- *Text* (refers to text added in the graphics editor)

- *Background* (the area behind the graph)

- *Map* (the colors in the underlying graph)

Changing the color of text and lines was discussed earlier in the chapter. In this section, we will concentrate on the three other color options (Inside, Background, and Map).

WORKING IN BLACK-AND-WHITE MODE

If you have a color monitor but don't have a color output device, you may want to tell Wysiwyg to work in black-and-white mode. That way, you can see your graph with the exact shades that will be printed. Follow these steps if you wish to work in black-and-white mode:

1. Choose Quit to exit the graphics editor.

2. Press : to display the Wysiwyg menu and choose:

   Display
   Mode
   B&W
   Quit

3. To go back into the graphics editor, double-click on the graph or choose :Graph Edit.

If you have a color monitor, your graph will now display with gray-shaded bars.

CHANGING COLORS AND SHADES

When you choose Inside or Background on the Color menu, you are presented with a full screen of numbered colors or gray shades, as shown in Figure 11.10. This screen is called the *color palette*. The current color/shade has a box drawn around it (color number 1 in Figure 11.10). To choose a different shade, point to the new color with the mouse or arrow keys, and then click or press Enter.

Refer to the color palette in Figure 11.10, and notice that there is a lot of repetition of shades when you are working in black-and-white. For example, colors 1, 33, and 49 are white and colors 201 and 217 are black. (Note: If the background color of your screen is black, the black and white in the color palette are the opposite of the normal settings. For example,

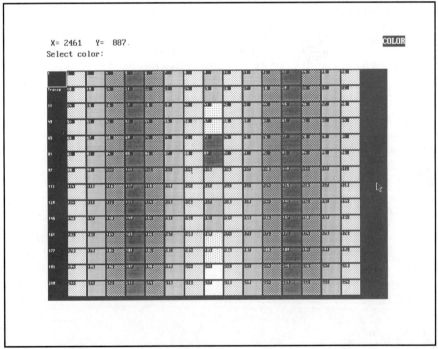

Figure 11.10: The color palette

colors 1, 33, and 49 are black, and colors 201 and 207 are white.) Those of you who are working in color will notice repetition to a lesser degree. In case of duplicate colors or shades, it doesn't matter which one you choose.

By default, all shapes you add are transparent, meaning that anything underneath the shape will show through. For example, when you drew the ellipse on top of existing text, you didn't have any problem seeing the text underneath. It's as if you had drawn the shape on a clear piece of plastic and placed it over the graph. As you will see in the following exercise, when you change the color from transparent to a gray shade or color, the text underneath is temporarily covered up.

Before you shade the ellipse, you should preselect the object. With the mouse, click on the outline of the ellipse. With the keyboard, choose:

Select

One

Then move the cursor to the outline of the ellipse and press Enter.

The reason you preselected the object is that the Color Inside command automatically colorizes any selected objects. If a different object had been selected before you issued the Color Inside command, that object would be colorized, not the ellipse. If no object is selected, it is not necessary to preselect.

Follow these steps to shade the ellipse:

1. Choose:

   Color

   Inside

2. The color is currently transparent (the box marked *Transp*). Place the mouse pointer on color 213. With the keyboard, press ↓ and → to move the box to color 213.

3. Click the mouse button or press Enter. Your screen should look similar to Figure 11.11.

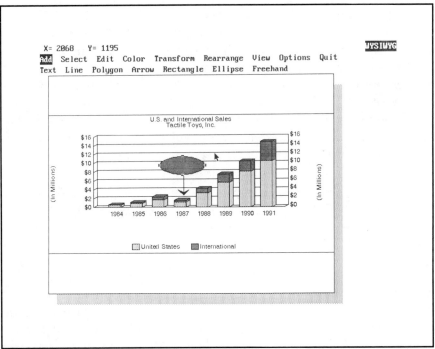

Figure 11.11: The text is hidden underneath the shaded ellipse.

THE CASE OF THE DISAPPEARING OBJECT

When the ellipse was transparent, you had no problem seeing the text. But now that you have shaded the ellipse, the text is hidden underneath it (see Figure 11.11). To rectify this situation, you need to bring the text in front of the ellipse or place the ellipse in back of the text. This is done with the Back and Front commands on the Rearrange menu. Because the ellipse is selected, you will use the Back option.

To place the ellipse behind the text, as shown in Figure 11.12, choose:

Rearrange

Back

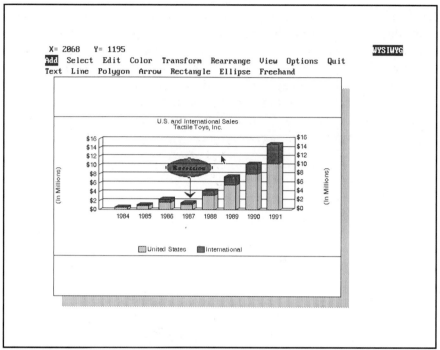

Figure 11.12: The text reappears once the shaded ellipse is sent to the back

COLOR MAPPING

The Map option on the Color menu lets you change the colors in the underlying 1-2-3 graph. Color mapping is similar to PrintGraph's Range-Colors option, yet it is more powerful. You can choose different colors or shades for almost every part of the graph:

- the data ranges (for example, the colors of the bars in a bar graph)

- text (titles, legends, and other labels)

- lines (the frame and grid lines)

When you choose Map on the Color menu, the control panel displays the numbers 1 through 8. These numbers are codes for different areas of the graph. Code 1 controls the color of the frame around the graph, grid lines, the outline around the bars and legend boxes, the numbers on the y-scale, the x-axis labels, and the titles. Codes 2 through 7 control the color of the six data ranges, A–F. Table 11.1 describes each of the codes. It would be nice if the menu options were more descriptive, or even if the Help key explained what the codes stand for, but no such luck.

Let's say you prefer a different color/shade for the B range (code 3). Follow these steps to assign a new color:

1. Choose:

    Color

    Map

    3

2. Choose color 121 (Cyan) in the color palette.

3. Choose Quit.

The bars and legend for the international sales data are now Cyan (or a different gray shade if you are working in black-and-white mode).

Table 11.1: Color Mapping Codes

CODE	AREA	DEFAULT COLOR (NUMBER)
1	Text and Lines	White (1)
2	A range	Blue (137)
3	B range	Green (73)
4	C range	Cyan (105)
5	D range	Red (9)
6	E range	Magenta (169)
7	F range	Yellow (41)
8	Undefined	Black (201)

UP CLOSE AND PERSONAL

For precise positioning of objects, you may want to zoom or magnify a portion of the screen. The View menu provides a number of options for getting "up close and personal" with your graph:

Full In Pan + – Up Down Left Right

The easiest way to zero in on a particular portion of the screen is with the In option. With this option, you draw a box around the area you want to magnify. The graphics editing window will then focus on this enlarged area. To further enlarge it, choose the + option on the View menu. Each time you choose +, the area is enlarged with a greater level of magnification. Five levels are available. To reduce the area, choose the – option. Actually, you don't even need to go to the View menu to zoom: Press + or – from the main graphics editing menu, and the graph will enlarge or reduce. To view a different part of the graph, choose the Up, Down, Left, or Right commands on the View menu. Each of these options moves you a half-screen in the direction you indicate.

Another way to position and magnify the graph is with the Pan option. When you choose View Pan, you can press + to enlarge, – to reduce, and the four arrow keys to move one half-screen in the direction of the arrow. The advantage of the Pan option is that you can do all your positioning and zooming at once, without having to return repeatedly to the View menu.

The Full option on the View menu returns the graph to its original size in the graphics editing window.

Let's zoom in on the ellipse and arrow:

1. From the main graphics editing menu, choose:

    View

    In

2. If you have a mouse, use the click-and-drag technique to draw a box around the ellipse and arrow. The screen is now focused on this area, as shown in Figure 11.13.

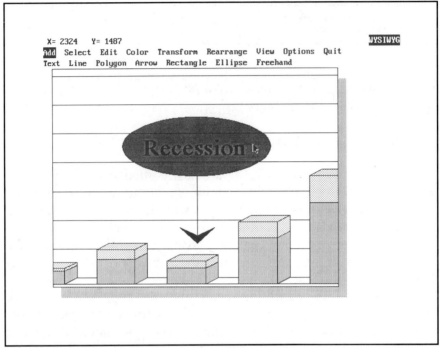

Figure 11.13: Zooming in on a portion of the graph

3. If you don't have a mouse, place the cursor above and to the left of the ellipse, and press the spacebar. Move the cursor below and to the right of the arrow and press Enter. The screen is now focused on this area, as shown in Figure 11.13.

To view other parts of the graph, use the Pan option as follows:

1. From the graphics editor's main menu, choose:

   View

   Pan

2. As the top of the screen instructs you, use ↑, ↓, →, and ← to view other parts of the graph.

3. To zoom in further, press +.

4. To zoom out, press –.

5. Press Enter to leave the panning screen.

6. To return the graph to full-screen size, choose:

   View

   Full

FINE-TUNING YOUR OBJECTS' SIZE AND POSITION

No one can draw every object perfectly. It's inevitable that sooner or later you will draw an object too small or too big or in the wrong place. That's why the graphics editor contains the Rearrange and Transform menus. With the options on these menus, you can delete, move, copy, and re-size objects created in the graphics editor.

The graphics editor offers several tools to help you align, place, and size objects. First, it frequently helps to magnify the area you are working with. Second, you can display the spreadsheet's grid lines with the Grid option on the Options menu. The dotted grid lines don't print, but they can help you align elements on the screen. If the grid lines don't fall in the right place, you can create your own guides by drawing temporary lines. I used this last technique to align the baselines of the three objects in Figure 11.7. After aligning the objects, I deleted the temporary guideline.

Before you rearrange or change the size of your objects, it's a good idea to save your file—even if Undo is enabled. Alt-F4 (Undo) does not work on certain operations in the graphics editor. You can quit the graphics editor and press Alt-F4, but 1-2-3 undoes *everything* you just did in the graphics editor: *all* additions, deletions, repositioning, and resizing. If the file is saved and then you make a big mistake, you can retrieve the file and try again. To save the file, you must quit the graphics editor. Follow these steps:

1. Quit the graphics editor.

2. Save the file with the same name (SALESHIS).

3. Reload the graph into the graphics editor.

DELETING OBJECTS

To remove an object you no longer want, select it, and choose the Delete option on the Rearrange menu. A faster way is to select the object and press the Del key. To bring back the last item you deleted, choose Restore on the Rearrange menu.

MOVING OBJECTS

You can reposition an object or a group of objects with the Move command on the Rearrange menu. While you are in the process of moving an item, a copy of the object appears inside a dotted rectangle called the *bounding box*, and a pudgy little hand appears inside the copy. It is the bounding box that you position—not the actual object. As soon as you press Enter or click the mouse button, the object moves into its new location.

If you have a mouse, you don't need to choose a menu option—just select the object(s) and use the click-and-drag technique to move the objects into their new position.

It's more than likely that the ellipse, text, or arrow is slightly out of position. Follow these steps to zoom in on this area and then move objects if necessary:

1. Use the In command on the View menu to zoom in on the ellipse area. (See the previous exercise for complete steps on this process.)

2. Study the screen to see whether the text is centered inside the ellipse and the arrow begins at the ellipse edge. If you find an object that is out of position, select it.

3. From the main graphics editing menu, choose:

   Rearrange

   Move

4. With the mouse or arrow keys, move the bounding box into the new location.

5. Press Enter or click the mouse button to move the object.

6. Repeat steps 3 through 5 for each object you need to move.

RESIZING AN OBJECT

While you are zoomed-in on the annotated area of your graph, you may also notice that the ellipse is the wrong size or the arrow is too long or too short. The Size command on the Transform menu lets you adjust the size of all objects except text.

When you are sizing an object, a bounding box appears around it. The upper-left corner of the box is fixed while the lower-right corner is adjustable. For example, to make the object longer, move the lower-right corner down by pressing ↓ or by moving the mouse down. Because you are forced to size the object from the lower-right corner, you may end up having to move the object after you have sized it.

1. Study the screen to see if the arrow is too long or too short, or if the ellipse is incorrectly sized. If you find an object that needs to be resized, select it.

2. From the main graphics editing menu, choose:

    Transform

    Size

3. With the mouse or arrow keys, make the bounding box the desired size.

4. Press Enter or click the mouse button to move the object.

5. Repeat steps 2 through 4 for each object you need to resize.

You are now finished with your annotated graph. To print the final graph (as shown in Figure 11.14), follow these steps:

1. Quit the graphics editor.

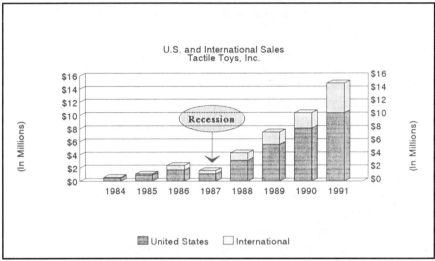

Figure 11.14: The annotated graph printed on an HP LaserJet II

2. To print, press **:** to display the Wysiwyg menu and choose:

   Print

   Range

   Set

3. Specify the graph range, A16..E26, and press Enter.

4. Choose a high-density printer.

5. Set left and right margins of 1.5 inches.

6. Choose Go.

7. Save the file.

COPYING OBJECTS

If you need an object to be the same size and shape as an existing one, you can clone the original with the Copy command on the Rearrange menu. This command also comes in handy when you are experimenting with different options: you can make copies of an item, try different options on each one, and then decide which one you prefer. The Copy command copies the object's size, shape, font, line-style, width, arrowheads, smoothing, and color.

The Copy command does not ask you for a target location. The clone is placed on top of the original, but is offset slightly so you can easily see the duplicate. You will then need to use the Move command to place the duplicate in the desired target location. Therefore, copying is actually a two-step process.

Another way to copy an object is to select it and press the Ins key.

CREATING
AN ORIGINAL GRAPHIC

So far, you have used the graphics editor only to enhance a 1-2-3 graph. As mentioned at the beginning of this chapter, you can also use the graphics editor to create your own designs and images. While Wysiwyg's graphics-manipulation capabilities are impressive for a spreadsheet program, they do not rival the features included in dedicated graphics programs, such as CorelDRAW or Arts & Letters.

In this section, you will create the logo shown at the top of the report in Figure 11.15. This logo was created in a separate file and then imported into the SALESHIS file. The design consists of two ellipses (a solid-black ellipse behind a shaded one) and two text strings (*tactile* and *toys*). The words and the ellipses are rotated to create a playful effect.

If you intend to draw a graphic from scratch, you must first create an empty graph range with :Graph Add Blank; the size of the range should correspond to the approximate size of the graphic you will be creating.

Follow these steps to begin creating the logo:

1. Clear the screen (/Worksheet Erase).

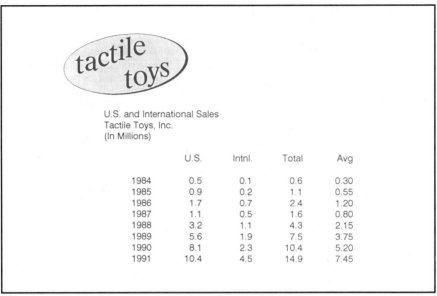

U.S. and International Sales
Tactile Toys, Inc.
(In Millions)

	U.S.	Intnl.	Total	Avg
1984	0.5	0.1	0.6	0.30
1985	0.9	0.2	1.1	0.55
1986	1.7	0.7	2.4	1.20
1987	1.1	0.5	1.6	0.80
1988	3.2	1.1	4.3	2.15
1989	5.6	1.9	7.5	3.75
1990	8.1	2.3	10.4	5.20
1991	10.4	4.5	14.9	7.45

Figure 11.15: The logo was created in the graphics editor.

2. Press **:** to display the Wysiwyg menu and choose:

   Graph

   Add

   Blank

3. Paint the range A1..C6 and press Enter.

4. Load the graphics editor (:Graph Edit or double-click on the graph range).

Add and format the text:

1. Use the Add Text command to add the word **tactile** and place it approximately in the middle of the window (Add Text).

2. Then type the word **toys** and place it underneath *tactile*.

3. Select both items and change the font to 12-point Dutch (Edit Font 7). This type size is much too small for the logo, so you need to use the Font-Magnification option to enlarge the text.

4. To enlarge the text, choose:

   Options

   Font-Magnification

5. Type **900** and press Enter. This number enlarges the text 900 percent.

6. Move the text so that each line is positioned as in Figure 11.16.

Create the two ellipses:

1. Draw an ellipse around the text (Add Ellipse). Refer to Figure 11.16 for the size of this ellipse.

2. Fill the inside of the ellipse with Green, color 74 (Color Inside).

3. Send the ellipse to the back (Rearrange Back).

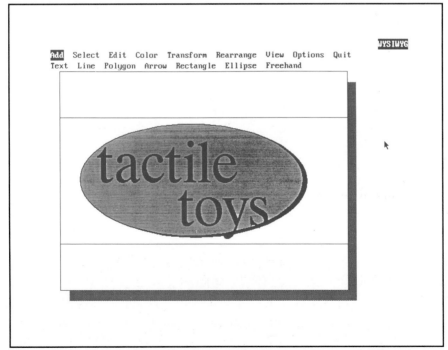

Figure 11.16: The shadow effect is created with two ellipses of different colors.

4. Press Ins to create a copy of the ellipse.

5. Fill the inside of this ellipse with Black, color 1. (Note: If the background of your screen is black, choose white. When you print, the white converts to black.)

6. Move the black (or white) ellipse up and to the left so that all of the green ellipse is obscured except for its upper-left edge.

7. Send the black (or white) ellipse to the back. Your logo should look similar to Figure 11.16. If you don't get a pleasing shadow effect, bring the black (or white) ellipse to the front, and try moving it again.

When your logo is just right, save the file, as follows:

1. Quit the graphics editor.

2. Save the file with the name **LOGO**.

3. Reload the logo into the graphics editor.

TRANSFORMING YOUR IMAGES

With the options on the Transform menu, you can make your graphics do backflips, somersaults, and cartwheels. You can slant or rotate your text and objects (for example, sideways or upside-down) and stretch standard objects to create new shapes (for example, to create a parallelogram out of a rectangle). In the upcoming exercise, you will get an opportunity to see some of these gymnastics in action.

ROTATING AN OBJECT IN 90-DEGREE INCREMENTS

The Quarter-Turn option on the Transform menu rotates the selected objects in 90-degree increments. Each time you choose Quarter-Turn, the selected objects are rotated 90 degrees, counterclockwise. This option is typically used to print a few lines of text in an orientation different from the rest of the page. Figure 11.17 shows text rotated one quarter-turn.

ROTATING
AN OBJECT IN ANY INCREMENT

Object rotation is not limited to 90-degree increments. With the Rotate option on the Transform menu, you can rotate an object in any increment. This option was used to create the slanted text in the logo shown in Figure 11.18.

While you are rotating an object, an axis extends from the center of the object. This axis is like a handle that rotates the object in the direction you press the arrow keys or move the mouse. Actually, you rotate a copy of the selected object, but as soon as you press Enter or click the mouse button, the original is moved into position.

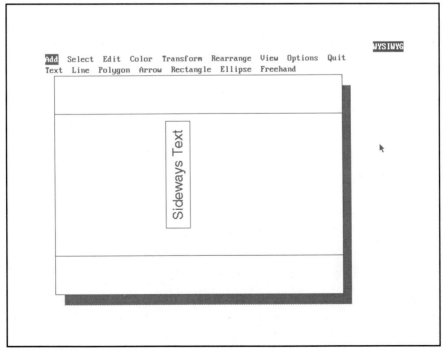

Figure 11.17: Text rotated one quarter-turn

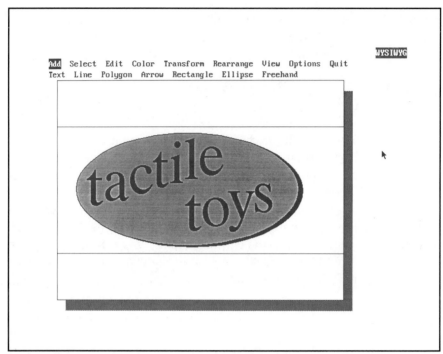

Figure 11.18: The slanted text was created with the Rotate option.

Follow these steps to rotate the text:

1. Select *tactile* and *toys*. (The ellipses should *not* be selected.)

2. From the main graphics editing menu, choose:

   Transform

   Rotate

3. Press ↑ or move the mouse up until the bounding box is rotated approximately 15 degrees counterclockwise.

4. Press Enter or click the mouse button.

5. If necessary, move the text so that it matches Figure 11.18.

FLIPPING OBJECTS

The X-Flip and Y-Flip options are two additional ways of rotating objects. The Y-Flip option turns an object upside down while the X-Flip option faces the object in the opposite direction. If you flip the object in the wrong direction, you can reverse your action by choosing the same option again (X-Flip or Y-Flip).

SKEWING AN OBJECT

The Horizontal and Vertical options on the Transform menu allow you to change the angles and size of an object. This process is sometimes referred to as *skewing*. When you transform an object horizontally, the upper part of the bounding box remains stationary as you freely move the other three sides of the bounding box in any direction. When you transform vertically, the left side of the bounding box is stationary.

To place the logo at a slight upward angle, skew it vertically, as follows:

1. To select all objects in the logo, choose:

   Select

   All

2. To skew the logo, choose:

   Transform

   Vertical

3. Press ↑ or move the mouse up until the bounding box is rotated approximately 15 degrees counterclockwise.

4. Press → or move the mouse to the right until the bounding box is slightly elongated.

5. Press Enter or click the mouse button.

6. If the top of the ellipse doesn't fit on the screen, move the logo down. Your logo should now look similar to Figure 11.19.

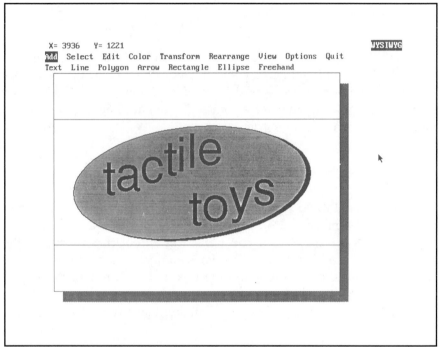

Figure 11.19: A skewed logo

If you aren't satisfied with your results, choose the Clear option on the Transform menu. This option returns the selected objects to their original size, angles, and rotation.

LOCKING OBJECTS

Once an object is the perfect size, in the perfect position, with the exact options you want, it's a good idea to use the Lock option on the Rearrange menu to prevent it from being accidentally changed. A locked object cannot be deleted, moved, sized, rotated, colorized, or edited. The one thing you can do to a locked object is copy it. If you later need to change a locked object, choose the Unlock option on the Rearrange menu.

IMPORTING THE LOGO

The logo is finished. All that's left to do before you import it into a spreadsheet is to move it into the upper-left corner of the graph range. This position is important because this is where you want the logo to appear when it's imported.

1. To select all elements of the logo, choose:

    Select

    All

2. Move the logo into the upper-left corner of the graphics editing window. Make sure all four sides of the bounding box are inside the window.

3. Quit the graphics editor.

4. Save the file.

Now that you have finished your logo, you are ready to import it into a spreadsheet where it will appear at the top of the report (see Figure 11.20). To copy a graphic between files, you will use the :Special Import Graphs command.

1. Retrieve SALESHIS.

2. Insert eight rows at the top of the spreadsheet (/Worksheet Insert Row).

3. Insert one column to the left of the spreadsheet (/Worksheet Insert Column).

4. To import the logo, press : to display the Wysiwyg menu and choose:

    Special

    Import

    Graphs

402

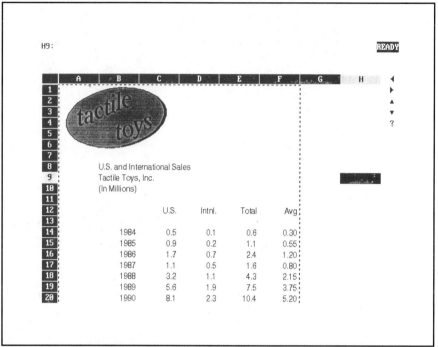

Figure 11.20: The imported logo

5. Select the file named LOGO.FMT. The logo is imported into the current spreadsheet, as shown in Figure 11.20.

6. Set one-inch left and right margins, and print the range A1..F22. The printed report should resemble Figure 11.15.

7. Save the file.

WORKING WITH
EXTERNAL GRAPHIC IMAGES

The graphics editor can import only two types of external graphic images—1-2-3 picture files (extension .PIC) and computer graphic metafiles (extension .CGM). *Metafile* is a standard format that most graphics packages can import and export. For example, if you have created a graphic image in CorelDRAW, you can export it to metafile format and import it into the graphics editor. You can also purchase stand-alone clip art packages that contain a selection of .CGM files. *Clip art* refers to simple drawings of animals, people, holiday items, buildings, office equipment, and so on. The tiger in Figure 11.21 is an example of a .CGM file.

VIEWING METAFILES

1-2-3 includes a few sample metafiles that you can import. These .CGM files are located in the 1-2-3 program directory (for example, C:\123R23). To view a metafile before you import it, use the :Graph View command.

Follow these steps to look at several of the metafiles included with 1-2-3:

1. Press **:** to display the Wysiwyg menu and choose:

    Graph

Figure 11.21: The tiger is a .CGM file.

View

Metafile

2. If necessary, change the path to your 1-2-3 directory (for example, *C:\123R23*) and press Enter.

3. Press F3 to see a complete list of metafile names.

4. Choose one of the .CGM files.

5. Repeat steps 1 through 4 to view other metafiles.

IMPORTING A METAFILE

To import a metafile, use the :Graph Add Metafile command. Just as when you add 1-2-3 graphs, you need to choose a name and define a graph range. The graph range can be an empty spreadsheet range or it can overlay a range of data or another graph range. Figure 11.22 shows a car graphic (range C31..E33) that was added to a 1-2-3 graph (range A16..H35). When you overlay a graphic over data or another graphic, you may need to make the graphic transparent. Use :Graph Settings Opaque No to see underlying data or graphics.

The size of your graph range determines the size of the imported metafile. Pay attention to the proportions of the original graphic when defining your graph range. If the original metafile is short and fat and you define a tall and narrow range, your imported graphic will be distorted. However, there are times when you may want this distortion. Compare the cars in Figure 11.23. The cars appear to be two completely different models because of the dimensions of the graph ranges.

Follow these steps to create the no-smoking sign shown in Figure 11.24:

1. Clear the screen (/Worksheet Erase).

2. Press : to display the Wysiwyg menu and choose:

Graph

Add

Metafile

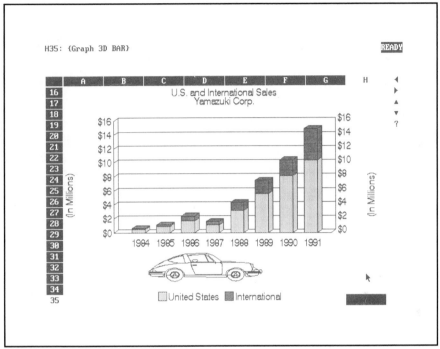

Figure 11.22: The car is a .CGM file added to a 1-2-3 graph.

3. If necessary, change the path to your 1-2-3 directory (for ex-
    ample, *C:\123R23*) and press Enter.

4. Press F3 to see a complete list of metafile names.

5. Choose NOSMOKE.CGM. If you don't have this file, choose a
    different one.

6. Define the range A1..F17 and press Enter.

Once a metafile is imported, there are a limited number of things you
can do to change it. You can bring it into the graphics editor, but you can't
shade or add color to the different areas. (You can only change the color of
the entire graph range.) You can add new objects (such as text) but you
can't edit or delete existing elements. You are able to flip and rotate an

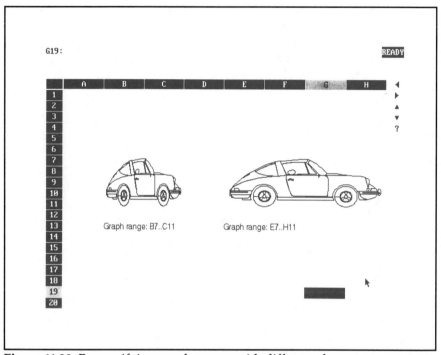

Figure 11.23: By specifying graph ranges with different shapes, you can create two graphics that look very different.

imported metafile. For example, you can use the X-Flip option on the Transform menu to make the car face left instead of right (see Figure 11.25). To preselect the metafile, use the Graph option on the Select menu.

Let's bring the metafile into the graphics editor and add the words *No Smoking* inside the puff of smoke. If you have imported a different file, you may want to type something more appropriate.

1. Load the graphics editor (:Graph Edit or double-click the mouse).

2. To add the text, choose:

   Add

   Text

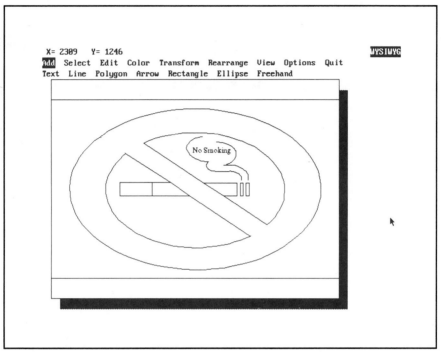

Figure 11.24: The no-smoking sign is an imported metafile.

3. Type **No Smoking** and press Enter.

4. Place the text inside the puff of smoke (see Figure 11.24) and press Enter or click the mouse.

5. To change the font to 10-point Dutch, choose:

   Edit

   Font

   6

6. Exit the graphics editor, print the sign, and save the file if you want to keep it.

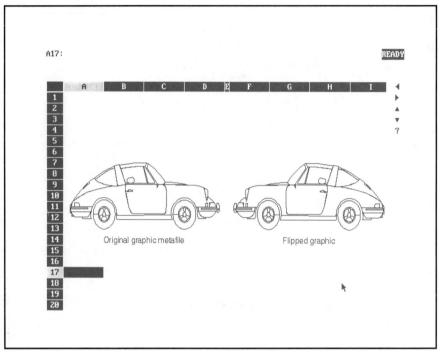

Figure 11.25: Use the X-Flip option to make the car face in the opposite direction.

PART I

PART II

PART III

PART IV

PART V

Databases

Chapter 10

Chapter 11

Chapter 12

Chapter 13

Chapter 14

Manipulating a Database

◀︎||||| FAST TRACK ||||▶

To enter a date: 420

Type @DATE(YY,MM,DD) where *YY* is the year, *MM* is the month, and *DD* is the day, for example, @DATE(91,5,26).

To automatically fill a range with numbers: 423

Choose /Data Fill. When prompted, specify the fill range, start value, step value, and stop value.

To sort a database: 425

Invoke the /Data Sort command. Select Data-Range and specify the records to be sorted. Choose Primary-Key and indicate one cell in the column to be sorted. If necessary, specify a Secondary-Key. Choose Go to sort the records.

To specify database ranges for a query: 431

First, create the database. Make two copies of the field names and label them *Criteria Range* and *Output Range*. Invoke the /Data Query command. Choose Input and specify the database range (including field names). Choose Criteria and specify the range where you will enter search criteria (a row of field names and the blank row underneath). Finally, choose Output and specify where the extracted records should be placed (a row of field names).

To find a record: 431

Setup and specify your input and criteria ranges. Enter criteria under the appropriate field names in the criteria range and then choose /Data Query Find.

To extract records to an output range: 431

Setup and specify your input, criteria, and output ranges. Enter criteria under the appropriate field names in the criteria range and choose /Data Query Extract Quit.

1-2-3's database commands allow you to keep track of many related pieces of information. Think about the different types of information you manage in your home or business. At work you may need to keep track of customers, vendors, inventory, sales leads, invoices, and employees. At home you may keep a phone and address list of friends and relatives, records of your assets and debts, credit-card information, and lists of your collectibles (cassette tapes, stamps, coins, baseball cards, etc.)

Now think about your current methods for keeping track of information. You probably use file folders, a Rolodex, and index cards. These paper methods of information management have several disadvantages compared to a computerized system:

- It's tedious to alphabetize or otherwise order the folders or cards.

- It's time-consuming to look up information (especially if it's not where it's supposed to be).

- It's difficult to summarize the information.

A computerized database solves all these problems. To sort information in alphabetical order, you issue the Sort command, and an entire database is quickly organized. The Query command lets you look up information (such as a particular customer's account balance) and summarize your data into reports (for example, a summary of customer purchases).

What does the term *database* mean exactly? A database is a collection of information on one particular subject that is organized in such a way that data can be quickly and easily retrieved. One example of a database is the telephone book—it's a collection of names, addresses, and phone numbers in one geographical area. The book is organized alphabetically by last name so that you can easily look up a phone number or address. A novel, on the other hand, is not a database—the information is not organized for easy retrieval.

The computerized equivalent of your telephone book is Directory Assistance (for example, 4-1-1). When you call Directory Assistance, the operator does not thumb through telephone books to find the requested phone number; he or she searches a computerized database for the city and name and usually locates the number in seconds.

An electronic database is organized into fields and records. A *field* is a piece of data that has a descriptive name assigned to it. For example, a customer database might have the following fields: Company, Contact, Telephone, Street, City, State, and Zip. An inventory database might have these fields: Part Number, Description, Quantity, Price, etc. A *record* contains all the information (fields) about a particular item or person in the database. In a customer database, each customer has a different record. In an inventory database, each part or product has a different record.

1-2-3 uses the layout of your spreadsheet grid for the structure of the database. The column headings are the database's field names, each record is in its own row, and field data is entered into individual cells. Figure 12.1 is the database you will be creating in this chapter. This database, which keeps track of employee data, has nine fields and nineteen records. For the sake of brevity, this database has fewer fields and records than an actual employee database would probably have.

```
I20:  +G20*H20+G20                                              READY
```

	A	B	C	D	E	F	G	H	I	
1	ID	Last	First	Dept	Exempt	Hire Date	Salary	Raise %	New Sal.	
2	1000	Peterson	Pete	MIS	Yes	07/21/82	21,000	12.0%	23,520	
3	1001	Jones	Mary	Sales	No	10/15/88	29,500	11.0%	32,745	
4	1002	Anderson	Jane	MIS	Yes	08/02/85	34,000	13.0%	38,420	
5	1003	Wilson	Robert	Eng.	Yes	10/14/83	36,000	15.0%	41,400	
6	1004	Meyers	Andrew	MIS	Yes	12/01/88	41,000	9.0%	44,690	
7	1005	Bradford	William	Sales	Yes	09/10/86	60,000	10.0%	66,000	
8	1006	Bradley	Brad	Sales	No	02/26/85	54,000	8.0%	58,320	
9	1007	Manley	Martin	Mfg.	No	03/09/91	26,000	7.0%	27,820	
10	1008	Smith	Paul	Mfg.	No	06/10/87	24,000	10.0%	26,400	
11	1009	Kline	Harry	Sales	No	03/25/88	26,000	7.0%	27,820	
12	1010	Smythe	Jennifer	Eng.	Yes	11/13/90	34,000	6.0%	36,040	
13	1011	Gibson	Pamela	Eng.	No	11/26/89	45,000	12.0%	50,400	
14	1012	Ingram	Greg	Mfg.	No	09/30/90	21,000	6.5%	22,365	
15	1013	Smothers	Stacey	Mfg.	No	05/01/87	24,000	7.5%	25,800	
16	1014	Tucker	Brian	Eng.	Yes	04/22/88	39,000	9.0%	42,510	
17	1015	Slater	Peter	Mfg.	No	01/05/82	20,000	8.0%	21,600	
18	1016	Smith	Charles	Mfg.	Yes	06/29/84	25,000	7.0%	26,750	
19	1017	Jones	Carolyn	MIS	Yes	10/17/84	62,000	11.0%	68,820	
20	1018	Andrews	Andy	MIS	Yes	08/27/89	61,000	14.0%	69,540	

Figure 12.1: The employee database

CREATING A DATABASE

The first step in creating a database is to get out the old-fashioned paper and pencil—don't turn your computer on yet. In this planning stage, you need to decide what types of information you want the database to track and then write down descriptive names for the information. These descriptive names will be your *field names*. They can be as long as you like (up to 240 characters), but it is wise to keep them fairly short, since they will be your column headings. You should also note the maximum number of characters that will be entered into each field. This number will be the field's column width.

When you are designing your database, you should make your fields as specific as possible; they should contain only one piece of information. For example, don't create a single field called *Address* that contains the street address, city, state, and zip code. Instead, create four separate fields (Street, City, State, and Zip). When the information is in separate fields, you have a lot more flexibility in searching, sorting, and reporting.

Creating a database is not too different from creating a spreadsheet. It doesn't matter where in the grid you create the database, though most often databases begin at the home position (A1). There are a few special rules to follow when you set up a database:

- The field names must be in the row directly above the first record. Notice in Figure 12.1 that the field names are in row 1 and the first record is in row 2. Although it would be nice to have some separation here, you cannot have a blank row or a row of dashes between the field names and the first record. In Wysiwyg, though, you can create a solid line under the field names, as shown in Figure 12.1.

- Each field name must be unique.

- Field names are restricted to a single row. You can create two-line column headings but the top line is not officially part of the field name or the database.

- While not imperative, it's best not to leave blank rows between records or blank columns between fields. (This is true for any spreadsheet, not just databases.)

CREATING THE EMPLOYEE DATABASE

To create the employee database, follow these steps:

1. Clear the screen (/Worksheet Erase).

2. Enter the field names in row 1.

3. Right-align the field names in F1..I1 and center the label in A1 (/Range Label).

4. Leave the global column width at its default (9 characters), but set the following special column widths:

Column	Width
A	5
D	6
E	7

5. Place a solid line under the field names (:Format Lines Bottom).

6. Enter the nineteen records shown in Figure 12.2. Leave the ID, Hire Date, and New Sal. columns blank for now.

7. Format the Raise % column to Percent format with 1 decimal place (/Range Format).

8. Change the global format to comma (/Worksheet Global Format).

9. Save the file with the name **EMPLOYEE**.

ENTERING DATES

In Chapter 2, you learned how to enter a date in a cell: you must convert it to a label by typing an apostrophe before the date. Otherwise 1-2-3

```
 120:                                                                    READY

      A      B       C      D       E        F       G        H       I
 1   ID    Last    First   Dept   Exempt  Hire Date  Salary  Raise % New Sal.
 2         Peterson Pete    MIS    Yes                21000    0.12
 3         Jones    Mary    Sales  No                 29500    0.11
 4         Anderson Jane    MIS    Yes                34000    0.13
 5         Wilson   Robert  Eng.   Yes                36000    0.15
 6         Meyers   Andrew  MIS    Yes                41000    0.09
 7         Bradford William Sales  Yes                60000    0.1
 8         Bradley  Brad    Sales  No                 54000    0.08
 9         Manley   Martin  Mfg.   No                 26000    0.07
 10        Smith    Paul    Mfg.   No                 24000    0.1
 11        Kline    Harry   Sales  No                 26000    0.07
 12        Smythe   Jennifer Eng.  Yes                34000    0.06
 13        Gibson   Pamela  Eng.   No                 45000    0.12
 14        Ingram   Greg    Mfg.   No                 21000    0.065
 15        Smothers Stacey  Mfg.   No                 24000    0.075
 16        Tucker   Brian   Eng.   Yes                39000    0.09
 17        Slater   Peter   Mfg.   No                 20000    0.08
 18        Smith    Charles Mfg.   Yes                25000    0.07
 19        Jones    Carolyn MIS    Yes                62000    0.11
 20        Andrews  Andy    MIS    Yes                61000    0.14
```

Figure 12.2: Enter these records

thinks you are typing a value and it performs a calculation. However, there are several problems with entering dates as labels. First, you cannot sort date-labels chronologically. Second, you cannot perform calculations on the dates. (For instance, you cannot determine from a date-label how many years an employee has worked for the company.) Third, you cannot do comparisons with date-labels. (For example, you can't get a report of all employees who have worked for the company more than five years.)

In order to manipulate dates, you must enter them as *values*, not *labels*, using the @DATE function. The syntax for this function is as follows:

@DATE(YY,MM,DD)

Substitute the last two digits of the year for *YY*, the month number for *MM*, and the day for *DD*. To enter the date 2/5/91, type **@DATE(91,2,5)**. This method requires a little extra work as you are entering the data, but opens up powerful possibilities for data manipulation. If you will be entering a lot of dates, you should create a date macro to speed up the process. (Macros are described in Chapter 14.) For the first 99 years in the year 2000, add 100 to the number. For example, to enter the date May 26, 2010, type **@DATE(110,5,26)**.

After you enter a date function, you will see a number in the cell, for example, @DATE(91,2,5) gives the result 33274. This value represents the number of days since December 31, 1899; it's called a *serial date number*. While *you* don't really care what the serial number is, *the computer* needs it to be able to sort and manipulate dates. Since not too many people can readily convert serial numbers into dates, 1-2-3 offers a way to format these numbers into recognizable dates. The /Range Format Date command offers several ways to format your dates, as illustrated below:

Menu	Option Example
1 (DD-MMM-YY)	05-DEC-91
2 (DD-MMM)	05-DEC
3 (MMM-YY)	DEC-91
4 (Long Intn'l)	12/05/91
5 (Short Intn'l)	12/05

The fourth option, long international, is the most common format. Follow these steps to enter the dates in Figure 12.3:

1. Move the pointer to cell F2.

2. Type **@DATE(82,7,21)** and press Enter. The serial date number *30153* appears in the cell—you need to format the column to date format.

3. Press / to display the 1-2-3 menu and choose:

   Range

   Format

   Date

   4 (Long Intn'l)

4. Paint the range F2..F20 and press Enter.

5. Go to the next cell down, type **@DATE(88,10,15)** and press ↓.

```
F2: (D4) @DATE(82,7,21)                                              READY
```

	A	B	C	D	E	F	G	H	I	
1	ID	Last	First	Dept	Exempt	Hire Date	Salary	Raise %	New Sal.	
2		Peterson	Pete	MIS	Yes	07/21/82	21,000	12.0%		
3		Jones	Mary	Sales	No	10/15/88	29,500	11.0%		
4		Anderson	Jane	MIS	Yes	08/02/85	34,000	13.0%		
5		Wilson	Robert	Eng.	Yes	10/14/83	36,000	15.0%		
6		Meyers	Andrew	MIS	Yes	12/01/88	41,000	9.0%		
7		Bradford	William	Sales	Yes	09/10/86	60,000	10.0%		
8		Bradley	Brad	Sales	No	02/26/85	54,000	8.0%		
9		Manley	Martin	Mfg.	No	03/09/91	26,000	7.0%		
10		Smith	Paul	Mfg.	No	06/10/87	24,000	10.0%		
11		Kline	Harry	Sales	No	03/25/88	26,000	7.0%		
12		Smythe	Jennifer	Eng.	Yes	11/13/90	34,000	6.0%		
13		Gibson	Pamela	Eng.	No	11/26/89	45,000	12.0%		
14		Ingram	Greg	Mfg.	No	09/30/90	21,000	6.5%		
15		Smothers	Stacey	Mfg.	No	05/01/87	24,000	7.5%		
16		Tucker	Brian	Eng.	Yes	04/22/88	39,000	9.0%		
17		Slater	Peter	Mfg.	No	01/05/82	20,000	8.0%		
18		Smith	Charles	Mfg.	Yes	06/29/84	25,000	7.0%		
19		Jones	Carolyn	MIS	Yes	10/17/84	62,000	11.0%		
20		Andrews	Andy	MIS	Yes	08/27/89	61,000	14.0%		

Figure 12.3: Enter the dates in column F with the @DATE(YY,MM,DD) function.

6. Refer to Figure 12.3 to enter the remaining dates. Remember, you must use the proper syntax, @DATE(YY,MM,DD).

CREATING A CALCULATED FIELD

A database can contain fields that perform calculations on other fields. In an invoice database, for instance, you can have a field called Total that is the product of the Price and Quantity fields. Or you can have a field called Tax that multiplies the Total field by seven percent. These calculated fields are simply spreadsheet formulas—nothing new to you.

In the employee database, you will create a formula for the New Salary field (see Figure 12.4). This formula calculates an employee's salary after a raise. It multiplies the Salary and Raise % fields and then adds that number to the original salary. Follow these steps:

1. Place the pointer in cell I2.

```
I2: +G2*H2+G2                                                            READY

      A      B         C       D      E      F        G       H        I       ◄
  1  ID   Last      First    Dept   Exempt Hire Date Salary  Raise %  New Sal.  ▶
  2       Peterson  Pete     MIS    Yes    07/21/82  21,000   12.0%    23,520   ▲
  3       Jones     Mary     Sales  No     10/15/88  29,500   11.0%    32,745   ▼
  4       Anderson  Jane     MIS    Yes    08/02/85  34,000   13.0%    38,420   ?
  5       Wilson    Robert   Eng.   Yes    10/14/83  36,000   15.0%    41,400
  6       Meyers    Andrew   MIS    Yes    12/01/88  41,000    9.0%    44,690
  7       Bradford  William  Sales  Yes    09/10/86  60,000   10.0%    66,000
  8       Bradley   Brad     Sales  No     02/26/85  54,000    8.0%    58,320
  9       Manley    Martin   Mfg.   No     03/09/91  26,000    7.0%    27,820
 10       Smith     Paul     Mfg.   No     06/10/87  24,000   10.0%    26,400
 11       Kline     Harry    Sales  No     03/25/88  26,000    7.0%    27,820
 12       Smythe    Jennifer Eng.   Yes    11/13/90  34,000    6.0%    36,040
 13       Gibson    Pamela   Eng.   No     11/26/89  45,000   12.0%    50,400
 14       Ingram    Greg     Mfg.   No     09/30/90  21,000    6.5%    22,365
 15       Smothers  Stacey   Mfg.   No     05/01/87  24,000    7.5%    25,800
 16       Tucker    Brian    Eng.   Yes    04/22/88  39,000    9.0%    42,510
 17       Slater    Peter    Mfg.   No     01/05/82  20,000    8.0%    21,600      �k
 18       Smith     Charles  Mfg.   Yes    06/29/84  25,000    7.0%    26,750
 19       Jones     Carolyn  MIS    Yes    10/17/84  62,000   11.0%    68,820
 20       Andrews   Andy     MIS    Yes    08/27/89  61,000   14.0%    69,540
```

Figure 12.4: The New Salary column is a calculated field.

2. Type **+G2*H2+G2** and press Enter.

3. Copy this formula to the range I3..I20. Your screen should look similar to Figure 12.4.

If you were to add more records to the database, you would need to copy the formula to these new rows.

AUTOMATIC NUMBERING

The /Data Fill command lets you automatically fill in a range of numbers that have regular increments. You can use this command in your employee database to assign employee identification numbers that begin with 1000 and increase by increments of 1 (see Figure 12.5). Rather than typing in the data yourself, you can have 1-2-3 fill it in for you.

Instead of offering menu options and a dialog box, the /Data Fill command prompts you with a series of questions in the control panel. The first

```
A2: (G) [W5] 1000                                              READY

     A      B        C        D     E       F        G       H        I      ◄
 1  ID  Last    First     Dept  Exempt Hire Date  Salary  Raise %  New Sal.  ►
 2  1000 Peterson Pete     MIS   Yes   07/21/82   21,000   12.0%   23,520    ▲
 3  1001 Jones    Mary     Sales No    10/15/88   29,500   11.0%   32,745    ▼
 4  1002 Anderson Jane     MIS   Yes   08/02/85   34,000   13.0%   38,420    ?
 5  1003 Wilson   Robert   Eng.  Yes   10/14/83   36,000   15.0%   41,400
 6  1004 Meyers   Andrew   MIS   Yes   12/01/88   41,000    9.0%   44,690
 7  1005 Bradford William  Sales Yes   09/10/86   60,000   10.0%   66,000
 8  1006 Bradley  Brad     Sales No    02/26/85   54,000    8.0%   58,320
 9  1007 Manley   Martin   Mfg.  No    03/09/91   26,000    7.0%   27,820
10  1008 Smith    Paul     Mfg.  No    06/10/87   24,000   10.0%   26,400
11  1009 Kline    Harry    Sales No    03/25/88   26,000    7.0%   27,820
12  1010 Smythe   Jennifer Eng.  Yes   11/13/90   34,000    6.0%   36,040
13  1011 Gibson   Pamela   Eng.  No    11/26/89   45,000   12.0%   50,400
14  1012 Ingram   Greg     Mfg.  No    09/30/90   21,000    6.5%   22,365
15  1013 Smothers Stacey   Mfg.  No    05/01/87   24,000    7.5%   25,800
16  1014 Tucker   Brian    Eng.  Yes   04/22/88   39,000    9.0%   42,510
17  1015 Slater   Peter    Mfg.  No    01/05/82   20,000    8.0%   21,600    ▸
18  1016 Smith    Charles  Mfg.  Yes   06/29/84   25,000    7.0%   26,750
19  1017 Jones    Carolyn  MIS   Yes   10/17/84   62,000   11.0%   68,820
20  1018 Andrews  Andy     MIS   Yes   08/27/89   61,000   14.0%   69,540
```

Figure 12.5: The values in the ID field are filled in automatically.

question pertains to the fill range—A2..A20 in the employee database. The remaining questions are:

- *Start*—the first value in the range (0 is the default)
- *Step*—the incremental value (1 is the default)
- *Stop*—the last value in the range (8191 is the default)

1-2-3 stops numbering at whichever comes first—the stop value or the end of the fill range. Therefore, if you know that the last value in the range will be less than the default stop value (8191), you do not need to change the stop value; simply press Enter to accept the default.

The step value can be positive or negative. A negative step value will create a list of descending numbers. For example, if the start value is 100 and the step value is –1, the range will be filled with 100, 99, 98, and so forth.

Follow these steps to fill in the data for the ID field:

1. Place the pointer in A2.

2. Press **/** to display the 1-2-3 menu and choose:

    Data

    Fill

3. For the fill range, paint the range A2..A20 and press Enter.

4. Type **1000** for the start value and press Enter.

5. Press Enter to accept the default step value (1).

6. Press Enter to accept the default stop value (8191).

7. To remove the commas in the numbers, format them to General format (/Range Format General). Your screen should look similar to Figure 12.5.

Because dates are values, you can use the /Data Fill command to create a series of chronological dates. For example, to create a list of dates in January 1992, use the following specifications:

- Fill range: a range of at least 31 cells

- Start value: @DATE(92,1,1)

- Step value: 1

- Stop value: @DATE(92,1,31)

The range will be filled with serial date numbers so you will need to format the cells with /Range Format Date.

SORTING RECORDS

Records appear in the order you enter them, usually in a random order. Most likely, though, you will want to organize records alphabetically, numerically, or chronologically. You can sort by any field in the database, in either ascending or descending order. *Ascending* order is more common: It sorts text from A–Z, numbers from lowest to highest, and dates from earliest to latest. Choosing *descending* sorts data in reverse order from ascending.

You can use the /Data Sort command to organize rows in any type of spreadsheet, not just databases. You will see the Sort Settings dialog box shown in Figure 12.6 when you choose /Data Sort. You can either edit this box directly or use the appropriate menu options. Sorting a database is similar to printing one. You specify a range, choose options, and then select Go to execute the command.

The range you specify when you sort is called the *data range*. The data range consists of all records and columns in the database, but does not include the field names. In the employee database, the data range is A2..I20. If you inadvertently include the field names in your data range, this row will be sorted into the database. That's one good reason why you should save your file before sorting (or make sure Undo is enabled). Also, if there are any blank rows in the data range, they will be moved to the top or bottom of the database, depending on whether you are sorting in ascending or descending order.

The Primary-Key option tells 1-2-3 which column to order the records by. To sort by the last name field in your employee database, you would specify a cell in column B as the sort key. Or, to sort by the hire-date field,

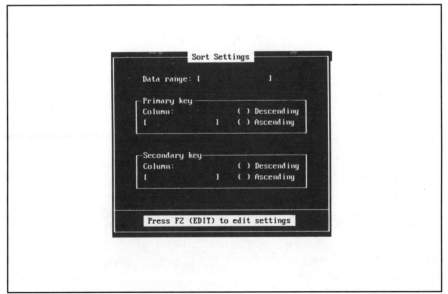

Figure 12.6: The Sort Settings dialog box

you would indicate a cell in column F. 1-2-3 doesn't care which cell you choose—to sort the last names, B2 works just as well as B2000. We'll discuss the Secondary-Key option later.

SORTING THE EMPLOYEE DATABASE

Follow these steps to sort the employee data, such that the most recent hire dates appear first:

1. Press / to display the 1-2-3 menu and choose:

    Data

    Sort

    Data-Range

2. Paint the range A2..I20 and press Enter.

3. Choose Primary-Key.

4. Move the pointer to any cell in column F (the hire-date field) and press Enter. You are then prompted for the sort order (ascending or descending).

5. Press Enter to accept *D* (the default).

6. Choose Go to sort the database. As shown in Figure 12.7, the records are now sorted by the hire-date field, with the most recently hired employees at the beginning.

Now, sort by a different field—let's sort the last names in alphabetical order. Before you sort the data, think about which sort settings have changed. Do you need to set up a new data range? No, the records you want to sort are still in A2..I20, and 1-2-3 remembers the last data range entered in the Sort Settings dialog box. Will you need to specify a new primary key? Yes, because you want to sort by a different field (the last names in column B).

Follow these steps to sort by the last name field:

1. Press / to display the 1-2-3 menu and choose:

    Data

Sort

Primary-Key

2. Move the pointer to any cell in column B and press Enter.

3. Type **A** for Ascending and press Enter.

4. Choose Go. The records are now sorted alphabetically by last name.

SECONDARY SORT KEYS: THE TIEBREAKER

When you have duplicate entries in the primary sort field, you should specify a secondary sort key to function as a "tiebreaker." In this example, two people have the last name Jones and two people have the name Smith. Therefore, you need to tell 1-2-3 to sort by the first name field when there is duplicate entry (a "tie"). The tiebreaking field is called the Secondary-Key.

```
F2: (D4) @DATE(91,3,9)                                              READY

      A      B        C         D      E        F         G        H        I      ◄
 1   ID    Last     First     Dept   Exempt  Hire Date  Salary  Raise %  New Sal.  ►
 2   1007  Manley   Martin    Mfg.   No      03/09/91   26,000    7.0%   27,820    ▲
 3   1010  Smythe   Jennifer  Eng.   Yes     11/13/90   34,000    6.0%   36,040    ▼
 4   1012  Ingram   Greg      Mfg.   No      09/30/90   21,000    6.5%   22,365    ?
 5   1011  Gibson   Pamela    Eng.   No      11/26/89   45,000   12.0%   50,400
 6   1018  Andrews  Andy      MIS    Yes     08/27/89   61,000   14.0%   69,540
 7   1004  Meyers   Andrew    MIS    Yes     12/01/88   41,000    9.0%   44,690
 8   1001  Jones    Mary      Sales  No      10/15/88   29,500   11.0%   32,745
 9   1014  Tucker   Brian     Eng.   Yes     04/22/88   39,000    9.0%   42,510
10   1009  Kline    Harry     Sales  No      03/25/88   26,000    7.0%   27,820
11   1008  Smith    Paul      Mfg.   No      06/10/87   24,000   10.0%   26,400
12   1013  Smothers Stacey    Mfg.   No      05/01/87   24,000    7.5%   25,800
13   1005  Bradford William   Sales  Yes     09/10/86   60,000   10.0%   66,000
14   1002  Anderson Jane      MIS    Yes     08/02/85   34,000   13.0%   38,420
15   1006  Bradley  Brad      Sales  No      02/26/85   54,000    8.0%   58,320
16   1017  Jones    Carolyn   MIS    Yes     10/17/84   62,000   11.0%   68,820
17   1016  Smith    Charles   Mfg.   Yes     06/29/84   25,000    7.0%   26,750
18   1003  Wilson   Robert    Eng.   Yes     10/14/83   36,000   15.0%   41,400
19   1000  Peterson Pete      MIS    Yes     07/21/82   21,000   12.0%   23,520
20   1015  Slater   Peter     Mfg.   No      01/05/82   20,000    8.0%   21,600
```

Figure 12.7: The database sorted by the hire-date field

Follow these steps to specify a secondary sort key:

1. Press **/** to display the 1-2-3 menu and choose:

    Data

    Sort

    Secondary-Key

2. Move the pointer to any cell in column C and press Enter.

3. Type **A** for Ascending order and press Enter.

4. Choose Go. The records are now sorted alphabetically by last name, and when a last name appears more than once, the first names are sorted. Your database should look similar to Figure 12.8.

Here's another example of when you need to use a secondary sort key. In the employee database, let's suppose you want to group together all the

```
B3: 'Andrews                                                          READY

     A     B          C         D     E       F          G        H        I      ◀
 1   ID  Last       First     Dept  Exempt  Hire Date  Salary  Raise % New Sal.    ▶
 2  1002 Anderson  Jane      MIS   Yes     08/02/85   34,000   13.0%   38,420     ▲
 3  1018 Andrews   Andy      MIS   Yes     08/27/89   61,000   14.0%   69,540     ▼
 4  1005 Bradford  William   Sales Yes     09/10/86   60,000   10.0%   66,000     ?
 5  1006 Bradley   Brad      Sales No      02/26/85   54,000    8.0%   58,320
 6  1011 Gibson    Pamela    Eng.  No      11/26/89   45,000   12.0%   50,400
 7  1012 Ingram    Greg      Mfg.  No      09/30/90   21,000    6.5%   22,365
 8  1017 Jones     Carolyn   MIS   Yes     10/17/84   62,000   11.0%   68,820
 9  1001 Jones     Mary      Sales No      10/15/88   29,500   11.0%   32,745
10  1009 Kline     Harry     Sales No      03/25/88   26,000    7.0%   27,820
11  1007 Manley    Martin    Mfg.  No      03/09/91   26,000    7.0%   27,820
12  1004 Meyers    Andrew    MIS   Yes     12/01/88   41,000    9.0%   44,690
13  1000 Peterson  Pete      MIS   Yes     07/21/82   21,000   12.0%   23,520     ↖
14  1015 Slater    Peter     Mfg.  No      01/05/82   20,000    8.0%   21,600
15  1016 Smith     Charles   Mfg.  Yes     06/29/84   25,000    7.0%   26,750
16  1008 Smith     Paul      Mfg.  No      06/10/87   24,000   10.0%   26,400
17  1013 Smothers  Stacey    Mfg.  No      05/01/87   24,000    7.5%   25,800
18  1010 Smythe    Jennifer  Eng.  Yes     11/13/90   34,000    6.0%   36,040
19  1014 Tucker    Brian     Eng.  Yes     04/22/88   39,000    9.0%   42,510
20  1003 Wilson    Robert    Eng.  Yes     10/14/83   36,000   15.0%   41,400
```

Figure 12.8: The last name field is the Primary-Key and the first name field is the Secondary-Key.

people in the same department and alphabetize the names within each department, as shown in Figure 12.9. As you can see, all the people in the Engineering department are grouped together and they are alphabetized by last name. The primary sort key in this example is the department field (column D) and the secondary key is the last name field (column B).

THE NUMBER ONE SORT PROBLEM

The most common mistake people make with the sort command is not including all columns in the database when specifying the data range. Here's a typical scenario. You want to sort the last names in alphabetical order so you specify B1..B20 as the Data-Range and B2 as the Primary-Key. When you choose Go, you are pleased and proud because the names alphabetized perfectly. Or so it appears at first glance...

B3: 'Smythe   READY

	A	B	C	D	E	F	G	H	I
1	ID	Last	First	Dept	Exempt	Hire Date	Salary	Raise %	New Sal.
2	1011	Gibson	Pamela	Eng.	No	11/26/89	45,000	12.0%	50,400
3	1010	Smythe	Jennifer	Eng.	Yes	11/13/90	34,000	6.0%	36,040
4	1014	Tucker	Brian	Eng.	Yes	04/22/88	39,000	9.0%	42,510
5	1003	Wilson	Robert	Eng.	Yes	10/14/83	36,000	15.0%	41,400
6	1012	Ingram	Greg	Mfg.	No	09/30/90	21,000	6.5%	22,365
7	1007	Manley	Martin	Mfg.	No	03/09/91	26,000	7.0%	27,820
8	1015	Slater	Peter	Mfg.	No	01/05/82	20,000	8.0%	21,600
9	1016	Smith	Charles	Mfg.	Yes	06/29/84	25,000	7.0%	26,750
10	1008	Smith	Paul	Mfg.	No	06/10/87	24,000	10.0%	26,400
11	1013	Smothers	Stacey	Mfg.	No	05/01/87	24,000	7.5%	25,800
12	1002	Anderson	Jane	MIS	Yes	08/02/85	34,000	13.0%	38,420
13	1018	Andrews	Andy	MIS	Yes	08/27/89	61,000	14.0%	69,540
14	1017	Jones	Carolyn	MIS	Yes	10/17/84	62,000	11.0%	68,820
15	1004	Meyers	Andrew	MIS	Yes	12/01/88	41,000	9.0%	44,690
16	1000	Peterson	Pete	MIS	Yes	07/21/82	21,000	12.0%	23,520
17	1005	Bradford	William	Sales	Yes	09/10/86	60,000	10.0%	66,000
18	1006	Bradley	Brad	Sales	No	02/26/85	54,000	8.0%	58,320
19	1001	Jones	Mary	Sales	No	10/15/88	29,500	11.0%	32,745
20	1009	Kline	Harry	Sales	No	03/25/88	26,000	7.0%	27,820

Figure 12.9: The department field is the Primary-Key and the last name field is the Secondary-Key.

After studying the data, though, you realize there's a problem. While the names are indeed alphabetized, the other columns in the database didn't move along with the names. Everybody has the wrong first name, department, and salary. In other words, your data is garbage. This is what happens when you don't include the entire database in your data range.

If you recognize your mistake before you give any other commands *and* if Undo is enabled, you can press Alt-F4 to reverse the sort operation. Otherwise, you must abandon the file, and retrieve your last-saved version. This is another validation of the argument for saving before you sort a database.

QUERYING THE DATABASE

One of the reasons for creating a database is to be able to retrieve information quickly. 1-2-3's /Data Query command offers two ways to do this: Find and Extract. The *Find* option is similar to the /Range Search command discussed in Chapter 5: You indicate what you want to search for and the cell pointer moves to that particular record. For example, you can search for Pete Peterson's record to give him a raise. You will typically use the Find option to look up or update information.

The *Extract* option allows you to create reports that are a subset of your database. For example, you may want to print out a list of the employees in the sales department or of all the employees who make more than $50,000 a year. Because databases are inclined to be quite large, the data tends to be hard to analyze unless it is summarized or organized. By limiting the number of records or fields in a report, the Extract option lets you turn raw data into meaningful information.

QUERY RANGES

When you are querying your database, you need to set up several special ranges, as indicated in the Query Settings dialog box in Figure 12.10. You already have one of these ranges—the database. The Query command calls your database the *input range*. It includes all fields, records, and field names. In the employee database, the input range is A1..I20. Notice that the Query command's input range includes the field names—when 1-2-3 performs database queries, it needs to know the names of your fields.

The *criteria range* is where you type your queries. It consists of two rows—the field names and one blank row below the names. Figure 12.11 shows the criteria range for the employee database, A27..I28.

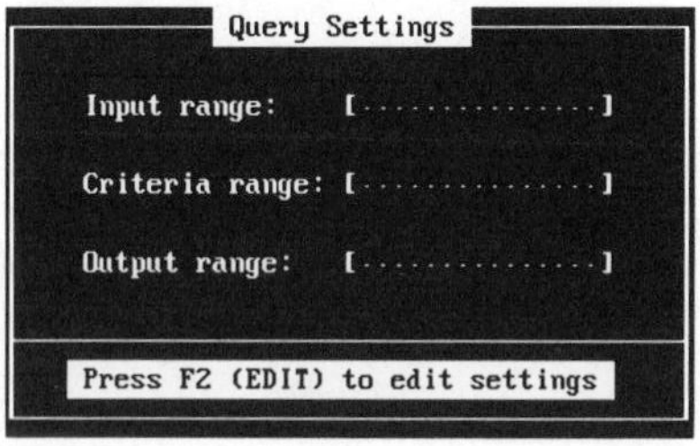

Figure 12.10: The Query Settings dialog box

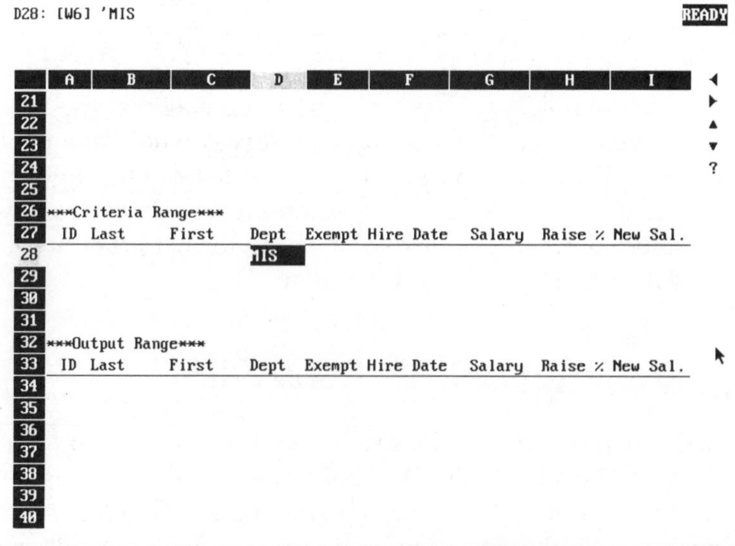

Figure 12.11: The criteria and output ranges for the employee database

One criterion is entered into this range: MIS under the Dept field name. This criterion indicates that you want to locate all employees in the MIS department. As you can see, you enter your search criteria directly in the spreadsheet (under the appropriate field name in the criteria range) rather than in a dialog box. Later in this section, you will learn different ways to specify search criteria.

The *output range*, or your report range, is where the matching records are placed when you use the Extract command. For example, if MIS is typed under the Dept field name in the criteria range and you do an Extract operation, all records for employees in the MIS department will be copied into the output range. This range consists of a single row of field names, A32..I32 in Figure 12.11. *You* decide which field names are in the output range. If you want only names and salaries in your report, you enter these field names in your output range.

You can set up your criteria and output ranges anywhere in the spreadsheet. In the employee database, we created the ranges below the records. If your database had many records, you might want to create the criteria and output ranges to the right of the input range. Make sure you do *not* place the output range above any data. When you issue the Extract command, 1-2-3 automatically erases everything under the output range—all the way to row 8192, whether or not the extracted records need the space.

If you really want to put data under the output range, there is a way to prevent disasters. When defining your output range, include the field names *and* a range of blank rows. The number of rows you highlight depends on the maximum number of records you think you will extract. When you define a fixed length to your output range, 1-2-3 will not erase data underneath the output range. However, if your output range is too small, you will get the following error message:

Too many records for Output range

1-2-3 will then extract as many records as can fit in the output range, but you will be left with an incomplete report. If this occurs you should define a longer output range and extract the records again.

Admittedly, creating and specifying the three database ranges requires a bit of work, but once the ranges are in place, querying the database is fast. You can type a criterion in the criteria range, give the /Data Query Extract command (or simply press the Query key, F7), and you instantly have a report in the output range. After printing this report, you can produce another report by typing a new criterion and pressing F7.

In your employee database, you need to create and define the criteria and output ranges. The easiest way to create them is to use the /Copy command to copy the field names to each range. Follow these steps:

1. Use the /Copy command to copy A1..I1 to A27..I27. The copied field names will be part of the criteria range.

2. Copy the field names again to A33..I33 (the output range).

3. To remind yourself what each range represents, type ***Criteria Range*** in cell A26 and ***Output Range*** in A32. These labels are for *your* information only—they are not required.

4. If desired, use the :Format Lines Bottom command to place a solid line under the field names in the criteria and output ranges.

5. Press / to display the 1-2-3 menu and choose:

   Data

   Query

   Input

6. To define the input range, paint the range A1..I20 and press Enter. The Query Settings dialog box will display this range next to Input. It's important that the field names in row 1 are included in the input range.

7. Choose Criteria.

8. To define the criteria range, paint the range A27..I28 and press Enter. Make sure the range contains the field names *and* the blank row underneath.

9. Choose Output.

10. To define the output range, paint the range A33..I33 and press Enter. The output range should be only one row long. Your Query Settings dialog box should match the one in Figure 12.12.

11. Choose Quit.

Keep in mind that all this prep work needs to be done only once for each database.

ENTERING CRITERIA

To specify which records you want to find or extract, enter search criterion under the appropriate field name in the criteria range. To locate Bradford's record, the criteria range should have *Bradford* typed under the last name field (cell B28). Or to get a list of people in the sales department, the criteria range should have *Sales* typed under the Dept field name (cell D28). Once you have entered the search criterion, issue the /Data Query Find or /Data Query Extract command, depending on whether you want to look up the data (Find) or create a report (Extract).

Each type of field (labels, values, and dates) has specific rules for how you must enter the criteria. Label fields are the easiest to query, so we will cover them first. We'll tackle values and dates later.

For your first query, follow these steps to display a list of all the employees in the MIS department:

1. Move the pointer to cell D28.

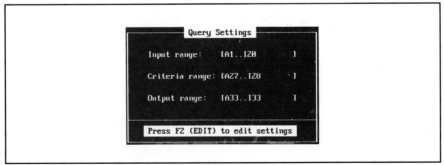

Figure 12.12: The Query Settings dialog box for the employee database

2. Type **MIS** and press Enter. You can type the text in upper- or lowercase but make sure you type the word correctly; the query text must match the database text, character for character.

3. To extract the records, press / to display the 1-2-3 menu and choose:

   Data

   Query

   Extract

   Quit

The list of matching records—only employees in the MIS department—is displayed under the output range (see Figure 12.13). You can now edit, delete, sort, or print this partial list. In the rest of this chapter, you are going to perform many different queries, one after another, to see how this command works. In your actual work, though, you would probably do a single query and then print a report, do another query and then print, etc. Note that you do not need to erase one report before performing the next query; 1-2-3 does this for you automatically.

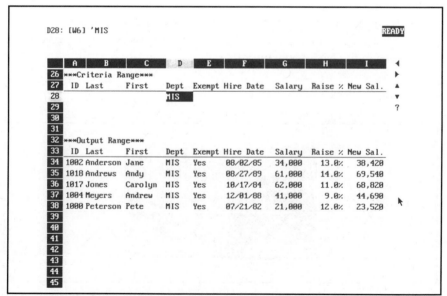

Figure 12.13: A list of employees in the MIS department

SPECIFYING MULTIPLE CRITERIA

Sometimes you will want to enter several different criteria as part of a single query. For example, you may want to get a list of all people in the engineering department who are exempt from overtime. When you enter multiple search criteria, all criteria must be met in order for a record to be found or extracted. Enter each criterion under the appropriate field, as follows:

1. In cell D28, type **Eng.** and press Enter. (Don't forget the period after *Eng.* If you do not include it, the query will not work.)

2. In cell E28, type **Yes** and press Enter.

3. Press F7. The Query key repeats the operation you last performed in the /Data Query menu (either Find or Extract). Since you just did an Extract, the output range displays a list of exempt employees in the engineering department. Your list should look similar to the one in Figure 12.14.

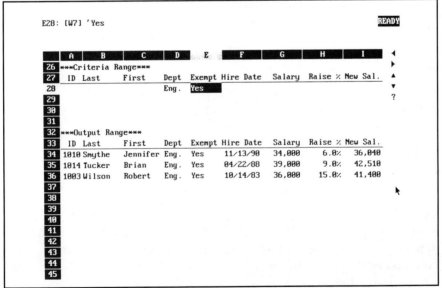

Figure 12.14: A list of exempt employees in the engineering department

COMMON PROBLEMS WITH DATA QUERIES

After years of teaching 1-2-3 in a classroom environment, I have seen just about everything that can possibly go wrong with a query. Allow me to share some of these pitfalls, so you can avoid making the same mistakes. If your query is not working, go through the following checklist:

- Display the Query Settings dialog box, and make sure the ranges exist (you may have inadvertently cleared the ranges with the Reset option on the /Data Query menu).

- Make sure the database ranges are accurately defined. The input range should include the field names and all the records. The criteria range should include a row of field names and a single blank row beneath, for a total of two rows. The output range should include only a row of field names.

- Compare the field names in the input range with those in the criteria and output ranges. Except for upper- and lowercase, the names must be identical in all three ranges. Perhaps one of the names has a space or a period after it. I recommend that you use the /Copy command to ensure identical field names in the ranges.

- Study the second row of the criteria range (row 28 in the employee database). Make sure it doesn't contain old criteria from your last query. Be sure to erase cells with the Del key or /Range Erase—if you use the spacebar, your queries will not work.

USING WILDCARDS

In your previous queries, the criteria you entered had to match the data in the database exactly in order for the record to be extracted. When you can't be so exact, you can use *wildcards* to take the place of the characters you aren't sure of. The asterisk and question mark are the query wildcards. Use these wildcards in your criteria when you don't know (or don't feel like typing) the complete, exact contents of a field. The asterisk matches any group of characters in the position where you type it; the question mark is a placeholder for a single character. These wildcards can be used only with labels. Here are a few examples:

- The criteria *t** matches all words that start with the letter *t*.

- The criteria *Peter** matches all labels that start with *Peter* (like Peter, Peters, Peterson, and Petersburg).

- The criteria *Thomps?n* lists all labels that have a single character in the position of the question mark (like Thompsen and Thompson).

- The criteria *Sm?th** matches all labels that start with *Sm*, followed by any character, followed by *th*, followed by any number of characters (like Smith, Smythe, Smothers, and Smithsonian).

Notice that in the above examples, the asterisk wildcard appears only at the end of the label. This placement is not a coincidence—it's a requirement. You cannot type **son* to locate all labels that end in *son*, nor can you type *T*son* to find all labels that start with *T* and end in *son*. 1-2-3 has another way of handling these types of queries, discussed later in the chapter.

One way of using the wildcard is as a shortcut for entering your search criteria. For example, you can simply type *s** to match *sales*. Of course, this works only if there are no other departments that begin with *s*.

USING THE FIND OPERATION

Let's suppose you want to look up information about someone whose first name begins with the letter *P*. Because you want to look up information (as opposed to producing a report), use the Find command. Follow these steps:

1. Use the Del key or /Range Erase to clear the old criteria from cells D28 and E28.

2. In C28, type **P*** and press Enter.

3. To find the matching records, press / to display the 1-2-3 menu and choose:

   Data

   Query

   Find

The first matching record (Pamela Gibson) is highlighted, as shown in Figure 12.15. To find the next matching record, press ↓. Keep pressing ↓ until 1-2-3 beeps at you—this means you are on the last matching record. Table 12.1 explains how special keys operate when you are in FIND mode.

One of the reasons for using the Find operation is to update data once you have located a record. Let's give Paul Smith a raise:

1. Highlight Paul Smith's record.

2. Press → to move to the salary field. (To see which cell you are in, look at the control panel or find the shaded column letter in the spreadsheet frame.)

```
A6: (G) [W5] 1011                                              FIND

      A     B        C        D      E      F        G      H      I       ◀
 1   ID    Last     First    Dept   Exempt Hire Date Salary Raise % New Sal. ▶
 2  1002 Anderson  Jane      MIS    Yes    08/02/85 34,000  13.0%  38,420   ▲
 3  1018 Andrews   Andy      MIS    Yes    08/27/89 61,000  14.0%  69,540   ▼
 4  1005 Bradford  William   Sales  Yes    09/10/86 60,000  10.0%  66,000   ?
 5  1006 Bradley   Brad      Sales  No     02/26/85 54,000   8.0%  58,320
 6  1011 Gibson    Pamela    Eng.   No     11/26/89 45,000  12.0%  50,400
 7  1012 Ingram    Greg      Mfg.   No     09/30/90 21,000   6.5%  22,365
 8  1017 Jones     Carolyn   MIS    Yes    10/17/84 62,000  11.0%  68,820
 9  1001 Jones     Mary      Sales  No     10/15/88 29,500  11.0%  32,745
10  1009 Kline     Harry     Sales  No     03/25/88 26,000   7.0%  27,820
11  1007 Manley    Martin    Mfg.   No     03/09/91 26,000   7.0%  27,820
12  1004 Meyers    Andrew    MIS    Yes    12/01/88 41,000   9.0%  44,690
13  1000 Peterson  Pete      MIS    Yes    07/21/82 21,000  12.0%  23,520   ➤
14  1015 Slater    Peter     Mfg.   No     01/05/82 20,000   8.0%  21,600
15  1016 Smith     Charles   Mfg.   Yes    06/29/84 25,000   7.0%  26,750
16  1008 Smith     Paul      Mfg.   No     06/10/87 24,000  10.0%  26,400
17  1013 Smothers  Stacey    Mfg.   No     05/01/87 24,000   7.5%  25,800
18  1010 Smythe    Jennifer  Eng.   Yes    11/13/90 34,000   6.0%  36,040
19  1014 Tucker    Brian     Eng.   Yes    04/22/88 39,000   9.0%  42,510
20  1003 Wilson    Robert    Eng.   Yes    10/14/83 36,000  15.0%  41,400
```

Figure 12.15: The first record found is highlighted.

Table 12.1: Special Keys in FIND Mode

KEY	DESCRIPTION
↓	Next matching record
↑	Previous matching record
Home	First record in input range
End	Last record in input range
→	Next cell in current record
←	Previous cell in current record
Enter	Exits FIND mode
Esc	Exits FIND mode
Ctrl-Break	Quits to READY mode
F2	Edits contents of current cell

3. Type **27000** and press Enter.

4. Press Ctrl-Break to exit the Find command and return to READY mode.

QUERYING NUMERIC FIELDS

There are two types of queries you can do on numeric fields. *Exact-match* queries are entered the same way as those for text fields: Type the criteria underneath the appropriate field name in the criteria range. Thus, to locate all employees who will be getting a fifteen percent raise, you would type **15%** in H28.

However, with numeric fields, you rarely do exact-match queries; more often, you display a range of values. For example, you may want to create a report listing employees who have a salary greater than $40,000. To enter this type of criteria, you type a *conditional formula*. A conditional formula is a test that has only two possible answers: true or false. Conditional formulas use the following relational operators:

Symbol	Description
>	Greater than
<	Less than
=	Equal to
>=	Greater than or equal to
<=	Less than or equal to
<>	Not equal to

The conditional formula to list those whose salary is $40,000 or more is:

+G2>=40000

You are probably wondering what the *G2* signifies in this formula. When you are creating conditional formulas, you refer to the first database record (row 2) in the field you are querying (column G). Thus, you refer to cell G2 in this formula. It would be more straightforward if you could type *+SALARY>=40000* or simply *>=40000*, but you must reference the first record in the field you are querying to get results. (Actually, if you use the /Range Name command to assign the name *SALARY* to cell G2, you could enter the criterion *+SALARY>=40000*.)

When you enter a formula, you see the result in the cell and the formula in the control panel. Therefore, you will not see your criterion (+G2>=40000); you will see a 0 if the condition is false (i.e., G2 is not greater than 40000) or a 1 if the condition is true (G2 is 40000 or higher). When you are working with conditional formulas, the true/false information is of no importance. It would be much more meaningful to display the *formula* in the criteria range rather than the 0 or 1. The /Range Format Text command allows you to do this.

Enough discussion—let's get to work:

1. Erase the old criteria in row 28.

2. In G28, type **+G2>=40000** and press Enter. The result of this formula, 0, displays in the cell.

3. To see the formula in the cell, press / to display the 1-2-3 menu and choose:

> Range
>
> Format
>
> Text

4. Indicate the range A28..I28 and press Enter. (It's a good idea to format *all* cells in the criteria range.) You should now see the formula in the cell, as shown in Figure 12.16.

5. To list the matching records in the output range, press / to display the 1-2-3 menu and choose:

> Data
>
> Query
>
> Extract
>
> Quit

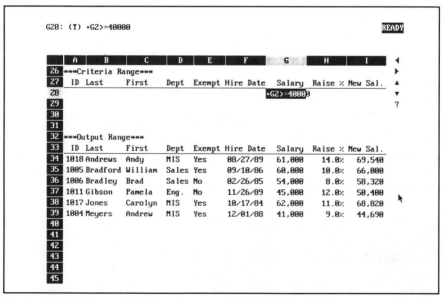

Figure 12.16: Format the criteria range to Text format so that you can see the conditional formulas.

The list of employees who make more than $40,000 is displayed in the output range (see Figure 12.16).

Let's try another example. List the employees who will be getting less than a ten percent raise:

1. Erase the old criteria in row 28.

2. In H28, type **+H2<0.1** and press Enter. The formula displays in the cell because you formatted it to text in the previous exercise.

3. Press F7 and the list displays in the output range.

COMBINING CRITERIA
IN A SINGLE FORMULA

Let's suppose you want to list the employees who are in the $30,000 to $40,000 salary range. This query actually requires two conditions: salary greater than $30,000 and salary less than $40,000. To specify multiple conditions in a single field, you can link the conditions with the following logical operators: #AND# and #OR#. Let's look at examples of each.

The query formula that finds a range of salaries between $30,000 and $40,000 is:

    +G2>=30000#AND#G2<=40000

When the #AND# operator is used, both conditions must be met in order for a record to be found or extracted. In this example, a record is located only if the salary is greater than or equal to $30,000 *and* less than or equal to $40,000. This condition matches four records, as shown in Figure 12.17.

With the #OR# operator, only one of the conditions has to be true for a record to be found or extracted. You can use this operator to find values at the lower or upper end of a scale, for example,

    +G2<25000#OR#G2>60000

This search criteria would find or extract records of employees who make less than $25,000 or more than $60,000. Six records match this criteria.

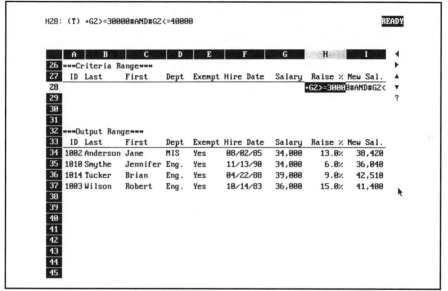

H28: (T) +G2>=30000#AND#G2<=40000   READY

	A	B	C	D	E	F	G	H	I	
26	***Criteria Range***									◄
27	ID Last	First		Dept	Exempt	Hire Date	Salary	Raise % New Sal.		►
28								+G2>=30000#AND#G2<		▲
29										▼
30										?
31										
32	***Output Range***									
33	ID Last	First		Dept	Exempt	Hire Date	Salary	Raise % New Sal.		
34	1002 Anderson	Jane		MIS	Yes	08/02/85	34,000	13.0%	38,420	
35	1010 Smythe	Jennifer	Eng.		Yes	11/13/90	34,000	6.0%	36,040	
36	1014 Tucker	Brian	Eng.		Yes	04/22/88	39,000	9.0%	42,510	
37	1003 Wilson	Robert	Eng.		Yes	10/14/83	36,000	15.0%	41,400	
38										
39										
40										
41										
42										
43										
44										
45										

Figure 12.17: The output range lists the employees who make between $30,000 and $40,000.

If you like, try each of the queries mentioned above, or make up some of your own.

QUERYING DATE FIELDS

With date field queries, you usually want to match a range of dates. For example, you may want to see all records before a certain date, or in a certain year or month. Therefore, most of your date queries will be conditional formulas. Here is an example of a date query:

    +F2>=@DATE(89,1,1)

This criterion would locate all employees hired on or after January 1, 1989. In order for this formula to work, the database dates must be entered using the @DATE function (as you did when you created the database). If they are entered as labels (for example, '12/15/88), you can query the field but you will need a different formula:

@DATEVALUE(F2)>=@DATE(89,1,1)

This formula converts the label in cell F2 to a date value that can be queried.

Create a report of all employees who were hired before January 1, 1986:

1. Erase any old criteria in row 28.

2. In F28, type **+F2<@DATE(86,1,1)** and press Enter.

3. Press F7 to display the matching records in the output range. Your list should look similar to the one in Figure 12.18.

In addition to @DATE and @DATEVALUE, 1-2-3 has many other built-in functions that manipulate dates. The two most useful ones for database querying are @MONTH and @YEAR. These functions allow you to locate

```
F28:  (T)  +F2<@DATE(86,1,1)                                          READY

          A      B        C      D     E       F        G        H        I      ◄
      26 ***Criteria Range***                                                    ►
      27  ID  Last     First   Dept  Exempt  Hire Date  Salary  Raise %  New Sal. ▲
      28                                      +F2<@DATE(86,1,1)                   ▼
      29                                                                          ?
      30
      31
      32 ***Output Range***
      33  ID  Last     First   Dept  Exempt  Hire Date  Salary  Raise %  New Sal.
      34 1002 Anderson Jane    MIS   Yes     08/02/85   34,000   13.0%    38,420
      35 1006 Bradley  Brad    Sales No      02/26/85   54,000    8.0%    58,320
      36 1017 Jones    Carolyn MIS   Yes     10/17/84   62,000   11.0%    68,820
      37 1000 Peterson Pete    MIS   Yes     07/21/82   21,000   12.0%    23,520
      38 1015 Slater   Peter   Mfg.  No      01/05/82   20,000    8.0%    21,600   ◄
      39 1016 Smith    Charles Mfg.  Yes     06/29/84   25,000    7.0%    26,750
      40 1003 Wilson   Robert  Eng.  Yes     10/14/83   36,000   15.0%    41,400
      41
      42
      43
      44
      45
```

Figure 12.18: A list of employees who were hired before January 1, 1986

all dates within a certain month or year. For example,

    @MONTH(F2)=6
    @YEAR(F2)=88

The first conditional formula finds or extracts the records of employees hired in month six (June). The second formula locates all employees hired in 1988.

Here's an example of another useful date query:

    91-@YEAR(F2)>=5

This formula locates the employees who have worked for the company more than five years. It takes the current year (91 in this example), subtracts the year the employee was hired and checks to see if the result is greater than or equal to five.

ADVANCED QUERIES

So far you have seen two ways to query text fields: with an exact match or with wildcards. While wildcards give you greater flexibility than exact matches, you are still somewhat limited in what you can enter as your search criteria. For example, you cannot use wildcards at the beginning of the text string (e.g., *son or *other*), nor can you locate a range of values (for example, all names that begin with the first half of the alphabet). 1-2-3 offers sophisticated techniques for creating these and other types of queries.

Using the @FIND Function

To enter a criteria that matches text *anywhere* in the field, use the @FIND function. This comes in handy in fields that contain several words. For example, if a field contains *Santa Barbara, CA*, you can use the @FIND function to search for *CA*. Or, if a field contains *Janet Jackson*, you can locate *Jackson*. You would not be able to do these kinds of searches with wildcards.

In a database of recording stars, you would enter the following formula in the criteria range to find all the Jacksons:

@FIND("Jackson",B2,0)

In this formula, *Jackson* is the string you are searching for—text strings must always be enclosed in quotes. *B2* is the first record in the field you are querying. The *0* tells 1-2-3 to start looking for the string at the first character position in the cell. (Have you ever noticed that computers always start counting with zero instead of one?) In other words, 1-2-3 searches the entire cell for the text string.

Before or after entering an @FIND formula in the criteria range, you should format the cell to Text format. Otherwise, you will see ERR (if the first record doesn't contain the search string) or a number (corresponding to the character position in which the string is located). In the employee database, you have already formatted row 28 to Text format.

Unlike exact-match or wildcard queries, the text string used in the @FIND function is case sensitive. The text inside the quotes must have the same upper- and lowercase letters as the data in the database.

Follow these steps to find all employees whose last name ends in *son*:

1. Erase the old criteria from the criteria range.

2. In B28, type **@FIND("son",B2,0)** and press Enter.

3. Press **/** to display the 1-2-3 menu and choose:

    Data

    Query

    Find

4. Press ↓ to highlight each record (Anderson, Gibson, Peterson, and Wilson).

5. Press Ctrl-Break to quit to READY mode.

Using Conditional Formulas on Text Fields

The conditional formulas you used on numeric fields also work on text fields. They work much the same way as the ones for numeric fields except the data must be enclosed in quotes. For example,

> +B2>="M"

This formula finds or extracts the records in which the last name begins with a letter between *M* and *Z*. To restrict the range further, you can combine two criteria into a single formula:

> +B2>="J"#AND#B2<="R"

The above formula locates the last names that start with a letter between *J* and *R*. The results of a /Data Query Extract are shown in Figure 12.19.

Suppose you want a report of everyone in the engineering and manufacturing departments. You can build a two-criteria conditional formula, as follows:

> +D2="Eng."#OR#D2="Mfg."

```
B28: (T) +B2>="J"#AND#B2<="R"                                    READY

      A       B       C       D    E      F        G       H        I
26  ***Criteria Range***
27   ID Last      First      Dept  Exempt Hire Date Salary  Raise % New Sal.
28        +B2>="J"#AND#B2<="R"
29
30
31
32  ***Output Range***
33   ID Last      First      Dept  Exempt Hire Date Salary  Raise % New Sal.
34  1017 Jones    Carolyn    MIS   Yes    10/17/84  62,000   11.0%  68,820
35  1001 Jones    Mary       Sales No     10/15/88  29,500   11.0%  32,745
36  1009 Kline    Harry      Sales No     03/25/88  26,000    7.0%  27,820
37  1007 Manley   Martin     Mfg.  No     03/09/91  26,000    7.0%  27,820
38  1004 Meyers   Andrew     MIS   Yes    12/01/88  41,000    9.0%  44,690
39  1000 Peterson Pete       MIS   Yes    07/21/82  21,000   12.0%  23,520
40
41
42
43
44
45
```

Figure 12.19: A list of employees whose last names begin with a letter between *J* and *R*

Multiple-Line Criteria Range

1-2-3 offers another way to produce the report of employees in the engineering and manufacturing departments. Figure 12.20 shows an example of how to set up this query. Each criterion (Eng., Mfg.) is entered on a separate row under the Dept field. For this technique to work, the criteria range must be expanded to include the additional row; in this example, the criteria range would be A27..I29. On the plus side, this technique doesn't require conditional formulas. On the down side, you must temporarily change the criteria range and remember to change it back when you are finished with the query.

When a criteria range contains multiple lines of queries, only one of the lines must be true for the record to be found or extracted. In other words, a multiple-line criteria range is similar to the #OR# operator.

Excluding Data

There are several operators you can use to exclude data from a query operation. Suppose you want a list of all employees except for those in the

D29: [W6] 'Mfg.									READY

	A	B	C	D	E	F	G	H	I
26	***Criteria Range***								
27	ID	Last	First	Dept	Exempt	Hire Date	Salary	Raise %	New Sal.
28				Eng.					
29				Mfg.					
30									
31									
32	***Output Range***								
33	ID	Last	First	Dept	Exempt	Hire Date	Salary	Raise %	New Sal.
34	1011	Gibson	Pamela	Eng.	No	11/26/89	45,000	12.0%	50,400
35	1012	Ingram	Greg	Mfg.	No	09/30/90	21,000	6.5%	22,365
36	1007	Manley	Martin	Mfg.	No	03/09/91	26,000	7.0%	27,820
37	1015	Slater	Peter	Mfg.	No	01/05/82	20,000	8.0%	21,600
38	1016	Smith	Charles	Mfg.	Yes	06/29/84	25,000	7.0%	26,750
39	1008	Smith	Paul	Mfg.	No	06/10/87	27,000	10.0%	29,700
40	1013	Smothers	Stacey	Mfg.	No	05/01/87	24,000	7.5%	25,800
41	1010	Smythe	Jennifer	Eng.	Yes	11/13/90	34,000	6.0%	36,040
42	1014	Tucker	Brian	Eng.	Yes	04/22/88	39,000	9.0%	42,510
43	1003	Wilson	Robert	Eng.	Yes	10/14/83	36,000	15.0%	41,400
44									
45									

Figure 12.20: The criteria range in this example is A27..I29.

sales department. There are three ways to do this:

```
~Sales
#NOT#D2="Sales"
+D2<>"Sales"
```

The tilde (~) is a special symbol that stands for *except for* or *not*. It can be used with labels only. The #NOT# and <> (not equal to) operators, on the other hand, can be used with labels, values, or dates.

OTHER QUERY OPTIONS

So far, you have performed two query operations: Find and Extract. There are two others, though: Unique and Delete. Unique is quite similar to Extract. The only difference is that duplicate records are not extracted to the output range. Because records are occasionally entered twice into a database, the Unique option is a great way to weed out redundant data. Records are considered to be duplicates only if *all* fields are identical.

The Delete query operation is dangerous. When you choose /Data Query Delete, all records that match the criteria in the criteria range are permanently deleted from the input range. Fortunately, 1-2-3 asks you to confirm the command before it deletes the records. You can use this command to update a database. For example, suppose you have a membership database with a field that contains the date that members owe their dues, and if dues aren't paid by a certain date, the member should be deleted from the database. Each month you can set up a criterion that locates a range of dates (for example, in a certain month and year) and then issue the /Data Query Delete command to purge the database of unpaying members.

Chapter 10

Chapter 11

Chapter 12

Chapter 13

Chapter 14

Analyzing
Your Data

◀||| FAST TRACK |||▶

To use database statistical functions: 457

Set up input and criteria ranges. If desired, enter search criteria in the criteria range. To enter the formula, type the appropriate function (@DSUM, @DAVG, @DMAX, @DMIN, @DCOUNT, @DVAR,@DSTD) followed by (*input range,field number,criteria range*).

To create a one-variable data table: 460

Create the framework of the data table. The first column contains the variables and the first row contains the formulas you want to calculate. Then, choose /Data Table 1. When prompted, indicate the table range and the input cell.

To create a two-variable data table: 463

Create the framework of the data table. The first column and row contain the variables; the upper-left corner of the table contains the formula you want to calculate. Then, choose /Data Table 2. When prompted, indicate the table range and the two input cells.

To calculate a frequency distribution: 468

Set up the values range (the data you want to analyze) and the bin range (the list of numeric intervals). Then, choose /Data Distribution. When prompted, indicate the values range and the bin range.

To perform a regression analysis: 470

Enter the data to be analyzed. You need one column of dependent variables and at least one column of independent variables. Choose /Data Regression. Select X-Range and specify the range of independent variables. Choose Y-Range and indicate the range of dependent variables. Choose Output-Range and indicate where you want the output to appear. To generate the statistics, choose Go. The closer the R-Squared value is to 1 (100 percent), the higher the degree of correlation.

In Chapter 12 you learned how to use the sort and query operations to analyze a database. In this chapter you will learn several other data-analysis techniques that produce summary statistics on your database. For example, you can find out the average salary for employees in the engineering department or the highest salary in each department. You can also determine the salary distribution—how many people make less than $20,000, how many make between $20,000 and $30,000, and so on.

DATABASE FUNCTIONS

1-2-3 offers seven @ functions that are specifically designed to work with databases:

Function	Description
@DSUM	Totals the specified field
@DAVG	Averages the specified field
@DCOUNT	Counts the number of records in the specified field
@DMAX	Finds the maximum value in the specified field
@DMIN	Finds the minimum value in the specified field
@DSTD	Calculates the standard deviation of the specified field
@DVAR	Calculates the variance of the specified field

At first glance, these functions do not look too different from the standard @ functions (@SUM, @AVG, and so forth). What makes the database functions so powerful is that they are linked to the database criteria range. Thus, if there are any conditions entered in the criteria range, a database function performs its calculation on only those records that match the criteria.

Let's look at an example—suppose you want to find the average salary in the engineering department. If *Eng.* were entered in the criteria range, the @DAVG function would calculate an average for the employees in the engineering department.

The syntax for the @DAVG function is:

@DAVG(input,field,criteria)

All database functions require three pieces of information: the *input* range, the *field* you want to perform the calculation on, and the *criteria* range. The *field* is not a cell coordinate, nor is it a range or field name; rather, it refers to the number of the field in the database. For example, salary is the seventh field in the database. But, since computers start counting with zero, the field value in the database function should be 6.

The formula to calculate the average salary in the employee database would be:

@DAVG(A1..I20,6,A27..I28)

A1..I20 is the input range, *6* means that you want to average the seventh field in the database, and *A27..I28* is the criteria range. When you work with database formulas, it's a good idea to assign range names to the input and criteria ranges. That way, your formulas will be much easier to understand, plus you don't have to memorize the specific range coordinates. If you were to name the ranges, the formula would be:

@DAVG(INPUT,6,CRIT)

Retrieve the EMPLOYEE file and follow these steps to name the ranges:

1. Press / to display the 1-2-3 menu and choose:

    Range

    Name

    Create

2. Type **INPUT** and press Enter.

3. Paint the range A1..I20 and press Enter.

4. Follow the above steps to assign the name **CRIT** to A27..I28.

ANALYZING THE SALARY FIELD

Now, let's do a statistical analysis of the salary field in the employee database. In this first exercise, you will analyze the entire database without entering any specific criteria. (If there are no criteria specified, the database functions will perform the calculations on all records in the database.) You'll create a statistical summary above the criteria range (see Figure 13.1) so you can enter new criteria and see the results without having to move off the screen.

1. Erase the old criteria in row 28.

2. Insert four rows above row 26 (/Worksheet Insert Row).

3. Type the labels in A24..A28 as shown in Figure 13.1.

4. Enter the following formulas in the specified locations:

Cell	Contents
B24	@DSUM(INPUT,6,CRIT)
B25	@DAVG(INPUT,6,CRIT)
B26	@DCOUNT(INPUT,6,CRIT)
B27	@DMAX(INPUT,6,CRIT)
B28	@DMIN(INPUT,6,CRIT)

SPECIFYING CRITERIA IN DATABASE FUNCTIONS

You can see the real power of the database functions when you enter conditions in the criteria range. When you have search criteria, the database functions restrict their analyses to the records that match the specified conditions. Thus, if *sales* were entered under the Dept field in the criteria range, the database formulas would display the summary statistics for the sales department.

To display salary statistics for the sales department, enter **Sales** in cell D32. 1-2-3 automatically recalculates the new statistics in B24..B28, as

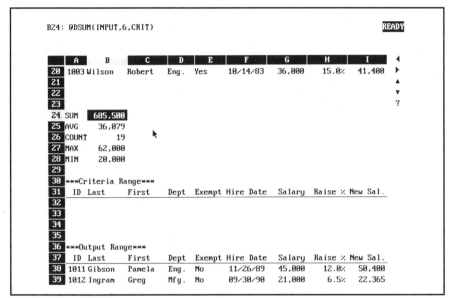

Figure 13.1: A statistical summary of the salary field in the employee
database

shown in Figure 13.2. Enter other departments (Eng., Mfg., and MIS) in
D32 and study the salary statistics. When you are finished, erase cell D32.

Each time you enter a different department, the database formulas display the salary statistics for the department. But what if you want to compare data from the various departments? With the way the formulas
are currently structured, every time you enter a new criterion, the statistics
for the last criterion are replaced with the new statistics. You could print
out the results for each department and then compare them on paper, but
the /Data Table command offers an easier way.

DATA TABLES

The data table feature plugs different values into a formula and displays the results in a nice, compact table. When you are working with
database functions, the data table command places different search criteria

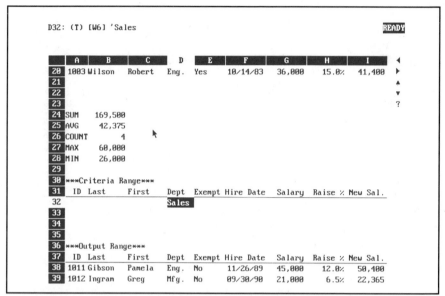

Figure 13.2: The salary statistics for the sales department

into the criteria range and displays statistics for each. The result is a table such as the one shown in Figure 13.3. This table calculates database averages, maximums, and minimums for each department. The values in E25..G28 are not formulas—they are the end-product of the /Data Table command.

Figure 13.4 shows the framework of a data table before the /Data Table command has been issued. The first column (D25..D28) contains the variables that will be plugged into the criteria range—the department names in this example. The first row (E24..G24) contains the database functions you want to calculate. You do not see these formulas in Figure 13.3 because the cells are hidden with the /Range Format Hidden command. Follow these steps to construct the framework of the data table:

1. Type the department names in D25..D28 as shown in Figure 13.4.

2. Enter and right-align the column headings in E23..G23.

3. Enter the following formulas:

Cell	Contents
E24	@DAVG(INPUT,6,CRIT)
F24	@DMAX(INPUT,6,CRIT)
G24	@DMIN(INPUT,6,CRIT)

To fill in the table with the appropriate statistics, use the /Data Table command. This command prompts you for two pieces of information: a table range and an input cell. The *table range* includes the variables and the formulas; the range is D24..G28 in the current example. The *input cell* is where 1-2-3 plugs the variables in, one at a time. In this example, each department name is placed, one by one, under the Dept field name (cell D32) in the criteria range.

Data tables can have either one or two variables. The table in this example uses only one variable (department). Later on, you will build a table that has two variables (department and exempt status). Choose /Data Table 1 if you have one variable and /Data Table 2 if you have two.

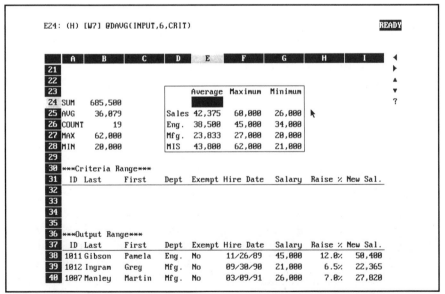

Figure 13.3: A data table that summarizes salary statistics by department

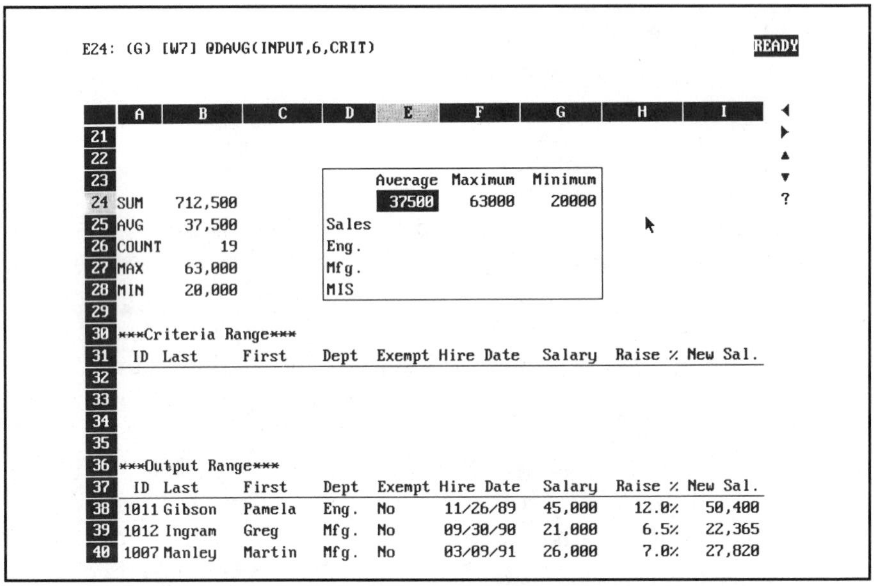

```
E24: (G) [W7] @DAVG(INPUT,6,CRIT)                              READY

        A       B       C       D       E       F       G       H       I      ◄
21                                                                              ►
22                                                                              ▲
23                                  Average  Maximum  Minimum                   ▼
24 SUM    712,500                    37500    63000    20000                    ?
25 AVG     37,500            Sales
26 COUNT       19            Eng.                                  ►
27 MAX     63,000            Mfg.
28 MIN     20,000            MIS
29
30 ***Criteria Range***
31   ID Last     First     Dept  Exempt Hire Date  Salary  Raise % New Sal.
32
33
34
35
36 ***Output Range***
37   ID Last     First     Dept  Exempt Hire Date  Salary  Raise % New Sal.
38 1011 Gibson   Pamela    Eng.  No    11/26/89   45,000   12.0%   50,400
39 1012 Ingram   Greg      Mfg.  No    09/30/90   21,000    6.5%   22,365
40 1007 Manley   Martin    Mfg.  No    03/09/91   26,000    7.0%   27,820
```

Figure 13.4: The framework of a data table (D24..G28)

Follow these steps to calculate the data table:

1. Press / to display the 1-2-3 menu and choose:

   Data

   Table

   1

2. Paint the range D24..G28 and press Enter. You are then prompted for the input cell.

3. Move the pointer to cell D32 and press Enter.

The formulas in E24..G24 are required for the /Data Table command but they are confusing when displayed above the table. You can erase them after the table is calculated, but you will have to reenter them if you ever need to recalculate the table. The best solution is to hide them. Follow these steps to finish your data table so that it looks like the one in Figure 13.3.

1. Move the pointer to E24.

2. Press / to display the 1-2-3 menu and choose:

    Range

    Format

    Hidden

3. Paint the range E24..G24 and press Enter.

RECALCULATING THE TABLE

Data tables are not dynamic. If you were to change an employee's salary in the database, the existing data table would not automatically reflect the change. However, assuming the table range and input cell haven't changed, you can quickly recalculate the data table with the Table key, F8. Let's try it.

1. Change Robert Wilson's salary to **63000**. When you press Enter, notice that the engineering row in the data table does not reflect the revised data.

2. With your eye on the engineering row, press F8 to recalculate the data table. The table now displays new statistics for the engineering department.

If you change the table range or input cell of a data table, the F8 key will not work—you must reissue the /Data Table command and respecify the ranges.

CREATING
A TWO-VARIABLE DATA TABLE

With the /Data Table 2 command, you can create data tables that make calculations based on two variables. For example, you can build a table that displays the average salaries for exempt and non-exempt employees in each department (see Figure 13.5). The first set of variables (the departments) is listed down the first column of the table range while the second

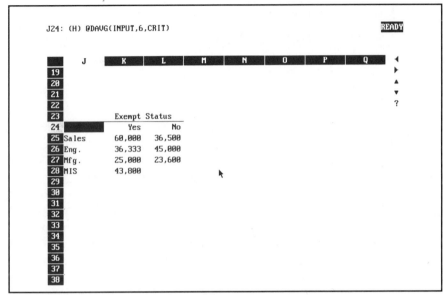

Figure 13.5: A two-variable data table

set of variables (the exempt status) is listed across the first row. The formula is placed in the upper-left corner of the table (J24)—it is hidden in Figure 13.5.

Note that two-variable data tables can calculate statistics on only one formula. With one-variable data tables, you can display results to as many formulas as you like. The data table you created earlier has three formulas—average, maximum, and minimum salaries.

Follow these steps to construct the framework of the data table:

1. Type the department names in J25..J28 as shown in Figure 13.6. These labels are the first set of variables in the data table.

2. Type and right-align the exempt statuses (*Yes* and *No*) in K24..L24. These labels are the second set of variables.

3. In J24, type **@DAVG(INPUT,6,CRIT)** and press Enter.

Your table should look similar to Figure 13.6. Now, calculate the data table as follows:

1. Press / to display the 1-2-3 menu and choose:

   Data

   Table

   2

2. Press Backspace to clear the previous table range.

3. Paint the range J24..L28 and press Enter. You are then prompted for the first input cell.

4. Make sure the pointer is on cell D32 and press Enter. You are prompted for the second input cell.

5. Move the pointer to cell E32 and press Enter. 1-2-3 then calculates your two-variable data table. L28 displays ERR because there are no non-exempt employees in the MIS department.

So that your data table matches the one in Figure 13.5, format J24 to hidden format, enter the *Exempt Status* heading, and erase cell L28. Save your file.

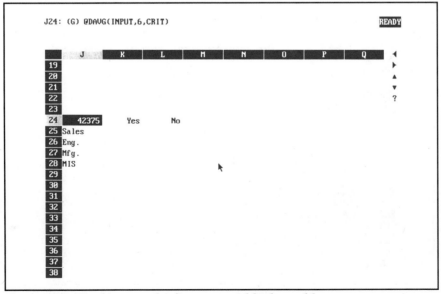

Figure 13.6: The framework of a two-variable data table

PLAYING WHAT-IF GAMES WITH MORTGAGE PAYMENTS

1-2-3's data tables and mortgage payment function (@PMT) are ideal tools for potential home buyers. You can create a data table, such as the one pictured in Figure 13.7, to calculate mortgage payments for a range of fixed interest rates. When we were house hunting, my husband and I relied heavily on this type of data table to see what our mortgage payments would be like with varying home prices and interest rates.

This spreadsheet has only two formulas. The formula in B3 calculates the loan amount based on the home price and the percentage of the down payment. The @PMT function is entered at the top of the second column of the data table. The syntax for the @PMT function is:

@PMT(principal,interest,term)

In this example, the principal amount is entered in B3, the interest rate is in B4, and the term of the loan is in B5. Because you typically want to

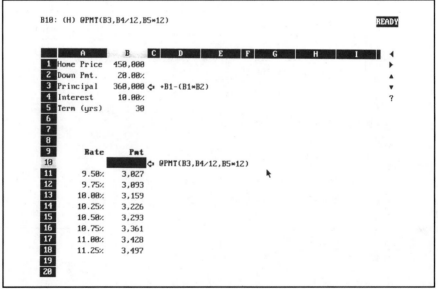

Figure 13.7: A data table to calculate mortgage payments at different interest rates

calculate *monthly* mortgage payments, you must convert the interest rate and term into months. You can make these conversions in the @PMT formula by dividing the yearly interest rate by 12 and multiplying the number of years by 12. The complete formula is:

@PMT(B3,B4/12,B5*12)

To calculate the mortgage payments for each interest rate, give the /Data Table 1 command and specify A10..B18 as the table range and B4 as the input cell. Once the table is generated, you are ready to play what-if games. What if you buy a $400,000 house? Type the new home price in B1 and press F8 to calculate the table based on this new assumption. Or, what if you give a 25 percent down payment instead of 20? What if you get a fifteen-year loan? To play these what-if games, enter your new assumptions in the appropriate cells and press F8 to regenerate the data table.

You may want to set up a data table that accounts for two variables such as the table shown in Figure 13.8. This table calculates mortgage payments for different interest rates and home prices. (Note: The sideways text in Figure 13.8 was created in the graphics editor.)

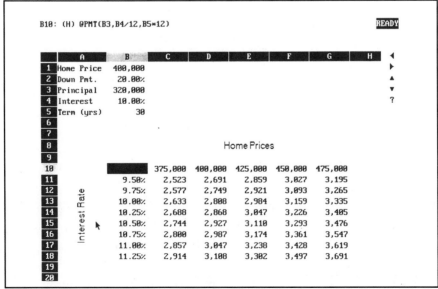

Figure 13.8: A two-variable data table to calculate mortgage payments

FREQUENCY DISTRIBUTION

With the /Data Distribution command you can determine how many values in a range fall within specific intervals. In your employee database, it might be interesting to know how many employees make between $20,000 and $30,000, between $30,000 and $40,000, and so forth. The statistical world calls this type of analysis *frequency distribution*. Figure 13.9 shows the frequency distribution of salaries for each $10,000 interval.

Frequency distributions are useful for tabulating survey responses. For example, if you have a column of numerically-coded responses (1=Yes, 0=No), the /Data Distribution command can count the number of yes and no responses. Another use for frequency distributions is in the classroom: Teachers can calculate the distribution of test scores. Remember from your school days when teachers used to post a list of how many people scored in the 60s, 70s, 80s, and 90s? This was a frequency distribution—but it was probably calculated manually instead of in 1-2-3. (At least in *my* school days it was!)

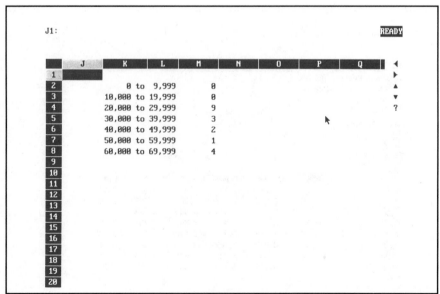

Figure 13.9: A frequency distribution of salaries in the employee database

Before you can issue the /Data Distribution command, you must have two ranges set up. The *values range* is the data you want to analyze—the salaries in G2..G20 in this example. The *bin range* is the list of numeric intervals—L2..L8 in Figure 13.9. The easiest way to create your bin range is with the /Data Fill command. The labels in column K in Figure 13.9 are not a formal part of the frequency distribution but they are helpful for interpreting the data.

Use the /Data Fill command to create the bin range, as follows:

1. If necessary, retrieve EMPLOYEE.

2. Place the pointer in cell L2.

3. Press / to display the 1-2-3 menu and choose:

   Data

   Fill

4. Paint the range L2..L8 and press Enter.

5. When prompted, specify a start value of **9999**, a step value of **10000**, and a stop value of **69999**. Column L now lists the intervals (bins).

6. Enter the descriptive labels shown in column K of Figure 13.9. Because the labels begin with a value character, you must precede each description with a label prefix (use the quotation mark to right-align the labels).

Now, let's calculate the frequency distribution:

1. Press / to display the 1-2-3 menu and choose:

   Data

   Distribution

2. When prompted for the values range, paint the range G2..G20 and press Enter.

3. When prompted for the bin range, paint the range L2..L8 and press Enter.

4. Save the file.

The frequencies are placed to the right of the bin range. The frequencies in column M indicate how many salaries are less than or equal to the adjacent value in the bin range, but greater than the preceding interval. Your distribution table should look similar to Figure 13.9. The only difference between your screen and the figure is that your screen will have a zero at the bottom of the frequency list. This extra value indicates how many salaries are greater than the highest interval (none in this case); it can be deleted.

PERFORMING
A REGRESSION ANALYSIS

Regression analysis is a statistical process that determines whether there is a correlation between two sets of data and predicts future values based on current data. Statisticians and other analysts use regression analysis to test the effect of one or more variables on another variable. Here are a few examples of ways you can use regression analysis:

- To determine whether age, sex, and race have any effect on salary level in a certain profession

- To predict a child's IQ level based on his or her parents' IQ test results

- To see if there is any correlation between a tariff and the balance of trade

There are two types of variables in regression analysis. *Dependent variables* are data whose values depend on outside factors. *Independent variables* are the outside factors themselves. In the examples above, the dependent and independent variables are:

Dependent	Independent
Salary	Age, Sex, Race
Child's IQ	Mother's IQ, Father's IQ

Dependent	Independent
Balance of trade	Tariff

Notice that each dependent variable can have one or more independent variables.

GENERATING THE STATISTICS

The best way to understand regression analysis is through a simple example. Our hypothesis in this example is that a park vendor's daily sales of ice cream cones is dependent upon the high temperature of the day (in Fahrenheit). Our goal is to determine whether there is indeed a correlation between sales and temperature, and if so, to predict future sales according to temperatures forecasted by the weatherman.

The more sample data you collect, the more meaningful your regression analysis will be. To keep our example simple, we are testing only a handful of days; in a real analysis you would want to compare several months of data. Follow these steps to build the spreadsheet shown in Figure 13.10:

1. Clear the screen (/Worksheet Erase).

2. Enter the labels and values shown in Figure 13.10. If Wysiwyg is attached, boldface the column headings and place a line underneath.

3. Change the width of column A to 5 and column B to 7.

4. Save the file with the name **ICECREAM**.

In this example, temperature is the independent variable and the number of cones sold is the dependent variable. 1-2-3 refers to the independent variable as the *X-Range* and the dependent variable as the *Y-Range*. The *Output-Range* is an empty area of the spreadsheet where 1-2-3 will place the results of the regression analysis.

Follow these steps to generate the regression statistics:

1. Press / to display the 1-2-3 menu and choose:

   Data

   Regression

2. Choose X-Range and indicate the range B4..B8.

3. Choose Y-Range and indicate the range C4..C8.

4. Choose Output-Range and specify cell C11 (you don't have to paint the entire range—one cell is sufficient—but make sure you have nine blank rows and four empty columns).

5. To generate the statistics, choose Go. Your screen should look similar to Figure 13.11.

UNDERSTANDING THE OUTPUT

Unless you are a statistician, you may be confused by the regression output. While I don't claim to be a statistician, let me try to give you a

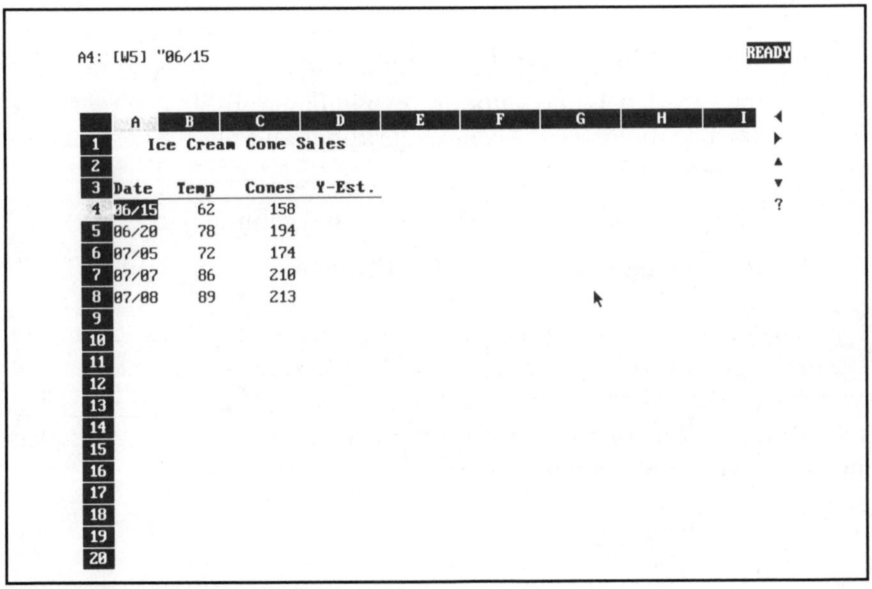

Figure 13.10: The sample data

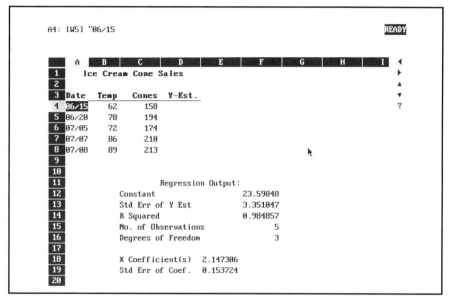

Figure 13.11: The regression output is placed in C11..F19.

layman's explanation of the regression results. To check for a correlation, look at the value for *R Squared* (0.984857). The closer this value is to 1 (100 percent), the higher the degree of correlation. A value of 0.98 (98 percent) indicates that there is a very high level of correlation between ice cream sales and temperature.

The *Constant* and the *X-Coefficient* can be used in an equation to estimate or predict *y*-values. When plotted on an XY graph, the estimated *y*-values form a straight line. If there is a high level of correlation, the actual *y*-values will appear very close to this line. Figure 13.12 shows an XY graph of the ice cream data.

Before you can create this graph, you need to calculate the estimated *y*-values in column D. The formula to compute the *y*-values is a linear equation, as follows:

$$Y=A+B*X$$

A is the constant (23.598 in cell F12), *B* is the *x*-coefficient (2.147 in E18), and *X* is the independent variable (temperature—for example, B4). Follow these steps to create this formula:

1. In D4, type **+$F$12+$E$18*B4** and press Enter. (The dollar signs make the cell references absolute so that they won't change when you copy the formula.)

2. Format the cell to Fixed with 0 decimal places.

3. Copy the formula to D5..D8. Your screen should look similar to Figure 13.13.

Compare the estimated sales in column D with the actual sales in column C. Because of the correlation that exists between sales and temperature, the values are very close. In fact, 98 percent of the time (the R-squared value), the estimated *y*-values will be correct within 3.35 cones (the *Std Err of Y est*).

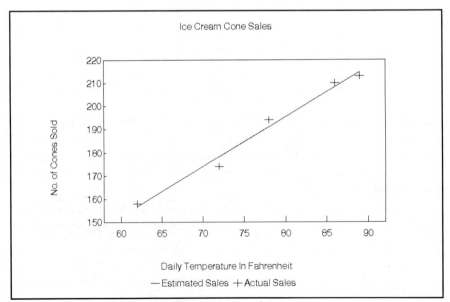

Figure 13.12: An XY graph of the ice cream data

CREATING AN XY GRAPH

An easier way to interpret regression data is with an XY graph. By definition, the estimated *y*-values create a straight line. The actual *y*-values will be points on, above, or below this line. Follow these steps to create the XY graph shown in Figure 13.12:

1. Press / to display the 1-2-3 menu and choose:

    Graph

    Type

    XY

2. Choose X and specify the temperatures in B4..B8.

3. Choose A and specify the estimated sales in D4..D8.

4. Choose B and specify the actual sales in C4..C8.

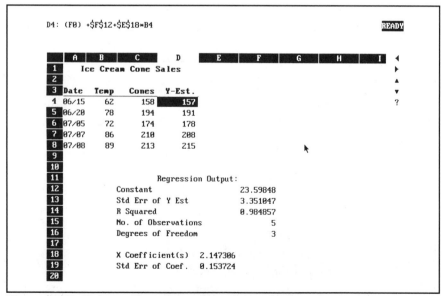

Figure 13.13: Column D contains the estimated sales values.

5. View the graph. This graph is difficult to interpret because the actual sales data points are connected with lines—they should have symbols only. Also, the regression line should have lines without symbols.

6. From the main /Graph menu, choose:

   Options

   Format

   A

   Lines

   B

   Symbols

   Quit

7. Press F10 to view the graph. It is now easy to see how the actual values are scattered in relation to the regression line.

8. Add titles and legends as shown in Figure 13.12.

PREDICTING FUTURE VALUES

Now that we have determined that ice cream sales are related to temperature, we can use the regression statistics to predict future sales. Let's build a table that predicts ice cream cone sales for a variety of temperatures. The temperatures will be in five-degree increments. Follow these steps to set up a prediction table:

1. Enter the titles and column headings shown in Figure 13.14.

2. Enter the temperatures in column B. (The fastest way is to use /Data Fill.)

3. In C27, type **+$F$12+$E$18*B27** and press Enter. This is the same linear equation you used earlier.

4. Format the cell to Fixed with 0 decimal places.

5. Copy the formula to C28..C36.

6. Save the ICECREAM file.

```
C27: (F8) +$F$12+$E$18*B27                           READY
```

	A	B	C	D	E	F	G	H	I
21	Estimated Ice Cream Cone Sales								
22	Based on Forecasted Temperatures								
23									
24		High	Pred.						
25		Temp.	Sales						
26									
27		60	152						
28		65	163						
29		70	174						
30		75	185						
31		80	195						
32		85	206						
33		90	217						
34		95	228						
35		100	238						
36		105	249						
37									
38									
39									
40									

Figure 13.14: A table that predicts ice cream cone sales

Now, let's suppose that the weatherman forecasts tomorrow's high temperature will be 95 degrees. According to our regression analysis, the vendor should sell 228 ice cream cones.

MULTIPLE INDEPENDENT VARIABLES

In the regression analysis you performed on the ice cream cone data, you had one independent (temperature) and one dependent variable (sales). Frequently, though, dependent variables depend on more than one factor. For example, ice cream sales can also depend on the number of hours the sun is shining. 1-2-3's linear regression allows for multiple independent variables—in fact, you can have up to 255 independent variables.

Figure 13.15 shows ice cream sales data for a different range of dates with two independent variables (temperature and hours of sun). The independent variables (the X-Range) are located in B4..C8. The sales in D4..D8 are the dependent variables (the Y-Range). The Output-Range is still C11. Notice that the regression output contains several additional statistics. Because you have two independent variables, 1-2-3 calculates *x*-coefficients for each variable. Thus, the *x*-coefficient for the temperature variable is 1.3 (cell E18) and the *x*-coefficient for the sun variable is 1.86 (cell F18). The additional coefficient must be included in the linear equation. The formula for the estimated *y*-values in column E is:

+$F$12+($E$18*B4)+($F$18*C4)

Therefore, when you have multiple independent variables, the linear equation multiplies each *x*-coefficient by its corresponding *x*-value.

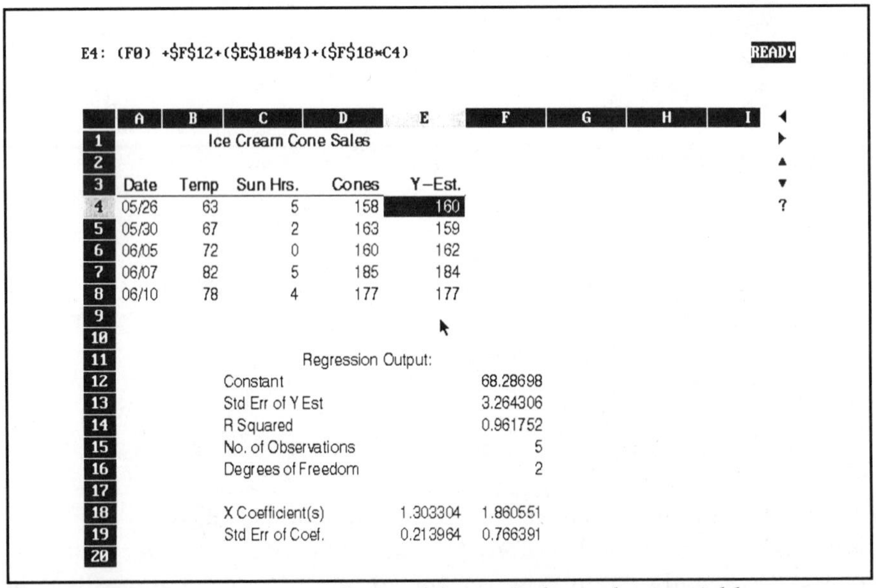

Figure 13.15: A regression analysis with two independent variables

PART I

PART II

PART III

PART IV

PART V

Macros

Chapter 10

Chapter 11

Chapter 12

Chapter 13

Chapter 14

Automating Your Keystrokes with Macros

To create a macro: 486

On a piece of paper, write down the keystrokes you want the macro to perform, and then enter these keystrokes into a cell as a label (for example, '/fs). Name the macro with the /Range Name Create command; macro names typically start with a backslash followed by a single letter (for example, \S).

To execute a macro: 488

Press Alt with the letter you have assigned as the name (for example, *Alt-S*). You can also press Alt-F3 and choose the macro name from a list.

To assign special keys in a macro: 488

Each key on your keyboard has a way of being identified in a macro. For example, the tilde (~) represents the Enter key, {RIGHT} stands for →, and {GOTO} signifies the Goto key (F5). Table 14.1 gives a complete list of these keys.

To pause a macro: 501

Type {?} where you want the macro to pause.

When a macro doesn't work, 506

Check to make sure it is named properly and that it doesn't have any typing mistakes. If you can't determine the problem, use step mode: Press Alt-F2 to turn on step mode, invoke the macro, and press the spacebar to execute the keystrokes one step at a time. When you locate the problem, press Ctrl-Break to cancel the macro, press Alt-F2 to turn off step mode, and correct the mistake by editing the macro.

To record a macro: 508

Define a learn range with the /Worksheet Learn Range command. Turn on the learn feature with Alt-F5 and enter the commands and keystrokes you want recorded (don't use the mouse). Turn off the learn feature with Alt-F5.

To copy a macro file into the current file: 511

Place the cell pointer in a remote location of the spreadsheet where you want the macros to go. Choose /File Combine Copy Entire-File and select the file that contains the macros. Rename the macros with the /Range Name Labels Right command.

Imagine a hand coming out of your computer and typing on the keyboard for you. While 1-2-3 can't do anything so dramatic, it does offer an equivalent—macros. With 1-2-3's macro feature, you can automate lengthy command sequences, reducing them to a few shortcut keys. Then, all you have to do is press the shortcut keys, and 1-2-3 takes care of the rest.

Let's look at an example. Printing a report requires quite a few keystrokes. In 1-2-3, you choose /Print Printer Range, specify the range, and then choose Align Go Page Quit. With a macro, you can print with only two keystrokes (Alt-P, for example). As you can clearly see, macros are a big time-saver.

Occasionally you will want to create temporary macros to help you with tedious editing jobs. Usually these tasks are one-time jobs, such as converting a column of dates from labels to date functions. It is unlikely you would want to keep this type of macro permanently, so after using such a macro, you could delete it.

But macros can do more than just automate your commands; they can automate your typing as well. For example, you can create a macro that types your signature block at the end of a letter, or one that creates monthly column headings (Jan., Feb., and so on) across a row.

The macros you will create in this chapter are commonly called *keystroke macros* because they automate your keystrokes. However, macros go beyond commands and typing: 1-2-3 includes a powerful programming language that allows you to customize the program to your own needs. For those who are interested in exploring the programming aspect of macros, be sure to read Chapters 16 and 17, which explain 1-2-3's programming language in detail.

CREATING A MACRO

We saved macros for the final part of the book for a very good reason: You need to be familiar with the 1-2-3 and Wysiwyg commands before you can create macros to automate them. The first step to creating a macro is actually giving the commands at the keyboard and writing down the keystrokes on a piece of paper as you issue the commands. For example, let's say you want to create a macro to save a file. You should go through the motions of saving a file and write down the keystrokes (/fs). Notice that you need to write down only the first letter of each command.

BUILDING A MACRO

To build a macro, you enter the keystrokes in an empty cell. Because the keystrokes must be entered as a label, you will usually need to begin the cell entry with an apostrophe. In the file-save example, you would enter the following keystrokes into a cell (don't do this now):

'/fs

The apostrophe is the label prefix, and the keystrokes issue the /File Save command. It doesn't matter whether you enter the keystrokes in upper- or lowercase.

Another way to build a macro is to record the keystrokes in much the same way you would record a song on a tape recorder. Instead of recording on a cassette tape, though, you record into a spreadsheet range. The recording feature is discussed later in the chapter.

NAMING A MACRO

The final step to creating a macro is assigning it a name with the /Range Name Create command. Macros have special names: They begin with a backslash (\) followed by a single letter. If possible, you should make the name mnemonic: \P for a print macro, \S for a save macro, and so on. The letter can be entered in upper- or lowercase—macros are not case sensitive.

You can have up to 26 macros named with the backslash-letter combination (A–Z). If you need more than 26 macros, or if you want macros with more descriptive names, you can assign regular range names to your macros (such as PRINT or SAVE). These macro names can be up to fifteen characters long; however, macros with regular range names cannot be executed as quickly.

RUNNING A MACRO

After you have named a macro, you should test it out to make sure it works. How you execute or run a macro depends on the type of name you have assigned to it. To execute a macro that you have named with the backslash-letter combination, press Alt with the letter, for example, Alt-P or Alt-S. To run a macro that has a longer name, press Alt-F3 (the Run key) and then choose the macro name (such as PRINT or SAVE) from the displayed list.

Because names with the backslash-letter combination can be executed with fewer keystrokes, we will use these types of names for most of the examples in this chapter. The main drawback to the backslash names is that they are not as easy to remember or recognize.

DOCUMENTING YOUR MACROS

Macro keystrokes are somewhat cryptic so it's a good idea to provide additional documentation in the adjacent cells. Figure 14.1 shows the three-column format commonly used for macros. The first column contains the macro name, the second column is the macro, and the third column is a brief description. While the first and third columns are optional, they are extremely helpful for deciphering your (or someone else's) macros.

Notice that a blank line separates each macro. This empty row is not simply for clarity. It is actually the macro's stop sign. Because some macros automate many keystrokes, they run over into multiple rows (such as the \H and \T macros in Figure 14.1). A blank cell lets 1-2-3 know the macro is finished.

ASSIGNING SPECIAL KEYS IN MACROS

Every key on your keyboard has some way of being represented in a macro. For example, to tell the macro to press the Enter key, type a tilde (~). To represent →, type {**RIGHT**} or {**R**}. To indicate the F2 (Edit) key in a macro, type {**EDIT**}. A complete list of the special keys appears in Table 14.1.

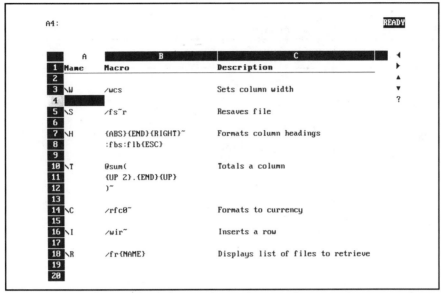

Figure 14.1: In the standard three-column format, the macro's name and
purpose are immediately apparent.

Table 14.1: Macro Key Names

KEY	MACRO KEY NAME
Enter	~
↓	{DOWN} or {D}
↑	{UP} or {U}
←	{LEFT} or {L}
→	{RIGHT} or {R}
Ctrl-←	{BIGLEFT}
Ctrl-→	{BIGRIGHT}
PgUp	{PGUP}
PgDn	{PGDN}
Home	{HOME}
End	{END}
Backspace	{BACKSPACE} or {BS}

Table 14.1: Macro Key Names (*continued*)

KEY	MACRO KEY NAME
Esc	{ESCAPE} or {ESC}
Ctrl-Break	{BREAK}
Del	{DELETE} or {DEL}
Ins	{INSERT} or {INS}
F1	{HELP}
F2	{EDIT}
F3	{NAME}
F4	{ABS}
F5	{GOTO}
F6	{WINDOW}
F7	{QUERY}
F8	{TABLE}
F9	{CALC}
F10	{GRAPH}
Alt-F7	{APP1}
Alt-F8	{APP2}
Alt-F9	{APP3}
Alt-F10	{APP4}

Several of the macros in Figure 14.1 make use of the special keys. For example, here are the macro keystrokes to resave a file:

```
/fs~r
```

This macro issues the /File Save command, presses Enter to accept the same name, and then chooses Replace.

Now look at the macro to format column headings:

```
{ABS}{END}{RIGHT}~
:fbs:flb{ESC}
```

This macro prespecifies the range before issuing several Wysiwyg formatting commands. The {ABS} presses the F4 key, which anchors the cell pointer. The {END} and {RIGHT} macro commands move the cell pointer to the last entry in the row, and the ~ enters the range. The end result is that the row of column headings is painted before the bold (:fbs) and bottom line (:flb) commands are issued. {ESC} represents the Escape key (it clears the range in this example).

WHERE DO MACROS GO?

You are probably wondering where you create your macros. There are several approaches you can take. One technique is to place them in a remote area of the spreadsheet. The safest place to put them is to the right of and below the active spreadsheet. This way, if you delete or insert rows and columns, the macros will not be affected. Figure 14.2 is a diagram that illustrates this location. Using this approach, you must enter or copy the macros into each spreadsheet file. Later on in this chapter, you will learn how to copy the macros into other files.

Another option is to use 1-2-3's Macro Library Manager add-in. With this approach, the macros are loaded into memory (RAM) and are always available. This second method offers two advantages: You don't need to bother copying the macros into each file, and your spreadsheet is not cluttered with macros. Chapter 15 discusses the Macro Library Manager in detail.

Many of the macros you will create will be generic and can be used in any spreadsheet file. Macros that fall into the generic category include those that save files, format column headings, insert rows, add up columns of numbers, and so forth. Your generic macros should all go into a single master file. That way, they can easily be transferred into other files or into a macro library.

Some macros may be spreadsheet-specific, such as one that prints three named ranges, one after another. This type of macro should be entered into a remote area of the spreadsheet as indicated in Figure 14.2.

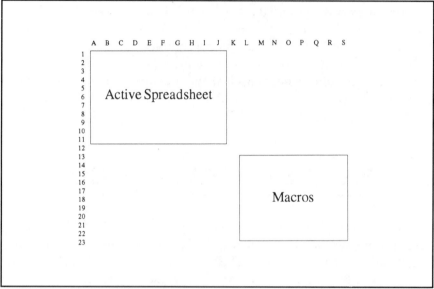

Figure 14.2: The safest place to enter your macros is to the right of and below the active spreadsheet.

CREATING A SET OF GENERIC MACROS

Now that you have learned the basics, you are ready to start creating your own macros. In the upcoming exercises, you will compile a set of generic macros that could be useful in just about any spreadsheet file. You will create these macros in their own file. Once the macro set is complete, you can copy it into another spreadsheet file or into a macro library.

Follow these steps to create your macro file:

1. If necessary, clear the screen (/Worksheet Erase).

2. Enter the following column headings:

Cell	Label
A1:	Name
B1:	Macro
C1:	Description

3. Save the file with the name **MACROS**.

CREATING A COLUMN-WIDTH MACRO

To begin, let's create a macro that changes the width of a column. This macro will not set the width to any specific size; rather, it will prompt you for the column width. The command this macro will issue is /Worksheet Column Set-Width.

To create the macro:

1. In B3, type **'/wcs** and press Enter. Be sure to type the apostrophe—if you don't, you will bring up the 1-2-3 menu.

2. To name the macro, press / to display the 1-2-3 menu and choose:

    Range

    Name

    Create

3. Type **\W** for the name and press Enter. (Make sure you type the backslash and not the forward slash.)

4. Press Enter to accept B3..B3 as the range.

5. For documentation purposes, enter **'\W** in A3 and **Sets column width** in C3. Compare your screen to Figure 14.3.

Now, run the macro:

1. Place the pointer in any cell in column B.

2. Press Alt-W. You are prompted for the column width. You can either type in the number or use the arrow keys to expand or contract the width one character at a time.

3. Type **25** and press Enter.

4. Move the pointer to column C.

5. Press Alt-W and set the width to 35.

If your macro doesn't work properly, refer to the section *Debugging a Macro*, later in the chapter.

CREATING A FILE-SAVING MACRO

Now let's create a macro that resaves a file (in other words, that uses the Replace option). Naturally, this macro assumes you have already saved the file once and given the file a name.

To create the macro:

1. In B5, type **'/fs~r** and press Enter. Remember, the tilde (~) represents the Enter key.

2. To name the macro, press / to display the 1-2-3 menu and

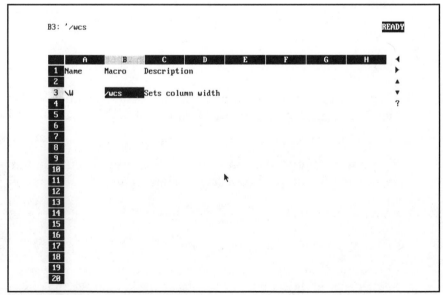

Figure 14.3: Row 3 contains the column-width macro.

choose:

> Range
>
> Name
>
> Create

3. Type **\S** for the name and press Enter.

4. Press Enter to accept B5..B5 as the range.

5. For documentation purposes, enter '**\S** in A5 and **Resaves file** in C5. Compare your screen to Figure 14.4.

Before you run the macro, make sure you have given the file a name (MACROS). If you run this macro on a file that has not yet been named, it saves the file with the first name on your list. Thus, the contents of this first file will be replaced with your macros—you will essentially lose your first file.

To run the macro, press Alt-S. The file will be resaved under the same name (MACROS). If your macro doesn't work, refer to the section *Debugging a Macro,* later in the chapter.

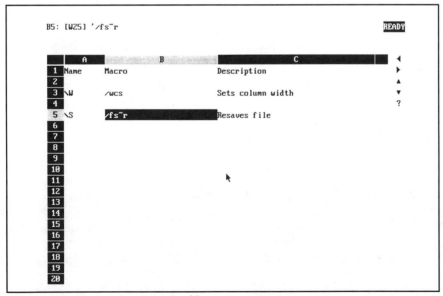

Figure 14.4: Row 5 contains the file-saving macro.

CREATING A MACRO
TO FORMAT COLUMN HEADINGS

Macros can automate Wysiwyg commands as well as 1-2-3 commands. Let's say you want to create a macro to bold and underline some column headings. Because you want to format the range with two Wysiwyg formatting commands, it's more efficient to specify the range before you bring up the Wysiwyg menu. Remember, to prespecify a range, press the F4 key to anchor and then use the arrow keys to paint the desired range. Since column headings are in consecutive cells in a row, you can easily specify the entire row by pressing End and →. End and → highlight all headings, regardless of how many there are.

Since this macro has two steps (specifying the range and formatting), let's divide the macro into two cells (B7 and B8).

Create the macro:

1. In B7, type **{ABS}{END}{RIGHT}~** and press Enter. A label prefix (apostrophe) is not necessary here because the cell entry begins with a label character.

2. In B8, type **':fbs:flb{ESC}** and press Enter. (The *{ESC}* at the end of the macro clears the highlighting from the prespecified range.)

3. Move the cell pointer up to the first cell in the macro (B7). For multiple-cell macros, you name only the first cell.

4. To name the macro, press / to display the 1-2-3 menu and choose:

    Range

    Name

    Create

5. Type **\H** for the name and press Enter.

6. Press Enter to accept B7..B7 as the range.

7. For documentation purposes, enter **'\H** in A7 and **Formats column headings** in C7. Compare your screen to Figure 14.5.

Note that this macro assumes Wysiwyg is attached. To run the macro:

1. Place the pointer in A1.

2. Press Alt-H to format the column headings. If your macro doesn't work properly, refer to the section *Debugging a Macro*.

3. Press Alt-S to save the file.

CREATING A MACRO TO SUM A COLUMN

Macros are not limited to menu commands—you can also create macros that enter part or all of a formula. The @SUM function is a perfect candidate for a macro because you use it all the time and it requires quite a few keystrokes. This macro will enter the complete @SUM function, including the range. It adds up any column of numbers, no matter how large the range is. For the macro to work, two conditions must be met:

- the last cell to be summed must be two cells above the formula

- there can't be any blank cells in the middle of the column

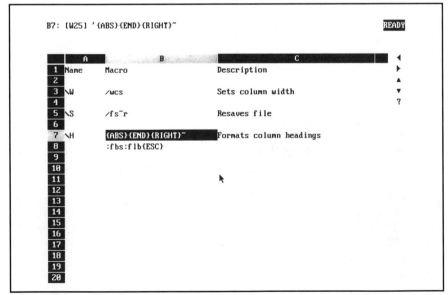

Figure 14.5: Rows 7 and 8 contain the formatting macro.

Figure 14.6 demonstrates which ranges of numbers will and won't work with the macro.

To create the macro:

1. In B10, type **'@sum(** and press Enter. Don't forget the apostrophe at the beginning!

2. In B11, type **{UP 2}.{END}{UP}** and press Enter. This part of the macro paints the sum range. *{UP 2}* moves the cell pointer up two cells; it's the same as typing *{UP}{UP}*.

3. In B12, type **')~** and press Enter to finish the macro.

4. Move the pointer to the first cell of the macro (B10) and assign the name **\T** (for Total).

5. Enter the documentation shown in Figure 14.7.

Before you can run this macro, you need a sample column of numbers. Follow these steps to test the macro:

1. In A14..A17, enter four numbers.

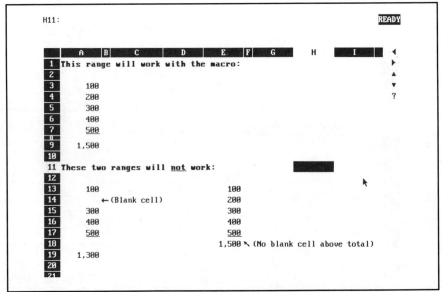

Figure 14.6: The \T macro works only if the sum range is set up properly.

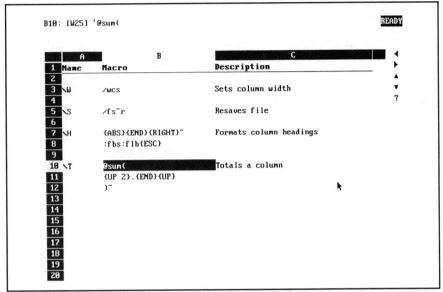

B10: [W25] '@sum(READY

	A	B	C
1	Name	Macro	Description
2			
3	\W	/wcs	Sets column width
4			
5	\S	/fs~r	Resaves file
6			
7	\H	{ABS}{END}{RIGHT}~	Formats column headings
8		:fbs:flb{ESC}	
9			
10	\T	@sum(	Totals a column
11		{UP 2}.{END}{UP}	
12		)~	
13			
14			
15			
16			
17			
18			
19			
20			

Figure 14.7: The macro to total a column is entered in rows 10 through 12.

2. Move the pointer to where you want the total to appear (A19).

3. Press Alt-T to total the column. If your macro doesn't work properly, refer to the section *Debugging a Macro*.

4. Erase the sample data (A14..A19).

5. Save the file with the Alt-S macro.

Later in the chapter you will learn how to create a more versatile macro that sums either a row or a column and allows you to have blank cells in the sum range.

A SHORTCUT
FOR NAMING MACROS

In the four macros you have created so far, you used the /Range Name Create command to name each macro. A faster way to name macros is with the /Range Name Labels Right command. This command assumes you have entered the range names in a column that is adjacent to the cells to be named. All you have to do is indicate the range of cells containing the range names (column A in the current example) and the command assigns the names to the cells to the right of the range. With this command, you don't have to type each individual name—you just tell 1-2-3 where the names are located.

Figure 14.8 shows several new macros added to the macro file. (Note: The titles were frozen on the screen with the /Worksheet Titles Horizontal command.) Rather than naming each macro with /Range Name Create, choose /Range Name Labels Right and specify the label range A14..A18. 1-2-3 will then assign the name \C to B14, \I to B16, and \R to B18.

To add these new macros to your file, follow these steps:

1. Type the names, macros, and descriptions as shown in Figure 14.8. Don't forget to use the apostrophe for the entries in columns A and B.

2. Move the pointer to A14.

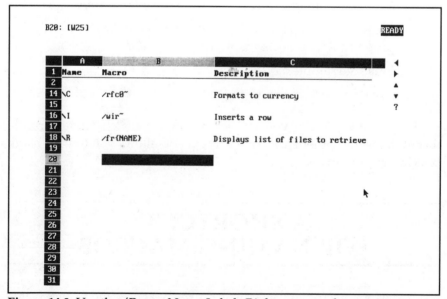

Figure 14.8: Use the /Range Name Labels Right command to name a group of macros with a single command.

3. To name the three macros, press / to display the 1-2-3 menu and choose:

   Range

   Name

   Labels

   Right

4. Paint the range A14..A18 and press Enter.

5. Press Alt-S to save the file.

6. Test each of the macros to make sure they work properly. Before testing the Alt-C macro, you will need to enter sample numbers. Erase these numbers after you have tested the macro. Be sure to delete any rows you insert with the Alt-I macro.

PAUSING A MACRO

In some of your macros, you will want the macro to pause so you can respond to a prompt in the control panel (for example, to specify a range). The macro pause command is {?}; enter this command at the point where you want the macro to pause. Then, when you invoke the macro, it will pause until you press Enter. To cancel a macro while it's pausing, press Ctrl-Break and Esc.

Each of the three macros in Figure 14.9 uses pause commands. The date macro (\D) pauses so you can enter a date in the format *MM/DD/YY* (for example, *3/4/92*). When you press Enter, the date function is completed and the cell is formatted to date format.

The find macro (\F) pauses so you can enter a text string to search for. After you type the string and press Enter, the first occurrence of the word will be highlighted.

The print macro (\P) pauses so you can specify a range. You can indicate the range by painting, by typing the range coordinates, by typing a range name, or by pressing F3 and choosing a range name. As soon as you press Enter, the macro continues.

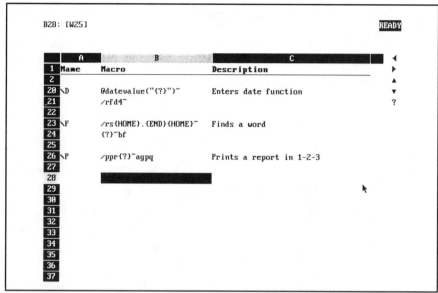

Figure 14.9: These macros use the {?} command to pause the macro.

To add these three macros to your file, follow these steps:

1. Type the names, macros, and descriptions as shown in Figure 14.9. Don't forget to use the apostrophe for the entries in columns A and B.

2. Move the pointer to cell A20.

3. To name the macros, press / to display the 1-2-3 menu and choose:

   Range

   Name

   Labels

   Right

4. Paint the range A20..A26 and press Enter.

5. Press Alt-S to save the file.

You are now ready to test the new macros to see how the pause command works. Follow these steps to test the date macro:

1. Go to a blank cell (for example, A29) and press Alt-D. The macro pauses and the control panel displays the beginning of the @DATEVALUE function. The status line at the bottom of the screen displays *CMD* (for Command) when the macro is paused.

2. Type the date **10/15/91**.

3. Press Enter to tell the macro to continue. The date is entered and formatted.

4. Erase this cell.

To test the find macro, follow these steps:

1. Press Alt-F. The macro pauses as the control panel prompts you for a search string.

2. Type **file** for the search string.

3. Press Enter to continue the macro. The first occurrence of the word *file* is highlighted and the control panel displays two choices, Next and Quit. Note that at this point 1-2-3 has executed all the keystrokes in the macro. The macro is no longer in control—*you* are back in the driver's seat.

4. Choose Next to find the next occurrence.

5. Choose Quit.

To test the print macro, let's print the macro list shown in Figure 14.10. It's always wise to print your macros so you can refer to the list if you can't remember a macro's name.

1. Press Alt-P. The macro pauses so you can specify the print range.

2. Paint the entire three-column range (A1..C26).

3. Press Enter to continue the macro. Your printout should look similar to the one in Figure 14.10.

4. Press Alt-S to save the file.

```
Name      Macro                        Description

\W        /wcs                         Sets column width

\S        /fs˜r                        Resaves file

\H        {ABS}{END}{RIGHT}˜           Formats column headings
          :fbs:flb{ESC}

\T        @sum(                        Totals a column
          {UP 2}.{END}{UP}
          )˜

\C        /rfc0˜                       Formats to currency

\I        /wir˜                        Inserts a row

\R        /fr{NAME}                    Displays list of files to retrieve

\D        @datevalue("{?}")˜           Enters date function
          /rfd4˜

\F        /rs{HOME}.{END}{HOME}˜       Finds a word
          {?}˜bf

\P        /ppr{?}˜agpq                 Prints a report in 1-2-3
```

Figure 14.10: A printout of the macros

The Alt-T macro you created earlier would be more versatile with a pause command. Instead of the macro defining the sum range, the macro can pause to allow you to enter the range yourself. This version of the Alt-T macro would have the following keystrokes:

@sum({?})~

DEBUGGING A MACRO

Many different things can go wrong with a macro. Here is a list of some common problems you might have:

- You have typed the keystrokes incorrectly. Analyze the macro and check to be sure you didn't make a typo or leave out a keystroke.

- You have forgotten a tilde. It's all too easy to forget to include a tilde where you want the macro to press Enter.

- You haven't left a blank row between macros. Blank cells are macro stop signs. If you don't leave a blank cell between two macros, 1-2-3 thinks the range is a single macro and will execute all keystrokes until it finds a blank cell.

- You have forgotten to name the cell. Be sure to use /Range Name Create or /Range Name Labels Right to name the macro.

- You have assigned the wrong name to the macro. Common mistakes are to type the forward slash or to forget the backslash.

- You have assigned the name to the wrong cell. The cell that should be named is the one containing the macro keystrokes. If the macro is several rows long, you need only name the first cell.

Refer to the above list whenever you have problems with your macros. If 1-2-3 beeps at you and does nothing when you press the macro keys, you have a problem with your range name. Either you didn't name the macro or you named it incorrectly. Use the /Range Name Create command to rename the macro. To see a list of range names and their corresponding ranges, use the /Range Name Table command. This produces a list such as the one shown in Figure 14.11. Study this list and make sure the macros are properly named.

If the macro starts to execute commands and then beeps or displays a syntax error message, the macro contains incorrect keystrokes. Study the macro keystrokes and check their accuracy. In particular, look for missing tildes and braces. Once you locate the problem, edit the cell to correct the mistake and try the macro again. (You don't need to rename the macro.) If you still can't locate the problem, use *step mode*.

USING STEP MODE

Because macros execute so quickly, it's not always easy to pinpoint the problem when a macro doesn't work. *Step mode* allows you to slow things down to see what's happening one keystroke at a time. Each time you press a key (any key), a single keystroke or macro command is executed.

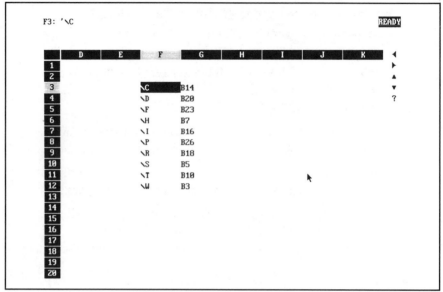

Figure 14.11: A range-name table

Because macro execution is slowed down, you can easily determine where the problem occurs.

To see how this works, let's introduce a mistake into one of your macros and then use step mode to locate the problem. Let's alter the contents of B16 so that the keystrokes are incorrect.

1. Change B16 to **'/wri~** instead of *'/wir~*.

2. Press Alt-I to insert a row. You hear a beep and the control panel prompts you for a column insert range—not what you wanted the macro to do.

3. Press Ctrl-Break to cancel the command.

Now, use step mode to figure out where the macro is going wrong:

1. Press Alt-F2 to turn on step mode. The status line displays *STEP*.

2. Press Alt-I to invoke the insert-row macro. The bottom-left corner of the screen displays the macro keystrokes (*/wri~*). The first keystroke is highlighted as shown in Figure 14.12.

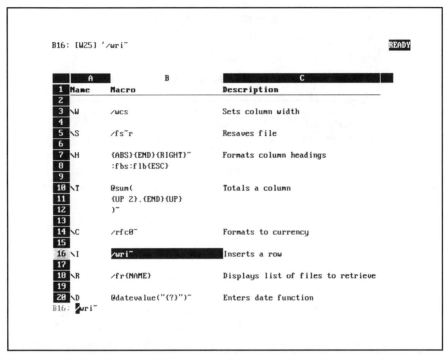

```
B16: [W25] '/wri~                                              READY

              A                 B                        C
     1  Name        Macro                   Description
     2
     3  \W          /wcs                     Sets column width
     4
     5  \S          /fs~r                    Resaves file
     6
     7  \H          {ABS}{END}{RIGHT}~       Formats column headings
     8              :fbs:flb{ESC}
     9
     10 \T          @sum(                    Totals a column
     11             {UP 2}.{END}{UP}
     12             )~
     13
     14 \C          /rfc0~                   Formats to currency
     15
     16 \I          /wri~                    Inserts a row
     17
     18 \R          /fr{NAME}                Displays list of files to retrieve
     19
     20 \D          @datevalue("{?}")~       Enters date function
     B16: /wri~
```

Figure 14.12: The bottom-left corner of the screen lists the macro keystrokes that are being stepped out in step mode.

3. Press any key (such as the spacebar) to begin executing keystrokes. The 1-2-3 menu displays in the control panel, and the next keystroke (*w* for *Worksheet*) is highlighted in the status line. So far so good.

4. Press any key. The Worksheet option is selected and the control panel displays the /Worksheet menu. The next keystroke (*r* for *Row*) is highlighted in the status line.

5. Press any key. Because Row is not an option on the /Worksheet menu, 1-2-3 beeps at you. You have located the problem.

6. Press Ctrl-Break to cancel the macro.

7. Press Alt-F2 to turn off step mode.

8. To correct the mistake, edit cell B16 so that it reads */wir~*.

9. Press Alt-I to run the macro. The corrected macro should now successfully insert a row.

10. Delete the inserted row before you continue.

RECORDING A MACRO

If you find that you make a lot of typing mistakes when building your macros, you may want to consider recording your keystrokes with 1-2-3's *learn* feature. By recording, you can eliminate several steps of macro creation—you don't need to write the keystrokes down on a piece of paper, nor do you need to type the keystrokes into a cell. Another advantage of recording your keystrokes is that typos are not a concern.

Recording keystrokes in 1-2-3 is similar to recording your voice on a tape recorder. To begin recording, press Alt-F5; this is the equivalent of your tape recorder's Record button. Then go through the commands and keystrokes that you want to record. For example, to record the keystrokes for saving a file, issue the /File Save command. To stop recording, press Alt-F5 again; this is the equivalent of your tape recorder's Stop button. The recorded keystrokes are then entered into a predefined spreadsheet range called the *learn range*. To define the learn range, use the /Worksheet Learn Range command.

In summary, here are the basic steps to recording a macro:

- Define a learn range with the /Worksheet Learn Range command.

- Turn on the learn feature with Alt-F5.

- Enter the commands and keystrokes you want recorded. Note that you must issue all commands with the keyboard—mouse operations are not recorded.

- Turn off the learn feature with Alt-F5.

If you choose the wrong command or make a typo while recording a macro, go ahead and correct the mistake. The mistakes will be recorded, but so will the steps you took to correct them. Later on, you can edit out these mistakes and corrections if you want to. (I usually do because I don't want a permanent record of my mistakes.) If you really botch the recording, you can turn off learn mode (Alt-F5) and clear the learn range with the /Worksheet Learn Erase command. You can then record from the beginning.

   Let's record a macro to print a range in Wysiwyg:

1. To define the learn range, press / to display the 1-2-3 menu and choose:

    Worksheet

    Learn

    Range

2. Paint the range B28..B40 and press Enter. Notice that this is the same column in which you have been entering your keystrokes manually. It doesn't matter how many rows you specify in the learn range as long as the range is long enough to hold all the keystrokes you will be recording.

3. Press Alt-F5 to turn on the learn feature. *LEARN* appears in the status line to let you know you are in learn mode.

4. Press : to display the Wysiwyg menu.

5. Type **P** to choose Print.

6. Type **C** to choose Config.

7. Type **P** to choose Printer.

8. With ↓, highlight the desired print density and press Enter.

9. Type **Q** to choose Quit.

10. Type **R** to choose Range.

11. Type **S** to choose Set. You are prompted for the print range, but we want the macro to pause at this point (just like in the other print macro you created). You cannot insert a pause command in the middle of a recording session, though, so you will have to insert it after the fact.

12. Press Enter to accept the print range.

13. Type **G** to choose Go.

14. Press Alt-F5 to turn off the learn feature. The LEARN indicator disappears, but the learn range is empty.

15. To see your recorded keystrokes in the learn range, press any key, such as Enter or an arrow key. Your screen should look similar to Figure 14.13. The {D 3} instruction refers to the number of times you pressed ↓ to highlight the printer driver. Your macro may have a different number here.

As mentioned earlier, you need to manually insert the pause command into the macro. Follow these steps to add the pause instruction and to name the macro:

1. Move the pointer to B28 and press F2 to edit.

2. Place the cursor on the second tilde (after the *s*).

3. Type {?} and press Enter. The macro should now read as follows:

　:pcp{D 3}~qrs{?}~g

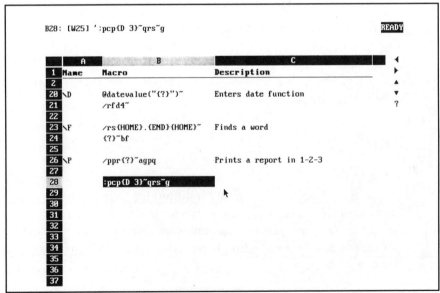

Figure 14.13: The recorded keystrokes appear in the first cell of the learn range.

4. Assign the name **WWPRINT** to the macro.

5. Enter the name (**WWPRINT**) and description (**Prints a report in Wysiwyg**) in the adjacent cells.

Because you have assigned a regular range name to the macro, you must invoke it with the Run key, Alt-F3. Let's try this:

1. Press Alt-F3. A list of range names appears in the control panel. To see all the names at once, you can press the Name key, F3.

2. Highlight WWPRINT and press Enter. After executing the initial keystrokes, the macro pauses and prompts you for the range to print.

3. Press Esc to unanchor the previous print range and then indicate the macro range (A1..C28).

4. Press Enter to continue the macro execution. The Wysiwyg-formatted list of macros will print.

The learn range you specified earlier is valid for any number of recording sessions—until the bottom of the range is reached. If you were to turn on learn mode and record another macro, the keystrokes would be placed in the next empty cell in the learn range (B29 in this example). 1-2-3 does not automatically leave a blank cell between each macro, so you will have to insert rows after recording the macros. This isn't so bad, though—you can insert rows with the Alt-I macro.

COPYING MACROS INTO OTHER FILES

The macros you have created in this chapter will work in only one file—the current one, MACROS.WK1. To use them in other files, you must either create a macro library (see Chapter 15) or copy them into each file. In Chapter 5 you learned how to use the /File Combine Copy command

to copy all or part of a spreadsheet into another file. You will use this command now to copy your macros.

Follow these steps to copy your macros into the SALESHIS file:

1. Press Alt-S to save your macros.

2. Press Alt-R to invoke the file-retrieve macro.

3. Highlight the name SALESHIS.WK1 and press Enter.

4. Move the cell pointer to a remote area of the spreadsheet, such
   as AA100.

5. Press / to display the 1-2-3 menu and choose:

   File

   Combine

   Copy

   Entire-File

   MACROS.WK1

The macros are copied into the current spreadsheet. However, the
/File Combine command is somewhat limited in what it imports. It does
not bring in Wysiwyg formatting, column width settings, or range names.
If you were to invoke one of your macros right now (for example, Alt-S),
1-2-3 would beep at you because the name doesn't exist in this file. While
this limitation is annoying, at least there is an easy way to name all the
macros at once: with the /Range Name Labels command. Follow these
steps to name the macros:

1. Move the pointer to AA102.

2. Press / to display the 1-2-3 menu and choose:

   Range

   Name

   Labels

   Right

3. Paint the range AA102..AA127 and press Enter.

4. Press Alt-S to save the file.

5. Use the Alt-W macro to change the width of column AB to 25 and AC to 35 characters.

6. Use the Alt-H macro to format the column headings in AA100..AC100 and in C13..F13.

7. Press Alt-S to save the file again.

It's a good idea to assign a name to the macro range, in the event you need to edit or create a macro. If you were to name the range MACROS, for example, you could then simply press F5 (the Goto key), F3 (the Name key), and choose the name from the list; the cell pointer would then move directly to the macro area.

AUTOEXECUTING MACROS

If you have a task that needs to be executed every time you retrieve a spreadsheet file, you can create an *autoexecuting macro*. This type of macro is executed immediately upon file retrieval—you don't need to press Alt-F3 or Alt with a letter. To create an autoexecuting macro, simply name the macro \0 (zero). When you retrieve a file with a macro named \0, 1-2-3 will automatically execute the keystrokes in this macro. Autoexecuting macros are frequently used for macro-menus (discussed in Chapter 16) and file-combining.

To temporarily turn off the execution of an auto macro, issue the /Worksheet Global Default Autoexec No command. When you wish to reinstate the autoexec macro, use /Worksheet Global Default Autoexec Yes.

Note that you cannot execute a \0 macro with Alt-0. To manually invoke this type of macro, you must press Alt-F3 and choose \0 from the list.

You can take automation one step further by naming a file AUTO123. A file with this name will be automatically retrieved when you load 1-2-3. When you combine an auto-retrieving file with an autoexecuting macro, you can do some pretty powerful and exciting things. Here is one of my favorite autoexecuting macros in an auto-retrieving file:

```
'/fr{NAME}
```

This macro displays a list of files to retrieve (just like the Alt-R macro you created earlier). It's a perfect autoexecuting macro for an AUTO123 file because usually the first thing you want to do in 1-2-3 is retrieve a file.

But what if you don't want to retrieve a file—what if you want to create a new spreadsheet? The easiest way to handle this situation is to create an empty file named **00000000.WK1** (eight zeros). A file with this name will show up as the first file on the list, so you can simply press Enter to retrieve this file. Because the file doesn't contain any data, you are starting with a fresh spreadsheet. The only difference is that when you save the file, the name *00000000.WK1* will appear; make sure you type a new name or 00000000.WK1 will no longer be empty.

Follow these steps to create the automated system just discussed:

1. Clear the screen (/Worksheet Erase).

2. In cell A1, type **'/fr{NAME}** and press Enter.

3. Name the macro **\0** (zero).

4. Save the file with the name **AUTO123**.

5. Clear the screen.

6. Save the empty spreadsheet with the name **00000000**.

7. Quit 1-2-3.

8. Load 1-2-3. Assuming your macro has worked correctly, you should now see a list of files to retrieve. Notice that the empty spreadsheet, 00000000.WK1, is the first file on the list. If you want to create a new spreadsheet at this point, simply press Enter.

9. Choose SAMPMACS.WK1. (This is a file that comes with 1-2-3—it is discussed in the next section.)

When you no longer want to retrieve files automatically, rename or delete the AUTO123.WK1 file.

USING SAMPMACS.WK1

SAMPMACS.WK1 is a file of sample macros that is included with 1-2-3, Release 2.3. If you find any that are useful, you can copy them into your master macros file (MACROS.WK1). You may need to rename them because some of their names are identical to the ones in your file. Here is a brief description of each macro in SAMPMACS:

Alt-G   Displays a list of range names to go to

Alt-S   Shifts the current row to the top of the screen

Alt-D   Enters today's date

Alt-R   Rounds a number to the number of decimal places you specify

Alt-C   Displays a menu of options related to columns (setting column widths, hiding, inserting, deleting, and so forth)

The Alt-R and Alt-C macros (shown in Figure 14.14) are different from the macros you created in this chapter—they use commands from 1-2-3's powerful macro programming language. You might want to try out these macros just to see how they differ from your regular keystroke macros. If they pique your interest, read Chapters 16 and 17, which discusses macro programming in detail.

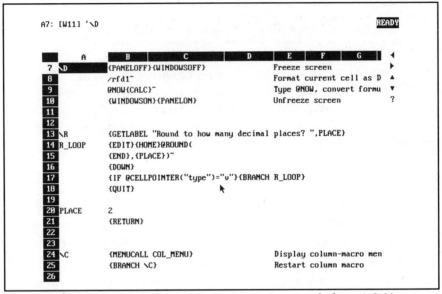

```
A7: [W11] '\D                                                    READY

        A       B        C        D       E      F      G        ◄
  7  \D        {PANELOFF}{WINDOWSOFF}         Freeze screen      ►
  8            /rfd1~                         Format current cell as D  ▲
  9            @NOW{CALC}~                    Type @NOW, convert formu  ▼
 10            {WINDOWSON}{PANELON}           Unfreeze screen    ?
 11
 12
 13  \R        {GETLABEL "Round to how many decimal places? ",PLACE}
 14  R_LOOP    {EDIT}{HOME}@ROUND(
 15            {END},{PLACE})~
 16            {DOWN}
 17            {IF @CELLPOINTER("type")="v"}{BRANCH R_LOOP}
 18            {QUIT}
 19
 20  PLACE     2
 21            {RETURN}
 22
 23
 24  \C        {MENUCALL COL_MENU}           Display column-macro men
 25            {BRANCH \C}                   Restart column macro
 26
```

Figure 14.14: The Alt-R and Alt-C macros use commands from 1-2-3's programming language.

Using the Macro Library Manager

To attach the Macro Library Manager: 522

Choose /Add-In Attach and select MACROMGR.ADN. Choose an invoke function key (7–10).

To invoke the Macro Library Manager: 522

Press Alt with the invoke function key (for example, Alt-F9 if the invoke key is 9).

To create a macro library: 524

Create and name a set of macros. Make sure the Macro Library Manager is attached and then display the macro menu (for example, press Alt-F9). Choose Save and enter a library file name. Specify the macro library range. When asked if you want to assign a password, choose Yes or No, depending on whether you want to protect your library from prying eyes.

To load a macro library: 525

Make sure the Macro Library Manager is attached and then display the macro menu (for example, press Alt-F9). Choose Load and select the library file name.

To modify a macro library: 526

Make sure the Macro Library Manager is attached, and then clear the screen. Display the macro menu (for example, press Alt-F9) and choose Edit. Select the library file name. Choose Overwrite. When asked for the library range, place the pointer in A1 and press Enter. The macros are inserted into the spreadsheet. You can then edit the existing macros or create new ones. When you are finished modifying the library, you need to save all the macros to the same library file name. (See the instructions for creating a macro library.)

To attach the Macro Library Manager Automatically: 531

Choose /Worksheet Global Default Other Add-In Set 2. From the list of add-ins that is displayed, highlight MACROMGR.ADN and press

Enter. Choose an invoke function key. When asked if you want to automatically invoke the add-in, choose Yes or No. (Note: Be sure to choose Update on the Default menu to permanently save this setting.)

To automatically load a macro library: 532

Create an autoexecuting macro (\0) in the auto-retrieving file (AUTO-123.WK1). This macro will invoke the macro add-in and then load the macro library.

The Macro Library Manager, an add-in program included with 1-2-3, allows you to use your macros without having to actually store them in each spreadsheet file. With the macro manager, you can simply load the macros into memory (RAM) and have them available for use in any file you retrieve.

ATTACHING THE MACRO LIBRARY MANAGER

Because the macro manager is an add-in program not actually built-in to 1-2-3, you must attach it to make it accessible. The add-in consumes only 14K of memory. Follow these steps to attach the add-in:

1. Press / to display the 1-2-3 menu and choose:

    Add-In

    Attach

2. Highlight MACROMGR.ADN from the list of add-ins and press Enter.

3. Choose 9 for the invoke-key. This choice indicates that you will bring up the Macro Library Manager menu with Alt-F9.

4. Choose Quit.

INVOKING THE MACRO LIBRARY MANAGER

To display the Macro Library Manager menu, press Alt-F9—the invoke key you assigned when you attached the add-in. Alternatively, you can choose / Add-In Invoke and select MACROMGR. Either way, you will see the menu shown in Figure 15.1.

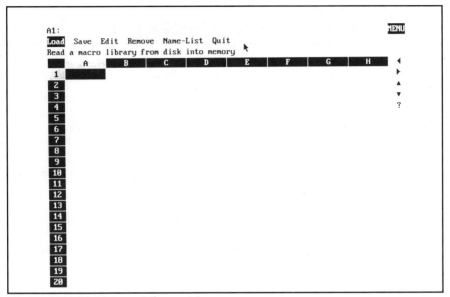

Figure 15.1: The Macro Library Manager menu

Here is a brief explanation of each option:

Option	Description
Load	Loads an existing macro library file into memory
Save	Creates a macro library file and loads the library into memory
Edit	Copies a macro library file into the current spreadsheet
Remove	Removes a macro library file from memory
Name-List	Inserts a list of macro names into the current spreadsheet
Quit	Returns to READY mode

These options will be discussed in more detail throughout the chapter.

CREATING A MACRO LIBRARY

If you have created a set of macros in a spreadsheet file, you already have the contents of your macro library—you just need to use the Macro Library Manager to move them into a special macro library file. To create a macro library, use the Save option on the macro menu. This option performs two tasks:

- It moves the macros out of the spreadsheet into a file that has an .MLB extension (in other words, a macro library file).

- It loads the macros into memory so you can use them in any file.

Follow these steps to move your macros into a macro library file:

1. Retrieve MACROS.WK1.

2. Press Home.

3. Press Alt-F9 to display the macro menu.

4. Choose Save and enter **GENERIC** for the library file name. This name indicates that the file contains generic macros. You are then prompted for the macro library range. The important part of this range is the macros themselves in column B. However, it's a good idea to include the documentation in case you ever need to edit the library.

5. Paint the range A1..C28 and press Enter. You are asked if you want to use a password to lock the library. If you choose Yes, you will need to enter a password whenever you edit the library. Only use passwords if other people are likely to monkey around with your macro library.

6. Choose No.

Your macros and their documentation disappear from the spreadsheet as they are moved into the macro library file and loaded into memory. Even though the macros are not in the spreadsheet, they are available for use with any file. To see how this works, retrieve and format the memo you created in Chapter 8. Follow these steps to format the memo like Figure 15.2.

1. Press Alt-R to invoke the file-retrieve macro.

2. Choose JANMEMO.WK1 and press Enter.

3. Format the column headings in row 22 with the Alt-H macro.

4. Boldface cell E21.

5. Using the Alt-W macro, widen column A to 11 characters.

6. Format the numbers in column D with the Alt-C macro.

7. Print the memo with the WWPRINT macro. (Hint: You need to press Alt-F3 to run this macro.) Your memo should look similar to Figure 15.2.

8. Save the file with the Alt-S macro.

USING A MACRO LIBRARY

The Save command on the macro menu loads the library into memory. The macro library remains in memory until you do one of the following:

• Remove it from memory with the Remove option on the macro menu

• Detach the Macro Library Manager add-in with the / Add-In Detach command

• Quit 1-2-3

To use the macros when the library is no longer in memory, choose the Load option on the macro menu to load the library back into memory. Of course, the Macro Library Manager add-in must be attached before you can invoke the macro menu with Alt-F9.

Assuming you will want to use your macro library on a regular basis, you will need to attach the Macro Library Manager add-in and load the macro library (GENERIC.MLB in our example) each time you load 1-2-3.

Memorandum

To: Richard Bell
From: Paula Montgomery
Date: February 25, 1992
Subject: January Sales

Below are the January sales figures for the people in your district. As you can see, *Becky Andrews* had an <u>outstanding</u> month. She sold 25% of the district total.   Becky deserves special recognition, don't you think?   Have any ideas of what we can do to reward her for these amazing sales efforts?

Randy Cauldwell, on the other hand, is not pulling his weight.   Perhaps you should talk to him to see what the problem is.

Please give me a call if you have any questions.

Last Name	First Name	Sales	% of Total
Anderson	Robert	$24,000	2.78%
Andrews	Rebecca	$220,000	25.49%
Cauldwell	Randy	$10,000	1.16%
Goldstein	George	$65,000	7.53%
Haldeman	Ann–Marie	$92,000	10.66%
Jackson	John	$26,000	3.01%
Jameson	George	$47,000	5.45%
Lansberg	Jackson	$26,000	3.01%
Patterson	Margaret	$100,000	11.59%
Pauley	Barbara	$45,000	5.21%
Peterson	Paul	$79,000	9.15%
Smith	Betsy	$54,000	6.26%
Smith	Ruth	$75,000	8.69%
Total		$863,000	

Figure 15.2: The memo after being formatted with the macros in the GENERIC library

To go through the procedure of using your macro library in another 1-2-3 session, quit and reload the program.

1. Quit 1-2-3 (/Quit Yes).

2. Type **123** and press Enter to reload the program.

3. If your AUTO123 file displays a list of files to retrieve, press Enter to choose 00000000.WK1.

4. To attach the Macro Library Manager add-in, press / to display the 1-2-3 menu and choose:

    Add-In

    Attach

5. From the list of add-ins that is displayed, highlight MACRO-MGR.ADN and press Enter.

6. Choose 9 for the invoke-key.

7. Choose Quit.

Now that the Macro Library Manager is attached, follow these steps to load your macro library:

1. Press Alt-F9 to display the macro menu.

2. Choose Load.

3. Highlight the library GENERIC.MLB and press Enter.

4. Choose Quit.

Your macros are now available for use. For example, you can press Alt-R to retrieve a file. If you can't remember your macro names, you have two ways of looking them up:

- Press the Run key, Alt-F3, to choose the name from a list.

- Press Alt-F9 and choose Name-List. This command inserts the range names from a macro library into a spreadsheet range, as shown in Figure 15.3. (The command prompts you for the library name and the spreadsheet range.)

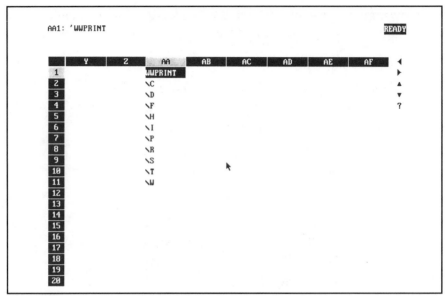

Figure 15.3: A list of names in the macro library

Both of these methods have limited usefulness, because they give you only the names, not the descriptions. But sometimes the name is enough to jog your memory. For more complete information about your macros, refer to your macro printout (if you have one) or insert the macros back into the spreadsheet (discussed in the next section).

MODIFYING A MACRO LIBRARY

To add new macros to your macro library or revise any of the existing macros, use the Edit option on the macro menu. This command copies the contents of a macro library into the current spreadsheet. You can then modify any of the macros or create new ones at the bottom of the list.

After you have finished modifying the macros, you must save them again into the macro library. Note that you must save *all* of the macros, not just the new ones you added or the old ones you modified.

Follow these steps to copy your macros into an empty spreadsheet:

1. If necessary, clear the screen (/Worksheet Erase).

2. Press Alt-F9 to display the macro menu.

3. Choose Edit.

4. Select GENERIC.MLB as the macro library to edit.

5. Choose Ignore or Overwrite. (It doesn't matter which option you choose here since you are copying the library into an empty spreadsheet. The Ignore option will not bring in a macro name if the name already exists in the current spreadsheet. The Overwrite option will overwrite conflicting range names in the spreadsheet.)

6. For the library range, place the pointer in A1 and press Enter. The macros are inserted into the spreadsheet.

7. Use the Alt-W macro to set the width of column B to 25 and C to 35.

Now, add a new macro to your library:

1. In B30, type **':wrs~3~** and press Enter. This Wysiwyg macro sets the height of a row to 3 points—a common height for the blank row above column totals.

2. Assign the name **\L** (for line height—yes, I'm stretching the mnemonics here, but only because better candidates were already taken).

3. Enter the documentation as shown in Figure 15.4.

4. On a blank row, test the Alt-L macro. (You should always test and debug a macro before adding it to the macro library.)

5. After testing the macro, return the row to its original height (:Worksheet Row Auto).

Resave the modified macro library:

1. Press Home.

2. Press Alt-F9 to display the macro menu.

3. Choose Save.

4. Select the same name (GENERIC.MLB) for your macro file. 1-2-3 warns you that the file already exists and asks if you want to overwrite the existing file.

5. Choose Yes.

6. For the macro range, paint the range A1..C30 and press Enter.

7. Answer No to the password question. Your macros and their documentation are then saved into the macro library file.

Now use Alt-R to retrieve JANMEMO and Alt-L to set the height of row 37. Save the file with Alt-S.

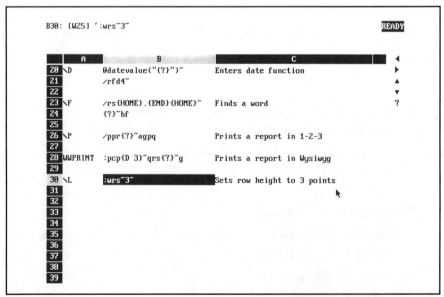

Figure 15.4: The Alt-L macro is a new addition to the macro library.

AUTOMATING THE MACRO LIBRARY MANAGER

If you plan to use your macros every time you work in 1-2-3, you should attach the add-in automatically, just as you did for Wysiwyg. Furthermore, you can modify your AUTO123 file so that the autoexecuting macro loads your macro library.

ATTACHING THE MACRO MANAGER AUTOMATICALLY

To automatically attach the Macro Library Manager every time you load 1-2-3, follow these steps:

1. Press / to display the 1-2-3 menu and choose:

   Worksheet

   Global

   Default

   Other

   Add-In

   Set

   2

2. From the list of add-ins that is displayed, highlight MACRO-MGR.ADN and press Enter.

3. Choose 9 for the invoke-key. You are then asked if you want to automatically invoke the add-in. By your choosing Yes, the macro menu will automatically display after 1-2-3 is loaded and the add-ins are attached. This auto-invoke setting saves you from having to press Alt-F9 to display the macro menu. This assumes the first thing you want to do when you begin a 1-2-3 session is load your macro library. In this exercise, however, we will not automatically invoke the add-in because we will create

an auto-macro that will do this *and* load the macro library.

4. Choose No.

5. To save the setting, choose:

Quit

Update

Quit

Now, the next time you load 1-2-3, the Macro Library Manager add-in will be attached automatically. The following section explains how to automatically load your macro library (GENERIC.MLB) as well.

AUTOMATICALLY LOADING A MACRO LIBRARY

To automatically load your macro library, you need to modify the AUTO123 file you created in Chapter 14. Currently, the autoexecuting macro displays a list of files to retrieve. You will now expand this macro so that it invokes the macro library manager and loads the GENERIC macro library.

Follow these steps to edit your AUTO123 file:

1. Retrieve AUTO123. The \0 macro is automatically executed and the list of files to retrieve is displayed.

2. Press Ctrl-Break to return to READY mode.

3. Enter the following macro keystrokes in the indicated cells:

Cell	Contents
A1	'/aiMACROMGR~
A2	LGENERIC~q
A3	'/fr{NAME}

4. Make sure cell A1 is still named \0 (zero).

5. Save the file with the same name (AUTO123).

6. To test out this automated system, quit 1-2-3 and reload the program. If all goes well, you should see a list of files to retrieve.

7. Choose any file (except AUTO123.WK1).

8. To make sure your macro library is indeed loaded, press Alt-S to save the file. If your library is loaded, the file will be saved successfully. If 1-2-3 beeps at you, your library did not load. You should retrieve AUTO123 and check the keystrokes in your macro.

CREATING ADDITIONAL MACRO LIBRARIES

If you don't have a lot of macros, you can easily fit them in a single library. But as your library starts to grow, you might want to consider dividing the macros up into smaller files. There are several reasons to do this. First of all, the larger your macro library, the less memory you will have available for the current spreadsheet. With large spreadsheets and macro libraries, you might not be able to fit both the macro library and the spreadsheet in memory. Second, you might have certain macros designed for specific tasks (such as database queries and graph creation) that don't apply to all spreadsheets. It makes sense to put related macros into their own library file and load them as you need them. The Macro Library Manager allows you to have up to ten macro libraries in memory at any one time.

Figure 15.5 shows a macro library for graphing tasks. The Alt-Q macro prompts you for a graph file name, saves the spreadsheet, and then quits 1-2-3 so that you can load PrintGraph. Alt-A creates an area graph with no margins and Alt-B creates a three-dimensional bar graph. The Alt-A and Alt-B macros assume you have already defined the graph ranges. All three macros begin with {BREAK}; this macro command represents the Ctrl-Break key combination; the purpose of this command is to go to READY mode. That way, you can run the macro while you are in READY or MENU mode.

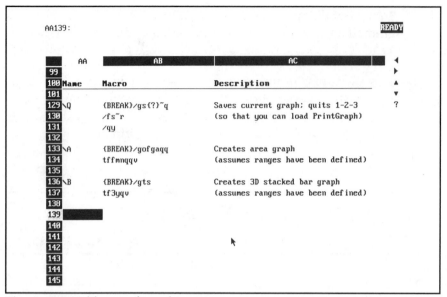

Figure 15.5: A library of graphing macros

Follow these steps to create a library for these graphing macros:

1. Retrieve the SALESHIS file.

2. Go to cell AA129 and create the macros shown in Figure 15.5. (Don't forget to name them with /Range Name.)

3. Retrieve the COMPARISON graph (/Graph Name Use) and test the macros to make sure they work properly.

4. Move the pointer to cell AA129.

5. Press Alt-F9 to display the macro menu.

6. Choose Save and enter **GRAPHING** for the library file name. You are then prompted for the macro library range.

7. Paint the range AA129..AC137 and press Enter.

8. In response to the password question, choose No.

You now have two macro libraries in memory: GENERIC and GRAPH-ING. If you want only the GRAPHING macros in memory, use the Remove option on the graph menu and choose GENERIC.MLB. In the future, you can load either GENERIC or GRAPHING or both.

If macro libraries contain conflicting names, 1-2-3 uses the macro from whichever library was loaded first. For example, if both GENERIC and GRAPHING contain an Alt-S macro, the file-saving macro would be executed since GENERIC was loaded first. However, there is a way to run either macro. Press Alt-F3 and F3 to display a full-screen list of macros to run (see Figure 15.6). When you highlight a range name, the control panel indicates the macro library where the name is located. In Figure 15.6, the \S macro is highlighted, and the control panel indicates the macro is located in the GENERIC.MLB file.

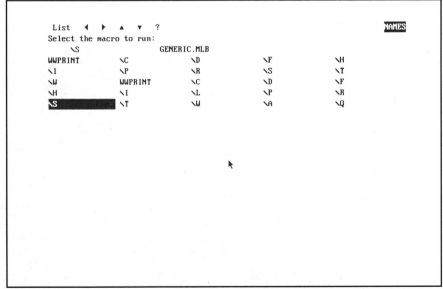

Figure 15.6: The control panel indicates which macro library the macro is in.

Chapter 13

Chapter 14

Chapter 15

Chapter 16

Chapter 17

Writing
a Macro Program

To write a macro program: 542

In your own words (not with programming commands), write down the series of steps you want the macro to perform. Organize the tasks into subroutines, and then translate your written steps into macro commands. Type the program into a spreadsheet range and assign names to the macros and subroutines.

To create custom prompts: 547

Use the {GETLABEL prompt-string,location} command to store the response as a label or the {GETNUMBER *prompt-string,location*}command to store the reply as a value. *Prompt-string* is the question that appears in the control panel. Enclose the prompt-string in quotation marks if the text contains commas or semi-colons. *Location* is the cell in which the response is stored.

To create conditional {IF} statements: 549

Use the {IF *condition*} command. If the *condition* is true, the keystrokes to the right of the {IF} statement are executed. If the condition is false, the commands on the next line are executed.

To change the indicator: 550

Use the {INDICATE *string*} command where *string* is the text to appear in the indicator. To return to the standard indicator, use the {INDICATE} command with no string.

To branch to a subroutine: 553

Use the {BRANCH *subroutine*} command. *Subroutine* is the cell in which macro execution is continued.

To call a subroutine: 553

Type the subroutine's name inside braces—for example, {REPORT}.

To turn off screen and panel redrawing: 556

Use the {WINDOWSOFF} and {PANELOFF} commands. To turn them back on, use {WINDOWSON} and {PANELON}.

To design a custom menu   558

You need to type the menu options in adjacent cells across a single row, and enter a brief description directly below each option. In subsequent rows, enter the macro instructions (or subroutine calls) that should be executed when the option is selected.

To display a custom menu: 560

First, write a macro that uses the {MENUBRANCH *location*} command. *Location* is the cell that contains the first menu option. Give the macro a name (such as \M). To display the menu, invoke the macro (for example, press Alt-M).

In Chapter 14 you learned how to create simple macros to execute commands automatically. But macros can do much more than automate your keystrokes. Here are a few examples of what you can do:

- build your own menus that work just like 1-2-3 menus

- display your own messages and questions in the control panel

- perform different tasks, depending on your response to custom prompts

- repeat a task a specified number of times

1-2-3 comes with an extensive set of special macro commands that allow you to write *macro programs*. A program is a list of instructions that performs specific functions or tasks; the instructions are executed in the order they are listed. While programming may seem like a scary concept to many of you, don't be intimidated—you created many programs in Chapter 14, albeit simple ones. In this chapter, you will increase the power and complexity of the programs you write.

1-2-3's programming language is similar to the popular, easy-to-use language called *BASIC* (Beginners All-Purpose Symbolic Instruction Code). If you are an experienced programmer, you should have no problem learning 1-2-3's language; as with any computer language, you can create subroutines, loops, conditional statements, etc.

I personally am not a professional programmer, though I did take a beginning computer programming class in college. Despite my lack of formal training, I have written many sophisticated 1-2-3 macro programs— and so can you. One of the aspects of computer programming that appeals to me most is the challenge of debugging a program and the subsequent joy of getting the program to operate successfully. Programming definitely has its frustrating moments, but the thrill of victory far surpasses the frustrations.

For an example of a macro program, look at the date macro in Figure 16.1. This macro creates serial date numbers out of dates entered as labels. Suppose you entered a column of dates by preceding each date with an apostrophe (such as '3/15/92). The date macro converts each label in the column to an @DATEVALUE function so that you can then sort them properly or do date comparisons and queries. Don't you wish you had a macro like this when you entered the employee hire dates in Chapter 12?

Let's analyze each line of this program. The first four lines of the program are no different from the keystroke macros you created in Chapter 14. Line 1 edits the cell and deletes the apostrophe at the beginning of the cell. Line 2 begins the @DATEVALUE function while Line 3 finishes it. Line 4 moves the cell pointer down to the next cell. The next two lines are the "meaty" stuff. Line 5 is a conditional {IF} statement that checks the current cell to see if it's blank. If the cell is blank, the program branches (goes to) to a subsidiary program named FORMAT which displays the dates in the MM/DD/YY format and then quits the macro program. (Subsidiary programs that support the main macro program are called *subroutines*.) If the current cell is not blank, the command in line 6 is executed. The {BRANCH DATE} command loops back to the beginning of the program and runs the DATE program again.

The above discussion of the date macro is intended as a quick introduction to macro programming. The macro commands discussed here will be explained in full detail later in the chapter and in Chapter 17. In the remainder of this chapter, you will write a program that automates

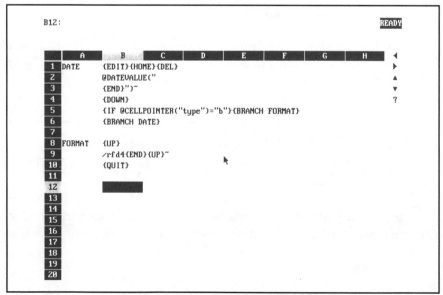

Figure 16.1: A date macro program

database queries. In the process of writing this program you will learn a dozen of the most commonly used macro commands. Chapter 17 is a complete reference of all the commands in 1-2-3's programming language.

PLANNING A PROGRAM

Before you actually start typing a program into a spreadsheet, it's a good idea to write down the series of steps you want the program to perform. Write down the steps in your own words—not in programming lingo. In the date macro, for example, you might write down the following:

1. Edit cell.

2. Delete apostrophe and insert the @DATEVALUE function.

3. Go down to the next cell.

4. Test this cell to see if it's blank.

5. If it is blank, format the range to date format and quit the macro.

6. If it's not blank, repeat the macro.

Once you have written the program in terms *you* can understand, you will find it easier to rewrite it in terms that 1-2-3 can understand (i.e., with 1-2-3 macro commands).

DEVELOPING A PROGRAM TO AUTOMATE DATABASE QUERIES

The program that you will write here automates queries performed on the employee database created in Chapter 12. The program, shown in

Figure 16.2, has the following subroutines:

Name	Description
NAME_SEARCH	Asks you which last name you want to search for and then highlights the records in FIND mode
DEPT_RPT	Asks you which department you want to list records for and then runs the REPORT subroutine (see REPORT below) to extract the matching records
REPORT	Extracts the matching records and asks if you want to print the report—if you answer yes, the output range is printed

```
            AA            AB          AC          AD          AE          AF
100   NAME_SEARCH  {HOME}{BLANK QUERIES}
101                {GETLABEL "Enter last name to search for: ",LAST}
102                /dqf{?} ~ {BREAK}
103
104   DEPT_RPT     {HOME}{BLANK QUERIES}
105                {GETLABEL "List employees for which department? ",DEPT}
106                {REPORT}
107
108   REPORT       /dqeq{GOTO}OUTPUT ~
109                {GETLABEL "Do you wish to print this report (Y/N)? ",REPLY}
110                {IF @UPPER(REPLY)="N"}{QUIT}
111                :prcrs.{END}{RIGHT}{END}{DOWN} ~
112                lmr.25 ~ l.25 ~ qq
113                {INDICATE PRINTING...}g
114                {INDICATE}
115
116   REPLY
117
118   SALARY_RPT   {HOME}{BLANK QUERIES}
119                {GETNUMBER "List employees with salaries greater than what? ",SALARY}
120                {IF @ISERR(SALARY)}{BRANCH SALARY_RPT}
121                {GOTO}SALARY ~ {EDIT}{HOME}+G2> ~
122                {REPORT}
123
124   DATE_RPT     {HOME}{BLANK QUERIES}
125                {GETNUMBER "List employees hired within the last how many years? ",HIRE}
126                {IF @ISERR(HIRE)}{BRANCH DATE_RPT}
127                {OFF}{GOTO}HIRE ~ {EDIT}{HOME}@YEAR(@NOW) – @YEAR(F2) <= ~
128                {REPORT}
```

Figure 16.2: The data query macro program

Name	Description
SALARY_RPT	Asks you for a salary amount and then runs the REPORT subroutine to list the employees who make more than the specified salary
DATE_RPT	Asks you to enter a number (how many years) and then runs the REPORT subroutine to list the employees hired within the number of years specified

Once you create and debug all the subroutines, you will write a menu program that allows you to choose and execute the query options from a menu, instead of with the Run key, Alt-F3. This custom menu is shown in the control panel of Figure 16.3.

```
A1: {B} [W5] ^ID                                              MENU
Name  Dept  Salary  Hire Date   Quit
Search for name
        A      B         C        D       E        F         G        H        I
   1   ID    Last      First    Dept   Exempt  Hire Date  Salary  Raise %  New Sal.
   2  1002 Anderson   Jane     MIS    Yes     08/02/85   34,000   13.0%    38,420
   3  1018 Andrews    Andy     MIS    Yes     08/27/89   61,000   14.0%    69,540
   4  1005 Bradford   William  Sales  Yes     09/10/86   60,000   10.0%    66,000
   5  1006 Bradley    Brad     Sales  No      02/26/85   54,000    8.0%    58,320
   6  1011 Gibson     Pamela   Eng.   No      11/26/89   45,000   12.0%    50,400
   7  1012 Ingram     Greg     Mfg.   No      09/30/90   21,000    6.5%    22,365
   8  1017 Jones      Carolyn  MIS    Yes     10/17/84   62,000   11.0%    68,820
   9  1001 Jones      Mary     Sales  No      10/15/88   30,000   11.0%    33,300
  10  1009 Kline      Harry    Sales  No      03/25/88   26,000    7.0%    27,820
  11  1007 Manley     Martin   Mfg.   No      03/09/91   26,000    7.0%    27,820
  12  1004 Meyers     Andrew   MIS    Yes     12/01/88   41,000    9.0%    44,690
  13  1000 Peterson   Pete     MIS    Yes     07/21/82   21,000   12.0%    23,520
  14  1015 Slater     Peter    Mfg.   No      01/05/82   20,000    8.0%    21,600
  15  1016 Smith      Charles  Mfg.   Yes     06/29/84   25,000    7.0%    26,750
  16  1008 Smith      Paul     Mfg.   No      06/10/87   27,000   10.0%    29,700
  17  1013 Smothers   Stacey   Mfg.   No      05/01/87   24,000    7.5%    25,800
  18  1010 Smythe     Jennifer Eng.   Yes     11/13/90   34,000    6.0%    36,040
  19  1014 Tucker     Brian    Eng.   Yes     04/22/88   39,000    9.0%    42,510
  20  1003 Wilson     Robert   Eng.   Yes     10/14/83   36,000   15.0%    41,400
                                        CMD
```

Figure 16.3: The custom menu for data queries

USING RANGE NAMES
IN MACRO PROGRAMS

Subroutine names follow the same rules as macro names. First, you need to name only the top cell, for example, cell AB100 in the NAME_SEARCH subroutine. Second, the names can be a combination of one to fifteen characters (letters, numbers, spaces, and special symbols) or a backslash followed by a single letter (such as \A). In general, try to make the subroutine name descriptive of its task so that your programs are easier to decipher.

As much as possible, use range names rather than cell coordinates in your macro programs. Look over the macro program in Figure 16.2 and notice that there are very few cell references, but there are many range names (*QUERIES, NAME, DEPT, SALARY, HIRE, OUTPUT, REPLY*). The reason for this is simple: Cell locations may change when you modify your spreadsheet (such as when you insert rows or columns, delete rows or columns, or move cells). If your macro program contains references to specific cells and those cell locations change, you have a problem on your hands—the program will be referring to the wrong cells. (Unfortunately, macro commands don't dynamically change cell references like formulas do.) You won't experience these kinds of problems, though, if your macros refer to range names.

For the database query program in the EMPLOYEE file, you will need the following range names:

Name	Range	Description
QUERIES	A32..I32	The second row in the criteria range
OUTPUT	A37..I37	The row of field names in the output range
LAST	B32	The cell under the Last field name in the criteria range
DEPT	D32	The cell under the Dept field name in the criteria range

Name	Range	Description
HIRE	F32	The cell under the Hire Date field name in the criteria range
SALARY	G32	The cell under the Salary field name in the criteria range

Follow the steps below to create these range names:

1. Retrieve EMPLOYEE.WK1.

2. Use the /Range Name Create command to assign the name *QUERIES* to the range A32..I32.

3. Use /Range Name Create to assign the name *OUTPUT* to the range A37..I37.

4. Because the LAST, DEPT, and SALARY names already exist as labels, you can use the /Range Name Labels Down command to name them. To name LAST, place the cell pointer in B31, choose /Range Name Labels Down, and press Enter. Repeat this for the DEPT and SALARY names.

5. Use the /Range Name Create command to name cell F32 *HIRE*.

CREATING THE
NAME_SEARCH SUBROUTINE

The NAME_SEARCH subroutine contains just three lines, shown in Figure 16.4. {BLANK QUERIES} erases cells in the range named *QUERIES*. The {BLANK} macro command is the equivalent of the /Range Erase command except it executes a bit faster. The macro instructions '/reQUERIES~ would give you the same end result.

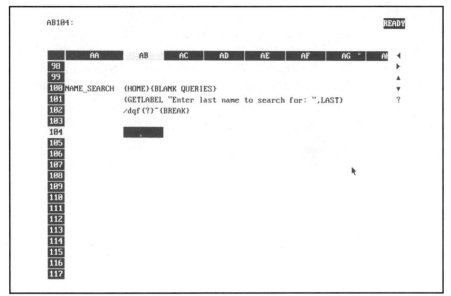

Figure 16.4: The NAME_SEARCH subroutine

ASKING QUESTIONS
WITH THE {GETLABEL} COMMAND

The {GETLABEL} macro command displays the prompt *Enter last name to search for:* in the control panel, waits for you to enter a response, and then stores your answer in the cell named *LAST*. This command has the following syntax:

{GETLABEL *prompt-string,location*}

The *prompt-string* is the message or question that appears in the control panel. You should keep it to under 73 characters so your messages will fit in the control panel. The prompt-string needn't be enclosed in quotation marks unless the string contains a comma or semicolon. I usually insert quotation marks as a matter of habit (it certainly doesn't hurt to have them). The *location* is the cell in which the response is stored as a label. It can be either a cell coordinate, range, or range name. If you specify a range, the response is entered in the upper-left corner cell of the range.

The final line of the NAME_SEARCH subroutine issues the /Data Query Find command, pauses until you press Enter, and then returns to READY mode. This command assumes the input and criteria ranges have already been specified—you defined them in Chapter 12.

To create and test the NAME_SEARCH macro subroutine, follow these steps:

1. Go to cell AA100.

2. Widen column AA to 13 characters.

3. Type the labels shown in Figure 16.4.

4. Assign the name *NAME_SEARCH* to cell AB100.

5. Save the file with the same name (EMPLOYEE).

6. To run the macro, press Alt-F3 and choose NAME_SEARCH. The message *Enter last name to search for:* appears in the control panel.

7. Type **jones** and press Enter. The first employee with the last name of Jones is highlighted. You can either edit this record, or press ↓ to highlight additional matching records. As soon as you press Enter, the macro continues.

8. Press ↓ to highlight the next record.

9. Move to the Salary field, type **30000**, and press Enter. The salary is updated and you are returned to READY mode.

CREATING THE DEPT_RPT AND REPORT SUBROUTINES

The DEPT_RPT and REPORT subroutines are shown in Figure 16.5. The first two lines of DEPT_RPT are similar to the ones in NAME_SEARCH. The third line simply runs the REPORT subroutine.

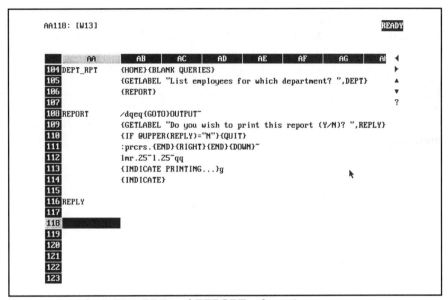

Figure 16.5: The DEPT_RPT and REPORT subroutines

The first line of the REPORT subroutine issues the /Data Query Extract Quit command and then moves the cell pointer to the range named *OUTPUT*. The second line uses a {GETLABEL} command to ask if you want to print the report. Notice the *(Y/N)* at the end of the prompt-string. When applicable, it's always a good idea to indicate what type of response is expected. The response (*Y* for Yes or *N* for No) is stored in the cell named *REPLY* (AB116).

CONDITIONAL {IF} STATEMENTS

The next line of the program is a conditional {IF} statement that checks the contents of REPLY to see if a yes or no response was entered. If the reply is *N*, the macro quits. Otherwise, the program continues to the subsequent lines and prints the report. The syntax of the {IF} command is:

{IF *condition*}true
false

The *condition* is a logical expression that evaluates to true or false. In this example, the condition is @UPPER(REPLY)="N". The @UPPER function converts REPLY to uppercase so that 1-2-3 considers N and n to be the same response. (You don't want to be forced to be case-specific in your reply.)

If the condition is true, 1-2-3 executes the commands to the right of the {IF} statement (they must be in the same cell). In this case, the {QUIT} command is executed. This command simply exits the macro program to READY mode.

If the condition is false, 1-2-3 executes the commands in the next cell (AB111).

CHANGING THE INDICATOR

The next line of the macro (AB111) clears the Wysiwyg print range before defining a new range. The cell pointer is already at the upper-left corner of the OUTPUT range, so all that needs to be done is anchor (.) and paint the range with {END}{RIGHT}{END}{DOWN}. The next line of the REPORT program (AB112) sets ¼-inch right and left margins.

The last two lines of the program use the {INDICATE} macro command. This command redefines the indicator in the upper-right corner of the screen. {INDICATE PRINTING...} displays *PRINTING...* while the report is printing. The {INDICATE} command returns the indicator to its standard message (such as READY).

To create and test the DEPT_RPT macro subroutine, follow these steps:

1. Go to cell AA104.

2. Type the labels shown in Figure 16.5.

3. Assign the following names:

Name	Range
DEPT_RPT	AB104
REPORT	AB108
REPLY	AB116

4. Save the file with the same name.

5. To run the macro, press Alt-F3 and choose DEPT_RPT. The message *List employees for which department?* appears in the control panel.

6. Type **sales** and press Enter. The list of employees in the sales department is displayed and the message *Do you wish to print this report (Y/N)?* appears in the control panel.

7. Type **y** and press Enter to print the report.

8. Run the program again, but this time display a list of the employees in the MIS department and do not print the report. (You need to make sure the program works for both *yes* and *no* responses.)

CREATING THE SALARY_RPT SUBROUTINE

The SALARY_RPT subroutine, shown in Figure 16.6, produces a list of employees whose salaries are greater than a specified amount. Like DEPT_RPT, SALARY_RPT calls the REPORT subroutine to actually perform the query and print the report.

ASKING QUESTIONS WITH THE {GETNUMBER} COMMAND

The second line of the SALARY_RPT program uses the {GETNUMBER} command. The syntax for this command is identical to {GETLABEL}'s:

{GETNUMBER *prompt-string,location*}

The only difference between the two commands is that {GETNUMBER} expects a numeric response. If you enter a valid number, it is stored as a value in *location*. But if you enter a label or a number that contains label characters, an ERR (error) message is stored in the cell location. For

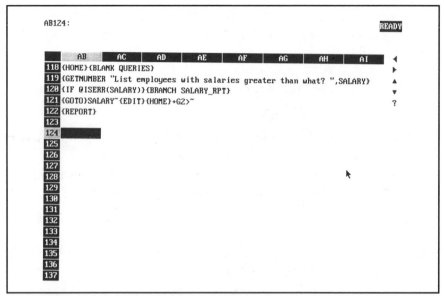

Figure 16.6: The SALARY_RPT subroutine

example, if you enter **35,000,** an error message results because the comma is a label character.

In the SALARY_RPT routine, the {GETNUMBER} command asks to *List employees with salaries greater than what?* Your response is then stored in the cell named *SALARY* in the criteria range.

TRAPPING ERRORS

Well-written macro programs look for possible input mistakes and handle the error before it makes the program dysfunctional. This process is sometimes called *error trapping.* Because a non-numeric response to the {GETNUMBER} command creates an error message, you should trap the error before the macro proceeds any further. Thus, the third line of the SALARY_RPT program looks for an error message in the SALARY cell. The command is:

{IF @ISERR(SALARY)}{BRANCH SALARY_RPT}

In English, this command reads: "If there is an error message in SALARY, then re-execute the SALARY_RPT subroutine." The {IF} statement is the primary vehicle to check for invalid responses to {GETNUMBER} and {GETLABEL} commands. The @*ISERR* function looks for an ERR message in a specific cell (SALARY, in this example). When you combine the @ISERR function with an {IF} statement, you can easily check for ERR messages in a {GETNUMBER} cell location.

If an error message is located in the SALARY cell, the {BRANCH SALARY_RPT} command is executed so you are prompted to enter the salary again. (The {BRANCH} command is discussed in the next section.) If SALARY doesn't contain an error, the commands on the next line (cell AB121) are executed. This line edits the SALARY cell (which contains the number you entered in response to the {GETNUMBER} command) and adds +G2> at the beginning of it. This forms a complete conditional formula (for example, +*G2>30000*). The final line of the program executes the REPORT subroutine.

BRANCHING TO A SUBROUTINE

There are two ways to tell a program to execute a subroutine: {BRANCH *subroutine*} or simply {*subroutine*}. For example, {REPORT} executes the REPORT subroutine and {BRANCH SALARY_RPT} executes the SALARY_RPT subroutine. There is a subtle difference between these two ways of executing a subroutine.

Both {BRANCH *subroutine*} and {*subroutine*} continue macro execution at a different cell but {*subroutine*} returns to the original routine after its has finished the commands in the subroutine; {BRANCH *subroutine*} does not return to the original program unless you explicitly tell it do so with another {BRANCH} command. In many cases, you can get away with using either command. For example, you can execute the REPORT subroutine with either {REPORT} or {BRANCH REPORT}.

In programming lingo, {BRANCH *subroutine*} is a *go to* and {*subroutine*} is a *call*.

To create and test the SALARY_RPT macro subroutine, follow these steps:

1. Go to cell AA118 and type **SALARY_RPT**.

2. Type the labels shown in Figure 16.6.

3. Assign the name *SALARY_RPT* to cell AB118.

4. Save the file.

5. To run the macro, press Alt-F3 and choose SALARY_RPT. The message *List employees with salaries greater than what?* appears in the control panel.

6. Type **50,000** and press Enter. Because you typed a comma in the number, an error message is entered in SALARY. You are immediately asked to enter another salary.

7. Type **50000** and press Enter. The list of employees with salaries greater than $50,000 is displayed, and the message *Do you wish to print this report (Y/N)?* appears in the control panel.

8. Type **y** and press Enter to print the report. While the report is printing, the indicator displays *PRINTING....*

CREATING THE DATE_RPT SUBROUTINE

The structure of the DATE_RPT routine (see Figure 16.7) is similar to that of SALARY_RPT. The QUERIES range is erased, the {GETNUMBER} command prompts with a question, the response is checked for errors, a conditional formula is entered into the criteria range, and the REPORT subroutine is executed.

The line that creates the conditional formula (cell AB127) requires additional explanation. This formula first determines how many years the employee has been working at the company by subtracting the hire date year—*@YEAR(F2)*—from the current year—*@YEAR(@NOW)*. It then checks to see if this number is less than or equal to the specified number of years. If you enter 5 in response to the *List employees hired within the last how many years?* question, the following conditional formula is created:

@YEAR(@NOW)-@YEAR(F2)<=5

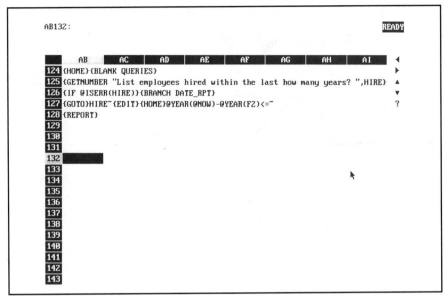

Figure 16.7: The DATE_RPT Subroutine

To create and test the DATE_RPT macro subroutine, follow these steps:

1. Go to cell AA124 and type **DATE_RPT**.

2. Type the labels shown in Figure 16.7.

3. Assign the name *DATE_RPT* to cell AB124.

4. Save the file.

5. To run the macro, press Alt-F3 and choose DATE_RPT. The message *List employees hired within the last how many years?* appears in the control panel.

6. Type **five** and press Enter. Because you typed a label, an error message is entered in HIRE. You are immediately asked to enter another number.

7. Type **5** and press Enter. The list of employees who have been hired within the last five years is displayed, and the message *Do*

you wish to print this report (Y/N)? appears in the control panel.

8. Type **n** and press Enter.

CONTROLLING
THE SCREEN DISPLAY

When your macro programs execute, you will see a lot of flashing on the screen as commands are chosen from the menu and the pointer is moved around to different cells in the spreadsheet. 1-2-3 offers two commands that prevent these distractions: {WINDOWSOFF} and {PANEL-OFF}. {WINDOWSOFF} suppresses screen redrawing except in the control panel. Thus, you don't see cell pointer movements nor can you see new or revised spreadsheet entries until the windows are turned back on with the {WINDOWSON} command or until the macro ends. {PANELOFF} freezes the contents of the control panel. Frequently, you will use {WINDOWS-OFF} and {PANELOFF} together. Because 1-2-3 doesn't have to keep redrawing the screen, the macro executes much faster.

Don't turn off the screen and panel display until after you have completely debugged your macro program. It's virtually impossible to see where your macro is going awry if you can't see what's going on.

Because {WINDOWSOFF}{PANELOFF} and {WINDOWSON}-{PANELON} commands are sprinkled throughout your programs, you might want to create subroutines called OFF and ON (see Figure 16.8). Then, whenever you want to turn off the screen and panel, you can type {**OFF**}, and when you want to turn them back on, simply type {**ON**}. Notice that subroutine calls are used here, not branches, because you want to run the subroutine and return to the original program.

In the following steps, you will first create the ON and OFF subroutines and then you will call these subroutine in various places in your macro programs (see Figure 16.9):

1. Go to cell AA130.

2. Type the labels shown in Figure 16.8.

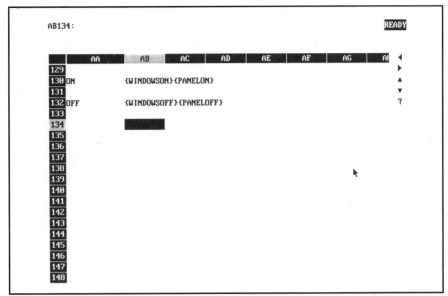

Figure 16.8: The ON and OFF subroutines

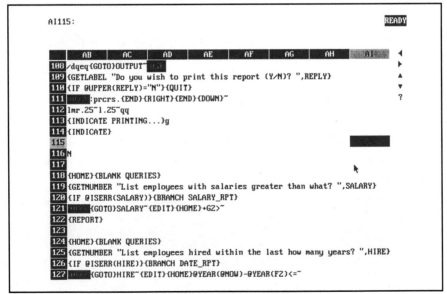

Figure 16.9: Insert the OFF and ON subroutine calls

3. Assign the name *ON* to AB130 and the name *OFF* to AB132.

4. Where indicated in Figure 16.9, insert the OFF and ON sub-routine calls. (Use the F2 key to edit the appropriate cells.)

5. Run one of the report programs (such as DEPT_RPT) and notice how much faster and cleaner it runs.

CREATING A CUSTOM MENU

The custom menus you can design with macro commands look and work just like standard 1-2-3 menus. The menu options appear in the control panel and the line below the options displays a one-line explanation describing the highlighted option. You can select an option by highlighting it and pressing Enter or by typing the first letter of the option. When you choose an option, a macro program associated with that option executes. Depending on how you set it up, this program could display a submenu, ask you questions, or immediately issue a command.

You display custom menus by invoking a macro (for example, by pressing Alt-M).

One reason to create a custom menu is to organize your macros. Instead of trying to memorize macro names, you can choose menu options that execute your macros. However, this usually makes sense only for longer macros such as the ones you created for database queries.

There are three steps to creating a custom menu:

- Design the menu: Type the menu options in adjacent cells across a single row, and enter a brief description directly below each option.

- Write the subroutines for each menu option, and specify subroutine calls in the menu.

- Build a short macro that displays the menu. This macro uses the {MENUBRANCH} command.

BUILDING A MENU
FOR DATABASE QUERIES

Figure 16.3 shows a custom menu with options for the database queries you created in this chapter. Notice that each menu option begins with a unique letter. Though it isn't a requirement, menu options should start with different letters so that you can choose commands by typing the first letter of the option. If two menu options begin with the same letter, the first option has priority; the only way to choose the second option is to highlight it and press Enter.

The programming commands for the menu are shown in Figure 16.10. The first row of the menu (row 134) contains the menu choices, the second row (135) has the menu descriptions, while the third row (136) calls the appropriate subroutine. Instead of calling a subroutine, you can enter the macro keystrokes in one or more rows under the appropriate menu option. However, the menu is more organized and easier to interpret if it references a descriptive subroutine name.

The macro that displays the custom menu is in AB139. This macro simply displays the menu which is located in the cell named *DATA_QUERY* (AB134). Thus, when you define the menu's name, you don't need to indicate the entire menu range—only the first menu option.

Because the name of the menu macro is \M, you can display the menu by pressing Alt-M.

Follow these steps to create and test the custom menu shown in Figure 16.10:

1. Go to cell AA134 and enter the labels shown in Figure 16.10. It's not absolutely necessary, but you might want to widen the

	AA	AB	AC	AD	AE	AF
134	DATA_QUERY	Name	Dept	Salary	HireDate	Quit
135		Search for name	Dept. Report	Salary Report	Hire Date Report	Quit menu
136		{NAME_SEARCH}	{DEPT_RPT}	{SALARY_RPT}	{DATE_RPT}	{QUIT}
137						
138						
139	\M	{MENUBRANCH DATA_QUERY}				

Figure 16.10: The program for the database query menu

columns so that you can see all of the labels.

2. Assign the name *DATA_QUERY* to cell AB134 and the name \M to AB139.

3. Save the file.

4. To display the custom menu, press Alt-M. The menu appears in the control panel (see Figure 16.3).

5. Highlight each option and read its description.

6. Choose the Salary option. The message *List employees with salaries greater than what?* appears in the control panel.

7. Type **40000** and press Enter. The list of employees with salaries greater than $40,000 is displayed, and the message *Do you wish to print this report (Y/N)?* appears in the control panel.

8. Type **y** and press Enter to print the report.

9. Press Alt-M to display the custom menu, and test each of the menu options to make sure the menu works properly.

AUTOMATICALLY REDISPLAYING THE MENU

As the menu is now designed, you return to READY mode after a menu option is executed; to choose another menu option, you must press Alt-M again to redisplay the menu. However, you can arrange for the menu to redisplay automatically after a subroutine has been executed, so you can immediately choose another option. Then, if you don't want to perform another database query, the Quit menu option takes you to READY mode.

To automatically redisplay the menu, call the \M macro after each subroutine has been executed. Figure 16.11 shows the revised database query menu. The only thing that's different here is that {\M} is added after each subroutine call. You will also want to edit cell AB110 in the REPORT subroutine so that it calls the \M macro instead of issuing the {QUIT} command. Make these revisions, save the file, and test each of the options to make sure the menu does indeed redisplay.

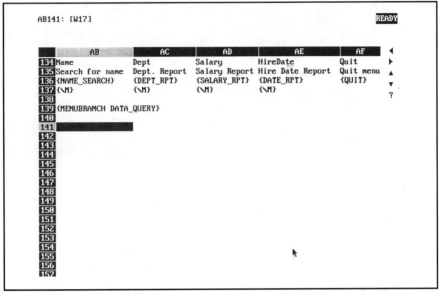

Figure 16.11: By adding *{\M}* below the subroutine call, you force the menu to redisplay automatically after each task has been completed.

Chapter 13

Chapter 14

Chapter 15

Chapter 16

Chapter 17

Macro Programming Commands

FAST TRACK

**The macro commands that
control the screen display are:**   **568**

> {BEEP}, {BORDERSOFF}, {BORDERSON}, {FRAMEOFF}, {FRAMEON}, {GRAPHOFF}, {GRAPHON}, {INDICATE}, {PANELOFF}, {PANELON}, {WINDOWSOFF}, and {WINDOWSON}.

The interactive macro commands are: **574**

> {?}, {BREAKOFF}, {BREAKON}, {FORM}, {FORMBREAK}, {GET}, {GET-LABEL}, {GETNUMBER}, {LOOK}, {MENUBRANCH}, {MENUCALL}, and {WAIT}.

To pause a macro: **574**

> Use the {?} command to pause a macro until you press Enter; use the {WAIT} command to pause for a fixed amount of time; use the {GET} command to pause for a single keystroke.

**To enter data into a form
and then move it into a database:**   **586**

> Unprotect the data entry range (/Range Unprotect) and then refer to this range in the {FORM} command. To copy the record to the bottom of the database range, use the {APPENDBELOW} command.

**The macro commands that
control the flow of a program are:**   **591**

> {BRANCH}, {DEFINE}, {DISPATCH}, {FOR}, {FORBREAK}, {IF}, {ON-ERROR}, {QUIT}, {RESTART}, {RETURN}, {*subroutine*}, and {SYSTEM}.

To repeat a task a certain number of times: **596**

> Create a subroutine for the task you want to repeat and then use the {FOR} command to repeat the task.

The data manipulation commands are: 602

{APPENDBELOW}, {APPENDRIGHT}, {BLANK}, {CONTENTS}, {LET}, {PUT}, {RECALC}, and {RECALCCOL}.

To place data in a cell: 606

Use the {LET} command if you know the exact cell address into which you want to place the data or use {PUT} to specify a relative location in a database table.

The file manipulation commands are: 609

{CLOSE}, {FILESIZE}, {GETPOS}, {OPEN}, {READ}, {READLN}, {SETPOS}, {WRITE}, and {WRITELN}.

To import data from an ASCII file: 610

Use the {OPEN} command to specify the file you want to import data from. Then use the {READLN} command to import data one line at a time or {READ} to import a specified number of characters.

Unlike the preceding sixteen chapters, this chapter is not a tutorial in which you will follow step-by-step instructions; it is a reference for the 53 commands in 1-2-3's programming language. The commands are grouped into five major categories: screen control, interactive, flow-of-control, data manipulation, and file manipulation. While there won't be any formal exercises, I will give you examples of ways to use each command. This chapter assumes that you have read Chapter 16 and understand programming terminology and concepts.

Table 17.1 is a list of 1-2-3's programming commands. The commands are grouped into the five categories.

Table 17.1: Macro Programming Commands

SCREEN CONTROL COMMANDS
{BEEP *tone-number*}
{BORDERSOFF}
{BORDERSON}
{FRAMEOFF}
{FRAMEON}
{GRAPHOFF}
{GRAPHON}
{INDICATE *string*}
{PANELOFF}
{PANELON}
{WINDOWSOFF}
{WINDOWSON}
INTERACTIVE COMMANDS
{?}
{BREAKOFF}
{BREAKON}
{FORM *input-location*}
{FORMBREAK}

Table 17.1: Macro Programming Commands (continued)

INTERACTIVE COMMANDS
{GET *location*}
{GETLABEL *prompt,location*}
{GETNUMBER *prompt,location*}
{LOOK *location*}
{MENUBRANCH *location*}
{MENUCALL *location*}
{WAIT *time-number*}

FLOW-OF-CONTROL COMMANDS
{BRANCH *location*}
{DEFINE *location1,location2,...*}
{DISPATCH *location*}
{FOR *counter,start,stop,step,subroutine*}
{FORBREAK}
{IF *condition*}
{ONERROR *branch-location*}
{QUIT}
{RESTART}
{RETURN}
{*subroutine*}
{SYSTEM *command*}

DATA MANIPULATION COMMANDS
{APPENDBELOW *target-location,source-location*}
{APPENDRIGHT *target-location,source-location*}
{BLANK *location*}
{CONTENTS *target-location,source-location*}

Table 17.1: Macro Programming Commands (continued)

DATA MANIPULATION COMMANDS
{LET *location,entry*}
{PUT *location,column-offset,row-offset,entry*}
{RECALC *location*}
{RECALCCOL *location*}

FILE MANIPULATION COMMANDS
{CLOSE}
{FILESIZE *location*}
{GETPOS *location*}
{OPEN *file-name,access-type*}
{READ *byte-count,location*}
{READLN *location*}
{SETPOS *offset-number*}
{WRITE *string*}
{WRITELN *string*}

MACRO COMMANDS THAT CONTROL THE SCREEN DISPLAY

There are a variety of commands that control the screen display. Most of these commands are ON/OFF toggles. The following commands are discussed in this section: {WINDOWSOFF}, {WINDOWSON}, {PANELOFF}, {PANEL-ON}, {BORDERSOFF}, {BORDERSON}, {FRAMEOFF}, {FRAMEON}, {INDI-CATE}, {GRAPHOFF}, {GRAPHON}, and {BEEP}.

ELIMINATING SCREEN REDRAWING: {WINDOWSOFF}

To speed up macro execution and to eliminate screen-redrawing, use the {WINDOWSOFF} command. When windows are turned off, the screen is frozen—you won't see the screen shift as the cell pointer is moved around, nor will you see new or revised spreadsheet entries. The only thing that changes on the screen when the windows are turned off is the control panel. When you need to update the screen during a macro, use the {WINDOWSON} command to unfreeze the screen. Note that the screen is automatically updated when the macro ends.

For further information and examples of the {WINDOWSOFF} and {WINDOWSON} commands, see the section *Controlling the Screen Display* in Chapter 16.

TURNING OFF THE CONTROL PANEL: {PANELOFF}

Another way to speed up macro execution is to turn off the control panel display with {PANELOFF}. When you include the {PANELOFF} command in a macro, the control panel is frozen—you don't see menus, prompts, or data. To undo this command, use the {PANELON} command.

See *Controlling the Screen Display* in Chapter 16 for macros that use the {PANELOFF} and {PANELON} commands.

REMOVING SPREADSHEET BORDERS: {BORDERSOFF} AND {FRAMEOFF}

1-2-3 offers two different macro commands to turn off the display of the column letters and row numbers in the spreadsheet borders: {BORDERSOFF} and {FRAMEOFF}. It doesn't matter which one you use because they are identical commands. The borders are removed until the macro ends or until you turn them back on with {BORDERSON} or {FRAMEON}.

The {BORDERSOFF} and {FRAMEOFF} commands do not work with Wysiwyg. However, you can eliminate the frame with a Wysiwyg command (:Display Options Frame None).

You might want to turn off the spreadsheet borders when it's not necessary to see the row numbers and column letters during macro execution—the screen looks cleaner without them. For example, if you have a macro that displays explanatory information or a data-entry form, there is no need to display the spreadsheet frame (see Figure 17.1).

CHANGING
THE INDICATOR: {INDICATE}

The mode indicator in the control panel gives you information about your current activity. For example, if you are entering a label, it says LABEL or if you are in the 1-2-3 menu, it displays MENU. Using the {INDICATE} macro command, you can change the indicator so that it displays a

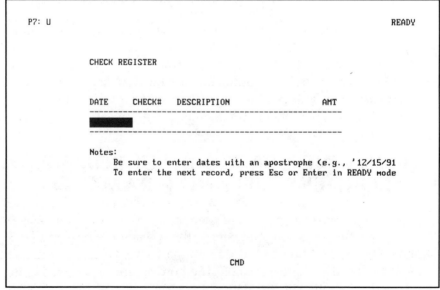

Figure 17.1: Use the {BORDERSOFF} command to eliminate the spreadsheet frame.

customized message during all or part of a macro's execution. The syntax of the command is:

{INDICATE *string}*

String can be a text string up to eighty characters long. For example, {INDICATE Please Wait} displays the message *Please Wait* as the mode indicator. If the string contains only values, you must enclose it in quotation marks, but if the string contains a combination of numbers and letters (even if it begins with a number), the quotation marks are optional. For example, to display *1-2-3* as the mode indicator, you would use the command {INDICATE "1-2-3"}. If you don't want any indicator displayed in the control panel, type **{INDICATE ""}**.

Instead of typing the string, you can refer to a cell that contains a label. The cell reference can be a range name or a cell coordinate. {INDICATE A50} displays the string located in cell A50 while {INDICATE MESSAGE} displays the string located in a cell named MESSAGE.

The indicator displays the string until you retrieve another file, clear the screen, exit 1-2-3, or use another {INDICATE} command. To return to the standard indicators, type **{INDICATE}**. The following macro demonstrates one way to use this command—to display an error message in the control panel:

{BEEP}
{INDICATE You did not enter a valid number}
{WAIT @NOW+@TIME(0,0,2)}
{INDICATE}

This subroutine beeps and displays the message *You did not enter a valid number.* The WAIT command displays the message for two seconds before the indicator is returned to its default status. (The WAIT and BEEP commands are discussed later in the chapter.) You can use this type of subroutine to verify that a valid number was entered in response to a GET-NUMBER prompt.

See the *Changing the Indicator* section of Chapter 16 for another example of the {INDICATE} command.

DISPLAYING A GRAPH: {GRAPHON}

There are several ways to display a graph in a macro:

- with the {GRAPH} keyword (the equivalent of the F10 key)
- with the /Graph View command
- with the /Graph Name Use command
- with the {GRAPHON} macro command

The first three methods display the graph and pause the macro until you press a key. With the {GRAPHON} command, however, the macro continues to run while the graph is displayed. The graph remains on the screen until the macro ends or until one of the following commands appears in the macro: {GRAPHOFF}, a {GRAPHON} command that displays a different graph, {INDICATE}, {?}, {GETLABEL}, {GETNUMBER}, {MENUBRANCH}, or {MENUCALL}.

{GRAPHON} displays the current graph. To display a different graph, specify the graph name. For example, type **{GRAPHON COMPARISON}** to display the COMPARISON chart. This command is equivalent to /Graph Name Use. You can also retrieve the settings of a particular graph without actually displaying the graph. For example, {GRAPHON AREA,NODISPLAY} retrieves the settings for the AREA graph but does not display it.

The complete syntax of this command is:

{GRAPHON *named-graph*,NODISPLAY}

Named-graph and *NODISPLAY* are optional.

To create a self-running slide show of your graphs, you can use a series of {GRAPHON} commands, as shown in Figure 17.2. The Alt-G macro displays a graph and waits for two seconds, then displays another graph and waits for two seconds, and so forth.

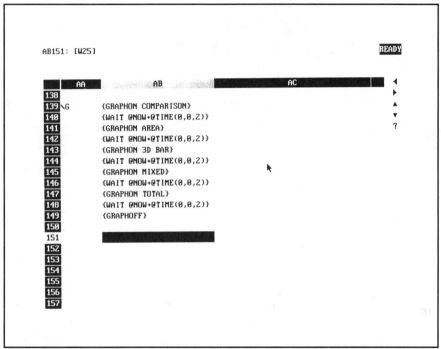

Figure 17.2: Use a series of {GRAPHON} commands to create a self-running slide show.

SOUNDING OFF: {BEEP}

While the {BEEP} command doesn't actually control the screen, it certainly draws your attention to it. Four different tones are offered, using the following syntax:

{BEEP *tone-number*}

The *tone-number* is a number 1 through 4, or a cell that contains a number. If you don't specify a tone number, tone 1 is used. Note that you won't hear the beep if you have turned off 1-2-3's beep option (/Worksheet Global Default Other Beep No).

Use the {BEEP} command to have 1-2-3 notify you when a long subroutine is finished or when an input error has been made.

INTERACTIVE MACRO COMMANDS

The interactive macro commands let you communicate with the macro while it is executing. These commands either prompt you for information in the control panel, or interpret your keystrokes. The commands discussed in this section are: {?}, {WAIT}, {GETLABEL}, {GETNUMBER}, {GET}, {LOOK}, {BREAKOFF}, {BREAKON}, {MENUBRANCH}, {MENU-CALL}, {FORM}, and {FORMBREAK}.

PAUSING A MACRO: {?} AND {WAIT}

Many of the interactive commands pause to allow you to enter information, choose menu options, or read messages. The {?} command, discussed in Chapter 14, pauses until you press Enter. This command pauses a macro so you can respond to a command in the control panel (for example, to specify a range). When you execute the macro, it will pause until you press Enter and then continue with the remaining keystrokes in the macro. To cancel a macro while it's pausing, press Ctrl-Break and Esc. Each of the macros in Figure 17.3 pauses so you can enter information. For example, the \D macro waits for you to enter a date.

The {WAIT} command pauses a macro for a specified amount of time. It is typically used to give you time to look over the spreadsheet, to read a message in the control panel, or to view a graph (see Figure 17.2). While the macro is paused, the WAIT mode indicator is displayed (unless the indicator has been changed with the {INDICATE} command).

The syntax of this command is:

{WAIT *time-number*}

Time-number is a future date-and-time serial number. (You learned about date serial numbers in Chapter 12). To indicate the current day and time, use the @NOW function; then, to specify a future time, add a fraction of a 24-hour day to the current time. For example, to pause the macro for half a day, type {**WAIT @NOW+0.5**}. However, you will typically want the

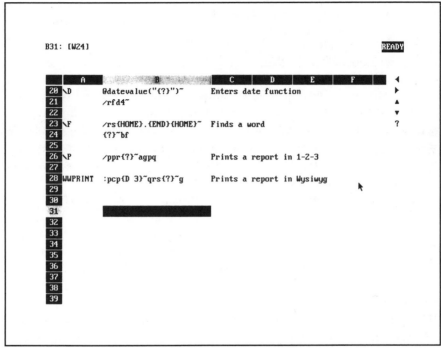

Figure 17.3: The {?} command pauses a macro until you press Enter.

macro to pause for mere seconds or minutes. No, you don't have to calculate how many seconds are in the day and then determine what fraction of a day a second is. The @TIME(hours,minutes,seconds) function offers a much easier way to enter the time. To pause the macro for five seconds, type **{WAIT @NOW+@TIME(0,0,5)}**; to pause for one minute, type **{WAIT @NOW+@TIME(0,1,0)}**.

CREATING CUSTOM PROMPTS: {GETLABEL} AND {GETNUMBER}

{GETLABEL} and {GETNUMBER} are data-input commands that display questions in the control panel and store your responses in a specified cell. {GETLABEL} stores the response as a label while {GETNUMBER} stores the reply as a value.

These commands have the following syntax:

{GETLABEL *prompt,location*}
{GETNUMBER *prompt,location*}

The *prompt* is the message or question that appears in the control panel. You should keep it under 73 characters long so the entire message will fit in the control panel. The prompt needn't be enclosed in quotation marks unless the string contains a comma or semicolon. The *location* is the cell in which the response is stored. It can be either an address or range name. The response can be up to eighty characters long.

If you don't enter a valid number in response to a {GETNUMBER} prompt, an ERR (error) message is stored in the cell location. Non-numeric responses include labels, numbers that contain label characters (such as *50,000*), or no response (you press Enter without typing a response). Because error messages could crash your program, you should check for errors with an IF statement (discussed later in this chapter and also in Chapter 16).

Figure 17.4 shows examples of the {GETLABEL} and {GETNUMBER} commands. This macro program enters data into a cash disbursements database. When this macro is run, it will first prompt you with *Enter check number.* Your response is stored as a label in the cell named *CHECK* (AB108). The next prompt is *Enter description.* Your response to this question is stored as a label in DESC (AC108). The final message prompts you to *Enter amount.* Your numeric response is stored in AMT (AD108). The {APPENDBELOW} command copies the range DATA_ENTRY (AB108..AD108) to the bottom of the INPUT range (not shown in Figure 17.4). The {APPENDBELOW} and {BLANK} commands are discussed later in the chapter.

Another way to enter custom prompts is with the /XN and /XL commands. For details, see the section *The /X Commands* later in this chapter.

Entering a Response into the Current Cell

The \E macro program in Figure 17.4 places responses into intermediary cells (CHECK, DESC, and AMT) before entering the data into a database. However, sometimes you may want your response to be entered

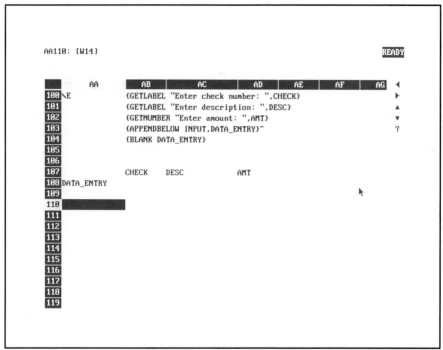

```
AA110: [W14]                                                      READY

             AA        AB           AC          AD       AE      AF      AG   ◄
100 \E             {GETLABEL "Enter check number: ",CHECK}                    ►
101                {GETLABEL "Enter description: ",DESC}                      ▲
102                {GETNUMBER "Enter amount: ",AMT}                           ▼
103                {APPENDBELOW INPUT,DATA_ENTRY}~                            ?
104                {BLANK DATA_ENTRY}
105
106
107                CHECK      DESC            AMT
108 DATA_ENTRY
109                                                          ▶
110
111
112
113
114
115
116
117
118
119
```

Figure 17.4: The {GETLABEL} and {GETNUMBER} commands prompt you
to enter data.

at the cell-pointer location—wherever that happens to be. Since the location is not constant, you can't indicate a specific cell here. Instead, use a
special @ function, as follows:

{GETLABEL *prompt*, @CELLPOINTER("address")}

The @CELLPOINTER("address") function stores the response in
the cell the pointer is currently highlighting. (For further information
on the @CELLPOINTER command, see Appendix B.) The \E macro in
Figure 17.5 enters the responses directly into the database. Notice that
the first line of the program moves the cell pointer to the beginning of the
database INPUT range and then moves down to the first empty row.
({END}{DOWN} moves the cell pointer to the last row in the database and
{DOWN} moves to the next row down.) Because the macro enters data into
the current cell, it's important that the cell pointer be in the correct place.

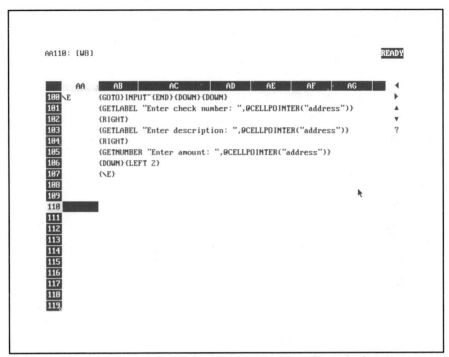

Figure 17.5: By specifying @CELLPOINTER("address") as the location, responses are stored in the current cell.

PAUSING FOR
A SINGLE KEYSTROKE: {GET}

The {?}, {GETLABEL}, and {GETNUMBER} commands pause until you press Enter, while the {WAIT} command pauses for a specified amount of time. A fifth data-input command, {GET}, pauses until you press a single key—you don't need to press Enter, and there is no time limit. The key you press is then stored in a cell. Thus, the syntax of this command is:

{GET *location*}

Figure 17.6 shows one way of using the {GET} command. In this example, an error message informs you to press any key to continue. The key you press is stored in the cell named KEY. Unlike the {GETNUMBER} and {GETLABEL} commands, {GET} does not display a prompt in the control panel. However, as Figure 17.6 shows, you can precede the {GET} command with a command to change the indicator. In essence, the indicator text string is functioning as a prompt. Just make sure you change the mode indicator back to its default setting after the {GET} command.

In the previous example, it doesn't matter what key is pressed; the key is stored in a cell but nothing is actually done with the response. Frequently, though, you will request a user to press certain keys to perform certain operations. The macro program can then evaluate the contents of the storage cell and execute different tasks based on the stored keystroke. Figure 17.7 shows an example of this type of program. Again, the {INDICATE} command is used to display a prompt. In this example, you are requested to *Press C to Continue; Q to Quit*. The keystroke is stored in a cell named KEY. If KEY contains a C, the \M macro is executed. If KEY

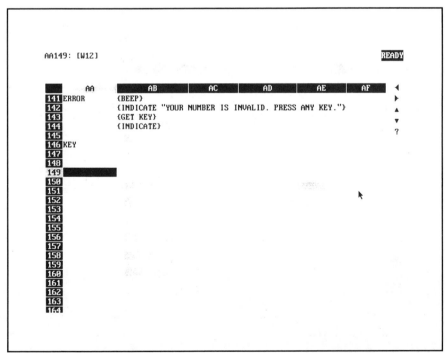

Figure 17.6: In the ERROR macro, the {GET} command pauses until you press a key.

contains a *Q*, the macro quits. If KEY contains any other keystroke, the CONTINUE program is run again. The {IF} command is discussed in Chapter 16 and later in this chapter.

LOOKING FOR A KEYSTROKE: {LOOK}

Like the {GET} command, the {LOOK} command stores a single keystroke in a specific cell. The difference between these two commands is that {LOOK} doesn't pause and wait for a keystroke. While a macro is running, it copies any keystrokes to a specified location (each new keystroke replaces the previous one). You will usually follow the {LOOK} command with an {IF} statement to evaluate the keystroke and perform an operation based on the key that is pressed. This macro command offers an

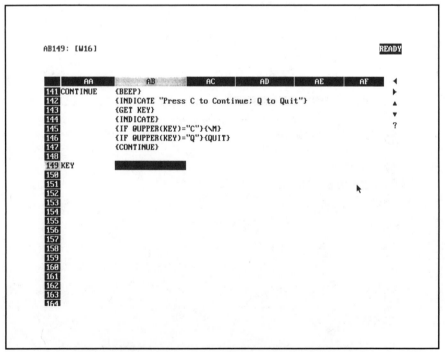

Figure 17.7: The CONTINUE macro evaluates the keystroke entered with the {GET} command, and performs different tasks depending on the response.

easy way to stop a long macro, to get out of an infinite loop, or to execute another subroutine.

Figure 17.8 shows an example of how you can use the {LOOK} command. The \G macro displays a series of graphs, pausing for two seconds between each graph. The STOP subroutine, which is executed after each graph is displayed, stops the \G macro if any key is pressed.

Let's analyze the STOP subroutine, line by line. The first line looks for a keystroke and stores it in the cell named KEY. The {IF} statement examines the contents of KEY. If it's blank (in other words, no key has been pressed), the macro returns to the original program (\G). Otherwise, the macro quits.

A variation of the STOP subroutine is shown in Figure 17.9. In this program, the \G macro stops only if the Home key is pressed; all other keystrokes will be ignored. This version of the STOP subroutine uses

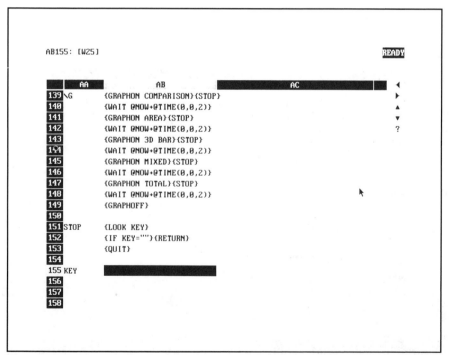

Figure 17.8: The STOP subroutine uses a {LOOK} command to stop the \G macro if any key is pressed.

both the {LOOK} and {GET} commands. (The {LOOK} command merely copies the keystroke while the {GET} command moves it into the storage cell.)

DISABLING THE BREAK COMMAND: {BREAKOFF}

As mentioned previously, Ctrl-Break cancels a macro while it is in the middle of executing commands or pausing for input. If you don't want macro processing to be interrupted, include the {BREAKOFF} command in your macro program. When you do this, the Ctrl-Break command will be ignored. There is no way to cancel the macro—you must let it finish

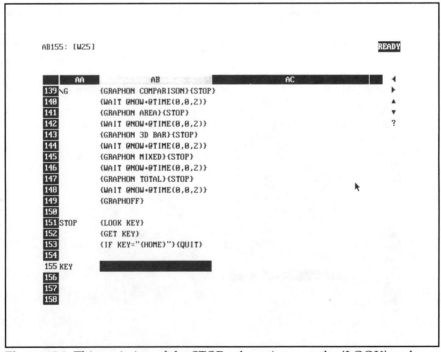

Figure 17.9: This variation of the STOP subroutine uses the {LOOK} and {GET} commands to stop the \G macro if the Home key is pressed.

naturally. *Don't use the {BREAKOFF} command until you have completely debugged the program!* You might create an infinite loop that issues the same commands over and over again. If you can't use Ctrl-Break to cancel the program, the only way to get out of such a loop is to turn off the computer.

{BREAKOFF} is typically used in macros that you develop for other people. It prevents them from stopping the macro and looking at or modifying sensitive data.

To re-enable the Ctrl-Break command, use the {BREAKON} command.

DISPLAYING CUSTOM MENUS: {MENUBRANCH} AND {MENUCALL}

The {MENUBRANCH} and {MENUCALL} commands display menus that you have laid out in the spreadsheet. Figure 17.10 shows an example of a custom menu (in the range AQ57..AR60) and the macro that displays

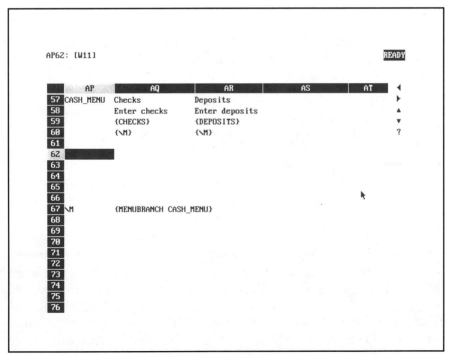

Figure 17.10: The programming commands for a custom menu

it (cell AQ67). The Checks and Deposits menu options run macros that enter data into a cash disbursements journal. Before we get into the specifics on designing the custom menu, let's look at the macro command that displays the menu:

{MENUBRANCH *location*}

This command displays a menu that begins in the specified location. *Location* can be a cell coordinate or a range name. In the \M macro in Figure 17.10, the menu begins in CASH_MENU (AQ57). While the menu is displayed in the control panel, the macro pauses so you can select a menu option. After you choose an option, 1-2-3 issues the macro commands associated with that option. For example, when you choose the Checks option, the CHECKS subroutine is executed.

The difference between {MENUBRANCH} and {MENUCALL} is subtle and is apparent only after the commands for a menu option have been executed. {MENUCALL} returns to the calling macro; {MENUBRANCH} does not.

Another way to display a custom menu is with the /XM command. For details, refer to the section *The /X Commands* later in this chapter.

If you want a menu to display automatically when you retrieve a file, name the macro \0 (see Chapter 14 for further information on autoexecuting macros).

Designing a Custom Menu

You can type your custom menus in any empty area of the spreadsheet—usually they are near your macros. Custom menus require a minimum of three lines: the menu options, menu descriptions, and macro instructions.

The menu options (up to eight) should be entered into adjacent cells across a single row. Do not leave empty cells between options because a blank cell indicates the end of the menu. The option titles can consist of letters, numbers, spaces, and special characters. However, it's a good idea to avoid spaces so each menu option is easily distinguishable. For multiple-word menu options, use a dash or underline. Though it isn't a requirement, menu options should start with different letters so you can choose commands by typing the first letter of the option. If two menu options begin with the same letter, the first option will have priority; the only way to choose the second option is to highlight it and press Enter.

The first option in the menu should be assigned a name; this name becomes the *location* in the {MENUBRANCH} or {MENUCALL} command. It is called CASH_MENU in Figure 17.10.

The second line of the menu contains brief descriptions for each option. These are the messages that appear in the control panel when you highlight an option.

Any subsequent lines of the menu contain instructions to be executed when an option is selected. For example, when the Deposits option is chosen, two subroutines are executed: {DEPOSITS} and {\M}. Therefore, the custom menu will automatically redisplay after the {DEPOSITS} subroutine is finished. Instead of calling a subroutine, you can enter the macro keystrokes in one or more rows under the appropriate menu option. However, the menu is more organized and easier to interpret if it references a descriptive subroutine name.

Creating Submenus

When you select an option in your 1-2-3 menu, you frequently will see a submenu with additional options. Your custom menus can also display submenus. To create a submenu, specify a {MENUBRANCH} or {MENUCALL} command under the appropriate option in your menu. For example, the Print option in Figure 17.11 displays a menu that is located in PRINT_MENU (cell AQ62). The submenu is set up identically to a master menu (in other words, the first row contains menu options, the second row contains descriptions, and any subsequent rows contain macro instructions).

Here is how the menu system in Figure 17.11 works: When you press Alt-M, the control panel displays the options Checks, Deposits, and Print. Then, when you choose Print, the items Income_Stmt and Journal are displayed. If you press Esc when you are in a submenu, the previous menu is displayed—just like with your 1-2-3 menus.

For another example of a custom menu system, see Chapter 16.

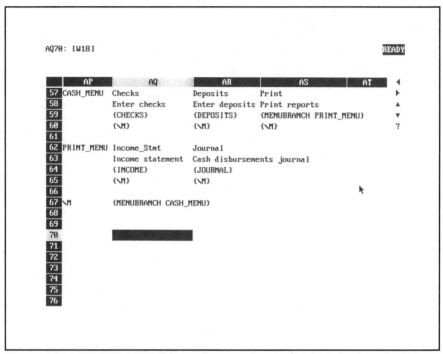

```
AQ70: [W18]                                                      READY

         AP              AQ              AR              AS         AT      ◄
  57 CASH_MENU   Checks          Deposits        Print                     ►
  58             Enter checks    Enter deposits  Print reports             ▲
  59             {CHECKS}        {DEPOSITS}      {MENUBRANCH PRINT_MENU}    ▼
  60             {\M}            {\M}            {\M}                       ?
  61
  62 PRINT_MENU  Income_Stmt     Journal
  63             Income statement Cash disbursements journal
  64             {INCOME}        {JOURNAL}
  65             {\M}            {\M}
  66
  67 \M          {MENUBRANCH CASH_MENU}
  68
  69
  70
  71
  72
  73
  74
  75
  76
```

Figure 17.11: PRINT_MENU is a submenu that is displayed when the Print option is selected.

FILLING IN
DATA-ENTRY FORMS: {FORM}

The {FORM} command pauses a macro and lets you enter data into the unprotected cells of a specified range. The macro pauses until you press Enter or Esc in READY mode. The data can then be copied to the bottom of the database range before you enter the next record. {FORM} works in much the same way as the /Range Input command except that it has several additional capabilities. The syntax of this command is:

{FORM *input-location*}

Input-location is the range of cells into which you want to enter data. The {FORM} command will not work unless the range is unprotected with the /Range Unprotect command. (However, global protection needn't be enabled.) In Figure 17.12, the input-location is P6..S6—an outline calls attention to this range. The notes underneath the form provide useful information on how to enter data into the form.

The following data-entry macro lets you enter data into the input form shown in Figure 17.12:

```
{GOTO}FORM_AREA~
{BLANK CHECK_FORM}~
{FORM CHECK_FORM}
{APPENDBELOW DBASE,CHECK_FORM}
{\E}
```

The first line of this macro positions the data-entry form on the screen. (FORM_AREA refers to the range O1..S11.) The second line of the macro

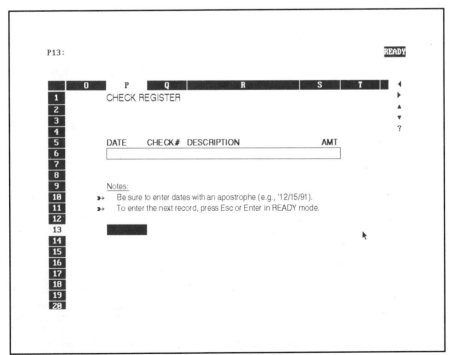

Figure 17.12: An outline is drawn around the data-entry range.

erases the range CHECK_FORM (P6..S6), ensuring that the form is blank before you enter a record. The third line pauses the macro so that you can enter data into the form. While the macro is paused, you can type, edit, and move the cell pointer. When you press Enter or Esc in READY mode, the next line of the macro is processed. The {APPENDBELOW} command adds the CHECK_FORM range to the bottom of the range named DBASE. (The {APPENDBELOW} command is discussed later in the chapter.) The final row of the macro loops back to the beginning of the \E macro so that you can enter the next record. The only way to stop this macro is with Ctrl-Break.

Creating Macros for a Data-Entry Form

The problem with this macro is that it creates an infinite loop. The \E macro is executed indefinitely and the only way to break out of it is with Ctrl-Break. A more elegant solution is to create a macro that allows you to end the macro when you are finished entering data. The macros that work when you are in the middle of the {FORM} command are even more powerful than your standard macros. First, you don't need to use the /Range Name command to assign a name to each macro. Second, the macro instructions are executed when you press a single key. For example, you can create a macro that is executed with the End key.

For the \E program, it might be useful to have macros that perform the following tasks:

- insert the current record and run the \E macro so you can enter another record

- erase the current record before it is entered into the database

- discontinue data entry

There are three steps to creating macros for a data-entry form. First, create a two-column list in the spreadsheet; this is called a *call-table*. The first column contains macro key names and the second column contains the keystrokes that will be executed when the key in the first column is pressed. This list appears in the range AB106..AC108 in Figure 17.13. Thus, when you press the Ins key, the INS_RECORD subroutine is executed. This subroutine adds the current record to the database, erases the

CHECK_FORM range, and then runs the \E macro again. When you press the Del key, the CHECK_FORM range is erased and the cell pointer is moved to the beginning of the data-entry range. When you press the End key, the {FORMBREAK} command ends data entry and returns macro execution to the line after the {FORM} command in the original program.

After you have created the call-table, you need to name it. In this example, the range AB106..AC108 is named CALL_KEYS. The final step is to tell the {FORM} command where the call-table is located. The syntax of the command is:

{FORM *input-location,call-table*}

In Figure 17.13, you can see that the third line of the \E macro includes a reference to the CALL_KEYS range.

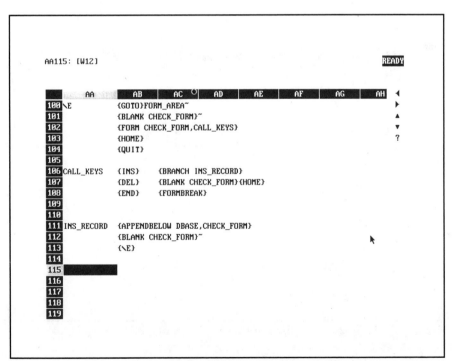

Figure 17.13: This variation of the data-entry program offers macros to insert and erase records as well as to end data entry.

Defining Keys Allowed During Data Entry

The {FORM} command offers two ways to control what keys are allowed during data entry. You can either create a list of keys that will be ignored when they are pressed (the *exclude-list*) or you can list the keys that are allowed (the *include-list*). 1-2-3 will beep when you press keys that are not allowed (keys on the exclude-list or keys not on the include-list). You cannot have both types of lists. Each cell in the list can contain one or more key names; be sure not to use any punctuation (such as spaces or commas). Figure 17.14 shows an exclude-list that ignores the F10 (Graph) key, ↑, and ↓. Table 14.1 lists all the macro key names that can be in an exclude- or include-list. The list can also contain letters, numbers, and special characters.

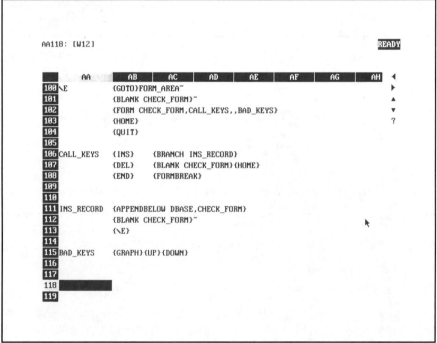

Figure 17.14: The exclude-list is located in the range BAD_KEYS (AB115).

The syntax of the {FORM} command, with all of its options, is:

{FORM *input-location,call-table,include-list,exclude-list*}

Even when you aren't using a particular option, you must still include the comma as a place-holder. For example, if you aren't using a call-table or an include-list, the syntax is:

{FORM input-location,,,exclude-list}

MACRO COMMANDS THAT CONTROL PROGRAM FLOW

The following commands direct the path of a macro program: {*subroutine*}, {BRANCH}, {DEFINE}, {DISPATCH}, {FOR}, {FORBREAK}, {IF}, {ONERROR}, {QUIT}, {RESTART}, {RETURN}, and {SYSTEM}.

EXECUTING SUBROUTINES: {SUBROUTINE} AND {BRANCH}

A *subroutine* is the location of a macro program. You can give subroutines descriptive names (such as REPORT) or the backslash-letter name (such as \R), or simply refer to the first cell in which the macro is located. Descriptive names are the most useful, however. 1-2-3's programming language offers two ways to tell a program to execute a subroutine: {BRANCH *subroutine*} or simply {*subroutine*}. For example, {REPORT} executes the REPORT subroutine and {BRANCH SALARY_RPT} executes the SALARY_RPT subroutine.

After executing the commands in a subroutine, the {*subroutine*} command returns to the original macro and performs the commands that follow the {*subroutine*} command. This is known as a *subroutine call*. The {BRANCH *subroutine*} command, on the other hand, does not return to the original macro; it transfers control to the subroutine. This is known as *subroutine branching*.

Examples of subroutine calls and branching appear throughout this chapter and Chapter 16. For example, the program in Figure 17.10 calls the CHECKS and DEPOSITS subroutines and the one in Figure 17.14 branches to the INS_RECORD subroutine.

Another way to call and branch to subroutines is with the /XC and /XG commands. For details, see the section *The /X Commands* later in this chapter.

BRANCHING TO A SUBROUTINE INDIRECTLY: {DISPATCH}

Like the {BRANCH} command, the {DISPATCH} command transfers macro control to a subroutine and does not return to the calling macro. However, instead of branching directly to a particular subroutine, the {DISPATCH} command refers to a cell that contains the name of a subroutine to execute. The syntax of this command is:

{DISPATCH *location*}

Location is the address or range name of the cell containing the subroutine name. This command allows you to branch to one of several different macros, depending on what subroutine name is listed in *location*. In other words, you can branch to different subroutines without using multiple {IF} statements.

The \E macro in Figure 17.15 demonstrates one way to use the {DISPATCH} command. The {GETLABEL} command prompts you to enter a C to record checks or a P to print; your response is stored in a cell named REPLY. The {DISPATCH REPLY} command then runs the subroutine whose name is stored in REPLY (either C or P). Thus, if you enter a C, the subroutine named C is executed; if you enter a P, the P subroutine is run. The {DISPATCH REPLY} command is a shorter way to say:

{IF REPLY="C"}{BRANCH C}
{IF REPLY="P"}{BRANCH P}

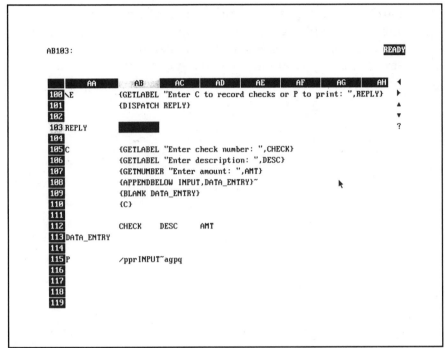

Figure 17.15: The {DISPATCH} command allows the flexibility of branching to different subroutines.

DEFINING
SUBROUTINE ARGUMENTS: {DEFINE}

The {subroutine} command can do more than just call a subroutine—it can also carry information to be used in the subroutine. This process is commonly called *passing arguments to a subroutine*. An argument can be a value, formula, label, range name, or cell address. Each argument is separated by a comma. For example,

{REPORT 1stqtr,|Q1 Report}

In the above example, the REPORT subroutine has two arguments. *1stqtr* is the name of the range to be printed in the REPORT subroutine and |*Q1 Report* is the report's header. The print macro in Figure 17.16 makes four subroutine calls—each with different arguments. Thus, the macro prints four reports with four different ranges and headers.

When you pass arguments to a subroutine, the first line of the subroutine must be a {DEFINE} statement that specifies where to store the arguments. The {DEFINE} statement for the REPORT subroutine is:

{DEFINE RANGE,HEADER}

This command stores the first argument in the cell named RANGE (cell AB107) and the second argument in the cell named HEADER (AB109).

As part of the definition of arguments, you can indicate how to store the data—as a label or a value. To store the data as a label, type **:s** or **:string** after

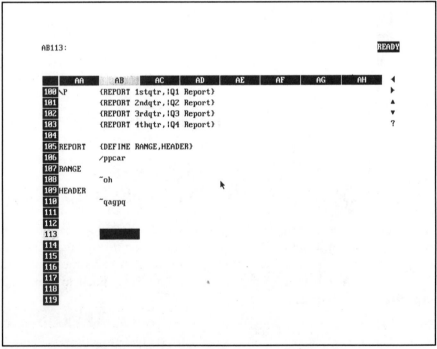

Figure 17.16: The {*subroutine*} command can carry information to a subroutine.

the location. To store the data as a value, type **:v** or **:value**. For example:

{DEFINE RANGE:s,HEADER:s}

If you don't specify the data type, 1-2-3 stores the data as a label.

ENTERING
CONDITIONAL STATEMENTS: {IF}

{IF} is one of the most widely used and powerful macro programming commands. It allows the program to do different tasks depending on the situation. For example, if the answer to a "Do you want to continue?" question is yes, a subroutine is re-executed; if the answer is no, the macro ends. The syntax of the {IF} command is:

{IF *condition*}

The *condition* is a logical expression that can only be either true or false. For example, *+SALES>30000* is a condition. Conditions use the following logical operators:

Operator	Description
=	Equal to
>	Greater than
>=	Greater than or equal to
<	Less than
<=	Less than or equal to
<>	Not equal to

To join together two logical expressions, use the #AND# or #OR# operators. When expressions are joined with #AND#, both expressions must be true for the condition to evaluate to true. When they are joined with #OR#, only one expression must be true for the condition to be true.

If the condition is true, 1-2-3 executes the commands to the right of the {IF} statement (they must be in the same cell). If the condition is false, 1-2-3 executes the commands in the next cell.

{IF} statements appear in many of the programs discussed in this chapter, such as the following excerpt from Figure 17.7:

```
{IF @UPPER(KEY)="C"}{\M}
{IF @UPPER(KEY)="Q"}{QUIT}
```

Another way to write an {IF} statement in a macro is with the /XI command. For details, see the section *The /X Commands* later in this chapter.

REPEATING A TASK: {FOR}

To repeat a task a certain number of times, create a *for-next loop* with the {FOR} command. The syntax of this command is:

```
{FOR counter,start,stop,step,subroutine}
```

Counter is where 1-2-3 keeps track of the number of times the *subroutine* has been executed; it is an address or range name of a blank cell. *Start* is the number with which the counter begins counting (usually 1). *Stop* is the number with which the counter ends counting. If the *start* value is 1, the *stop* value is the number of times you want the subroutine repeated. *Step* is the number added to the counter each time the subroutine is executed (usually 1). *Subroutine* is the address or range name of the subroutine to be repeated.

The print macro in Figure 17.17 prints a range a specified number of times. (1-2-3's /Print command does not have an option in which you can specify how many copies to print.) The macro begins with a {GETNUM-BER} command that prompts you for the number of copies to print; your response is stored in a cell named COPIES. The macro then issues the /Print Printer Range command and pauses for you to specify the print range. The next line of the program is the for-next loop:

```
{FOR COUNTER,1,COPIES,1,PRINT}
```

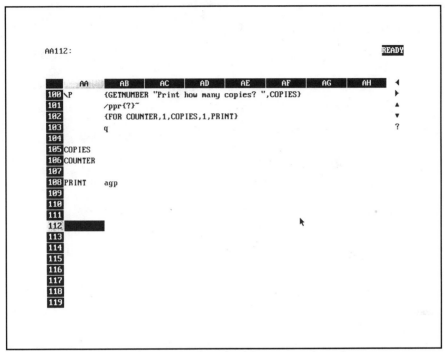

Figure 17.17: The {FOR} command in the \P macro prints the same range several times.

The counter is a cell named COUNTER, the start value is 1, the stop value is stored in the cell named COPIES, the step value is 1, and the subroutine that is executed multiple times is called PRINT. This subroutine simply issues the Align Go Page command.

To cancel a for-next loop before the stop value has been reached, use the {FORBREAK} command. The PRINT subroutine in Figure 17.18 will cancel the for-next loop if any key is pressed while the reports are printing. The {LOOK KEY} command stores any keystrokes in the cell named KEY. If KEY isn't blank, the {FORBREAK} command is issued. {FORBREAK} returns to the calling macro and executes the commands following the {FOR} command.

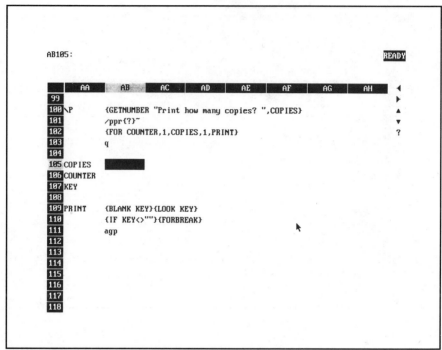

Figure 17.18: If any key is pressed during the PRINT subroutine, the for-next loop is cancelled.

HANDLING
ERROR MESSAGES: {ONERROR}

The {ONERROR} command prevents a macro from "crashing" when a 1-2-3 error occurs. Here are several examples of 1-2-3 errors:

- *Invalid cell or range address*
- *Invalid character in file name*
- *Disk drive not ready*
- *No print range specified*
- *Background print not in memory*
- *String not found*

- *No more matching strings*
- *Add-in is already attached*

Without the {ONERROR} command, a 1-2-3 error message will stop a macro dead in its tracks. An error message will appear on the screen (see Figure 17.19), and when you press Esc or Enter to clear the message, the macro will be aborted.

When there is a possibility of an error message, include an {ON-ERROR} command before the error is likely to occur. The syntax of this command is:

{ONERROR *branch-location,message-location*}

Branch-location is the name of a subroutine that will be executed when an error message is encountered. If you specify a *message-location* (it's optional), the error message is recorded in message-location.

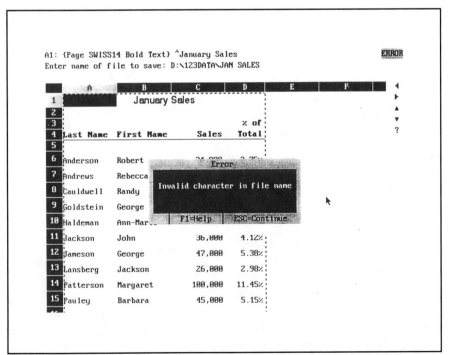

Figure 17.19: An error message, such as this one, typically aborts a macro.

The file-save macro in Figure 17.20 runs the NAME_ERROR sub-routine if an error message is encountered (for example, if you include a space in a file name). This subroutine displays the message *You entered an invalid character; press any key* in the mode indicator. When you press a key, the \S macro is re-executed.

Note that {ONERROR} does not trap error messages that result from syntax errors or typing mistakes in a macro program.

RETURNING TO THE ORIGINAL MACRO: {RETURN}

Whenever you want to return from a subroutine to the macro that called it, use the {RETURN} command. The {RETURN} command tells

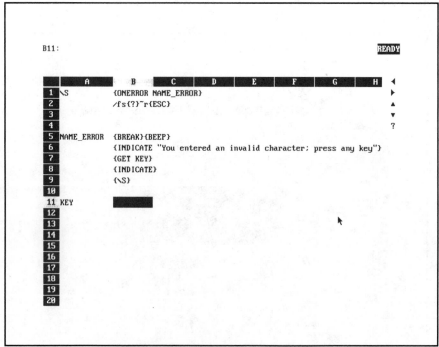

Figure 17.20: The NAME_ERROR subroutine is executed if an error message is encountered.

1-2-3 to process the commands or keystrokes in the cell immediately following the subroutine call.

You can also use {RETURN} in the subroutine that is called by a {FOR} command. {RETURN} will abort the current repetition and start the next repetition.

The {RETURN} command is most frequently used in conjunction with {IF} statements: If a certain condition is true, return to the original macro. For example:

```
{GETLABEL "Do you wish to continue? (Y/N) ",REPLY}
{IF @UPPER(REPLY)="N"}{RETURN}
{BRANCH START}
```

{RETURN} works only when you call a subroutine with the {*subroutine*} command; it does not work when you branch to a subroutine with {BRANCH *subroutine*}.

Another way to return to a subroutine is with the /XR command. For details, see the section *The /X Commands* later in this chapter.

CANCELING SUBROUTINE NESTING: {RESTART}

In your 1-2-3 programs, you can have one subroutine call another subroutine, which can call a third routine, which calls a fourth, and so on. When one subroutine calls another, your program has *nested subroutines*. Up to 32 subroutines can be nested in a program. 1-2-3 keeps track of the order in which nested subroutines are called and will automatically return from each subroutine to the one that called it—unless you use the {RESTART} command. When 1-2-3 finds a {RESTART} command, the remainder of the current subroutine is executed, but the link to the calling subroutine is broken.

QUITTING A MACRO PROGRAM: {QUIT}

To end a program before the last line is reached, use the {QUIT} command. The {QUIT} command is frequently used in conjunction with an {IF} statement. For example,

```
{IF REPLY="Q"}{QUIT}
{BRANCH START}
```

You may also want to place a {QUIT} command after the last line of a macro. It's not required, but it lets you know at a glance that you didn't lose the last lines of the macro.

Another way to quit a macro is with /XQ. For details, see the section *The /X Commands* later in this chapter.

RUNNING A DOS COMMAND: {SYSTEM}

The {SYSTEM} command goes to the DOS prompt, executes a DOS command, and returns to 1-2-3. The syntax for this command is:

```
{SYSTEM command}
```

Command can be either the actual DOS command to be executed or the name of a cell that contains the command. The following macro runs a batch file named BACKUP:

```
{SYSTEM BACKUP}
```

The BACKUP batch file copies all .WK1 and .FMT files to drive A.

COMMANDS THAT MANIPULATE DATA

The following macro commands manipulate (enter, copy, and erase) spreadsheet data: {APPENDBELOW}, {APPENDRIGHT}, {BLANK}, {CONTENTS}, {LET}, {PUT}, {RECALC}, and {RECALCCOL}.

APPENDING DATA: {APPENDBELOW} AND {APPENDRIGHT}

The {APPENDBELOW} command is an ideal way to add records to a database. This command copies a range of data (called the *source-location*) to the bottom of another range (called the *target-location*) and automatically redefines the target-location to include the new rows. The {APPENDRIGHT} command works in a similar fashion, except it copies the source-location to the right of the target-location. The syntax of these commands is:

    {APPENDBELOW *target-location,source-location*}
    {APPENDRIGHT *target-location,source-location*}

{APPENDBELOW} works well with the {FORM} command. You can use {FORM} to enter the data in a data-entry form and {APPENDBELOW} to copy the data to the database. For example:

    {GOTO}FORM_AREA~
    {BLANK CHECK_FORM}~
    {FORM CHECK_FORM}
    {APPENDBELOW DBASE,CHECK_FORM}
    {\E}

(See the section *Filling in Data-Entry Forms* for additional information on the {FORM} command.)

ERASING DATA: {BLANK}

The {BLANK} command offers an alternative way to erase data. It's the equivalent of /Range Erase, but {BLANK} is faster and doesn't recalculate the spreadsheet. The syntax of this command is:

    {BLANK *location*}

Location is the address or range name of the range to be erased. {BLANK} commands are used in many of the programs discussed in this chapter such as the PRINT subroutine in Figure 17.18.

Note that you don't see the results of the {BLANK} command until the screen is redrawn. The easiest way to do this is to include a tilde after the {BLANK} operation. (See the INS_RECORD subroutine in Figure 17.14.)

CONVERTING A VALUE TO A LABEL: {CONTENTS}

The {CONTENTS} command copies a value to another cell and converts it to a label. You might want to do this if you need to use the number in a text formula (see Appendix B for information about string functions). The syntax of this command is:

{CONTENTS *target-location,source-location*}

Target-location is the address or range name of the cell that will contain the label. *Source-location* is the address or range name of the cell containing the value to be converted.

Here is an example:

```
{CONTENTS SALARY_LABEL,SALARY_VALUE}
{GOTO}REPORT~
'+"The average salary is "&SALARY_LABEL&"for the sales dept."~
```

SALARY_VALUE is the name of a cell that contains a value and SALARY_LABEL is the name of a blank cell that will contain the label after the macro is run. If SALARY_VALUE contained the number $34,500, the following sentence would appear in the cell named REPORT:

The average salary is $34,500 for the sales dept.

{CONTENTS} has several options you can specify with the following syntax:

{CONTENTS *target-location,source-location,width,cell-format*}

Width determines the number of characters in the converted label; if you don't specify a width, the label's width is equivalent to the column width of the source-location. You will see asterisks in the string formula if the width is too small, extra spaces if the width is too large.

Cell-format specifies the format of the label (for example, Fixed, Currency, comma, and so forth). If you don't specify a format, the label has the same format of the cell in source-location. You must enter the appropriate numeric code for the cell-format you want to use (see Table 17.2). For example, to specify Currency format with 2 decimal places, the code would be 34.

Table 17.2: Cell Format Codes for the {CONTENTS} Command

CODE	FORMAT
0–15	Fixed, 0–15 decimal places
16–31	Scientific, 0–15 decimal places
32–47	Currency, 0–15 decimal places
48–63	Percent, 0–15 decimal places
64–79	Comma, 0–15 decimal places
112	+/−
113	General
114	Date (DD-MMM-YY)
115	Date (DD-MMM)
116	Date (MMM-YY)
117	Text
118	Hidden
119	Time (HH:MM:SS AM/PM)
120	Time (HH:MM AM/PM)
121	Date (MM/DD/YY)
122	Date (MM/DD)
123	Time (HH:MM:SS)
124	Time (HH:MM)
127	Global format

You cannot include a cell-format code unless you also specify a width. However, you can specify a width without entering a cell-format.

PLACING DATA IN A CELL: {LET}

The {LET} command places a label or value in a specified location. It is the equivalent of one of the following tasks:

- moving the cell pointer to a specific cell with the {GOTO} command and then typing data in that cell

- using the /Copy command to copy data from one cell to another

The syntax of this command is:

{LET *location,entry*}

Location is where you want to place the data; it can be an address or a range name. *Entry* is the data to be placed in *location*; it can be a label, value, formula, or a cell containing a label, value, or formula. For example,

{LET NEW_BALANCE,NEW_BALANCE-CHECK}

The above statement takes the value in NEW_BALANCE and subtracts the value in CHECK and places the result back in NEW_BALANCE.

{LET} statements are frequently used at the beginning of a subroutine to set a variable to a certain value. For example,

{LET COST,10}

PLACING DATA IN A TABLE: {PUT}

The {PUT} command is similar to {LET} in that it places data in a cell. You will use {PUT}, though, when you don't know the exact address or range name of the cell into which you want to enter data. With the {PUT} command, you specify a relative location. For example, a {PUT} command might translate to: "Put this data in the third column, fifth row in the range named TABLE."

The syntax of this command is:

{PUT *location,column-offset,row-offset,entry*}

Location is the table that contains a cell into which you want to enter data; *location* is frequently a database input range. *Entry* is the data to be entered into the table; it can be a label, value, formula, or a cell containing a label, value, or formula. 1-2-3 uses the *column-offset* and *row-offset* to determine where to enter the data. The column-offset indicates the column where the entry is to be placed; counting begins with 0 (the first column's number is 0, the second column's number is 1, etc.). The row-offset refers to the row in which the entry is to be placed. The intersection of the column- and row-offset identifies a specific cell in the table. The offset can be an address or range name of a cell containing the offset value.

The UPDATE macro in Figure 17.21 updates an employee's salary after a raise. It first prompts you for the employee's first and last name; the responses are stored in the appropriate cells (named FIRST and LAST) in the criteria range. The new salary is stored in a cell named NEWSAL. Then the /Data Query Find command is issued. The {LET} command stores the current row number in the cell named ROW. (This is the row number of the record you want to update.) The {PUT} command then enters the new salary (contained in the cell NEWSAL) into the appropriate cell in the database named INPUT. The row- and column-offset determine where the data is entered. Because the salary field is the seventh column in the INPUT range, the column-offset is 6 (remember, counting begins with 0). The row-offset is calculated by subtracting 1 from the value in ROW. The tilde after the {PUT} command redraws the screen so you can immediately see the change.

RECALCULATING A RANGE: {RECALC} AND {RECALCCOL}

The {CALC} command in a macro program updates all cells that have changed in the spreadsheet. Because recalculating a large spreadsheet can

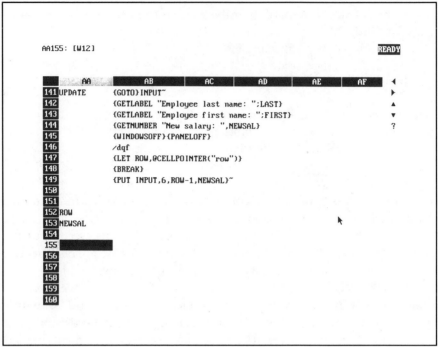

Figure 17.21: The {PUT} command enters data into a database table.

be slow, you can use the {RECALC} or {RECALCCOL} command to recalculate only part of a spreadsheet. Some macro commands, such as {LET} and {GETNUMBER}, aren't reflected in the spreadsheet until the cells are recalculated. You can use {RECALC} or {RECALCCOL} to recalculate the appropriate range.

{RECALC} recalculates the cells row-by-row while {RECALCCOL} recalculates column-by-column. The syntax for these commands is:

{RECALC *location,condition,iterations*}
{RECALCCOL *location,condition,iterations*}

Location is the address or name of the range to recalculate. *Condition* and *iterations* are options that can be included when the range must be recalculated multiple times (some formulas require several recalculations before they are updated). The *condition* is a logical expression that tells

1-2-3 to recalculate the range until the condition is true. The *iterations* option indicates how many times to recalculate the range.

If you include a condition and a number of iterations, the range is recalculated a specified number of times or until the condition is true, whichever comes first. You cannot include the number of iterations unless you also specify a condition. However, you can specify a condition without entering the iterations.

MACRO COMMANDS FOR TEXT-FILE MANIPULATION

1-2-3 offers several ways to create and import text files (also known as ASCII files). Chapter 6 explains how to create ASCII files with /Print File and Appendix C describes how to use /File Import to bring text files into a 1-2-3 spreadsheet. While these two commands are easy to use, they have their limitations. For instance, /Print File inserts spaces, instead of tabs, between columns, and /File Import cannot bring in more than 240 characters per line.

The file manipulation macro commands, on the other hand, are much more versatile and impose very few limitations. On the down side, they are cumbersome to work with. The commands are: {OPEN}, {CLOSE}, {READ}, {READLN}, {WRITE}, {WRITELN}, {FILESIZE}, {GETPOS}, and {SETPOS}.

Before studying the individual file commands, you need to get familiar with several terms. There are two basic operations you can perform on a text file: reading and writing. *Reading* imports data from the text file into the current spreadsheet. *Writing* exports data from the current spreadsheet to a new or existing text file.

To use the file commands properly, you need to understand the concept of a *byte pointer*. The byte pointer is like a cursor that moves around a text file. Some of the file commands place the byte pointer at the beginning or end of the text file while other commands move the byte pointer to different positions. The byte pointer is really what makes the file commands so powerful because you can read from and write to any part of the file.

OPENING A FILE: {OPEN}

The {OPEN} command makes a text file available for use. Once a file is open, you can write (save) data to it, read (copy) its data into the current spreadsheet, or both read and write. However, you do not see the contents of an open file on the screen. The syntax for this command is:

{OPEN *file-name,access-type*}

File-name is the complete file name, including extension. If the file is located in a directory or drive different from the default, you must also specify the path. You must enclose the name in quotation marks if you specify a path (for example, "C:\WP5\EMPLOYEE.TXT"), otherwise, quotes are optional. *Access-type* is a code that describes what type of action you will be performing on the file. The codes are:

Code	Action	Description
r	Read	Opens an existing file and lets you import data
w	Write	Creates a new file and lets you import and export data
m	Modify	Opens an existing file and lets you import and export data
a	Append	Opens an existing file and lets you export data to the end of the file; you can also import data

The code must be enclosed in quotes. The macro in Figure 17.22 opens the file named EMPLOYEE.TXT. The *r* code indicates that the file can be read from, but not written to.

1-2-3 can have only one file open at a time. If you open another file without closing the one currently open, the first file is closed automatically. Use the {CLOSE} command when you are finished reading from and writing to the file.

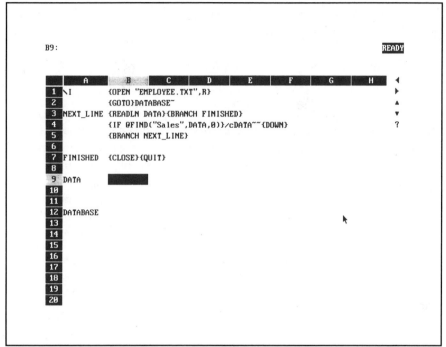

B9:   READY

	A	B	C	D	E	F	G	H
1	\I	{OPEN "EMPLOYEE.TXT",R}						
2		{GOTO}DATABASE~						
3	NEXT_LINE	{READLN DATA}{BRANCH FINISHED}						
4		{IF @FIND("Sales",DATA,0)}/cDATA~~{DOWN}						
5		{BRANCH NEXT_LINE}						
6								
7	FINISHED	{CLOSE}{QUIT}						
8								
9	DATA							
10								
11								
12	DATABASE							
13								
14								
15								
16								
17								
18								
19								
20								

Figure 17.22: The first line of the macro opens a file named
EMPLOYEE.TXT, allowing read-only access.

CLOSING A FILE: {CLOSE}

There isn't a whole lot to say about the {CLOSE} command except to
be sure to use it. Failing to close a file can cause unexpected results (such
as reading or writing incorrect information). If you forget to close a file, it
remains open until another file is opened or until you quit 1-2-3.

READING (IMPORTING)
DATA: {READ} AND {READLN}

The {READLN} command copies an entire line of data from the open
text file and places it in a specified location in the current spreadsheet. The

{READ} command is similar except it copies a specific number of characters. The syntax of these commands is:

> {READLN *location*}
> {READ *byte-count,location*}

Location is where you want to place the imported data; it can be an address or a range name. *Byte-count* is the number of characters to be imported; it must be a value (or a cell containing a value) between 0 and 240.

Exactly where in a text file do these commands begin reading? If you open a file with the read, write, or modify access-type, the byte-pointer will be at the beginning of the text file, so reading will begin there. If you open a file with the append access-type, the byte-pointer will be at the end of the file and there will be nothing to read. You can reposition the byte pointer with the {SETPOS} command.

After the {READLN} command imports a line of data, the byte pointer is moved to the beginning of the next line. The {READ} command positions the byte pointer at the next character in the file.

For an example of importing data from a text file, refer to Figure 17.22. This program imports data from an employee database file. However, it doesn't import every record—it only imports the employees in the sales department. This is a task that the /File Import command cannot do.

The \I program begins by moving the cell pointer to the DATABASE range—where you ultimately want the imported data to go. It then opens the file named EMPLOYEE.TXT and reads the first line of data into a cell named DATA (cell B9). DATA is not the final destination for the imported data—it is a temporary holding area. The {BRANCH FINISHED} command is not executed until there is no more data to read. The {IF} statement analyzes the contents of DATA to see if *Sales* appears anywhere in the cell. If it does, the imported data is copied to the database, the cell pointer is moved down to the next cell in the database range, and the next line of data is read. If the record does not contain the string *Sales*, the imported line of data is not placed in the database and the next line of data is read. When there is no more data to read (i.e., the byte pointer is at the end of the file), the macro branches to the FINISHED subroutine which closes the file and quits the macro.

WRITING (EXPORTING) DATA: {WRITE} AND {WRITELN}

Both {WRITE} and {WRITELN} copy a text string to an open file. The syntax of these commands is:

{WRITE *string*}
{WRITELN *string*}

String is text or a cell that contains a label. In the text file, the data is written to the current byte-pointer position.

The difference between these two commands is that {WRITELN} adds a carriage return and line feed after the text, while {WRITE} does not. {WRITELN} moves the byte pointer down to the beginning of the next line while {WRITE} keeps the byte pointer on the same line. Here is an example of a simple program that uses {WRITE} and {WRITELN} commands:

```
{OPEN NAME.TXT,"w"}
{WRITELN "John"}
{WRITELN "Smith"}
{WRITELN ""} {WRITE "John "}
{WRITELN "Smith"}
{CLOSE}
```

The text file that results from this program would look like this:

```
John
Smith

John Smith
```

Notice that the {WRITELN ""} command creates a blank line in the text file. A more involved macro program is shown in Figure 17.23. This is part of a program that my husband wrote to create a text file that has tabs between columns. A tab-delimited text file can be imported into a variety of software programs (such as Ventura Publisher, WordPerfect, Microsoft Word, and PageMaker) and printed with proportional fonts. (The /Print

File command creates a file with spaces between columns—with spaces, you cannot print with proportional fonts.)

The DATA subroutine writes the contents of each cell to a text file. The {WRITE @CHAR(9)} command in the WRTAB subroutine inserts a tab character between each column. The {WRITELN ""} command in the LINE subroutine inserts a carriage return/line feed after each line.

DETERMINING THE SIZE OF A TEXT FILE: {FILESIZE}

The {FILESIZE} command calculates the number of bytes (characters) in an open text file and places that number in a specified spreadsheet cell. You can use this information when reading data to determine if the end of

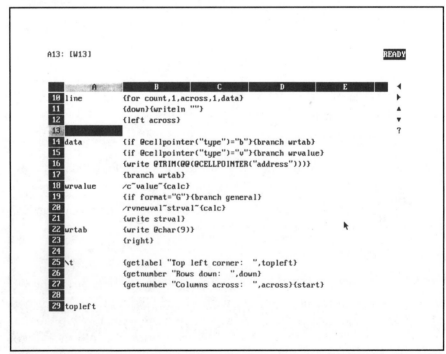

Figure 17.23: An excerpt from a program that creates a tab-delimited text file

the file has been reached. The syntax of this command is:

{FILESIZE *location*}

Location is the address or range name where the file size is stored.

DETERMINING THE POSITION OF THE BYTE POINTER: {GETPOS}

The {GETPOS} command enters the current character position of the byte pointer in a specified spreadsheet cell; it begins counting with 0. (In other words, the first character position in a text file is 0.) The syntax of this command is:

{GETPOS *location*}

Location is where the pointer location is stored; it can be an address or range name.

You can use this command in a subroutine to read data until the byte pointer is at a certain location. For example,

{GETPOS LOCATION}
{IF LOCATION<240}{BRANCH BEGIN}
{QUIT}

You can also use the {GETPOS} command before read and write commands to see if the pointer needs to be moved.

MOVING THE BYTE POINTER: {SETPOS}

The {SETPOS} command moves the byte pointer to a specified character position in an open text file. The syntax of this command is:

{SETPOS *offset-number*}

Offset-number is the character position to which you want to move the byte pointer; the first character in the file is numbered 0. You can use {SET-POS} in conjunction with {FILESIZE} to move the byte pointer to the last character in the file:

```
{FILESIZE SIZE}
{SETPOS SIZE}
```

THE /X COMMANDS

The /X commands are the original set of programming commands that were included with the first version of 1-2-3, Release 1A. These commands begin with /X and perform basic programming tasks such as branching to subroutines, prompting for input, evaluating data, displaying custom menus, and so forth. Thus, the /X commands have the same functionality as some of the macro commands explained earlier in this chapter. They are redundant, but they have remained available in subsequent releases of 1-2-3 so that programs written in Release 1A will run in all versions.

Table 17.3 lists the /X commands and their equivalent macro commands.

For the most part, the /X commands have awkward syntax, so you'll want to stick with the standard macro commands for most programming projects. However, there is one situation in which the /X commands offer an easier way to get the job done: when you want to enter a response in the current cell. With the {GETLABEL} command, you have to enter the following:

```
{GETLABEL prompt,@CELLPOINTER("address")}
```

The equivalent /X command is much simpler:

```
/XLprompt~~
```

Table 17.3: The /X Programming Commands

/X COMMAND	EQUIVALENT MACRO COMMAND
/XC*location~*	{*subroutine*}
/XG*location~*	{BRANCH *subroutine*}
/XI*condition~*	{IF *condition*}
/XL*prompt~location~*	{GETLABEL *prompt,location*}
/XM*location~*	{MENUBRANCH *location*}
/XN*prompt~location~*	{GETNUMBER *prompt,location*}
/XQ	{QUIT}
/XR	{RETURN}

Appendices

Appendix A

Appendix B

Appendix C

Appendix D

Installing
and Starting 1-2-3

Installing 1-2-3 on your computer is not difficult; Lotus provides a guided installation that holds your hand through the process of copying the program disks to your hard disk. Installation takes anywhere from 10 to 45 minutes, depending on which options you choose to install.

HARDWARE AND
SOFTWARE REQUIREMENTS

To run 1-2-3 on your computer, you need the following hardware and software setup:

- An IBM PC or compatible computer
- 640 kilobytes (K) of RAM memory
- DOS 2.1 or later
- Depending on how much of the package you install, 2–8Mb of free hard-disk space
- One floppy-disk drive, either 5¼ or 3½-inch, double or high density
- A video card, preferably with graphics capability (you need a graphics card to view graphs and to use the Wysiwyg add-in in graphics mode)
- A mouse (optional)
- A printer

You will also need the disks included with your 1-2-3 package.

UPGRADING
FROM RELEASE 2.2 TO 2.3

If you are upgrading from Release 2.2, you must install Release 2.3 in a different subdirectory from 2.2. If you don't have room on your hard disk or if you no longer want to keep Release 2.2, erase all your old 2.2 program files before you install the new program. Make sure you don't accidentally delete any of the following types of data files: worksheet (.WK1), Allways (.ALL), macro library (.MLB), or graph picture (.PIC). All of these files are compatible with Release 2.3.

RUNNING THE
INSTALL PROGRAM

The 1-2-3 disk labeled *Disk 1 (Install)* includes an installation program, called *INSTALL*, which takes you through the complete process of copying 1-2-3 to your hard disk. Do not use the DOS COPY command; the files are stored in a compressed format and INSTALL uncompresses them as it copies—the COPY command will not do this.

Follow these steps to run the INSTALL program:

1. Turn on your computer.

2. Once you see the DOS C:\> prompt, insert Disk 1 into your floppy-disk drive.

3. Type **A:** (or **B:** if you placed the disk in drive B) and press Enter.

4. Type **install** and press Enter.

RECORDING YOUR NAME

The first time you run the INSTALL program, you will be asked to enter both your name and that of your organization. This information will appear each time you load 1-2-3. When prompted, enter the information.

CHOOSING INSTALLATION OPTIONS

The next step in the installation process is choosing which parts of the program you want to copy to your hard disk (see Figure A.1). Here is a description of each of the choices:

1-2-3	The main program
Wysiwyg	An add-in that offers a graphical interface and extensive formatting capabilities
Add-Ins	Macro Library Manager, Auditor, and Viewer add-ins

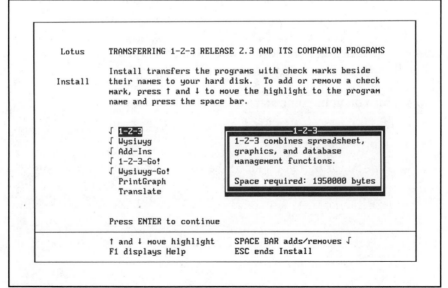

Figure A.1: The check marks indicate which options you want to install.

1-2-3 Go!	A tutorial to help you learn 1-2-3
Wysiwyg Go!	A tutorial to help you learn the Wysiwyg add-in
PrintGraph	A program that prints graphs created in 1-2-3
Translate	A program that imports and exports data files

By default, all options except for PrintGraph and Translate are selected—notice the check mark next to each one. At the very least, you need to install 1-2-3. However, to take advantage of 1-2-3's full potential, you should install Wysiwyg and the other add-ins (*add-ins* are programs that extend the capabilities of 1-2-3). Depending on your needs, you may also want to install PrintGraph and Translate. Because you are using this book to learn 1-2-3, you don't need to install the tutorials.

When deciding which parts of the program to install, look at each option's required disk space. As you highlight each option, the box to the right displays the space required for that particular option. Your hard disk may not have the capacity to hold all options. You can use the spacebar to toggle options on or off. If the option is already selected, the spacebar unselects it. If it's unselected, the spacebar selects it. Follow these steps to choose your options:

1. For each option you want to uncheck or check, use ↓ to highlight it and then press the spacebar.

2. When you are finished, press Enter to continue.

SPECIFYING A PATH

You now need to indicate where to install 1-2-3. The default path is C:\123R23. If there isn't enough space on your hard-disk drive, you will get an error message alerting you to this fact before INSTALL actually begins copying the files. If you get this error message, press Enter to select a different drive, or press Esc to end INSTALL. The Esc key will take you to the DOS prompt; once there, you can remove or archive files to open up additional space on the drive and then run INSTALL again.

Follow these steps to specify your path:

1. When prompted for the disk drive, press Enter to accept the default drive (C) or type a different drive letter and press Enter.

2. When prompted for the program directory, press Enter to accept the default (\123R23) or type a different name and press Enter.

3. At the confirmation screen, study the path you specified and type **Y** to accept it or **N** to re-enter it. Press Enter.

INSTALL begins copying the files to your hard disk, and the message *Please Wait* flashes at the bottom of the screen. The screen will indicate when you need to insert another floppy disk. Depending on which options you have selected to install, you may not use all the floppy disks in the package.

When all the files have been copied, the INSTALL program lets you know that the file transfer was successful; press Enter to continue.

SPECIFYING YOUR EQUIPMENT

The next part of the installation is to specify your video card and printer. If you don't know the type of video card your PC has, don't despair—INSTALL has a video detection process that determines your type of display (VGA, EGA, CGA, Hercules, and so forth).

Follow the steps below to select your video card (or *screen display* as INSTALL calls it):

1. From the Main Menu, make sure *Select Your Equipment* is high-lighted and press Enter. The Video Detection screen tells you what type of video card INSTALL thinks you have—make a note of this.

2. Press Enter to continue. The list of video-card options is displayed, as shown in Figure A.2.

3. Highlight the type of card that INSTALL has indicated on the Video Detection screen (unless you know that you have a

different one). Press Enter and you will be presented with a list of screen dimensions for the type of card you selected.

4. 80×25 is the standard dimension (80 characters across by 25 lines down) but most video cards offer additional dimensions. For example, the Video Graphics Array (VGA) offers 80×43 and 80×50 in addition to the standard dimension. Also, next to each screen dimension is *Black* or *White*; this refers to the background color of the screen when 1-2-3 displays graphs. I find a black background to be easier on the eyes. Highlight the screen dimension and background color you desire and press Enter.

SELECTING A PRINTER

In order to print reports and graphs in 1-2-3, you need to tell INSTALL what type of printer you have. 1-2-3 offers printer drivers for over 150 different printers. (A *printer driver* is a set of instructions about the printer's capabilities.)

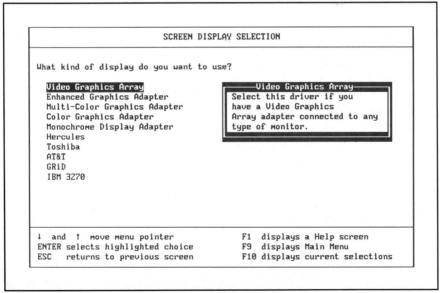

Figure A.2: The types of video cards supported by 1-2-3

The INSTALL program will ask you to specify two types of printers. 1-2-3 uses the *text printer driver* to print standard spreadsheet reports and the *graphics printer driver* to print graphs in the PrintGraph program and spreadsheet reports in Wysiwyg. It's entirely possible that your text and graphics printers are one and the same. Even so, you still need to specify both types of printers.

Follow these steps to choose your printer(s):

1. When asked if you have a text printer, press Enter to choose Yes. A list of printer manufacturers is displayed—press PgDn to see additional choices.

2. Highlight the name of your printer's manufacturer and press Enter.

3. Highlight your text printer's model number or name and press Enter.

4. If you have another text printer, choose Yes and repeat steps 2 and 3 above. Otherwise press Enter to choose No.

5. When asked if you have a graphics printer, choose Yes. (If you don't have a printer with graphics capabilities, choose No and skip the remaining steps below.) A list of printer manufacturers is displayed.

6. Highlight the name of your printer's manufacturer and press Enter.

7. Highlight your graphics printer's model number or name and press Enter.

8. If you have another graphics printer, choose Yes and repeat steps 6 and 7 above. Otherwise, press Enter to choose No.

SAVING YOUR DRIVER SET

When you are finished specifying your hardware equipment, it's time to save your selections in a *driver set*. A driver set is a file name with the extension .SET that contains information about your monitor and printer(s). The default driver set is called *123.SET*. I recommend that you save your standard driver set with this name. For some hardware configurations, you may want to create several driver sets, each containing a different combination of screen and printer types.

To save your driver set with the default name, press Enter to choose No. The file is saved with the name *123.SET*.

GENERATING FONTS

If you are installing Wysiwyg, you will see a screen that describes the font installation process. Read this screen and press Enter.

Before you generate fonts, you need to understand a few terms:

- In Wysiwyg, a *font* refers to a specific typeface—Helvetica, Times Roman, Courier, Line Printer, etc.—in a specific size.

- *Soft fonts* are disk files that tell the printer how to produce a font. Release 2.3 comes with four soft fonts: Dutch, Swiss, Courier, and XSymbol.

- Character sizes are measured in *points*. Points refer to a character's height and width in a given typeface.

The soft fonts are created after you select a font set: Basic, Medium, or Extended. Each set generates Swiss, Dutch, Courier, and XSymbol fonts in the following point sizes:

Basic	4, 6, 8, 10, 12, 14, 18, and 24
Medium	4, 6, 8, 9, 10, 11, 12, 14, 16, 18, 20, 24, and 36
Extended	4, 5, 6, 7, 8, 9, 10, 11, 12, 13, 14, 16, 18, 20, 24, 30, 36, 48, 60, and 72

The Extended set offers the greatest variation in sizes but takes a long time to generate and consumes more disk space. The exact time depends on what type of printer you are generating fonts for and on the speed of your computer. If you generate the Extended font set, be prepared to take at least a half-hour break while INSTALL creates the fonts.

When you have decided which font set to generate, highlight it and press Enter. During font generation, the screen continually updates to let you know which typeface and size is being created. When font generation is finished, press any key to return to the DOS prompt.

CREATING A DATA DIRECTORY

While you can store your spreadsheets in the 1-2-3 program directory (for example, C:\123R23), you might want to organize your files into one or more *data directories*. These directories can be anywhere on your hard disk. For example, to create a directory named *123DATA* off the root directory, type:

MD\123DATA

Or, to create a directory named *BUDGETS* located off the 123R23 directory, type:

MD\123R23\BUDGETS

If you are going to be creating a lot of spreadsheets, it's a good idea to organize them into different subdirectories. The kinds of spreadsheets you create determines how you will structure your subdirectories. You can group your files by project, date, subject, and so forth.

STARTING 1-2-3

There are two ways to load 1-2-3. You can type either **123** or **lotus** from the DOS prompt. The *123* command loads the main 1-2-3 spreadsheet program. The *lotus* command displays the Lotus Access Menu shown in Figure A.3. This menu gives you access to several other programs (Print-Graph, Translate, and Install) in addition to the 1-2-3 spreadsheet. To load 1-2-3 from the Access Menu, make sure 1-2-3 is highlighted and press Enter. If you know that you aren't going to be using the other programs, it's faster to simply type **123** to go directly into the spreadsheet program.

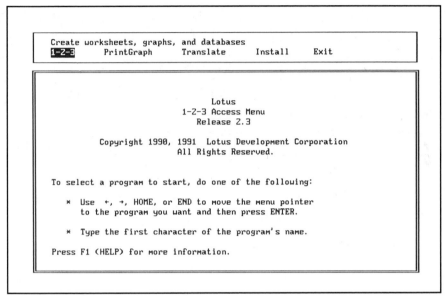

```
    ┌──────────────────────────────────────────────────────┐
    │ Create worksheets, graphs, and databases              │
    │ ▌1-2-3▐    PrintGraph    Translate    Install    Exit  │
    └──────────────────────────────────────────────────────┘
    ╔════════════════════════════════════════════════════════╗
    ║                                                          ║
    ║                          Lotus                           ║
    ║                    1-2-3 Access Menu                     ║
    ║                       Release 2.3                        ║
    ║                                                          ║
    ║        Copyright 1990, 1991  Lotus Development Corporation║
    ║                   All Rights Reserved.                   ║
    ║                                                          ║
    ║                                                          ║
    ║   To select a program to start, do one of the following:║
    ║                                                          ║
    ║     *  Use ←, →, HOME, or END to move the menu pointer   ║
    ║        to the program you want and then press ENTER.     ║
    ║                                                          ║
    ║     *  Type the first character of the program's name.   ║
    ║                                                          ║
    ║   Press F1 <HELP> for more information.                  ║
    ║                                                          ║
    ╚════════════════════════════════════════════════════════╝
```

Figure A.3: The Lotus Access Menu

Follow these steps to load 1-2-3:

1. At the DOS C:\> prompt, change to the subdirectory where you copied 1-2-3. For example, if you named the subdirectory 123R23, type **CD\123R23** and press Enter.

2. To start the program, type **123** or **lotus** and press Enter.

3. If you typed *lotus*, press Enter to select 1-2-3 from the Lotus Access Menu.

LOADING AN ALTERNATE DRIVER SET

To use an alternate driver set you have created in the INSTALL program, you must type the name of the driver set when you load 1-2-3. For example, at the DOS prompt, type:

    123 radius

This command loads 1-2-3 and uses the driver set named *RADIUS.SET.*

LOADING 1-2-3 AND A SPREADSHEET

If you know the name of the spreadsheet you want to work on, you can simultaneously load 1-2-3 and retrieve the spreadsheet file. For example, to retrieve a file named *INVEST,* type the following:

    123 -wINVEST

The *-w* must precede the filename. If the file is located in a different subdirectory, you must include the path. For example:

    123 -wC:\123R23\123DATA\INVEST

The above command loads 1-2-3 and retrieves the INVEST file located in C:\123R23\123DATA.

LOADING THE BACKGROUND PRINT UTILITY: BPRINT

1-2-3 Release 2.3 includes a feature that prints your reports in the background, allowing you to do other tasks while a report is printing. Whenever you want to print a report in the background, use the /Print Background or :Print Background command (see Chapters 6 and 7 for further information). However, you cannot use these commands unless you have first loaded a small 6K program called *BPRINT.* The BPRINT.EXE program is stored in your 1-2-3 directory, and must be loaded before you load 1-2-3. Thus, the steps to load BPRINT and 1-2-3 are:

1. At the DOS C:\> prompt, change to the subdirectory where you copied 1-2-3. For example, if you named the subdirectory 123R23, type **CD\123R23** and press Enter.

2. To load the utility that allows you to do background printing, type **BPRINT** and press Enter.

3. To start the spreadsheet program, type **123** and press Enter.

CREATING A BATCH FILE TO LOAD 1-2-3

Because it gets tiresome having to change to the 1-2-3 program directory before you type **123**, you will probably want to create a batch file that automates this procedure. A *batch file* is a text file that contains a series of DOS commands. You will want your 1-2-3 batch file to perform five DOS commands: change to the drive containing your 1-2-3 program, change to the appropriate directory, load BPRINT, load 1-2-3, and change back to the root directory after 1-2-3 is exited. If you name your batch file *123.BAT*, you can load 1-2-3 by typing **123** from the DOS prompt.

To create this batch file, follow these steps:

1. Type **CD** to change to the root directory. (Note: If you have a special subdirectory set up for batch files, change to this directory.)

2. Type **COPY CON 123.BAT** and press Enter. The commands you type next will be stored in a file named 123.BAT.

3. Type the command to change to the disk drive your 1-2-3 program is stored on. For example, type **C:** and press Enter. (This step is unnecessary if your system has only one hard drive.)

4. Type the command to change to your 1-2-3 subdirectory. For example, type **CD\123R23** and press Enter.

5. Type **BPRINT** and press Enter. (You can leave out this step if you don't want to use the background printing feature.)

6. Type **123** or **LOTUS** and press Enter.

7. Type **CD** and press Enter. (This command changes back to the root directory after you exit from 1-2-3.)

8. To save the file, press the function key F6 (you will see ^Z) and Enter.

To start 1-2-3 now, simply type **123** and press Enter. When you quit 1-2-3, you will end up in the root directory.

SETTING UP YOUR PRINTER

There is more to installing your printer than just indicating your model in the INSTALL program: You may also need to specify several options in 1-2-3 itself. Before you print in 1-2-3, you should check two options located on the /Worksheet Global Default Printer menu: Interface and Name.

Interface refers to your printer port, and the following choices are available: Parallel 1, Serial 1, Parallel 2, Serial 2, LPT1, LPT2, LPT3, and LPT4. Parallel 1, the most common, is the default. If you aren't sure which port your printer is connected to, check the back of your computer; the ports are sometimes labeled. If you choose a serial interface, you will be asked to specify a *baud rate*—the speed at which data is sent to your printer. The following baud rates are available: 110, 150, 300, 600, 1200, 2400, 4800, 9600, and 19200. The most common baud rate is 9600.

You need to worry about the *Name* option only if you have installed 1-2-3 for more than one text printer. Choose /Worksheet Global Default Printer and look next to the Name setting in the Default Printer Settings dialog box. If the printer you wish to use is not listed here, use the Name option to select a different printer.

After you print your first spreadsheet report, you may see that you need to adjust the *AutoLF* option. If your report is double-spaced, set AutoLF to Yes. If the lines print on top of each other, set AutoLF to No.

To permanently save your defaults, choose /Worksheet Global Default Update.

2.3 ▒▒▒▶ USING A MOUSE WITH 1-2-3

One of the new features in Release 2.3 is mouse support. With a mouse, you can choose commands, cancel commands, fill in dialog boxes, specify ranges, and move the cell pointer more quickly than with the keyboard. While a mouse is an optional piece of equipment, many people prefer this friendly critter to the keyboard. As you may have noticed, the INSTALL program didn't ask you any questions about your mouse; this is because your mouse software is independent of 1-2-3. Load your mouse software according to the directions that came with your mouse. With some mice, you will enter a command (DEVICE=MOUSE.SYS) in your CONFIG.SYS file. With other mice, you will enter a MOUSE command in your AUTOEXEC.BAT file.

To determine whether your mouse software is properly loaded, look for a *mouse pointer* after you load 1-2-3. (The mouse pointer is either a small square or arrow.) Assuming you see the pointer, move the mouse on your desktop; if all is well, the pointer will move in the direction you move the mouse.

MODIFYING YOUR HARDWARE SETUP

INSTALL is a dual-purpose program. You can use it to initially copy the program files to your hard disk and to tell 1-2-3 what type of hardware you have. As part of the original installation, the INSTALL program is copied to your hard disk. So, if your hardware setup changes, you can modify your driver set by running the INSTALL program from your hard disk. For example, you will need to re-run INSTALL if you purchase a new printer.

The INSTALL program is accessible from either the Lotus access system (see Figure A.3) or from the DOS prompt. To run INSTALL from the DOS prompt, change to the 1-2-3 program directory, type **install**, and press Enter.

Once you have loaded INSTALL, follow these steps to modify your hardware setup:

1. At the introductory screen, press Enter to continue.

2. From the Main Menu, highlight *Change Selected Equipment* and press Enter.

3. Choose *Modify the Current Driver Set*. You are asked to select the driver you want to change (see Figure A.4).

4. Select the type of driver (such as Graphics Display or Text Printer) you want to modify. A list of drivers will be displayed and your current choice will be marked with a ▶ symbol.

If you are selecting a new screen driver, you can simply choose the new driver—the new one will automatically replace the original one. This is not true for printer drivers, however. Because you are allowed to select multiple printer drivers, both the new and the original printer drivers are stored in the driver set. If you no longer want a printer driver in the set, you will need to explicitly remove it by highlighting the name and pressing Del.

At any time while you are in the INSTALL program, you can press F10 to view the current selections in your driver set. Be sure you do this before you save the driver set. When you are satisfied with your selections, follow these steps:

1. Choose *Return to Previous Menu*.

2. Choose *Save the Current Driver Set*.

3. Press Enter to save the drivers in the same driver set, or enter a new name.

Whenever you change screen or printer drivers, you will need to generate a new font set (Basic, Medium, or Extended). You will automatically be reminded of this after you save the driver set. For information about font generation, see the section *Generating Fonts* earlier in the chapter.

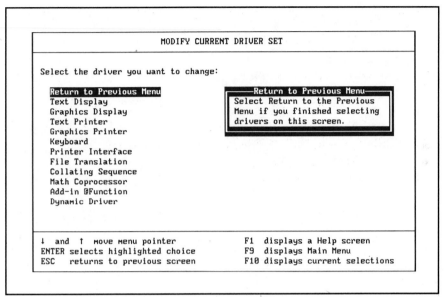

Figure A.4: A list of driver types you can modify

Appendices

Appendix A

Appendix B

Appendix C

Appendix D

Spreadsheet Functions

This appendix explains all 93 of 1-2-3's spreadsheet functions. These functions are grouped into nine categories:

Function Type	Example
Statistical	Summing or averaging a column
Mathematical	Rounding a number
Engineering	Computing a logarithm
Logical	Displaying different values in a cell depending on whether a condition is true or false
Special	Looking up a result in a table
Date and Time	Entering today's date
Financial	Calculating a mortgage payment
Database	Summarizing a field in a database
String	Converting the case (upper/lower) of a label

The following general rules apply to functions:

- They begin with an @ sign.

- They usually contain one or more arguments. An argument can be a number, formula, cell reference, or range. For example, the argument in the @SUM function is the cell range to be totalled.

- If a function has more than one argument, a comma must separate each one.

- Arguments are enclosed in parentheses.

STATISTICAL FUNCTIONS

Chapter 3 explains the two most common statistical functions: @SUM and @AVG. The other statistical functions are @COUNT, @MAX (maximum), @MIN (minimum), @STD (standard deviation), and @VAR (variance). In the following examples, refer to Figure B.1.

@AVG: Averaging a Range

The @AVG function totals the values in a range, counts how many values are in the range, and then divides the total by the number of values. Blank cells are not counted as values, but labels are treated as zero values. Therefore, do not include labels in the average range.

Syntax

@AVG(*range*)

Example

@AVG(B1..B6)

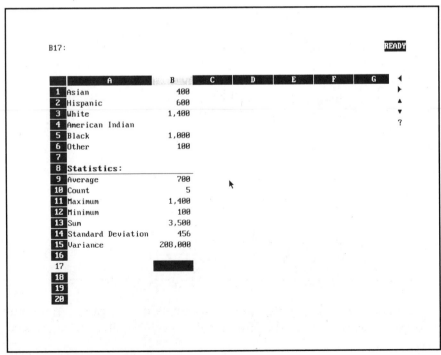

Figure B.1: Statistical functions

@COUNT: Counting the Number of Entries in a Range

The @COUNT function counts the number of non-blank cells in a range. Each cell that contains either a number, formula, or label counts as 1. Thus, if the range contains 25 cells, but three of them are blank, the count would be 22.

Syntax
@COUNT(*range*)

Example
@COUNT(B1..B6)

Though there are six cells in this range, the result of this formula is 5 because one of the cells is blank (see Figure B.1).

@MAX: Finding the Highest Value in a Range

The @MAX function displays the largest value in a range. You could use this function to determine which person, product, or division had made the most money, or who had achieved the highest score.

Syntax
@MAX(*range*)

Example
@MAX(B1..B6)

@MIN: Finding the Lowest Value in a Range

The @MIN function displays the lowest value in a range. You could use this function to quickly pinpoint the product with the worst sales record.

Syntax

@MIN(*range*)

Example

@MIN(B1..B6)

@SUM: Totalling a Range

The @SUM function totals the values in a range. You can use this function to add up a column or a row. Labels have a value of zero, so if there are any labels in the range, they will not affect the total.

Syntax

@SUM(*range*)

Example

@SUM(B1..B6)

@STD and @VAR: Measuring the Dispersion of a Range

The variance tells you how much the values in a range vary from the range's average. The standard deviation is simply the square root of the variance. The higher the standard deviation, the more widely dispersed the values are.

Syntax

@STD(*range*)
@VAR(*range*)

Examples

@VAR(B1..B6)
@STD(B1..B6)

MATHEMATICAL FUNCTIONS

The mathematical functions manipulate your numbers in different ways. You can take a number and round it (@ROUND), or find its square root (@SQRT), absolute value (@ABS), or integer value (@INT). You can also generate a random number (@RAND) and find a remainder after division (@MOD).

@ABS: Finding the Absolute Value of a Number

Absolute value is a mathematical term for a number's positive value. The *value* argument can be a number, a formula, or a cell reference.

Syntax

@ABS(*value*)

Examples

Formula	Result
@ABS(−20)	20
@ABS(−20*5)	100
@ABS(20)	20
@ABS(C3)	30

where C3= −30

@INT: Displaying a Number's Integer

An integer is a whole number without any decimal places—the numbers to the right of the decimal point are truncated without rounding the remaining number.

Syntax

@INT(*value*)

Examples

Formula	Result
@INT(125.67)	125
@INT(C3)	−100

where C3 = −100.456

@MOD: Finding the Remainder

@MOD is an abbreviation for modulus. *Modulus* is a mathematical term that refers to the remainder resulting from the division of two numbers. For example, if you divide 7 (the numerator) by 3 (the denominator), the remainder (modulus) is 1.

Syntax

@MOD(*numerator,denominator*)

Examples

Formula	Result
@MOD(18,4)	2
@MOD(20,4)	0
@MOD(C3,D3)	3

where C3= 23 and D3= 5

@RAND: Generating a Random Number

The @RAND function generates a random number between 0 and 1 (but not including 1). A new random number is generated each time the spreadsheet is recalculated. (The spreadsheet recalculates every time you make an entry or press F9.) To get larger random numbers you can multiply the function by a number such as 100 or 1000 as shown in the second example below. To get whole random numbers, you can use the @INT function as shown in the third example below. The @RAND function does not have any arguments.

Syntax
@RAND

Examples

Formula	Result
@RAND	a random number between 0 and 1
@RAND*1000	a random number between 0 and 1000
@INT(@RAND*1000)	a random whole number between 0 and 1000

@ROUND: Rounding Off to a Specified Number of Decimal Places

The numeric formatting commands change the number of decimal places that are displayed, but they do not alter the cell's actual contents; thus, when you refer to a formatted cell in a formula, 1-2-3 uses the actual number with all of its decimal places. If you want a formula to use a rounded number in a calculation, you can use the @ROUND function. In the function's arguments you must indicate which number or cell to round and the number of decimal places to round to.

Syntax
@ROUND(*value,decimals*)

Examples

Formula	Result
@ROUND(200.54,0)	201
@ROUND(A4,0)+@ROUND(B4,0)	2

where A4= 1.4 and B4= 1.4 (formatted to 0 decimal places)
Note: without rounding, the screen would show 1+1=3!

@SQRT: Calculating the Square Root of a Number

@SQRT calculates the square root of a number or formula.

Syntax

@SQRT(*value*)

Examples

Formula	Result
@SQRT(25)	5
@SQRT(A3*20)	10

where A3= 5

ENGINEERING FUNCTIONS

1-2-3 includes a set of functions intended for scientific and engineering applications. Most of these functions are trigonometric: sine, cosine, tangent, arcsine, arccosine, and arctangent. You can also compute pi and logarithms.

The trigonometric functions measure angles in radians, rather than in degrees. A *radian* is a unit of measurement based on pi.

@ACOS: Computing an Arccosine

The arccosine function converts a cosine into radians. *Cosine* is the function's argument. The cosine value must be between −1 and 1 (inclusive).

Syntax

@ACOS(*cosine value*)

Examples

Formula	Result
@ACOS(0)	1.571 radians
@ACOS(A5)	1.047 radians

where A5= 0.5

@ASIN: Computing an Arcsine

The arcsine function converts a sine into radians. *Sine* is the function's argument. The sine value must be between −1 and 1 (inclusive).

Syntax

@ASIN(*sine value*)

Examples

Formula	Result
@ASIN(1)	1.571 radians
@ASIN(A5)	−0.927 radians

where A5= −0.8

@ATAN: Computing an Arctangent

The arctangent function converts a tangent into radians. *Tangent* is the function's argument.

Syntax

@ATAN(*tangent value*)

Examples

Formula	Result
@ATAN(3)	1.249 radians

Formula	Result
@ATAN(A5)	−1.373 radians

where A5= −5

@ATAN2:
Computing a Four-Quadrant Arctangent

The arctangent function converts a tangent defined by x- and y-coordinates into radians. The coordinates are the function's two arguments.

Syntax

@ATAN2(*x-coordinate,y-coordinate*)

Examples

Formula	Result
@ATAN2(0,1)	1.571 radians
@ATAN2(A5,B5)	3.142 radians

where A5= −1, B5= 0

@COS: Computing a Cosine

The cosine function calculates the cosine of an angle measured in radians.

Syntax

@COS(*radians*)

Examples

Formula	Result
@COS(1.047)	0.500
@COS(A5)	0.866

where A5= 30*@PI/180

@EXP: Using Exponents

This function raises the *e constant* (2.71828...) to the specified power. It performs the inverse operation of the @LN (natural logarithm) function.

Syntax

@EXP(*power*)

Examples

Formula	Result
@EXP(1)	2.718
@EXP(2)	7.389

@LOG: Calculating Logarithms

This function calculates the base 10 logarithm of a number. The number cannot be zero or negative.

Syntax

@LOG(*value*)

Examples

Formula	Result
@LOG(10)	1
@LOG(A5)	2

where A5= 100

@LN: Calculating Natural Logarithms

Like @LOG, this function calculates a logarithm of a number, but @LN computes the log in base *e* (@LOG uses base 10). *Base e* is the constant

2.71828.... The value must be positive.

Syntax

@LN(*value*)

Examples

Formula	Result
@LN(2.7)	1 (formatted to 0 decimal places)
@LN(A5)	2 (formatted to 0 decimal places)

where A5= 7.389

@PI: Using Pi

This function, which doesn't have any arguments, displays the value of the pi constant (3.1415926536). *Pi* is the ratio of a circle's circumference to its diameter. Because the trigonometric functions use radians, which is based on pi, as their unit of measurement, you can use the @PI function to convert degrees into radians. The basic formula for converting degrees into radians is:

degrees * pi/180

The second example below converts a 90-degree angle into radians.

Syntax

@PI

Examples

Formula	Result
@PI	3.14...
90*@PI/180	1.571

@SIN: Computing a Sine

The @SIN function calculates the sine of an angle measured in radians.

Syntax

@SIN(*radians*)

Examples

Formula	Result
@SIN(1.047)	0.866
@SIN(A5)	0.500

where A5= 30*@PI/180

@TAN: Computing a Tangent

The @TAN function calculates the tangent of an angle measured in radians.

Syntax

@TAN(*radians*)

Examples

Formula	Result
@TAN(1.047)	1.731
@TAN(A5)	0.577

where A5= 30*@PI/180

LOGICAL FUNCTIONS

With 1-2-3's logical functions, you can look at the contents of a cell and display different results depending on what the cell contains. The main logical function is @IF; the other functions are usually arguments in @IF formulas: @ERR, @ISAAF, @ISAPP, @ISERR, @ISNA, @ISNUMBER, @ISSTRING, @NA, @TRUE, and @FALSE.

@ERR: Flagging an Error

The @ERR function displays ERR in a cell; it doesn't use any arguments. Any formula that references a cell containing an error message also displays ERR until the @ERR is removed. @ERR is frequently used as a *true value* or *false value* in an @IF formula. You can use it to flag error situations, such as when a cell contains a number outside of an acceptable range (see example below).

Syntax
    @ERR

Example
    @IF(B20>30000,@ERR,B20*1.07)

Assume that B20 contains a total invoice amount and that $30,000 is a credit limit. This formula reads as follows: "If cell B20 is greater than $30,000, then display ERR. Otherwise, multiply B20 by 1.07." This formula calls attention to a situation where a customer's order exceeds the credit limit.

@IF: Handling Two
Situations in One Formula

The @IF function places different values in a cell, depending on whether a condition is true or false. Conditions use the following logical operators:

Operator	Description
=	equal to
>	greater than
>=	greater than or equal to

Operator	Description
<	less than
<=	less than or equal to
<>	not equal to

The @IF function's *condition* argument uses one of the above operators to compare two values; the values can be numbers or labels typed into the formula, cell references, or field names in a database. Examples of valid conditions are: *B7>C7, B7=100, sales>50000,* and *B12="Y"*. Note that text strings must be enclosed in quotation marks.

The @IF function has three arguments. The *condition* tests to see if something is true or false. If the condition is true, the *true value* is displayed in the cell. But if the condition is false, the *false value* is displayed. Use the @IF function whenever you have more than one possible answer in a cell.

Syntax

@IF(*condition,true value,false value*)

Example

@IF(actual>quota,10%,0)

The above formula might be entered into a sales person's bonus field in a database. What this formula says is: "If the sales person's actual sales are greater than the quota (meaning the condition is true), then display 10% in the bonus field. Otherwise, if actual sales are not greater than the quota (meaning the condition is false), then display 0 in the field."

@ISAAF: Determining whether an Add-In @ Function Is Attached

If the 93 @ functions included with 1-2-3 don't satisfy all your needs, there are third-party add-in @ functions that you can purchase. You can use the @ISAAF function in a macro program to see if an add-in is attached before you try to use it. The argument for this function, *name*, is the name of the add-in @ function (without the @ sign) or a cell that contains the name.

@ISAAF displays a *1* (true) if the function is available or a *0* (false) if the appropriate add-in has not been attached. The @ISAAF function is typically used in a macro {IF} statement.

Syntax

@ISAAF(*name*)

Example

{IF @ISAAF("FTK_EFF")}{LET YIELD,@FTK_EFF(RATE,4)}~{QUIT}
/aaFTK~q
{\Y}

The first line of the above program checks to see if the @FTK_EFF function is available. If it is, the result of the @ function is entered into a cell. If the @ function is not available, the FTK (Finanical Toolkit) add-in is attached and the macro program (the \Y subroutine) is re-executed.

@ISAPP: Determining whether an Add-In Is Attached

A macro program can crash if you try to invoke an add-in that is not attached or if you attempt to attach an add-in that is already attached. If you include the @ISAPP function in your macro program, you can circumvent these errors—this function checks to see if an add-in is attached. The argument for this function, *name*, is the file name of the add-in (enclosed in quotation marks, without the .ADN extension) or a cell that contains the file name. The names of the add-ins included with Release 2.3 are: *WYSIWYG, AUDITOR, TUTOR, VIEWER,* and *MACROMGR.*

@ISAPP displays a *1* (true) if the specified add-in is attached or a *0* if the add-in is not attached. This function is typically used in a macro {IF} statement.

Syntax

@ISAPP(*name*)

Example

{IF @ISAPP("macromgr")}{APP2}IMACROS~q{QUIT}

/aaMACROMGR~8q{APP2}|MACROS~q

The first line in the above macro program checks to see if the Macro Library Manager is attached. If it is, the add-in is invoked and the library named *MACROS* is loaded. Otherwise, the second line of the program attaches the Macro Manager before invoking the add-in and loading the library.

@ISERR: Determining whether an Error Exists

The @ISERR function checks to see whether a cell contains an error message (*ERR*). If the tested cell contains *ERR*, *1* (true) displays in the cell; otherwise *0* (false) is displayed. A true result occurs if the cell contains @*ERR* or a formula that references a cell displaying *ERR*. @ISERR is most frequently used as a condition in an @IF function or an {IF} macro statement.

Syntax
@ISERR(*cell*)

Examples
@IF(@ISERR(A5/A6),0,A5/A6)

The purpose of the above formula is to prevent an error message from appearing if a cell is divided by 0. If A6 contains a 0, the division of A5 by A6 will produce *ERR*. This formula checks to see if A5/A6 results in an error. If it does, a *0* is displayed. Otherwise, the result of A5/A6 is displayed.

@ISNA: Determining whether Data Is Unavailable

The @ISNA function checks to see if a cell contains @NA (Not Available). If the tested cell contains @NA, *1* (true) displays in the cell; otherwise *0* (false) is displayed. A true result occurs if the cell contains @NA or a formula that references a cell containing @NA. @ISNA is most frequently used as a condition in an @IF function.

Syntax

@ISNA(*cell*)

Example

@IF(@ISNA(A5),10,5)

This formula reads as follows: "If A5 is not available, then display 10. Otherwise, display 5."

@ISNUMBER and @ISSTRING: Checking for Values and Labels

The @ISNUMBER function checks the contents of a cell to see if it is a value while the @ISSTRING function lets you know if a cell contains a label. @ISNUMBER displays a *1* (true) if the specified cell contains a value, *NA*, *ERR*, or is blank; if the cell contains a label, the result is *0* (false). @ISSTRING displays a *1* (true) if the specified cell is a label and a *0* (false) if it's not. These two functions are commonly used as conditions in @IF functions and {IF} macro statements. You can use them to make sure data is of the correct type (label or value).

Syntax

@ISNUMBER(*cell*)
@ISSTRING(*cell*)

Example

{IF @ISNUMBER(QTY)}{LET TOTAL,PRICE*QTY}~{QUIT}
{BRANCH INPUT}

The first line in the above macro checks to see if the cell named QTY is a number. If it is, QTY is multiplied by PRICE and the result is placed in a cell named TOTAL. Otherwise, the INPUT subroutine is executed.

@NA: When Data Is Not Available

When you are entering data into a spreadsheet, you might discover that an important number is missing. Rather than leaving the cell blank, you can enter the Not Available function, @NA. If you leave it blank, your results may be misleading. But if you enter the @NA function, any formula that uses the unavailable data also displays NA until the @NA is replaced with the actual number.

Syntax
    @NA

Example
    @NA

@TRUE and @FALSE: Finding the Truth

The @TRUE function displays a *1* and the @FALSE function displays a *0*. Neither function uses any arguments. They can be used as true and false values in @IF formulas to quickly see if you entered a complex condition correctly.

Syntax
    @TRUE
    @FALSE

Example
    @IF(A5/50>A6*100,@TRUE,@FALSE)

The above formula displays a *1* if the condition is true or a *0* if the condition is false.

SPECIAL FUNCTIONS

The Special Functions category is somewhat of a catch-all. Some of these functions look up information: @VLOOKUP (vertical lookup), @HLOOKUP (horizontal lookup), @INDEX (horizontal and vertical lookup), and @CHOOSE (lookup in a list). Think of these functions as ways to automatically enter data. Instead of referring to a table in a book or on a piece of paper, you can refer to a table in the spreadsheet and have 1-2-3 look up the value for you.

The other functions in this category are @CELL, @CELLPOINTER, @COLS, @ROWS, @@, and @?.

@CELL and @CELLPOINTER: Looking Up Information about a Cell

With the @CELL and @CELLPOINTER commands, you can find out a wide variety of information about a cell. For example, you can determine its type (blank, value, or label), alignment (left, right, or center), numeric format, or column width. The difference between these two functions is that @CELL analyzes a specific cell while @CELLPOINTER analyzes the current cell (the one the cell pointer is on).

These @ functions can determine ten different characteristics (*attributes*) of a cell; they are listed and described in Table B.1. Table B.2 provides further information on the format attribute. When you specify

Table B.1: Attributes for @CELL and @CELLPOINTER

ATTRIBUTE	DESCRIPTION
Address	Absolute cell address
Col	Column number (1–256)
Contents	Cell contents
Filename	Name and path of current file
Format	Numeric format (see Table B.2)
Prefix	Label prefix ('=left, "=right, ^=centered, \=repeating, |=nonprinting)
Protect	Protection status (1=protected, 0=unprotected)
Row	Row number (1–8192)
Type	Type of data (b=blank, v=value, l=label)
Width	Column width

the attribute argument in the @CELL or @CELLPOINTER function, you must enclose it in quotation marks, for example, *@CELLPOINTER("type")*.

The @CELL and @CELLPOINTER functions are typically used as conditions in @IF functions and {IF} macro statements.

Syntax
@CELL(*"attribute",cell*)
@CELLPOINTER(*"attribute"*)

Examples
Figure B.2 shows the results of all ten attributes for two different cells, B1 (*145*) and D1 (*Hello*). For example, the formula in cell B6 is:

@CELL("address",B1)

An example of a way to use @CELL in an @IF function is:

@IF(@CELL("type",D7)="b","",+C7/D7)

The above formula checks to see if cell D7 is blank. If it is, then nothing appears in the cell. (The "" displays nothing.) Otherwise, the result of the

Table B.2: Results for the Format Attribute

CODE	DESCRIPTION
C0 to C15	Currency, 0 to 15 decimal places
F0 to F15	Fixed, 0 to 15 decimal places
G	General
P0 to P15	Percent, 0 to 15 decimal places
S0 to S15	Scientific, 0 to 15 decimal places
,0 to ,15	Comma, 0 to 15 decimal places
+	+/−
D1 to D8	Date
T	Text
H	Hidden

```
A18: [W15]                                                      READY

            A              B        C        D        E        F        G      ◄
       1                 $145.00              Hello                            ►
       2                                                                       ▲
       3                                                                       ▼
       4  Attribute      Result (B1)          Result (D1)                      ?
       5
       6  Address        $B$1                 $D$1
       7  Col                       2                      4
       8  Contents                145          Hello
       9  Filename       D:\CELL.WK1          D:\CELL.WK1
      10  Format         C2                   G
      11  Prefix                              "
      12  Protect                   1                      1
      13  Row                       1                      1
      14  Type           v                    l
      15  Width                    11                     11
      16
      17
      18
      19
      20
```

Figure B.2: Attribute results of @CELL functions

formula *+C7/D7* displays. This formula prevents an ERR message from displaying when a formula divides by a blank cell.

@CHOOSE: Looking Up Values in a List

The @HLOOKUP, @VLOOKUP, and @INDEX functions all perform their lookups in a table. The @CHOOSE function looks up a value from a list of values entered as arguments in the formula (each value in the list is separated by a comma). Though the list can contain as many values as you want, you will probably use this function if you have only a few values to look up. If you have more than three or four values, one of the table functions would be more appropriate.

The first argument in the @CHOOSE function is *offset*. The offset indicates which of the values in the list you want to choose. The offset of the first value is 0, the second value is 1, the third value is 2, and so on.

Syntax

@CHOOSE(*offset,value 0,value 1,value 2, value n*)

Example

@CHOOSE(A3,15%,20%,25%)

If A3 contains 1, the result of this formula would be 20%. If A3 contains 0, the result would be 15%.

@COLS and @ROWS: Counting the Number of Columns and Rows

The @COLS function counts the number of columns in a range while the @ROWS function counts the number of rows. The range argument can be expressed as cell references or as a range name. You can use these functions to determine the size of a print range.

Syntax

@COLS(*range*)
@ROWS(*range*)

Examples

Formula	Result
@COLS(A4..L98)	12
@ROWS(A4..L98)	95

@HLOOKUP: Looking Up Values Indexed by Rows

The only difference between horizontal and vertical lookups is how the table is organized. In a vertical lookup, 1-2-3 looks down the first column to locate the lookup value. In a horizontal lookup, 1-2-3 looks across the first row to locate the lookup value.

The @HLOOKUP function has three arguments: *lookup value, table range*, and *row number*. The *lookup value* is the number you are looking up in the table. The *table range* is where the lookup table is entered into the spreadsheet. The *row number* refers to the row where the answer is located; the first row in the table is row 0, the second row is row 1, and so forth.

The first row of the horizontal lookup table must be in ascending order. If the lookup value does not exactly match an entry in the first row, the largest number less than the lookup value is chosen.

The entries in your lookup tables are not restricted to values—some of the rows can be values and others can be labels, or the entire table can be comprised of either values or labels. For example, you can look up the sales-tax rate for a particular city. The @HLOOKUP function is case-sensitive, so whatever text you are looking up must match the exact upper- and lowercase in the first row of the table.

Syntax
@HLOOKUP(*lookup value,table range,row number*)

Example
@HLOOKUP(B3,$A$15..$G$16,1)

Figure B.3 displays the spreadsheet and lookup table for this example. This formula tells 1-2-3 to look up the contents of cell B3 (15,000) in the lookup table (A15..G16) and find and display the discount located in row 1. Notice the dollar signs in the table range—these absolute reference symbols let you copy the formula without changing the table range references. (See Chapter 5 for more information on absolute references.)

@INDEX: Looking Up
Values Indexed by Rows and Columns

The @INDEX function allows you to look up values horizontally and vertically. This function has three arguments: *table range, column number,* and *row number*. The *table range* is where the lookup table is entered into the spreadsheet. The *column number* refers to the column where the answer is located; the first column in the table is numbered zero. The *row number* refers to the row where the answer is located; the first row in the table is numbered zero. The result of this function is the value in the cell at the intersection of the column and row numbers.

APPENDIX B

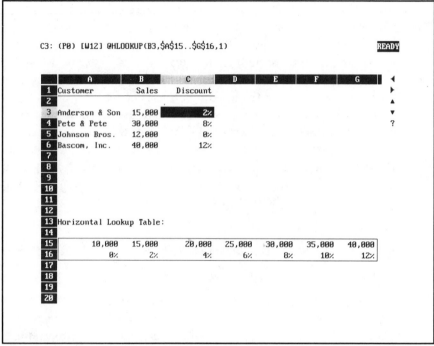

```
C3: (P0) [W12] @HLOOKUP(B3,$A$15..$G$16,1)                          READY

        A          B          C          D       E       F       G     ◄
  1  Customer     Sales    Discount                                     ►
  2                                                                     ▲
  3  Anderson & Son 15,000      2%                                      ▼
  4  Pete & Pete    30,000      8%                                      ?
  5  Johnson Bros.  12,000      8%
  6  Bascom, Inc.   40,000     12%
  7
  8
  9
 10
 11
 12
 13  Horizontal Lookup Table:
 14
 15       10,000     15,000     20,000   25,000   30,000   35,000   40,000
 16         0%         2%         4%       6%       8%      10%      12%
 17
 18
 19
 20
```

Figure B.3: Using a horizontal lookup table

The first row and first column of the lookup table must be numbered beginning with 1.

Syntax
@INDEX(*table range,column number,row number*)

Example
@INDEX($G$1..$I$11,B3,C3)

Figure B.4 displays the spreadsheet and index table for this example. The above formula tells 1-2-3 to look up the contents of cells B3 and C3 in the lookup table (G1..I11) and find and display the value in their intersection. Because B3 contains 2, 1-2-3 looks in the column numbered 2 at the top, and because C3 contains 5, 1-2-3 looks in the row numbered 5 at the left. The value at the intersection of the table's

```
D3: @INDEX($G$1..$I$11,B3,C3)                                    READY
```

	A	B	C	D	E	F	G	H	I	
1	Employee	Code	Yrs.	Rate		Index:		1	2	▶
2							1	20	15	▲
3	Johnson	2	5	56			2	30	23	▼
4	Jones	2	4	38			3	40	30	?
5	Smith	1	2	30			4	50	38	
6	Anderson	1	7	110			5	75	56	
7							6	100	75	
8							7	110	83	
9							8	115	86	
10							9	120	90	
11							10	125	94	
12										
13										
14										
15										
16										
17										
18										
19										
20										

Figure B.4: Using an index table

column 2 and row 5 is 56. Notice the dollar signs in the table range—these absolute reference symbols let you copy the formula without changing the table range references. (See Chapter 5 for more information on absolute references.)

@VLOOKUP: Looking Up Values Indexed by Columns

An income tax table is the perfect example of a vertical lookup table. You locate your income in the first column of the table. Then, you go across to the column associated with your filing status (single, married, filing jointly, etc.) and find your tax liability. The @VLOOKUP function has three arguments: *lookup value, table range,* and *column number.* The *lookup value* is the number you are looking up in the table (for example, your income). The *table range* is where the lookup table is entered into the spreadsheet. The *column number* refers to the column where the answer is located; the first column in the table is not included in the count. For example, if you were in the single filing status, the column number would be 1; if you were married, filing jointly, the column number would be 2.

The first column of the vertical lookup table must be in ascending order. If the lookup value does not exactly match an entry in the first column, the largest number less than the lookup value is chosen.

The entries in your lookup tables are not restricted to values—some of the columns can be values and others can be labels, or the entire table can comprise either values or labels. For example, you can look up the complete name for a particular person's initials. The @VLOOKUP function is case-sensitive so whatever text you are looking up must match the exact upper- and lowercase in the first column of the table.

Syntax
@VLOOKUP(*lookup value,table range,column number*)

Example
@VLOOKUP(B3,$A$13..$B$19,1)

Figure B.5 displays the spreadsheet and lookup table for this example. This formula tells 1-2-3 to look up the contents of cell B3 (15,000) in the lookup table (A13..B19) and find and display the discount in the first column. Notice the dollar signs in the table range—these absolute reference symbols let you copy the formula without changing the table range references. (See Chapter 5 for more information on absolute references.)

@@: Referencing a Cell Indirectly

The @@ function is an indirect cell reference. Instead of referring directly to a specific range in a formula, you can refer to a cell that contains the range.

Syntax
@@(*cell*)

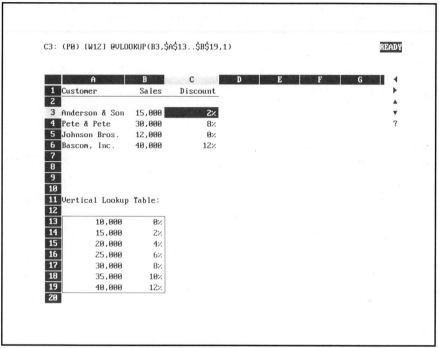

C3: (P0) [W12] @VLOOKUP(B3,$A$13..$B$19,1)   READY

	A	B	C	D	E	F	G
1	Customer	Sales	Discount				
2							
3	Anderson & Son	15,000	2%				
4	Pete & Pete	30,000	8%				
5	Johnson Bros.	12,000	0%				
6	Bascom, Inc.	40,000	12%				
7							
8							
9							
10							
11	Vertical Lookup Table:						
12							
13	10,000	0%					
14	15,000	2%					
15	20,000	4%					
16	25,000	6%					
17	30,000	8%					
18	35,000	10%					
19	40,000	12%					
20							

Figure B.5: Using a vertical lookup table

Example

@SUM(@@(G150))

where G150 contains the label *B2..B10*

@?: Unrecognized Add-In @ Function

If you used add-in @ functions in a spreadsheet and later retrieve the file without attaching the add-ins, the unrecognized functions will be replaced with @?, and *NA* will display in the cells. To rectify this problem, you must attach the add-in and retrieve the file again.

Note that *you* never enter the @? function—1-2-3 does.

DATE AND TIME FUNCTIONS

1-2-3 offers a variety of functions specific to dates and times. You can use the @NOW, @DATE, and @DATEVALUE functions to enter dates and the @TIME and @TIMEVALUE functions to enter time. The @DAY, @MONTH, @YEAR, @HOUR, @MINUTE, and @SECOND functions allow you to manipulate specific parts of the date or time.

Dates and times are actually stored as numbers so you can do calculations with them. For example, you can subtract two dates to see how many days have passed. The number associated with a date is the number of days since December 31, 1899. The number associated with a time is the fractional portion of the day. For example, 6 a.m. is a quarter of a day, so its time number is 0.25.

@DATE: Entering a Date

The @DATE function has three arguments: *YY* (the last two digits of the year), *MM* (the month number—one or two digits), and *DD* (the day number—one or two digits). The three arguments can be values entered directly in the function or cell references that contain the appropriate values. The result of this formula will be a serial number, which you can format to one of the date formats with /Range Format Date.

For the first 99 years in the year 2000, add 100 to the number. For example, to enter the date May 26, 2010, type **@DATE(110,5,26)**.

Syntax
    @DATE(*YY,MM,DD*)

Example

Function	Result	After Formatting
@DATE(92,5,15)	33739	05/15/92

@DATEVALUE:
Another Way to Enter a Date

The @DATE function requires you to enter the date in an awkward format. First of all, you must enter the year before the month which is not a natural instinct. Second, you place commas between the year, month, and day instead of dashes or slashes. The @DATEVALUE function alleviates some of this awkwardness.

The main advantage to @DATEVALUE is that you can enter dates in a format you are accustomed to: *MM/DD/YY*. The *string* argument for this function can be either the date, enclosed in quotation marks, or the address of a cell that contains a date, entered as a label. The numbers in the date must be separated by slashes—dashes will not work. Like @DATE, the result to the function is a serial number; you must format the cell with /Range Format Date.

Syntax

@DATEVALUE(*string*)

Examples

Function	Result	After Formatting
@DATEVALUE("5/15/92")	33739	05/15/92
@DATEVALUE(C5)	33739	05/15/92

where C5 contains the label *'5/15/92*

@DAY: Displaying the Day of the Month

The @DAY function extracts the day of the month from a date and displays it as a number between 1 and 31. The *date-number* argument can be a date function (@DATE, @DATEVALUE, or @NOW) or a cell containing a date function.

Syntax

@DAY(*date-number*)

Examples

Function	Result
@DAY(@DATE(92,5,15))	15
@DAY(@DATEVALUE("5/25/92"))	25
@DAY(A5)	10

where A5= @DATE(92,9,10)

@HOUR: Displaying the Hour

The @HOUR function extracts the hour from a given time and displays it as a number between 0 (midnight) and 23 (11 p.m.). The *time-number* argument can be a time function (@TIME, @TIMEVALUE, or @NOW) or a cell containing a time function.

Syntax

@HOUR(*time-number*)

Examples

Function	Result
@HOUR(@TIME(13,30,0))	13
@HOUR(@TIMEVALUE("9:30"))	9
@HOUR(A5)	15

where A5= @TIME(15,45,0)

@MINUTE: Displaying the Minute

The @MINUTE function extracts the minute from a given time and displays it as a number between 0 and 59. The *time-number* argument can be a time function (@TIME, @TIMEVALUE, or @NOW) or a cell containing a time function.

Syntax

@MINUTE(*time-number*)

Examples

Function	Result
@MINUTE(@TIMEVALUE("9:30"))	30
@MINUTE(A5)	45

where A5= @TIME(15,45,0)

@MONTH: Displaying the Month

The @MONTH function extracts the month from a date and displays it as a number between 1 and 12. The *date-number* argument can be a date function (@DATE, @DATEVALUE, or @NOW) or a cell containing a date function. This function can be used to query a date field in a database (see Chapter 12).

Syntax

@MONTH(*date-number*)

Examples

Function	Result
@MONTH(@DATE(92,5,15))	5
@MONTH(@DATEVALUE("5/25/92"))	5
@MONTH(A5)	9

where A5= @DATE(92,9,10)

@NOW: Entering the Current Date and Time

You will use this function to display the current date or time. It displays a serial number until you format the cell to either a date or time format with /Range Format Date. The @NOW function is dynamic and will update every time you retrieve a file. This function is only as accurate as your computer's system clock; so, if your clock is inaccurate, @NOW will be also.

Syntax
   @NOW

Example
   It is noon on April 17, 1992.

Function	Result	Date Format	Time Format
@NOW	33711.5	04/17/92	12:00 PM

Note: The integer portion (*33711*) represents the date; the decimal places (*.5*) represent the time.

@SECOND: Displaying the Second

The @SECOND function extracts the second from a given time and displays it as a number between 0 and 59. The *time-number* argument can be a time function (@TIME, @TIMEVALUE, or @NOW) or a cell containing a time function.

Syntax
   @SECOND(*time-number*)

Examples

Function	Result
@SECOND(@TIMEVALUE("9:30:0"))	0
@SECOND(A5)	30

where A5= @TIME(15,34,30)

@TIME: Entering a Time

The @TIME function has three arguments: *hour, minutes,* and *seconds.* The three arguments can be either values entered directly in the function or cell references that contain the appropriate values. The result of this formula will be a serial number, which you can format to one of the time formats with /Range Format Date Time.

The time should be entered using a 24-hour clock. Thus, the hour of 2 p.m. is 14, not 2. Even though you may not be concerned with seconds, you still must enter something (for example, a zero) for the second argument.

Syntax

@TIME(*hour,minutes,seconds*)

Examples

Function	Result	After Formatting
@TIME(9,30,0)	0.396	9:30 AM
@TIME(15,45,30)	0.657	3:45 PM

@TIMEVALUE: Another Way to Enter the Time

Another way to enter a time is with the @TIMEVALUE function. The main advantage to @TIMEVALUE is that you can enter time in a format you are accustomed to, for example *3:30 PM.* The *string* argument for this function can be either the time, enclosed in quotation marks, or the address of a cell that contains a time entered as a label. Like @TIME, the result to the function will be a serial number; you must format the cell with /Range Format Date Time.

String is a time entered in one of these formats: HH:MM:SS AM/PM, HH:MM AM/PM, HH:MM:SS (24-hour), or HH:MM (24-hour). In the first two formats, if a.m. or p.m. is not specified, a.m. is assumed.

Syntax

@TIMEVALUE(*string*)

Examples

Function	Result	After Formatting
@TIMEVALUE("9:30")	0.396	9:30 AM
@TIMEVALUE("15:45:30")	0.657	3:45 PM

@YEAR: Displaying the Year

The @YEAR function extracts the year from a date and displays it as a double-digit number (for example, *92* represents *1992*). The *date-number* argument can be a date function (@DATE, @DATEVALUE, or @NOW) or a cell containing a date function. This function can be used to query a date field in a database.

Syntax

@YEAR(*date-number*)

Examples

Function	Result
@YEAR(@DATE(92,5,15))	92
@YEAR(@DATEVALUE("5/25/92"))	92
@YEAR(A5)	93

where A5= @DATE(93,9,10)

FINANCIAL FUNCTIONS

If you are contemplating making an investment, you can use 1-2-3's financial functions to analyze the investment's feasibility and profitability. You can calculate an investment's future value (@FV), present value

(@PV), net present value (@NPV), rate of return (@RATE), and internal rate of return (@IRR). You can also calculate how long you need to hold onto an investment to reach a specified value in the future (@TERM, @CTERM). Probably the most commonly used financial function is @PMT which you can use to calculate monthly mortgage payments.

In addition, 1-2-3 offers three ways to calculate depreciation: straight-line (@SLN), double-declining balance (@DDB), and sum-of-the-years'-digits (@SYD). To use these functions, you need to know the asset's *cost* (the amount you purchased it for), *life* (the number of years you will use the asset), and *salvage value* (the amount the asset is worth at the end of its life).

@CTERM: Computing the Term on a Lump-Sum Payment

@CTERM calculates the number of years to reach a certain future value, given a fixed interest rate. This function, unlike @TERM, assumes that you make a single payment at the beginning of the period.

Syntax

@CTERM(*rate,future value,present value*)

Example

Formula	Result
@CTERM(11%,20000,10000)	6.6 years

If you make a single investment of $10,000 and it earns interest at a rate of eleven percent a year, this formula shows that it would take 6.6 years to double your money.

@DDB: Computing Depreciation with the Double-Declining Balance Method

With the double-declining balance method, the depreciation expense is higher in the earlier years of its life than in the latter years. To use the @DDB function, you need to know the asset's *cost, salvage value, life,* and *period*. Use the period argument to specify the year for which you want to calculate depreciation. (Depreciation expense for each year is different, unlike with straight-line depreciation.)

Syntax

@DDB(*cost,salvage value,life,period*)

Example

Formula	Result
@DDB(15000,3000,5,1)	$6,000

In the above example, you purchase a car for $15,000. You expect to use the car for five years at which time it will be worth $3000. This formula shows that, with the double-declining balance method, the depreciation expense for the first year is $6000.

@FV: Computing the Future Value of a Stream of Payments

The future value function, @FV, totals the amount of money you will have in the future if you invest a set amount each period, given a certain interest rate. The arguments in the @FV function are *payment* (amount invested each period), *rate* (the interest rate you expect to earn), and *term* (the number of periods you will invest).

Syntax

@FV(*payment,rate,term*)

Example

Formula	Result
@FV(2000,9%,35)	$431,421.50

In the above formula, you are investing $2000 each year for 35 years with an expected interest rate of nine percent a year. This formula shows that at the end of 35 years, you would have $431,421.50.

@NPV: Computing the Net Present Value

Net present value is similar to present value (see @PV) except that the payments are not equal, nor are they at fixed intervals. The payments are contained in a spreadsheet range and are referenced as an argument in the @NPV function.

Syntax

@NPV(*rate,range*)

Example

Formula	Result
@NPV(12%,A2..A5)	$5,418.76

In the above example, the discount rate is twelve percent and the payments are in the spreadsheet range A2..A5. This range contains the following payment amounts: 1000, 1500, 2000, and 3000. If you were considering investing in this annuity, you should pay no more than the net present value: $5,418.76.

@IRR: Computing the Internal Rate of Return on a Cash Flow

The @IRR function calculates the internal rate of return on a cash flow series (outgoing and incoming cash). This function requires two arguments. The first is a *guess* as to what you think the rate of return might be; it must be between 0 and 1. The guess does not affect the results unless your guess is off by more than 0.5. If the cell displays ERR, your guess was too far off; try another guess. The second argument is the *range* that contains the cash payments and receipts. Outgoing payments should be entered as negative numbers; cash receipts should be positive.

Syntax

@IRR(*rate,range*)

Example

Formula	Result
@IRR(15%,A2..A5)	12.7%

In the above example, you are guessing that the IRR is around fifteen percent. The cash flow series is in the spreadsheet range A2..A5. This range contains the following values: −5000 (your initial investment), 1500, 2000, and 3000. This formula shows that the internal rate of return is 12.7 percent.

@PMT: Computing Loan Payments

The @PMT function calculates loan payments based on a fixed interest rate. Besides the rate, the @PMT function requires two other arguments: *principal* (amount you are borrowing) and *term* (how long you are borrowing the money for). Make sure the term, rate, and payment use the same unit. For example, to calculate a monthly payment, the term and interest rate need to be expressed in months.

Syntax
@PMT(*principal,rate,term*)

Example

Formula	Result
@PMT(300000,0.1/12,30*12)	$2,632.71

In the above example, the principal amount is $300,000, the monthly interest rate is ten percent divided by 12, and the term is 30 years times 12. The monthly mortgage payment would be $2,632.71.

@PV: Computing the Present Value of an Annuity

The present value is what a future stream of payments would be worth today. The arguments in the @PV function are *payment* (amount paid to you each period), *rate* (the estimated discount rate), and *term* (the number of periods during which payments will be made to you).

Syntax

@PV(*payment,rate,term*)

Example

Formula	Result
@PV(50000,9%,20)	$456,427.20

In the above formula, you just won a million dollars in the state lottery. They are giving you $50,000 each year for twenty years, and the discount rate is assumed to be nine percent a year. This formula shows that the present value of the million dollars is $456,427.20. (This is how much the state would have to set aside for your winnings.)

@RATE: Calculating the Return on a Lump-Sum Payment

The @RATE function is similar to @IRR except that the investment's income comes in the form of a single payment at the end of a period. You need to specify the investment's *present value* (what you paid for it), *future value* (what you expect to sell it for), and the *term* (how long you will be holding the investment).

Syntax

@RATE(*future value,present value,term*)

Example

Formula	Result
@RATE(240000,168000,2)	19.5%

In the above example, you buy a house for $168,000 and you expect to sell it for $240,000 after owning it for two years. This formula shows that the rate of return on your investment is 19.5 percent.

@SLN: Computing Depreciation with the Straight-Line Method

With the straight-line depreciation method, the same amount is depreciated each year. To use the @SLN function, you need to know the asset's *cost*, *salvage value*, and *life*.

Syntax

@SLN(*cost,salvage value,life*)

Example

Formula	Result
@SLN(15000,3000,5)	$2,400

In the above example, you purchase a car for $15,000. You expect to use the car for five years at which time it will be worth $3000. This formula shows that, using the straight-line method, the depreciation expense for each year is $2,400.

@SYD: Computing Depreciation with the Sum-of-the-Years'-Digits Method

With the sum-of-the-years'-digits method, the depreciation expense is somewhat higher in the earlier years of its life than in the latter years, but it is more evenly distributed than the double-declining balance method. To use the @SYD function, you need to know the asset's *cost*, *salvage value*, *life*, and *period*. Use the period argument to specify which year you want to calculate depreciation for.

Syntax

@SYD(*cost,salvage value,life,period*)

Example

Formula	Result
@SYD(15000,3000,5,1)	$4,000

In the above example, you purchase a car for $15,000. You expect to use the car for five years at which time it will be worth $3000. This formula shows that, with the sum-of-the-years'-digits method, the depreciation expense for the first year is $4,000.

@TERM: Computing the Term on a Cash Flow

The @TERM function calculates the number of years to reach a certain future value, given a fixed interest rate. It assumes that a series of equal payments are made each period. (For unequal payments, see @CTERM.)

Syntax

@TERM(*payment,rate,future value*)

Example

Formula	Result
@TERM(10000,11%,100000)	7.1 years

The results of the above formula indicate that if you invested $10,000 a year at 11 percent, it would take 7.1 years to accumulate $100,000.

DATABASE FUNCTIONS

1-2-3 offers seven @ functions that are specifically designed to work with databases: @DAVG, @DCOUNT, @DMAX, @DMIN, @DSTD, @DSUM, and @DVAR.

Database functions are similar to the standard statistical functions (@SUM, @AVG, and so forth), except that they are linked to the database criteria range. Thus, if there are any conditions entered in the criteria range, a database function performs its calculation only on records that match the criteria.

All database functions require three pieces of information: the *input* range, the *field* you want to perform the calculation on, and the *criteria* range. The *field* is not a cell coordinate, nor is it a range or field name; rather, it refers to the number of the field in the database; the first column in the database is field 0, the second column is field 1, and so on. In the following examples, refer to Figure B.6. The input range (A1..D15) is named INPUT and the criteria range (A17..D18) is called CRIT. The condition entered into the criteria range is @MONTH(D2)=4. This condition means "locate all records with April dates."

For more information about database functions, refer to Chapter 13.

```
G5: {RT} (F2) @DAVG(INPUT,2,CRIT)                              READY

         A          B          C        D      E      F        G
  1  Part No. Description     Price    Date
  2     56321  Floppy Drive    45.00   02/01
  3     67509  Hard Disk Drive 450.00  02/04
  4     77767  Keyboard        129.00  02/15
  5     56432  Mouse           119.00  02/27       DAVG       40.67
  6     34342  Stop Watch        9.99  03/21       DCOUNT      4.00
  7     56321  Floppy Drive     50.00  03/26       DMAX      124.00
  8     87909  Modem           124.00  04/02       DMIN        9.99
  9     01231  Cables           15.67  04/03       DSUM      162.66
 10     87921  Labels            9.99  04/15       DSTD       40.16
 11     34291  Disk Box         13.00  04/17       DVAR     2318.95
 12     34291  Disk Box         12.00  05/05
 13     77767  Keyboard        129.00  05/06
 14     88858  Color Monitor   225.00  05/06
 15     56432  Mouse           119.00  05/12
 16
 17  Part No. Description     Price    Date
 18                                    @MONTH(D2)=4
 19
 20
```

Figure B.6: The input range is A1..D15 and the criteria range is A17..D18.

@DAVG: Averaging a Field

The @DAVG function averages the values in a particular database field; it averages only those records that satisfy the conditions entered in the criteria range. This function has three arguments: *input* (the database range), *field* (the column you want to average), and the *criteria* range. To determine the value to enter for the field argument, subtract one from the field number. For example, if the field you want to average is the fifth column in the database range, enter **4** for the field argument.

Any blank cells in the field are not counted as values, but labels are treated as zero values, so if you have labels in the field you are averaging, the average will be incorrect.

Syntax

@DAVG(*input,field,criteria*)

Example

@DAVG(INPUT,2,CRIT)

If the condition *@MONTH(D2)=4* is entered into the criteria range, the result of the above formula is *40.67* (see Figure B.6).

@DCOUNT: Counting the Number of Entries in a Field

The @DCOUNT function counts the number of non-blank cells in a particular database field; it counts only those records that satisfy the conditions entered in the criteria range. This function has three arguments: *input* (the database range), *field* (the column you want to count), and the *criteria* range. To determine the value to enter for the field argument, subtract one from the field number. For example, if the field you want to count is the fifth column in the database range, enter **4** for the field argument.

Syntax

@DCOUNT(*input,field,criteria*)

Example

@DCOUNT(INPUT,2,CRIT)

If the condition *@MONTH(D2)=4* is entered into the criteria range, the result of the above formula is *4* (see Figure B.6).

@DMAX: Finding the Highest Value in a Field

The @DMAX function displays the largest value in a particular database field; it looks at only those records that satisfy the conditions entered in the criteria range. This function has three arguments: *input* (the database range), *field* (the column you want to analyze), and the *criteria* range. To determine the value to enter for the field argument, subtract one from the field number. For example, if the field you want to analyze is the fifth column in the database range, enter **4** for the field argument.

Syntax

@DMAX(*input,field,criteria*)

Example

@DMAX(INPUT,2,CRIT)

If the condition *@MONTH(D2)=4* is entered into the criteria range, the result of the above formula is *124* (see Figure B.6).

@DMIN: Finding the Lowest Value in a Field

The @DMIN function displays the lowest value in a particular database field; it looks at only those records that satisfy the conditions entered in the criteria range. This function has three arguments: *input* (the database range), *field* (the column you want to analyze), and the *criteria* range. To determine the value to enter for the field argument, subtract one from the field number. For example, if the field you want to analyze is the fifth column in the database range, enter **4** for the field argument.

Syntax

@DMIN(*input,field,criteria*)

Example

@DMIN(INPUT,2,CRIT)

If the condition @*MONTH(D2)=4* is entered into the criteria range, the result of the above formula is *9.99* (see Figure B.6).

@DSUM: Totalling a Field

The @DSUM function totals the values in a particular database field; it sums only those records that satisfy the conditions entered in the criteria range. This function has three arguments: *input* (the database range), *field* (the column you want to sum), and the *criteria* range. To determine the value to enter for the field argument, subtract one from the field number. For example, if the field you want to sum is the fifth column in the database range, enter **4** for the field argument.

Syntax

@DSUM(*input,field,criteria*)

Example

@DSUM(INPUT,2,CRIT)

If the condition @*MONTH(D2)=4* is entered into the criteria range, the result of the above formula is *162.66* (see Figure B.6).

@DSTD and @DVAR:
Measuring the Dispersion of a Field

Variance tells you how much the values in a field vary from the field's average. The standard deviation is simply the square root of the variance. The higher the standard deviation, the more widely dispersed the values.

The @DSTD function displays the standard deviation for a particular database field; it looks only at those records that satisfy the conditions entered in the criteria range. The @DVAR function calculates the variance of a field. These functions have three arguments: *input* (the database range), *field* (the column you want to analyze), and the *criteria* range. To determine the value to enter for the field argument, subtract one from the field number. For example, if the field you want to analyze is the fifth column in the database range, enter **4** for the field argument.

Syntax
@DSTD(*input,field,criteria*)
@DVAR(*input,field,criteria*)

Example
@DSTD(INPUT,2,CRIT)
@DVAR(INPUT,2,CRIT)

If the condition *@MONTH(D2)=4* is entered into the criteria range, the standard deviation is *48.16* and the variance is *2318.95*. (see Figure B.6).

STRING FUNCTIONS

1-2-3 has the ability to create formulas out of labels and comes with a set of functions—called *string functions*—for label manipulation. A *string* is a series of alphanumeric characters; it can be text typed into a cell, part of a label, or text typed directly in a formula. Here are a few examples of what you can do with string functions:

- "add" together text in two cells, creating a third label that is a combination of the first two

- convert the case (upper/lower) of a label (@UPPER, @LOWER, @PROPER)

- locate a text string in a database field (@FIND)

- extract part of a long label and place it in a separate cell (@LEFT, @MID, @RIGHT)

- convert values into labels (@STRING) or labels into values (@VALUE)

- repeat a string a specified number of times (@REPEAT)

- compare two strings to see if they are exactly the same (@EXACT)

Other string functions are: @CHAR, @CLEAN, @CODE, @LENGTH, @N, @REPLACE, @S, and @TRIM.

CREATING STRING FORMULAS

To combine a text string with a label in a cell or to combine text from two cells, use an ampersand to "add" them together. Text strings must be enclosed in quotation marks. Here is an example of a string formula:

    +A1&" "&B1

The above formula combines the label in cell A1 with the label in B1, and places a space between them. If A1 contains the label *John* and B1 contains *Smith*, the result to this formula is *John Smith*. Here is another variation of this formula:

    +"Mr. "&A1&" "&B1

The above formula results in *Mr. John Smith*.

@CHAR: Creating Special Characters

1-2-3 lets you enter a variety of special characters such as bullets (•), copyright signs (©), pi (π), ½, ¼, and ≥. The set of special characters is called the *Lotus International Character Set* or simply *LICS*. Some of these special characters are shown in Figure B.7.

There are two ways to create special characters: by entering a compose sequence with Alt-F1 or by using the @CHAR function. The argument for @CHAR is a two- or three-digit code. The codes that produce the symbols in column C of Figure B.7 are shown in column A. The complete set of LICS codes and compose sequences is listed in Appendix A of the *User's Guide* that came with 1-2-3.

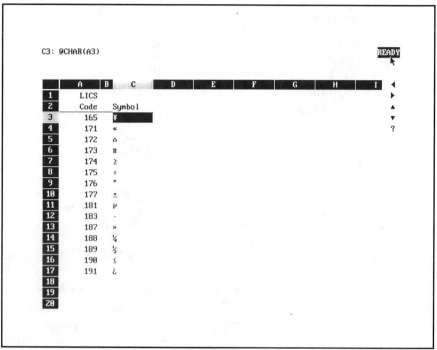

Figure B.7: Some of the codes and symbols in the Lotus International
Character Set (LICS)

Some of the codes do not appear exactly on the screen as they print.
For example, the copyright sign appears as a lowercase c, but prints as
either *(c)* or ©, depending on the font you are using.

Syntax

@CHAR(*code*)

Examples

Formula	Result
@CHAR(163)	£
@CHAR(A14)	¼

where A14 contains the LICS code 188

@CLEAN: Taking Out the Garbage

The @CLEAN function strips out unwanted control characters from a string. *Control characters* are codes that may not appear on the screen but can affect the printed report. You can use @CLEAN to remove extraneous, non-text characters from an ASCII file you have imported with /File Import. You can also use this function to remove Wysiwyg text formatting codes.

Syntax

@CLEAN(*string*)

Example

@CLEAN(A1)

where A1 contains text you have imported from a word-processing file

@CODE: Finding an LICS Code

The @CODE function is the opposite of the @CHAR function: It displays the Lotus International Character Set (LICS) code for a particular character. (See @CHAR for additional information about LICS codes.)

Syntax

@CODE(*string*)

Examples

Formula	Result
@CODE("£")	163
@CODE(C14)	188

where C14 contains ¼

Note: to enter the £ in the first formula, you must use a compose sequence—press Alt-F1 and type **L=**.

@EXACT: Comparing Two Strings

The @EXACT function compares two strings to see if they match exactly—including upper- and lowercase. The two arguments, *string1* and *string2*, can be cells that contain labels or text strings enclosed in quotation marks. The result to this function is a *1* (true) if the two labels match or a *0* (false) if the strings are different. Because @EXACT returns a true or false answer, it is ideal for conditions in database queries, @IF functions, or {IF} macro commands.

Syntax

@EXACT(*string1,string2*)

Example

@EXACT(B2,"Smith")

where B2 is the first record in a database

When you perform a database query (/Date Query Find) with this formula in the criteria range, 1-2-3 will locate only those records with *Smith* entered into column B. It will not locate *SMITH* or *smith*.

@FIND: Locating a Text String

The @FIND function looks for a string of characters (the *search-string* argument) within a particular cell or text string (the *string* argument), and begins searching the string at the position indicated (the *start-number* argument). It displays an error message if the search-string is not located. Otherwise, it displays the character position where it finds the first occurrence of the search-string.

The *start-number* argument is usually 0; this tells 1-2-3 to begin searching at the first character.

The @FIND function is frequently used as a criteria in a database query (see Chapter 12) or as an argument in other string functions (such as @LEFT and @MID).

Syntax

@FIND(*search-string,string,start-number*)

Examples

Formula	Result
@FIND(" ",A24,0)	8
@LEFT(A24,@FIND(" ",A24,0))	Jonathan
@MID(A24,@FIND(" ",A24,0)+1, @LENGTH(A24))	Ambers

where A24 contains the label *Jonathan Ambers*

The first formula determines the character position of the first space in cell A24. The purpose of the other two formulas is to extract the first and last name from a cell that contains a person's full name. Thanks to the @FIND function, these formulas will work on any name (assuming the first and last names are separated by a space).

@LEFT, @MID, @RIGHT: Extracting Part of a Label

The @LEFT, @MID, and @RIGHT functions place a portion of a label into another cell. The @LEFT function extracts the specified number of characters at the beginning of the label, @MID extracts characters in the middle, and @RIGHT extracts characters at the end of the label. For example, you can use @LEFT to copy the first ten characters of a label or @RIGHT to copy the last five.

The *number* argument is the number of characters to extract. The @MID function uses an additional argument, *start-number*; this argument indicates the position of the first character to be extracted (the first character in the label is position number zero). For example, if the first character you want to extract is the fifth character in the cell, the start-number will be 4.

To help you calculate the number or start-number arguments, you can use the @FIND function. For instance, you might want to extract the characters before or after a space or a comma (see @FIND).

Syntax

@LEFT(*string,number*)
@MID(*string,start-number,number*)
@RIGHT(*string,number*)

Examples

Formula	Result
@LEFT(B1,3)	Mr.
@MID(B1,4,4)	John
@RIGHT(B1,5)	Smith

where B1 contains the label *Mr. John Smith*

@LENGTH: Determining the Length of a String

The @LENGTH function calculates how many characters are in a particular cell or text string. You can use @LENGTH as a condition in an @IF function or {IF} macro command to make sure a label (such as a part code) is a certain length. This function is also useful for calculating the *number* or *start-number* arguments in the @LEFT, @MID, @REPEAT, and @RIGHT string functions.

If you use @LENGTH on a value, an error message will result.

Syntax

@LENGTH(*string*)

Examples

Formula	Result
@LENGTH(A24)	15
@MID(A24,@FIND(" ",A24,0)+1, @LENGTH(A24))	Ambers

where A24 contains the label *Jonathan Ambers*

In the second formula, the @LENGTH function is used as the *number* argument.

Another way to use @LENGTH is as a condition in a macro program:

```
{IF @LENGTH(CODE)<>8}{BRANCH INPUT}
```

The above command executes the INPUT subroutine if the length of the cell named CODE is not eight.

@LOWER, @UPPER, @PROPER: Converting Upper- and Lowercase

After a series of labels have been entered, you may discover that they have the wrong combination of upper- or lowercase characters. Perhaps they are in all capital letters when they should be in lowercase. The @UPPER, @LOWER, and @PROPER functions come to the rescue here. @UPPER converts the string to all capital letters, @LOWER converts the characters to lowercase, and @PROPER converts the first letter of each word to uppercase and the rest of the word to lowercase.

After converting the case of a column of labels, you might want to eliminate the original column. Don't do this until you have converted the string formulas to values with the /Range Value command (see Chapter 3).

Syntax

```
@LOWER(string)
@PROPER(string)
@UPPER(string)
```

Examples

Formula	Result
@PROPER("JOHN SMITH")	John Smith
@LOWER(B3)	january

where B3 contains the label *JANUARY*

The @UPPER command is frequently used in conditions for macro {IF} statements:

```
{GETLABEL "Print the report? (Y/N)",RESPONSE}
{IF @UPPER(RESPONSE)="Y"}{BRANCH REPORT}
```

By using the @UPPER function in the {IF} statement, the response to the *Print the report? (Y/N)* question can be entered in upper- or lowercase.

@N: Checking for a Numeric Entry

The @N function looks at the first (or only) cell in a range. If the entry is a number, the number is displayed. If it is a label or blank cell, a *0* is displayed. You can use this function in a conditional statement for @IF functions or {IF} macro commands to make sure a value is entered into a cell. In that way, it is quite similar to the @ISNUMBER function. The main difference is that @ISNUMBER considers blank cells to be values while @N does not.

Syntax

@N(*range*)

Example

```
{IF @N(DATA)=0}{BRANCH INPUT}
{REPORT}
```

In the above macro command, if the cell named DATA contains a label or a blank cell, the INPUT subroutine is executed. Otherwise, the macro runs the REPORT subroutine.

@REPEAT: Repeating a String

To repeat a series of characters a specified number of times, use the @REPEAT function. It is similar to the repeating label-prefix character (the backslash) except that @REPEAT lets you define how many times to repeat the string; the backslash, on the other hand, repeats the character across the entire width of the column.

Syntax

@REPEAT(*string,number*)

Example

Formula	Result
@REPEAT("-",@LENGTH(B20))	-------

where B20 contains *January*, a label seven characters long

@REPLACE: Replacing One String with Another

The @REPLACE function is similar to the Replace option of the /Range Search command: It replaces one text string with another. This function has four arguments. *Original-string* is a cell containing the characters you want to replace or a text string enclosed in quotation marks. You define which characters to replace in the original-string using the *start-number* and *number* arguments. The *number* argument is the number of characters to replace. The *start-number* argument indicates the position of the first character to be replaced (the first character in the label is position number zero). The *new-string* argument is the replacement text.

Syntax

@REPLACE(*original-string,start-number,number,new-string*)

Example

@IF(@LEFT(A5,3)="Mrs",@REPLACE(A5,0,3,"Ms"),A5)

where A5 contains the label *Mrs. Patricia Hamilton*

The above formula checks to see if the first three characters of A5 are *Mrs*. If they are, the @REPLACE function replaces these characters with *Ms* and the result is *Ms. Patricia Hamilton*.

@S: Converting a Value or Blank Cell to an Empty String

The @S function converts a value (or a blank cell) to an empty string. An *empty string* is the equivalent of a lone apostrophe. This conversion prevents an error message from displaying when a string formula references a blank cell or a value.

If the *range* contains a label, @S simply displays the label.

Syntax

@S(*range*)

Example

+@S(FIRST)&" "&@S(MIDDLE)&" "&@S(LAST)

Without the @S functions, an ERR message would result if any of the cells (FIRST, MIDDLE, or LAST) were blank.

@STRING: Converting a Value to a Label

In string formulas, you cannot combine text with values. If A3 contained the value 15 percent, the following formula would result in an error:

+"You will be receiving a "&A3&" percent raise."

To reference a value cell in a string formula, you must convert the value to a label with the @STRING function. This function requires that you specify a value or a cell containing a value, as well as the number of decimal places to round the number. The numeric format (Percent, Currency, and so forth) is ignored.

Syntax

@STRING(*value,decimals*)

Example

+"You will be receiving a "&@STRING(A3*100,0)&" percent raise."

where A3 contains 15 percent (*0.15*)

The result of this formula is:

You will be receiving a 15 percent raise.

@TRIM: Removing Extra Spaces

The @TRIM function eliminates extraneous spaces from a text string. This function removes one or more spaces at the beginning or end of the string and two or more consecutive spaces that appear in the middle of the string. You might need to use the @TRIM function to remove extra spaces from an imported text file. Another use for this function is to remove leading spaces that have been entered at the beginning of a cell. (For example, you may have used the spacebar to center a label before you learned about the /Range Label Center and :Text Align Center commands.)

Syntax
> @TRIM(*string*)

Example

Formula	Result
@TRIM(C1)	Sales Projection

where C1 contains the label ' *Sales Projection*

The above formula removes the leading spaces.

@VALUE: Converting Labels into Values

If you mistakenly enter a series of values as labels (in other words you type apostrophes in front of the numbers), you can convert them with the @VALUE command.

Syntax
@VALUE(*string*)

Example

Formula	Result
@VALUE(B5)	235.56

where B5 contains the label '*$235.56*

Appendices

Appendix A

Appendix B

Appendix C

Appendix D

Importing
and Exporting Data

No one lives in a vacuum, not even a dedicated 1-2-3 user. There are bound to be occasions when you will need to transfer data between 1-2-3 and another software package. For example, a work associate you need to share data with may use a different spreadsheet program. Or you might want to incorporate spreadsheet data into a WordPerfect document.

Because 1-2-3 is a spreadsheet standard, many programs can automatically import or export .WK1 files. MultiMate 4, WordStar, Excel, Quattro Pro, Microsoft Works, Harvard Graphics, and PageMaker are a few examples. While other programs may not be able to directly communicate with 1-2-3, you can transfer data back and forth using one of the following techniques:

- Use 1-2-3's Translate utility to convert files to other formats (for example, from 1-2-3 to dBASE III)

- Import or export ASCII files

USING THE TRANSLATE UTILITY

The Translate utility included with 1-2-3 can transfer data to and from a variety of file formats, as shown in Table C.1.

There are two ways to load the Translate program:

- From the Lotus Access Menu, highlight Translate and press Enter.

- From the DOS prompt, type **trans** and press Enter. (You must be in the 1-2-3 program directory—for example, C:\123R23—when you type this command.)

Once you have loaded Translate, you see the screen shown in Figure C.1. Notice that Translate gets right to the point—it immediately asks you to choose a program to translate from.

Here is the basic procedure for translating a file:

1. The first prompt, *What do you want to translate FROM?*, displays a list of program names. Choose the program that created the

Table C.1: Files Translate Can Convert

PROGRAM	FILE EXTENSION
1-2-3 Release 1A	WKS
1-2-3 Release 2–2.3	WK1
dBASE II	DBF
dBASE III	DBF
Data Interchange Format	DIF
Enable 2.0	SSF
MultiPlan SYLK	SLK
SuperCalc 4	CAL
Symphony 1.0	WRK
Symphony 1.1–2.2	WR1
VisiCalc†	VC

†VisiCalc data files can be converted into 1-2-3 files, but not vice versa.

file you want to convert. Use ↓ to highlight the name and press Enter.

2. The second prompt, *What do you want to translate TO?*, displays another list of programs. The list contains the programs that you can convert to. Select the program name and press Enter.

3. You are then presented with one or more information screens that let you know about any requirements, restrictions, or limitations of the file transfer. Read these screens carefully; it's possible that you will need to quit Translate to prepare the file according to these instructions. To read the next screen of information, press Enter; when you are ready to continue with the file translation, press Esc. If you need to quit Translate to prepare a file, keep pressing Esc until you are asked if you want to quit.

```
                Lotus  1-2-3  Release 2.3 Translate Utility
        Copr. 1985, 1991  Lotus Development Corporation  All Rights Reserved

What do you want to translate FROM?

              1-2-3 1A
              1-2-3 2 through 2.3
              dBase II
              dBase III
              DIF
              Enable 2.0
              Multiplan (SYLK)
              SuperCalc4
              Symphony 1.0
              Symphony 1.1 through 2.2
              VisiCalc



              Move the menu pointer to your selection and press ENTER
                   Press ESC to end the Translate utility
                   Press F1 (HELP) for more information
```

Figure C.1: The Translate program converts data to and from 1-2-3's file
format.

4. Translate then shows you a list of files that have the extension
   you are converting from (see Table C.1). By default, it lists files
   in the 1-2-3 program directory. To see files in another drive or
   subdirectory, press Esc to edit the path. Make the change and
   press Enter.

5. Highlight the name of the file you want to convert and press
   Enter.

6. Next to *Target file*, there is a suggested file name. It has the same
   first name as the source file, but with the appropriate extension
   for the target program; it is stored in the same path as the source
   file. If necessary, edit the target file path or name and press Enter.

7. At this point, some file translations require additional information. For example, to convert from 1-2-3 to dBASE, you are
   asked if you want to translate the entire worksheet or a range.
   Answer any questions.

8. Before the file conversion begins, you are asked if you want to proceed with the translation. Choose Yes. When the conversion is finished, you will (hopefully) see the message *Translation Successful* in the middle of your screen.

9. To return to the initial Translate screen, press Esc; or, to convert another file with the same source and target programs, press Enter.

While you are in Translate, you can press F1 at any time for help. To exit Translate, press Esc until you see the message *Do you want to leave Translate?*, and then choose Yes.

WORKING WITH ASCII FILES

If the program you want to convert to or from is not listed in Table C.1, you cannot use Translate to convert the file. Instead, you must use ASCII files. *ASCII* stands for *American Standard Code for Information Interchange*. It is a standard file format that is recognized by virtually all software packages, including 1-2-3.

CREATING ASCII FILES

1-2-3 offers two ways to create an ASCII file, which you can import into another program:

- The /Print File command, discussed in Chapter 6
- The {OPEN}, {WRITE}, and {WRITELN} macro commands, discussed in Chapter 17

Refer to these chapters for detailed information on these commands.

APPENDIX C

IMPORTING ASCII FILES

To copy an ASCII file into the current spreadsheet, use the /File Import command. This command offers two options: Text and Numbers. You must be familiar with the structure of your ASCII file before you can determine which option to choose. Compare the ASCII file in Figure C.2 with the one in C.3. The file in Figure C.2 has spaces between each field. (A *field*

```
56321 Floppy Drive       45.00 02/01/92
67509 Hard Disk Drive   450.00 02/04/92
77767 Keyboard          129.00 02/15/92
56432 Mouse             119.00 02/27/92
34342 Stop Watch          9.99 03/21/92
56321 Floppy Drive       50.00 03/26/92
87909 Modem             124.00 04/02/92
01231 Cables             15.67 04/03/92
87921 Labels              9.99 04/15/92
34291 Disk Box           13.00 04/17/92
34291 Disk Box           12.00 05/05/92
77767 Keyboard          129.00 05/06/92
88858 Color Monitor     225.00 05/06/92
56432 Mouse             119.00 05/12/92
78654 Video Card         56.79 05/17/92
56430 Floppy disks       12.95 05/21/92
67509 Hard Disk Drive   450.00 06/04/92
04321 Paper              22.50 07/12/92
```

Figure C.2: This ASCII file has spaces between each field.

```
"56321","Floppy Drive",45.00,19920201
"67509","Hard Disk Drive",450.00,19920204
"77767","Keyboard",129.00,19920215
"56432","Mouse",119.00,19920227
"34342","Stop Watch",9.99,19920321
"56321","Floppy Drive",50.00,19920326
"87909","Modem",124.00,19920402
"01231","Cables",15.67,19920403
"87921","Labels",9.99,19920415
"34291","Disk Box",13.00,19920417
"34291","Disk Box",12.00,19920505
"77767","Keyboard",129.00,19920506
"88858","Color Monitor",225.00,19920506
"56432","Mouse",119.00,19920512
"78654","Video Card",56.79,19920517
"56430","Floppy disks",12.95,19920521
"67509","Hard Disk Drive",450.00,19920604
"04321","Paper",22.50,19920712
```

Figure C.3: This ASCII file is delimited with commas and quotation marks.

is the equivalent of a single cell entry.) Figure C.3, on the other hand, has commas between fields and quotation marks around each label field (but not around values); this type of ASCII file is called a *delimited* file.

If you have produced an ASCII file in a database program, the file is most likely delimited (like Figure C.3). If you have created the text file in a word processor, the file will have spaces between fields (like Figure C.2). If you aren't sure of the file's structure, use the DOS TYPE command to view the file's contents. For example,

    TYPE PCUG.PRN

The above command displays the contents of a file named PCUG.PRN. Note: The /File Import command expects ASCII files to have a .PRN extension. If your file has a different extension, you must type it in yourself.

Choose /File Import Numbers if the file is delimited; otherwise, choose /File Import Text. When you import a delimited file with /File Import Numbers, each field is stored in a separate cell. When you import an ASCII file with /File Import Text, each line of data is stored as a long label in column A (or in whichever column you imported the data into). Look in the control panel of Figure C.4 and you can see that all the data for row 1 is stored in A1.

Delimited files are much more useful and easier to work with, since you can immediately begin formatting, performing calculations, querying, and sorting the imported data. You cannot do these types of operations on data imported from an undelimited file because each row is a single label. Fortunately, 1-2-3 offers a command to divide the data into separate cells: /Data Parse.

PARSING DATA INTO SEPARATE CELLS

The /Data Parse command takes a range of single-column labels and divides each label into separate cells of labels and values. Use this command to manipulate data imported with /File Import Text. The Parse operation requires you to create a format line that defines each cell's data type (Label, Value, Date, or Time) along with the maximum number of characters in each cell. Figure C.5 shows an example of a typical format line.

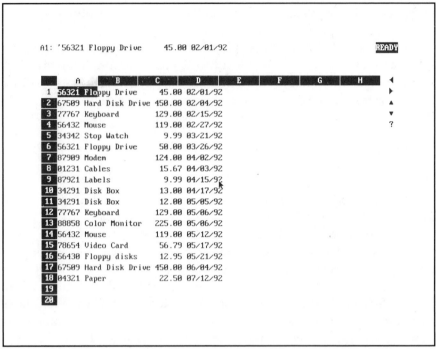

A1: '56321 Floppy Drive   45.00 02/01/92   **READY**

	A	B	C	D	E	F	G	H
1	56321 Floppy Drive		45.00	02/01/92				
2	67509 Hard Disk Drive		450.00	02/04/92				
3	77767 Keyboard		129.00	02/15/92				
4	56432 Mouse		119.00	02/27/92				
5	34342 Stop Watch		9.99	03/21/92				
6	56321 Floppy Drive		50.00	03/26/92				
7	87909 Modem		124.00	04/02/92				
8	01231 Cables		15.67	04/03/92				
9	87921 Labels		9.99	04/15/92				
10	34291 Disk Box		13.00	04/17/92				
11	34291 Disk Box		12.00	05/05/92				
12	77767 Keyboard		129.00	05/06/92				
13	88858 Color Monitor		225.00	05/06/92				
14	56432 Mouse		119.00	05/12/92				
15	78654 Video Card		56.79	05/17/92				
16	56430 Floppy disks		12.95	05/21/92				
17	67509 Hard Disk Drive		450.00	06/04/92				
18	04321 Paper		22.50	07/12/92				
19								
20								

Figure C.4: /File Import Text places each line of data in a single cell.

The beginning of each cell is defined with one of the following characters:

L   Label

V   Value

D   Date

T   Time

S   Skip (don't parse)

The maximum number of characters in each field is determined by the > symbols. Each > represents a single character. For example, L>>>>>>>>>> indicates that the longest piece of data in·this field is 10 characters. If you don't include enough > symbols, the data will be truncated. The asterisks represent blank spaces.

```
A1:  {L>>>>*L>>>>>>>>>>>>>*U>>>>>*D>>>>>>>                              READY

         A         B         C         D       E      F      G      H     ◄
   1  L>>>>*L>>>>>>>>>>>>>>>*U>>>>>*D>>>>>>>                                ►
   2  56321 Floppy Drive      45.00 02/01/92                               ▲
   3  67509 Hard Disk Drive 450.00 02/04/92                                ▼
   4  77767 Keyboard        129.00 02/15/92                                ?
   5  56432 Mouse           119.00 02/27/92
   6  34342 Stop Watch        9.99 03/21/92
   7  56321 Floppy Drive     50.00 03/26/92
   8  87909 Modem           124.00 04/02/92
   9  01231 Cables           15.67 04/03/92
  10  87921 Labels            9.99 04/15/92              ▾
  11  34291 Disk Box         13.00 04/17/92
  12  34291 Disk Box         12.00 05/05/92
  13  77767 Keyboard        129.00 05/06/92
  14  88858 Color Monitor   225.00 05/06/92
  15  56432 Mouse           119.00 05/12/92
  16  78654 Video Card       56.79 05/17/92
  17  56430 Floppy disks     12.95 05/21/92
  18  67509 Hard Disk Drive 450.00 06/04/92
  19  04321 Paper            22.50 07/12/92
  20
```

Figure C.5: Row 1 contains a format line used in data parsing operations.

While you can manually type the format line in an empty spreadsheet row, the easiest way to create it is with the /Data Parse Format-Line Create command. This command inserts the format line in the row above the cell pointer. 1-2-3 uses the first row of data as a sample for developing the format line. Because this row is not necessarily representative of all rows, you will almost always need to edit the format line—to make a field longer, to indicate a different data type, or to change where a field begins. Also, 1-2-3 uses spaces to determine where one field ends and the next begins. Since spaces appear between words as well as between columns, you will need to edit the format line to remove these extra fields. Figure C.6 shows a format line before it's been edited. Notice that the format line specifies two different label fields for *Floppy Disk* because of the space between words. This format line needs to be modified so that it looks like Figure C.5.

Before you parse data, either detach Wysiwyg or replace font 1 with a fixed-space font such as Courier. You will not be able to create a format line

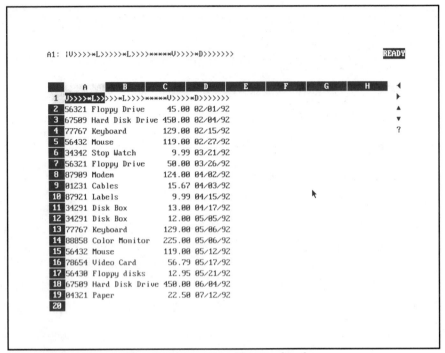

Figure C.6: A format line that has not yet been edited.

with proportional fonts (proportional spacing throws off the alignment of the columns). After the data is parsed, you can re-attach Wysiwyg or select a proportional font.

Follow this basic procedure to parse a range of data:

1. Place the cell pointer at the beginning of the first row of data to be parsed.

2. To create a format line, choose /Data Parse Format-Line Create.

3. To edit the format line, choose Format-Line Edit. Study the format-line to see if you need to make any changes. When you are editing a format line, you are in overtype mode; this means that any characters you type will replace existing format-line symbols. If necessary, replace incorrect data types (L, V, etc.) and define

longer field lengths (type additional > symbols). To view lines of data not on the screen, press ↓ or PgDn.

4. When the format line is correct, press Enter. (If you make a mistake and want to cancel the changes, hit Esc twice instead of pressing Enter.)

5. To define the parse range, choose Input-Column. Specify a single-column range of labels—make sure you include the format line.

6. To specify where to place the parsed data, choose Output-Range. You don't need to highlight a complete range—just the first cell. The output-range can be either an empty part of the spreadsheet or the first row of data in the Input-Column. If the Output-Range and Input-Column overlap, you will overwrite the original data; only do this when you are confident that your format line is precise.

7. Choose Go to perform the parse operation.

Move the cell pointer to the output-range so you can adjust column widths and format the data, as necessary. When you are satisfied that the data was parsed correctly, you can delete the original input range.

Appendices

Appendix A

Appendix B

Appendix C

Appendix D

Using
Release 2.3's
Auditor Add-In

The Auditor add-in, included with Release 2.3, can identify problems with your spreadsheet formulas. With the Auditor, you can:

- easily see that a formula has been inadvertently replaced with a value
- discover why a formula isn't calculating the correct answer
- locate all formulas containing references to the cells they are in (these are called *circular references*)

This add-in can perform five different tasks. The *Formulas* menu option identifies all formulas in all or part of the spreadsheet. The *Circs* option locates circular references. *Recalc-List* lets you know the order in which formulas are recalculated. The *Precedents* option identifies cells that are referenced in a specific formula while the *Dependents* option performs the reverse operation: it locates all the formulas that reference a specific cell.

ATTACHING AND INVOKING THE ADD-IN

As with any add-in, the Auditor must be attached before you can use it. This add-in consumes about 10K of conventional memory.

Follow these steps to attach the Auditor add-in:

1. Press / to display the 1-2-3 menu and choose:

   Add-In

   Attach

2. Highlight AUDITOR.ADN and press Enter.

3. Choose one of the available invoke-keys (7–10).

4. Choose Quit.

To display the Auditor's menu, press the appropriate invoke key. For example, if 7 is the invoke-key, press Alt-F7 to invoke the add-in. The Auditor's main menu is shown in Figure D.1.

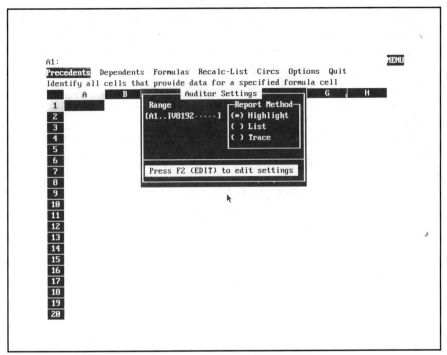

Figure D.1: The Auditor's main menu

REPORTING METHODS

The Auditor can report its findings in three ways. The *Highlight* option, the default method, displays the cells in a different color or screen intensity. The *List* option places the results in a spreadsheet range, which you can study on-screen or print out. The *Trace* option moves the pointer to each cell.

To better understand these reporting methods, let's look at an example in which you ask the Auditor to identify all formulas in a spreadsheet range. With the Highlight reporting method, the cells containing formulas will be brighter or in a different color. The List method creates a list of formulas, such as the one shown in Figure D.2. The Trace option moves the cell pointer to the first formula in the range and the control panel displays options for moving Forward and Backward to other formulas. If you choose Forward, the cell pointer is moved to the next cell containing a formula.

When you use the Highlight or List option, you usually must quit the Auditor menu to see the results.

Depending on the type of audit you are doing, one reporting method might be more appropriate than another. For example, to see if there are any values lurking in a formula range, use the Highlight method; an errant value will stand out when surrounded by a range of highlighted cells.

To select your reporting method, either directly edit the Auditor Settings dialog box (see Figure D.1), or use the Options command and choose Highlight, List, or Trace.

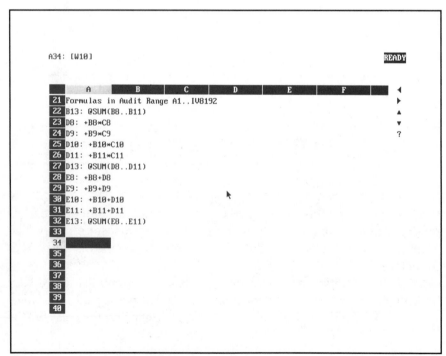

Figure D.2: A list of formulas in a spreadsheet

RESETTING HIGHLIGHTED CELLS

When you perform an audit using the Highlight reporting method, the cells remain highlighted until you:

- modify the spreadsheet with /Worksheet Insert, /Worksheet Delete, or /Move,

- retrieve the spreadsheet again, or

- use the Auditor's Options Reset Highlight command.

If you don't remove the highlighting from one audit, the cells remain highlighted for the next audit—even if they don't apply. Therefore, make sure you use the Options Reset Highlight command before you perform a subsequent auditing task.

AUDITING PART OF THE SPREADSHEET

Another setting in the Auditor Settings dialog box is Range. By default, the entire spreadsheet (A1..IV8192) is audited. To restrict the audit to a specific spreadsheet range, edit the dialog box or use the Options Audit-Range command.

IDENTIFYING FORMULAS

The Formulas option is appropriate for two different auditing tasks, depending on which reporting method you use. With the highlighting method, you can easily spot a cell that contains a value instead of a formula. These wayward values might sneak into your spreadsheet if you accidentally type a value into a cell that has a formula in it. With the naked eye, you might not notice this mistake, but the Highlight option makes it readily apparent.

If you print out the report created with the List reporting method, you will have a hard-copy record of your important formulas. For instance, you might have several complicated formulas that you need to recreate in other spreadsheets. The printed list offers an easy way to look up your formulas.

SNIFFING OUT
CIRCULAR REFERENCES

There are two types of circular references: direct and indirect. A direct circular reference occurs when a cell referenced in a formula is the cell containing the formula itself. For example, if cell B10 contains the formula @SUM(B3..B10), it is a direct circular reference. An indirect circular reference occurs when one formula references a cell with another formula that references the first. For example, if cell A15 contains the formula +B15+C15 and B15 contains the formula +A15+D15, it is an indirect circular reference. When a spreadsheet contains a circular reference, the status line displays *CIRC*. Furthermore, your spreadsheet will contain inaccurate results—each time the spreadsheet recalculates, the formulas with a circular reference will display different answers.

While 1-2-3's /Worksheet Status command indicates the cell address of a circular reference, this command has its limitations: It indicates only one cell that contains a circular reference. But spreadsheets frequently contain multiple circular references, especially if you copied the formula. That's where the Auditor's Circs option comes in handy; it lists *all* formulas containing circular references.

The Circs option first shows you an on-screen list of cells with circular references in their formulas (see Figure D.3). This screen is called the Circs window and the cells it lists are *source cells*. Choose one of these source cells and, depending on your reporting method, the cell will either be highlighted, listed, or traced.

The most useful reporting method is List. The list will display the circular path and all formulas involved in this circle (see Figure D.4). Contrary to what you might think (or the way you might think it should work), it doesn't list all circular references—only the source cell you select. However, the complete list of circular references appears when you first choose the Circs option (as shown in Figure D.3).

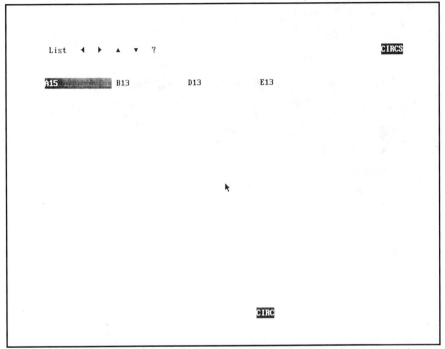

List ◀ ▶ ▲ ▼ ?   CIRCS

A15   B13   D13   E13

CIRC

Figure D.3: The Circs window lists all cells with circular references in their formulas.

Once you have used the Auditor to identify the circular references, you can correct the formulas. Note that the Auditor doesn't actually rectify problems—it simply identifies them.

IDENTIFYING THE ORDER OF RECALCULATION

When 1-2-3 recalculates a spreadsheet, it can do so in three different orders: Rowwise, Columnwise, or Natural. *Rowwise* calculates the formulas in row 1 first, then row 2, row 3, and so forth. *Columnwise* calculates the formulas in column A first, then column B, column C, etc. With the *Natural* order, all formulas on which a formula depends are recalculated

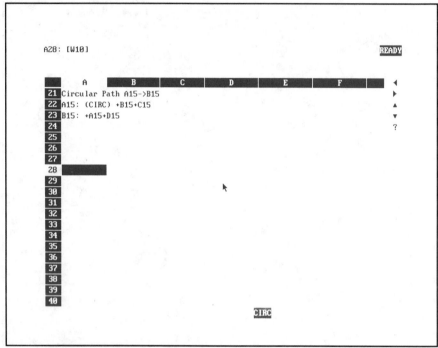

Figure D.4: The list generated by the Circs option indicates the cells and formulas involved in the circular path.

before recalculating a formula; it is neither columnwise nor rowwise. Natural is the default order and you should leave this as the default except in special, advanced applications. To change to a different order, use /Worksheet Global Recalculation.

If formulas aren't giving you accurate results, it's possible that they are recalculating in the wrong order. (This should only happen if the order of recalculation has been changed to Columnwise or Rowwise.) To identify the order in which formulas are recalculating, use the Recalc-List auditing option. With Recalc-List, you will want to specify either the Trace or List reporting method. Trace will jump to the formula that will be recalculated first; choose Forward to move the pointer to the next cell that will be recalculated. The List reporting method will identify the order of recalculation (Natural, Columnwise, or Rowwise) and list the formulas in the order they are recalculated. Figure D.5 contains two recalculation lists. The first one lists the Natural order of recalculation

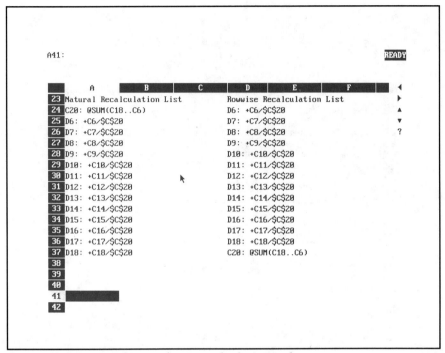

Figure D.5: A comparison of two recalculation orders

while the second one lists the Rowwise order. Notice that the Natural order calculates the @SUM formula in C20 first while the Rowwise order calculates it last. Because each of the formulas divides by the total in C20, the Rowwise order might calculate incorrect answers.

LISTING ALL CELLS REFERENCED IN A FORMULA

By indicating the cells that provide data to a formula, the Precedents Auditor option can help you determine why a formula is displaying an ERR message or an incorrect answer. For example, the averages in row 13 of Figure D.6 are incorrect. To find out why the averages are wrong, use

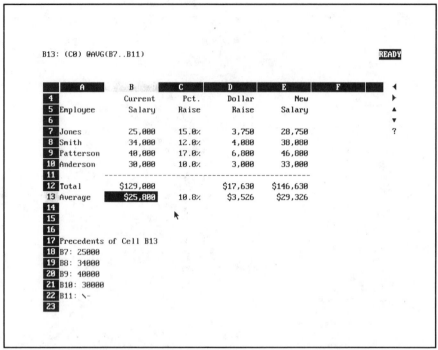

Figure D.6: The precedents report can help you determine why the averages in row 13 are incorrect.

the Precedents auditing option with the List reporting method. As you can see from the results shown in A17..A22 of Figure D.6, the formula in B13 is averaging five cells, instead of four. The dashed line in cell B11 is the culprit here.

Figure D.7 demonstrates another example of the Precedents option. In this example, there is obviously a problem with the formula in cell F7 because it is displaying an ERR message. After studying the results of a Precedents audit (A12..A16), you can see that cell E7 is the guilty party: It contains a label ("17") instead of a value.

When you choose the Precedents option, you are prompted to select a *precedent source cell*. This cell contains the formula you want to audit (for example, cell B13 in Figure D.6 and cell F7 in Figure D.7).

The precedents list displays cells that the formula references directly and indirectly. For instance, in Figure D.7, the source cell references a cell

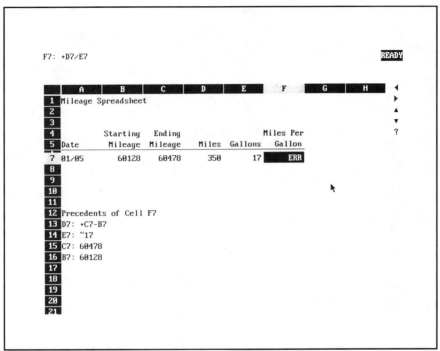

Figure D.7: The precedents report shows that the label in E7 is creating an ERR message in F7.

(D7) that contains a formula (+C7–B7); therefore, the audit report also lists these indirect references (C7 and B7) as precedents.

LISTING ALL FORMULAS THAT REFERENCE A CELL

The Dependents auditing task is the reverse operation of the Precedents option: It provides a list of formulas that refer to a specified cell. When you choose this option, you are prompted to select a *dependent source cell*. This cell can contain a label, value, or formula. Assuming you are using the List reporting method, the resulting report will display all formulas that reference the dependent source cell (see Figure D.8).

```
D7: +B7*C7                                                          READY

        A           B          C          D          E         F
   4              Current      Pct.     Dollar      New
   5  Employee    Salary       Raise    Raise       Salary
   6
   7  Jones       25,000       15.0%     3,750      28,750
   8  Smith       34,000       12.0%     4,080      38,080
   9  Patterson   40,000       17.0%     6,800      46,800
  10  Anderson    30,000       10.0%     3,000      33,000
  11
  12  Total      $129,000               $17,630   $146,630       ▲
  13
  14
  15
  16  Dependents of Cell D7
  17  E7:  +B7+D7
  18  D12: @SUM(D7..D10)
  19  E12: @SUM(E7..E10)
  20
  21
  22
  23
```

Figure D.8: The audit report in A16..A19 lists the formulas that are dependent on cell D7.

INDEX

Selections from The SYBEX Library

SPREADSHEETS AND INTEGRATED SOFTWARE

1-2-3 for Scientists and Engineers
William J. Orvis
371pp. Ref. 733-9
This up-to-date edition offers fast, elegant solutions to common problems in science and engineering. Complete, carefully explained techniques for plotting, curve fitting, statistics, derivatives, integrals and differentials, solving systems of equations, and more; plus useful Lotus add-ins.

The ABC's of 1-2-3 (Second Edition)
Chris Gilbert
Laurie Williams
245pp. Ref. 355-4
Online Today recommends it as "an easy and comfortable way to get started with the program." An essential tutorial for novices, it will remain on your desk as a valuable source of ongoing reference and support. For Release 2.

The ABC's of 1-2-3 Release 2.2
Chris Gilbert
Laurie Williams
340pp. Ref. 623-5
New Lotus 1-2-3 users delight in this book's step-by-step approach to building trouble-free spreadsheets, displaying graphs, and efficiently building databases. The authors cover the ins and outs of the latest version including easier calculations, file linking, and better graphic presentation.

The ABC's of 1-2-3 Release 3
Judd Robbins
290pp. Ref. 519-0
The ideal book for beginners who are new to Lotus or new to Release 3. This step-by-step approach to the 1-2-3 spreadsheet software gets the reader up and running with spreadsheet, database, graphics, and macro functions.

The ABC's of Excel on the IBM PC
Douglas Hergert
326pp. Ref. 567-0
This book is a brisk and friendly introduction to the most important features of Microsoft Excel for PC's. This beginner's book discusses worksheets, charts, database operations, and macros, all with hands-on examples. Written for all versions through Version 2.

The ABC's of Quattro Pro 3
Alan Simpson
Douglas Wolf
338pp. Ref. 836-6
This popular beginner's tutorial on Quattro Pro 2 shows first-time computer and spreadsheet users the essentials of electronic number-crunching. Topics range from business spreadsheet design to error-free formulas, presentation slide shows, the database, macros, more.

The Complete Lotus 1-2-3 Release 2.2 Handbook
Greg Harvey
750pp. Ref. 625-1
This comprehensive handbook discusses every 1-2-3 operation with clear instructions and practical tips. This volume especially emphasizes the new improved

graphics, high-speed recalculation techniques, and spreadsheet linking available with Release 2.2.

The Complete Lotus 1-2-3 Release 3 Handbook
Greg Harvey
700pp. Ref. 600-6

Everything you ever wanted to know about 1-2-3 is in this definitive handbook. As a Release 3 guide, it features the design and use of 3D worksheets, and improved graphics, along with using Lotus under DOS or OS/2. Problems, exercises, and helpful insights are included.

Lotus 1-2-3 2.2 On-Line Advisor Version 1.1
SYBAR, Software Division of SYBEX, Inc.
Ref. 935-8

Need Help fast? With a touch of a key, the Advisor pops up right on top of your Lotus 1-2-3 program to answer your spreadsheet questions. With over 4000 index citations and 1600 pre-linked cross-references, help has never been so easy to find. Just start typing your topic and the Lotus 1-2-3 Advisor does all the look-up for you. Covers versions 2.01 and 2.2. Software package comes with 3½″ and 5¼″ disks. **System Requirements:** IBM compatible with DOS 2.0 or higher, runs with Windows 3.0, uses 90K of RAM.

Lotus 1-2-3 Desktop Companion SYBEX Ready Reference Series
Greg Harvey
976pp. Ref. 501-8

A full-time consultant, right on your desk. Hundreds of self-contained entries cover every 1-2-3 feature, organized by topic, indexed and cross-referenced, and supplemented by tips, macros and working examples. For Release 2.

Lotus 1-2-3 Instant Reference Release 2.2 SYBEX Prompter Series
Greg Harvey
Kay Yarborough Nelson
254pp. Ref. 635-9

The reader gets quick and easy access to any operation in 1-2-3 Version 2.2 in this handy pocket-sized encyclopedia. Organized by menu function, each command and function has a summary description, the exact key sequence, and a discussion of the options.

Lotus 1-2-3 Tips and Tricks (2nd edition)
Gene Weisskopf
425pp. Ref. 668-5

This outstanding collection of tips, shortcuts and cautions for longtime Lotus users is in an expanded new edition covering Release 2.2. Topics include macros, range names, spreadsheet design, hardware and operating system tips, data analysis, printing, data interchange, applications development, and more.

Mastering 1-2-3 (Second Edition)
Carolyn Jorgensen
702pp. Ref. 528-X

Get the most from 1-2-3 Release 2.01 with this step-by-step guide emphasizing advanced features and practical uses. Topics include data sharing, macros, spreadsheet security, expanded memory, and graphics enhancements.

Mastering 1-2-3 Release 3
Carolyn Jorgensen
682pp. Ref. 517-4

For new Release 3 and experienced Release 2 users, "Mastering" starts with a basic spreadsheet, then introduces spreadsheet and database commands, functions, and macros, and then tells how to analyze 3D spreadsheets and make high-impact reports and graphs. Lotus add-ons are discussed and Fast Tracks are included.

Mastering Enable/OA
Christopher Van Buren
Robert Bixby
540pp. Ref 637-5

This is a structured, hands-on guide to integrated business computing, for users who want to achieve productivity in the shortest possible time. Separate in-depth sections cover word processing, spreadsheets, databases, telecommunications, task integration and macros.

Mastering Excel on the IBM PC
Carl Townsend
628pp. Ref. 403-8

A complete Excel handbook with step-by-step tutorials, sample applications and an extensive reference section. Topics include worksheet fundamentals, formulas and windows, graphics, database techniques, special features, macros and more.

Mastering Excel 3 for Windows
Carl Townsend
625pp. Ref. 643-X

A new edition of SYBEX's highly praised guide to the Excel super spreadsheet, under Windows 3.0. Includes full coverage of new features; dozens of tips and examples; in-depth treatment of specialized topics, including presentation graphics and macros; and sample applications for inventory control, financial management, trend analysis, and more.

Mastering Framework III
Douglas Hergert
Jonathan Kamin
613pp. Ref. 513-1

Thorough, hands-on treatment of the latest Framework release. An outstanding introduction to integrated software applications, with examples for outlining, spreadsheets, word processing, databases, and more; plus an introduction to FRED programming.

Mastering Freelance Plus
Donald Richard Read
411pp. Ref. 701-0

A detailed guide to high-powered graphing and charting with Freelance Plus. Part I is a practical overview of the software. Part II offers concise tutorials on creating specific chart types. Part III covers drawing functions in depth. Part IV shows how to organize and generate output, including printing and on-screen shows.

Mastering Quattro Pro 2
Gene Weisskopf
575pp. Ref. 792-4

This hands-on guide and reference takes readers from basic spreadsheets to creating three-dimensional graphs, spreadsheet databases, macros and advanced data analysis. Also covers Paradox Access and translating Lotus 1-2-3 2.2 work sheets. A great tutorial for beginning and intermediate users, this book also serves as a reference for users at all levels.

Mastering Quattro Pro 3
Gene Weisskopf
618pp. Ref. 841-6

A complete hands-on guide and on-the-job reference, offering practical tutorials on the basics; up-to-date treatment of advanced capabilities; highlighted coverage of new software features, and expert advice from author Gene Weisskopf, a seasoned spreadsheet specialist.

Mastering Smartware II
Jonathan Paul Bacon
634pp. Ref. 651-0

An easy-to-read, self-paced introduction to a powerful program. This book offers separate treatment of word processing, data file management, spreadsheets, and communications, with special sections on data integration between modules. Concrete examples from business are used throughout.

Mastering SuperCalc5
Greg Harvey
Mary Beth Andrasak
500pp. Ref. 624-3

This book offers a complete and unintimidating guided tour through each feature. With step-by-step lessons, readers learn about the full capabilities of spreadsheet, graphics, and data management functions. Multiple spreadsheets, linked spreadsheets, 3D graphics, and macros are also discussed.

Mastering Symphony (Fourth Edition)
Douglas Cobb
857pp. Ref. 494-1

Thoroughly revised to cover all aspects of the major upgrade of Symphony Version 2, this Fourth Edition of Doug Cobb's classic is still "the Symphony bible" to this complex but even more powerful package. All the new features are discussed and placed in context with prior versions so that both new and previous users will benefit from Cobb's insights.

Teach Yourself Lotus 1-2-3 Release 2.2
Jeff Woodward
250pp. Ref. 641-3

Readers match what they see on the screen with the book's screen-by-screen action sequences. For new Lotus users, topics include computer fundamentals, opening and editing a worksheet, using graphs, macros, and printing typeset-quality reports. For Release 2.2.

Understanding 1-2-3 Release 2.3
Rebecca Bridge Altman
700pp. Ref. 856-4

This comprehensive guide to 1-2-3 spreadsheet power covers everything from basic concepts to sophisticated business applications. New users will build a solid foundation; intermediate and experienced users will learn how to refine their spreadsheets, manage large projects, create effective graphics, analyze databases, master graphics, more.

Understanding PFS: First Choice
Gerry Litton
489pp. Ref. 568-9

From basic commands to complex features, this complete guide to the popular integrated package is loaded with step-by-step instructions. Lessons cover creating attractive documents, setting up easy-to-use databases, working with spreadsheets and graphics, and smoothly integrating tasks from different First Choice modules. For Version 3.0.

SYBEX ®

FREE CATALOG!

Mail us this form today, and we'll send you a full-color catalog of Sybex books.

Name _____

Street _____

City/State/Zip _____

Phone _____

Please supply the name of the Sybex book purchased.

_____

How would you rate it?

_____ Excellent   _____ Very Good   _____ Average   _____ Poor

Why did you select this particular book?

_____ Recommended to me by a friend

_____ Recommended to me by store personnel

_____ Saw an advertisement in _____

_____ Author's reputation

_____ Saw in Sybex catalog

_____ Required textbook

_____ Sybex reputation

_____ Read book review in _____

_____ In-store display

_____ Other _____

Where did you buy it?

_____ Bookstore

_____ Computer Store or Software Store

_____ Catalog (name: _____)

_____ Direct from Sybex

_____ Other: _____

Did you buy this book with your personal funds?

_____ Yes   _____ No

About how many computer books do you buy each year?

_____ 1-3   _____ 3-5   _____ 5-7   _____ 7-9   _____ 10+

About how many Sybex books do you own?

_____ 1-3   _____ 3-5   _____ 5-7   _____ 7-9   _____ 10+

Please indicate your level of experience with the software covered in this book:

_____ Beginner   _____ Intermediate   _____ Advanced

Which types of software packages do you use regularly?

_____ Accounting	_____ Databases	_____ Networks
_____ Amiga	_____ Desktop Publishing	_____ Operating Systems
_____ Apple/Mac	_____ File Utilities	_____ Spreadsheets
_____ CAD	_____ Money Management	_____ Word Processing
_____ Communications	_____ Languages	_____ Other _____
		(please specify)

Which of the following best describes your job title?

_____ Administrative/Secretarial	_____ President/CEO
_____ Director	_____ Manager/Supervisor
_____ Engineer/Technician	_____ Other _____
	(please specify)

Comments on the weaknesses/strengths of this book: _____

_____

_____

_____

_____

_____

PLEASE FOLD, SEAL, AND MAIL TO SYBEX

– –

SYBEX, INC.
Department M
2021 CHALLENGER DR.
ALAMEDA, CALIFORNIA USA
94501

SYBEX ®

SEAL

Top twenty wysiwyg commands

DESCRIPTION	COMMAND
Assigning a font	:Format Font 1–8
Bolding a range	:Format Bold Set
Centering a title	:Text Align Center
Changing the default font	:Format Font Replace 1
Copying a cell format	:Special Copy
Drawing a solid line under a range	:Format Lines Bottom
Fitting a report on one page	:Print Layout Compression Automatic
Inserting a page break	:Worksheet Page
Inserting a graph	:Graph Add
Loading the graphics editor	:Graph Edit
Loading the text editor	:Text Edit
Outlining a range	:Format Lines Outline
Printing	:Print
Printing in landscape	:Print Config Orientation Landscape
Setting row height	:Worksheet Row Set-Height
Setting margins	:Print Layout Margins
Shading a range	:Format Shade
Specifying a printer or print density	:Print Config Printer
Underlining a range	:Format Underline Single
Zooming in and out	:Display Zoom